2005

Dance Between Two Cultures

DANCE BETWEEN

Latino Caribbean Literature
Written in the United States

TWO CULTURES

William Luis

VANDERBILT UNIVERSITY PRESS
Nashville and London

This publication is made from recycled paper and meets the minimum requirements of American National Standard for Information Sciences—Permanence of Paper for Printed Library Materials. ⊚

Library of Congress Cataloging-in-Publication Data

Luis, William.
  Dance between two cultures : Latino Caribbean literature written in the United States / William Luis. -- 1st ed.
    p. cm.
  Includes bibliographical references and index.
  ISBN 0-8265-1302-6 (alk. paper)
  1. American literature--Caribbean American authors--History and criticism. 2. American literature--20th century--History and criticism. 3. Caribbean Americans--Intellectual life. 4. Ethnic groups in literature. 5. Minorities in literature. 6. Ethnicity in literature. I. Title.
PS153.C27L85 1997
810.9'868729--dc21   97-21192
                                                       CIP

Manufactured in the United States of America

Para mis hijos, Gabriel William y Diego Javier

CONTENTS

PREFACE

Latino Caribbean writers born or raised in the United States are at the vanguard of a literary movement that has opened up a new field in literary history and criticism. The movement, both Hispanic and North American in character, is helping to bring the two cultural groups and their literature together. The body of literature produced gives meaning to postmodern and postcolonial concerns and expresses the aspirations, disillusions, and sense of acceptance and rejection felt by Puerto Rican Americans, Cuban Americans, and Dominican Americans. Writing sometimes in Spanish but mainly in English, they speak both to Latino and all North American readers.[1]

In recent years, there has been a proliferation of Spanish American literature written in the United States. These Hispanic writers, born or educated in their countries of origin, left for economic or political reasons and took up residence in the United States. Authors such as Reinaldo Arenas (Cuba), Luis Rafael Sánchez (Puerto Rico), Luisa Valenzuela (Argentina), Laura Esquivel (Mexico), and Isabel Allende (Chile) write about their homelands. But as their stay in the United States becomes more permanent, the authors tend to incorporate a North American perspective into their works. Equally significant, they are also narrating their experiences in the United States and thus contributing to an existing body of Latino literature written by Chicanos such as Rudolfo Anaya and Gary Soto, Puerto Rican Americans such as Nicholasa Mohr and Tato Laviera, Cuban Americans such as Oscar Hijuelos and Cristina García, and Dominican Americans such as Franklin Gutiérrez and Julia Álvarez, who live and write in New York, Los Angeles, Miami, Newark, and other cities that have acquired a distinctly Latino character.[2]

Political events have helped to promote Latino Caribbean literature. During the turbulent decade of the sixties, organizations such as the Urban League, the National Council for the Advancement of Colored People NAACP, and the Black Panthers, as well as the Young Lords Party, drew attention to the plight of blacks, Hispanics, and Latinos in the United States. Latino Caribbean college students, many of them the sons and daughters of immigrants, were instrumental in creating and developing Latin American or Puerto Rican Studies programs throughout New York and other northeastern states. In search of an identity, they demanded relevant courses about life in Puerto Rico, the Dominican Republic, Cuba, and other Spanish-speaking countries and, equally important, about their own experiences in the United States. The newly created courses were different from traditional offerings insofar as they decentered the dominant perspective and incorporated an understanding of the lives of those being studied. The enthusiastic efforts of college students on U.S. campuses were paralleled by community activists and organizers who sponsored events to promote ethnic awareness and literary and artistic expressions emerging from the barrios and ghettos.

Latino Caribbean literature written in the United States has profited from the publicity received by the novel of the so-called Boom of Latin American literature, which during the 1960s brought Latin American literature to the attention of world readers.[3] North Americans who read Latin American writers in translation have also uncovered works written in English by Latinos living in the United States. Like their Latin American counterparts, the works written by Latinos also refer to the Hispanic experience, but within a familiar North American context. Similarly, Latino works written in Spanish and those in English translated into Spanish have made the Hispanic American culture accessible to the Spanish-speaking world.

My definition of *Latino,* which reflects the lives of those born or raised in the United States, differs from the one used by other scholars and by politicians.[4] Whereas the general tendency is to use the terms *Hispanic* and *Latino* interchangeably, I prefer to be more specific about the words' referentiality. Latino is a reappropriation of the nomenclature *Latin,* as in Latin American. The usage of Latin in the U.S. context is meant to distinguish those who reside in Latin America from those who live in the United States. But Latins or Latinos growing up within the North American cultural context are unique because they have experienced a tension between the culture of their parents and that of the United States. Those raised in metropolitan areas such as New York, Chicago, Miami, and Los Angeles were subjugated by the dominant culture and political establishment. They, in turn, developed a culture of resistance and a language that mediates between their parents' identity and the culture of their present reality. Their sacrifice and effort to establish a distinct identity contributed to an awareness of the Hispanic community throughout the United States.

The definition I propose for *Latino* is different from the broader term *Hispanic,* which refers to those born or raised in their parents' country of origin. *Hispanic* in North America does not have the same meaning in Spain or Spanish America. In the United States it can refer to those who travel for political or economic reasons to the United States. For the most part, Hispanics are Spanish speakers, and English is their second language. Although North Americans may view them also as being Latinos, their experiences in the United States are markedly different from those born or raised and educated in the Anglo-American environment. They, for example, have not been exposed to the same pressures as their U.S. counterparts. This is not to diminish the difficulties many Hispanic immigrants experience when traveling north, but to establish cultural referents that give Hispanics and Latinos meaning to their lives and experiences. It would be incongruous to group Hispanics from privileged families who have superior educational opportunities, traveling to the United States to pursue a post-secondary education, with Latinos living in the ghettos of East Harlem or East Los Angeles, attending inferior schools and lacking the economic, social, and political support necessary to overcome the limitations of their existence. Richard Rodríguez recongizes the difference between the two terms, and he was able to profit from opportunities others so desperately needed:

> The policy of affirmative action, however, was never able to distinguish someone like me (a graduate student of English, ambitious for a college teaching career) from a slightly educated Mexican-American who lived in a barrio and worked as a menial laborer, never expecting a future improved. Worse, affirmative action made me the beneficiary of this condition.[5]

Hispanic and Latino Caribbean literature written in the United States can be studied by country of origin and genre, but more appropriately should be divided into two main categories. The first consists of works by writers who were raised and educated in their native countries and later emigrated or were forced to flee to the United States. While in the United States, they continued to write in the vernacular, mostly about themes pertaining to their island of provenance. Some traveled to the United States for brief periods; others stayed longer. Regardless of the reasons for going to the United States or length of time spent there, the writers' presence in the United States has had a lasting effect on their lives and works.

The second category includes Latino writers who were born or raised in the United States and who for the most part write in English. As a group, Latinos write an ethnic literature that responds to concerns about their isolation within a dominant culture that has denied them an identity and access to mainstream U.S. society. For these writers, their parents' country of birth is a distant memory. They compose a literature that searches for their own identity and origins in the United States.

Hispanic and Latino Caribbean literature written in the United States is receiving much deserved attention. However, it is not new. It began as a literature of exile that can be traced to the first half of the nineteenth century, when Cuban, Puerto Rican, and Dominican intellectuals, seeking political asylum from the Spanish colonial government, traveled to and resided mainly in the northeastern part of the United States. New York became the center of operation against Spanish dominion over the islands and emerged as an important intellectual and publishing center for Hispanic Caribbean authors. Newspapers and journals contain the political and literary aspirations of generations of intellectuals fighting for their countries' independence and include the works of figures like Cirilo Villaverde, Enrique Piñeyro, and José Martí, of Cuba; Ramón Emeterio Betances, Eugenio María de Hostos, Francisco Gonzalo (Pachín) Marín, and Arturo Alfonso Schomburg, of Puerto Rico; and Gens. Narciso López and Máximo Gómez, of the Dominican Republic.

The number of Hispanics traveling to the United States increased after the Spanish-Cuban-American War of 1898, into the first decades of the twentieth century. After the Foraker Law of 1900, which made Puerto Rico a territory of the United States, and in particular the Jones Act of 1917, which gave Puerto Ricans U.S. citizenship, Puerto Ricans began to leave their native island to reside in New York City. Many of these immigrants joined their Cuban counterparts and worked as cigar makers. Later, after Operation Bootstrap went into effect during the 1940s and 1950s, Puerto Ricans migrated in greater numbers and were employed in New York's garment district.

The Puerto Ricans were soon joined by a large wave of Cubans, who were forced to leave their homeland shortly after the triumph of the Cuban Revolution in 1959. This group of professionally trained middle-class exiles sought refuge in San Juan but also in Miami, Newark, and New York City. Cubans arrived in four migratory waves: first, from 1959 to 1962; second, from 1965 to 1972; third, in 1980, as a result of the Mariel boatlift; and fourth, from 1989 to 1994, as *balseros*.[6] They added to a notable presence of Hispanics and Latinos in the United States, which continues to increase.

Dominicans are the newest members of a Caribbean population living in the United States. Their numbers rose as they began to leave their country concomitantly with the first two waves of Cubans, a period corresponding with the end of the Trujillo dictatorship in 1961 and the U.S. invasion of the Dominican Republic in 1965. But it was not until the 1970s and 1980s that the Dominicans became a noticeable presence in Latino communities. Like the Puerto Ricans, Dominicans fled their homeland to escape declining economic conditions.

Hispanics and Latinos living in the United States have indeed altered the cultural, racial, and linguistic complexion of North American society and are becoming a significant force to consider in this country's electoral campaigns. Demographers have shown that by the turn of the century, Latinos will be the largest minority in the United States.

   Although Chicano, Puerto Rican, Cuban, and Dominican communities make up most of the Latino population in the United States, people of Spanish descent have inhabited the North American continent since before the founding fathers transformed the British colony into an independent nation, living in territories that would later be incorporated into the growing United States. There were Spaniards living in the Southeast, on the peninsula that later became the state of Florida; and Mexicans in the Southwest, on land that encompassed the current states of Texas, New Mexico, Nevada, Utah, Arizona, Colorado, Wyoming, and California, land recognized as Aztlán, originally settled by the Aztecs. It is not uncommon for government officials and North Americans in general to consider all Hispanics or Latinos, with Spanish surnames, to be the same, and there are important similarities among them. As a region, the Spanish Caribbean islands share many similarities in geography, climactic conditions, history, culture, religion, diet, music, language, and economy.[7] However, their differences in development have led to varying political and economic conditions among these nations: Cuba as a Communist country, Puerto Rico as a colony of the United States, and the Dominican Republic as a struggling democracy.

   When Hispanics migrate to the United States, native differences are reinforced and others are created. They speak a "foreign" language many do not understand, and because of barriers in communication and widespread attitudes toward foreigners, stereotypes are created, promoted, and generalized. Hispanics with limited access to the political, educational, and economic systems in their homelands believe that in the United States they can have freer vertical movement. Once they arrive, these immigrants find that they cannot achieve those goals without encountering unexpected obstacles. Those who grew up under privileged conditions in their country of origin are dismayed when in the United States they are treated in a manner that denies them the status to which they were accustomed. Moreover, the racial situation on the mainland makes Afro-Hispanics understand more clearly that discrimination exists in their country of origin; and the racial prejudice in the United States forces many Hispanics and Latinos to seek refuge in African American culture.

   Historic events vary the experiences of Hispanics from the same country. For example, there are significant distinctions between Puerto Ricans who migrated to the mainland during the turn of the century and those who arrived in the 1940s; Cubans who fled Castro's island in the early stages of the revolution and Marielitos who arrived in 1980; and Dominicans who escaped the Dominican Republic before the downfall of Rafael Leónidas Trujillo Molina and those who migrated after the U.S. occupation of the island in 1965. And just as there are differences between

Puerto Ricans living on the island and those residing on the mainland, there are noticeable ones between Cubans from Miami and those from New York. More likely than not, Cubans living in New York have more political common ground with Puerto Ricans and Dominicans living in the city than they do with their compatriots from Miami.

But for many Anglo-Americans, the differences are negligible. Hispanics, whether born in the United States or abroad, from privileged or low socioeconomic classes, economic or political exiles, black or white, are grouped into a single category and viewed as foreigners. Even in classical times, Pliny the Elder's study of the monstrous races reveals that the differences travelers encountered, whether real or imaginary, when venturing outside Europe tended to reinforce European culture and identity.[8] In the postmodern and postcolonial period, travelers do not have to venture outside the United States; rather, travelers and foreigners occupy the same geographic setting. Separating Hispanics and Latinos from mainstream society is essential for preserving and reinforcing U.S. (European) national and racial identity. All Hispanics, whether living in crowded cities or in the suburbs, and blacks more so than whites, have been adversely affected by the dominant society. In some respects, they are treated as if they were members of Pliny the Elder's monstrous races. Regardless of the differences among them, Latinos share the same marginal experience in the United States, one that inevitably brings them together.

Generally speaking, Cubans have fared better than other Latino groups. As political refugees of a Communist regime, they have been welcomed with open arms. Cubans are exiles who may not return to their homeland, and an increasing number of them are putting the past behind them, accepting their destiny in the new environment. Their transition has been smoother. In comparison to other Latinos, white Cubans have reached a higher level of education. Puerto Ricans have fared the worst, in part because a large number of them are dark-skinned. Their situation is paradoxical. On the island, Puerto Ricans are subjected to a colonial status; on the mainland they do not escape a postcolonial condition, and they confront cultural and racial discrimination. Their double alienation, on the island and mainland, underscores Puerto Rican minority status and cultural identity.

Although it is true that some Latinos have made gains, the majority have not. Even those who have been able to transcend their parents' economic and educational situations continue to face cultural resistance from Anglo-Americans, who on the one hand demand homogeneity and conformity and on the other do not allow Hispanics to forget they are foreigners. Each of these attitudes is somewhat shortsighted. Latinos are ethnically, racially, and culturally diverse and can best understand both U.S. and Hispanic cultures and mediate the interrelationship of these two parts of the world. The Hispanic presence in the United States serves as a barometer of tolerance or intolerance of North American society and culture.

As conveyed in the title of this study, Latinos and their culture are engaged in a metaphorical dance with Anglo-Americans and the dominant culture. The dance suggests a coming together of the two and influences the way they dance, to the same tune in the same dance hall. Though the dance refers to Latino and U.S. cultures, it is not restricted to one dance or one partner; on the contrary, it includes others, such as African Americans and their culture. Once the two partners engage in the dance, both will change; neither one will ever remain the same.

Latinos will ultimately influence all aspects of life and culture in the United States. This is already evident in entertainment, music, sports, literature, and politics, with such controversial issues as bilingual education, the English-only movement, affirmative action, and California's propositions 187 and 206. The influence is also evident in higher education, as more and more Latinos enter the university and, with African Americans, impact the traditional offerings.

Latino literature and culture have affected the way we perceive Latin American and American studies. The migratory and exile experience of Hispanics in the United States is related to the internal circumstances of each Latin American country and to U.S. attitudes toward it. With regard to the Caribbean, the long-standing interest the U.S. government has had in acquiring politically or economically one or more of the Caribbean islands has directed foreign policy. The U.S. government's desire to intervene in other countries has made the notion of borders more fluid, allowing people to migrate with relative ease. Likewise, the type of relationship the United States has with its neighbors to the south is not totally independent of the way Latinos are treated in the United States. In some respects, Latinos also influence how the general public and government officials perceive Latin America and provide a counterdiscourse on their countries' conditions.

American studies programs do not concentrate on all of the Americas, but rather the United States. Even so, Hispanics have lived in territories that were later incorporated into the United States, like Florida and states in the Southwest. U.S. studies do pertain to the study of the Americas insofar as the cultural, ethnic, and racial complexities of the New World are also represented in the lives of Latinos living in the United States. Hispanics have been from the beginning an integral part of U.S. history, but their presence is barely perceptible in the curricula of American studies programs.

Latinos also influence the direction of African American studies programs. The interrelationship between black Latinos and African Americans points to the black presence in the diaspora, leading to comparative studies of slavery and race relations in Latin America, the Caribbean, and the United States. Racially speaking, countries such as Cuba, the Dominican Republic, Uruguay, Peru, Costa Rica, Nicaragua, and Mexico have a significant black population. Politically speaking, the issue of race and difference encompasses much more. It provides insight into history not from the victors' perspective, but from the victims'. And as more writers publish their works, literature departments, such as Romance languages, Spanish and Portuguese, English, and comparative literature, will adjust their course offerings. Equally important, a study of Latinos stimulates cross-disciplinary communication across colleges and universities, a requisite, according to François Lyotard, for a postmodern education.[9]

Latino literature will certainly figure prominently in postcolonial studies and have a shaping influence on past or present literary theories. Latinos living in the United States are subjected to a multilevel postcolonial existence. As a British colony the United States fought successfully for independence and has "written back" to the center. But this once peripheral country has also become a center.[10] The United States is an imperial country in the traditional sense: Puerto Rico continues to be its colony; and in the modern sense: Latin American countries are affected by decisions made in Washington. Whereas Spanish America was a colony of Spain and also "wrote back" to the imperial center, the United States has replaced the Spanish presence and continues to have a say in the economic and political systems of the region. Latinos are caught in a double bind, between the imperial influences of the U.S. and Spain (represented by the cultural dominance of their parents' country of origin). Within the Latino context, postcolonial studies indicate the presence of the periphery in the center. Latino literature incorporates the dynamic relationship between the center and the periphery and, equally important, between the periphery and the center. This is most visible in the language in which some writers choose to write, which speaks simultaneously to their marginality and centrality.

The idea for this book emerged from an essay Roberto González Echevarría and Enrique Pupo-Walker commissioned from me on "Latin American (Hispanic Caribbean) Literature Written in the United States" for the *Cambridge History of Latin American Literature.*[11] As I read everything I could put my hands on, I began to uncover a wealth of material, of which I had some prior knowledge. I was born and raised in New York City, and my parents were part of the migratory experience that has contributed to Latino literature and culture in the United States. Educated during the sixties, I read the works of up-and-coming writers such as Víctor Hernández Cruz and Piri Thomas, which at that time were not part of the traditional school curriculum. As I began to receive formal training in the traditional areas of our profession, I put on hold my social, political, racial, and economic background, which at that time seemed incompatible with postgraduate education. I specialized in Latin American literature, with a concentration in nineteenth- and twentieth-century Caribbean and Afro-Hispanic literatures. González Echevarría and Pupo-Walker's request allowed me to revisit my past and view it from critical and personal perspectives. Aspects of this study transported me back to my childhood on the Lower East Side and to memories of my junior high and high school friends. I reread my past experiences in such a manner that they served as an intertext for the works. I combined that viewpoint with my professional training to uncover a plurality of discourses contained in the lives of Latinos and present in their writings. Although I do recognize the sociological and political value of the works written by Latinos, as a literary critic I allow myself to be guided by the text. I have resisted imposing commonplace notions about Latinos on my readings, unless the text demands it of me. My methodology is not motivated from the outside. Rather, it is derived from the text and the text's context. I draw upon my knowledge of structuralism, poststructuralism, and postmodernism. The latter includes a dismantling of my own interpretations, a procedure I consider a fundamental proposition of postmodernism and which critics such as Lyotard do not consider. From a postmodern perspective, I do not see inconsistencies in combining the mentioned literary currents; on the contrary, they are all necessary in dismantling writing and the text.

I also draw upon the postcolonial debate. It is with Latinos that postcoloniality assumes another dimension, one that is relevant to U.S. criticism; the lives of Latinos gain significance, not within the colony, but within the colonizing country. In essence, both colony and colonizer, oppressor and oppressed share the same geographic time and space. Latino works provide a counterdiscourse to the discourse of power, one that questions and uncovers the strategies the dominant discourse masks as "truths."

The purpose of this study is not to provide a commentary on every Latino Caribbean author in the United States. Instead, I have chosen a representative number of writers whose works allow me to explore the lives of Latinos on the mainland and the literary traditions of which their works are a part. More often than not, literary critics study writers and movements after they have come to an end. Latino literature provides the distinct challenge of analyzing the movement as it unfolds. In this book, I study poetry and narrative. Rather than focus on one or two poets in each of the three sections, I have selected a variety of individual compositions published mainly, but not exclusively, in anthologies. As it is widely known, anthologies play a crucial role in the formation and promotion of the canon. There are already a representative number of anthologies in Spanish and English on Cuban Americans, Puerto Rican Americans, and Dominican American writers. I have concentrated on those works written in English or which appear in bilingual editions. The anthologies were compiled to reach a Latino and North American public and speak eloquently to the presence of Latino culture in the United States. It is too early to talk about a Latino canon, but anthologies, and the present study, will pave the way. When the anthologized selections were deficient, I included material from the authors' own works.

In narrative I chose to analyze contemporary works that have come to the attention of the public: two from Puerto Rican Americans, two from Cuban Americans, and one from a Dominican American writer. As with my study of poetry, I have selected narratives written in English or which have been translated from Spanish into English.

There are only a handful of book-length studies on Latino Caribbean literature. For the most part, they concentrate on one aspect of this literature, either the Cuban, Dominican, or Puerto Rican. Eugene Mohr's *The Nuyorican Experience: Literature of the Puerto Rican Minority*[12] (1982), whose subject is Puerto Rican American literature, has the distinction of being the first on any of the three literatures. As the title suggests, he focuses exclusively on Nuyorican literature and provides a useful overview of important works, from Bernardo Vega to the present. Of more academic rigor is Juan Flores's *Divided Borders: Essays on Puerto Rican Identity* (1993), a collection of essays that considers Puerto Rican popular culture as resisting the pressures to assimilate into the dominant culture.[13] The presence of Puerto Ricans in New York allows him to reinterpret island literature as well as understand the one that is unfolding in the city. Regarding Cuban American literature, Gustavo Pérez Firmat is the only critic of stature to treat the issues of that community. In *Life on the Hyphen: The Cuban-American Way* (1994) he looks at the translational properties of Cuban American literature, popular music, and other aspects of culture.[14] Pérez Firmat had begun to explore this idea in *The Cuban Condition: Translation and Identity in Modern Cuban Literature* (1989).[15] If Flores privileges New York as the source for Nuyorican literature, Pérez Firmat does the same with Miami and Cuban American culture. Of a broader perspective is Ilán Stavans's *The Hispanic Condition: Reflections on Culture and Identity in America* (1995), which expands on Pérez Firmat's position.[16] Stavans looks at Hispanic society as represented by Chicanos, Cubans, Puerto Ricans, and Central and South Americans, and he inserts himself into the same tradition. As a Mexican who identifies with Latino issues, Stavans gives the term a symbolic quality that goes beyond the parameters I have outlined. No full-length study on Dominican American literature exists.

I have found no study that gives a coherent overview of Latino Caribbean literature written in the United States. Although I do not consider myself to be a literary historian, I saw the need to fill a void in literary history. Therefore, in chapter 1, I provide an overview of Hispanic Caribbean and Latino literature and trace it from the early nineteenth century to the present. I discuss the reasons Cubans, Puerto Ricans, and Dominicans migrated to the United States and important figures and works that have helped to define this literature.

In chapter 2 I study contemporary Puerto Rican American poetry, which has two separate but interrelated origins: one is literary and relates to William Carlos Williams; the other is more social and political and has been influenced by the Last Poets and the Young Lords Party. The poems focus on aspects of the Puerto Rican experience in the United States. Some deal with the individual reactions to a new environment; others are more political and social and address the oppressive conditions to which Puerto Rican Americans and other Latinos have been subjected. The latter compositions are charged with emotions, with anger and frustration directed against the dominant society that has denied the poetic voices an identity and the American dream.

In chapter 3 I focus on *Memorias de Barnardo Vega* (1977; *Memoirs of Bernardo Vega*, 1984) and Piri Thomas's *Down These Mean Streets* (1967). Although these two works are not the most recent narratives written by Puerto Rican Americans, they are certainly the most important. Vega was the first writer to provide a historical understanding of the Puerto Rican presence in the United States. He supported the Hispanic community, but he also worked for Vito Marcantonio and was the national director of the Hispanic division of the committee to elect Henry Wallace. However, Vega died before publishing his memoirs; César Andreu Iglesias edited and published them twelve years later. I propose that Iglesias altered the manuscript and introduced changes that reflect the mediation and negotiation Puerto Ricans and other Latinos must endure when living in the United States. Thomas's *Down These Mean Streets* is already a classic among the works written by Puerto Rican American and Latino writers. Other Puerto Ricans had written about their experiences in the United States, but Thomas's narration was the first to come to the attention of a North American audience and opened the door for other writers and works. In his autobiographical account, Thomas describes the difficult and dangerous environment many Puerto Ricans and Latinos face and the racial and cultural conflicts he endured. In some respects, Thomas is a modern *pícaro*. Writing in the first person, Thomas describes traveling through different settings, constantly changing his identity, and attempts to convince the reader that he is a victim of his environment. Thomas's story is not only about his downfall and despair, but also about his rehabilitation and resurrection, as the act of writing itself indicates.

In chapter 4, I study several representative Cuban American poets. Although some of them look back with nostalgia to their parents' homeland, others are willing to put the island's past behind them and concentrate on the Cuban American experience in the United States. The compositions of the Cuban American poets covered in this chapter suggest a marked difference between the female and male poets. Whereas the men tend to be tied to a familiar time and space, the women are ready to put the past and Hispanic male culture behind them. As we will see with some of the Puerto Rican American women writers, this is especially evident in the works of Cuban American poets who embraced the women's movement.

In chapter 5, I analyze two Cuban American narratives, Oscar Hijuelos's *The Mambo Kings Play Songs of Love* (1989) and Cristina García's *Dreaming in Cuban* (1992). Hijuelos, who won the 1990 Pulitzer Prize, is the best-known Cuban American writer and already figures amongst the most popular contemporary North American authors. His work explores the development of Cuban music in the United States in the decades of the fifties, sixties, and seventies and in 1980. The novel pertains to music, love, and romance, but also to tragedy. The Castillo brothers achieve success and fame yet are still tied to the past, represented by Cuban and Hispanic cultures. García's novel takes place in the 1970s and concludes during the takeover of the Peruvian Embassy during the same year Hijuelos ends his novel, 1980. Whereas the Castillo brothers were trained musicians in Cuba, García's protagonist is an artist educated in the United States and is a product of the sixties. Typical of that generation, she rebels against society and her mother and embraces everything contrary to her mother's beliefs: she is close to her grandmother, who lives in Cuba and who supports the Castro government. The protagonist's trip to Cuba is a spiritual journey, to liberate her male cousin, and a reconciliation with her past and present.

In chapter 6 I discuss Dominican American poetry. Because Dominicans are the most recent immigrants, many feel more comfortable writing in their parents' language, even though their themes address the Dominican presence in the United States. Dominican authors are aware of the importance of reaching a broad audience and have produced several bilingual anthologies. Like Puerto Rican and Cuban American writers, they also suffer from an identity crisis. And like Cuban American writers, they look at their past and present from a contemporary North American perspective.

In chapter 7 I examine Julia Álvarez's *How the Garcia Girls Lost Their Accents* (1991), a work that explores the issue of identity, which in one form or another is present in all Latino writings, represented by the different points of view the four sisters offer. As with other works, the protagonist needs to find communion with the past, though not the one defined by current Dominican culture and politics. Rather, like other Latino writers, she looks for it in her childhood, which can never be recovered and only exists in the imagination—that is, in literature.

In chapter 8, I will explain in more detail the origin of the term *Latino* and provide a context for its use. I also will study Stavans's *The Hispanic Condition* and show the strategies he uses to redefine Latino identity.

As I conclude this book, I would like to thank first and foremost Roberto González Echevarría and Enrique Pupo-Walker, whose friendship and scholarly works have served as a constant source of inspiration. I am also deeply indebted to my Cuban mother, Petra Santos, who unfortunately passed away while I was writing the manuscript. I am grateful for her courage. As a single parent, she raised two sons in an inhospitable New York City environment. It was she who gave me the strength to stand up for what I believe is right.

I am also grateful to Eduardo Béjar and Evelina Félicité-Maurice for inviting me to participate in a symposium on Latinos in the United States at Middlebury College. While there, I had the opportunity to visit with Nicholasa Mohr and Dolores Prida and had the pleasure of meeting Julia Álvarez and Carlota Caulfield.

I would like to thank my Vanderbilt students, in particular those who enrolled in my humanities freshman seminars on Latino Caribbean literature written in the United States and those who signed up for an advanced undergraduate class and a graduate seminar on the same subject. Of these I recognize David García, for allowing me to test many of the ideas contained in this book. I am indebted to my colleagues in the Department of Spanish and Portuguese, especially to Christopher Maurer for encouraging me to design new courses and pursue my research in the area of Latino Caribbean literature. I also want to acknowledge the fellows of the Robert Penn Warren Center for the Humanities, who spent the academic year of 1993 to 1994 examining the direction of American studies. They are Lewis Perry, Vivian Fryd, Theresa Goddu, Jane Landers, Cecilia Tichi, Larry Griffin, John Lachs, Phyllis Frus, and Don Doyle. Special thanks go to Mona Frederick, the assistant director of the Robert Penn Warren Center, and Paula Covington, Vanderbilt's Latin American bibliographer. Colleagues outside of Vanderbilt have also been helpful: I am indebted to Randolph Pope and Enrico Mario Santí for their careful reading of the manuscript and invaluable suggestions. Roberto Márquez and Julio Marzán read and asked pertinent questions about the Puerto Rican section; and with Silvio Torres-Saillant I engaged in conversations about Dominican American literature.

I am grateful for the experience, expertise, and care with which the staff of Vanderbilt University Press has brought this project to completion. I especially want to thank the director, Charles Backus, and the editor, Bard

Young, whose enthusiasm and judgment have been a great resource. I would also like to thank the copy editor, Sonya Manes, and Sherrye Young for her excellent index.

This project could not have been accomplished without the financial support I received from the American Council of Learned Societies, for the calendar year of 1994, the Vanderbilt University Research Council, and the Office of Dean of Arts and Science. All provided the financial resources for me to dedicate my time to completing this book.

Last but not least, I am very grateful to my family, who have always stood by my side: my wife, Linda, and my two boys, Gabriel and Diego, who represent another generation of Latinos in the United States.

Dance Between Two Cultures

ONE

Setting New Roots
Latino Caribbean Literature in the United States

Criticism is worldly and in the world so long as it opposes *mono-centrism* in the narrowest as well as the widest sense of that too infrequently considered notion: for monocentrism is a concept that I take in conjunction with ethnocentrism, the assumption that culture masks itself as the sovereignty of *this* one and *this* human, whereas culture is the process of dominion and struggle always dissembling, always deceiving. Monocentrism is practiced when we mistake one idea as the only idea, instead of recognizing that an idea in history is always one among many. Monocentrism denies plurality, it totalizes structure, it sees profit where there is waste, it decrees the concentricity of Western culture instead of its eccentricity, it believes continuity to be given and will not try to understand, instead, how continuity as much as discontinuity is made.

—Edward Said, "The Text, the World, the Critic"

I

THE migratory histories of Caribbean people leaving their place of origin and going to the United States are essential for understanding their culture in the adopted country. Cuban migration to the United States takes place during the early to mid-nineteenth century, when Cubans who opposed Spain's dominion over the island and supported independence or annexation to the United States sought asylum abroad. Some fled to Jamaica, Nassau, and the Dominican Republic, but an even larger number of voluntary and forced Cuban exiles went to live in the United States and resided in cities such as New York, Baltimore, Jacksonville, Tampa, New Orleans, and Key West. Most of the countries of Spanish America concluded their wars of independence between 1810 and 1812, but Cuba and Puerto Rico remained under Spain's colonial rule until the end of the century.

The number of Cuban exiles increased during the 1860s and 1870s. They came to the United States as skilled craftsmen, the majority of whom were cigar makers and who worked in tobacco factories in cities like New York and Key West, where they continued to practice their craft. Cubans left primarily for two reasons: the declining economic conditions on the island and their opposition to colonial rule. Some had participated in the first tobacco strikes at the Hijos de Cabanas y Carbajal factory in 1865 and others supported the insurrection against the Spanish colonial government known as the Ten Years War, which lasted from 1868 to 1878.

Tobacco workers opposed Spanish colonialism and supported Cuba's independence from Spain. From the late eighteenth to the early nineteenth century, coffee, tobacco, and sugar became rival crops, sugar growing at the expense of the other two. Sugarcane required larger parcels of land; as the demand for sugar increased, cane fields began to infringe on land used to grow tobacco. By the time tobacco was manufactured in 1840, sugar had become the most important commercial product, tobacco had become a secondary crop, and coffee had ceased to be a significant export.

The cultivation of tobacco and sugar demanded different conditions, and their workers developed opposing political positions. Whereas sugar needed large extensions of land and was labor-intensive, tobacco required smaller parcels of land and fewer workers. Tobacco workers had a different perspective on slavery and Spanish dominion over the island from those who controlled the sugar industry. Sugar growers upheld slavery and colonialism; the tobacco workers favored independence, the abolition of slavery, and democratic ideals. Cigar makers commanded a high level of education. By the 1860s, the cigar industry had employed workers who read to cigar makers. The readings were varied and included literature, philosophy, and politics. Cigar workers founded the reformist newspaper *La Aurora* in 1865, and one year later created the first workers union, the Asociación de Tabaqueros de la Habana.

Exiled tobacco workers helped to create tobacco factories in the United States that rivaled the manufacture of the internationally known Cuban cigar, the Habano, which is made with leaves from the region of Vuelta Abajo. The Cuban émigré Juan Antonio Bances established the first Spanish-style cigar factory, in New York, with Cuban tobacco and workers; Vicente Martínez Ibor did the same in Key West with his factory El Príncipe de Gales. Those and other Cubans brought with them their ideas and customs, including their opposition to the colonial status of the island and readers for their cigar makers.

Cuban immigrants were active in politics in the United States. To counteract opinions that favored the colony, they founded newspapers such as *El Demócrata, La Revolución, La Independencia,* and *La Verdad* in New York; *La Patria* in New Orleans; and *El Republicano* in Key West. Cubans fought to change conditions in Cuba, but also in the United States. Key West and New York became the preferred areas for Cuban exiles; the first was chosen because of its proximity and similar climactic conditions to Cuba; the second because it was the political, cultural, and economic center for Cuban émigrés. Tobacco workers participated in labor strikes, such as the one held in 1875 in New York and Key West.

Cuban immigrants also played a fundamental role in island uprisings. Rolando Álvarez Estévez explains it as follows:

> The migratory current served as a catalyst of the revolutionary conscience of the most humble masses of the Cuban population, as well as the different sectors of the petite bourgeoisie, and to a lesser degree, of representatives of the agrarian and commercial bourgeoisie. The most important event produced by the migratory Cuban movement is determined by the creation and development of a proletariat whose participation would be decisive in the years to come, particularly between 1868 and 1898; that is, all of the insurrectionalist period against the Spanish colonial domination.[1]

Cuban émigrés contributed to the insurrection against Spanish colonialism. On June 15, 1878, *La Verdad* published a partial list of money collected for Cuban independence during the Ten Years War:

For Gen. Manuel Quesada's first expedition	$31,000
For Henry Bourden and Mary Lowell	53,000
For the schooner *Great Shot*	11,000
For the *Perit*	120,000
For the *Salvador*'s first expedition	20,000
For the *Cattierine White*	58,000
For the *Lylian*	200,000
For *Goicuria*	13,000
For the schooners *Violin* and *Tived*	15,000
For the *Cuba*	163,000
For the *Ana*	0,000
For the *Upton*	80,000
For the *Florida*	104,000
For the *Hornet*	70,000
For the *Codina*	2,000
For the *Mambi*	20,000
For the second of the *Virginius*	25,000
For the *Fany*	40,000
For the schooner *Villege Prige*	10,000
For the *Edgar Stward* [sic]	70,000

For the second of the *Salvador*	20,000
For the schooner *Velocity*	9,000
For the *U.*	70,000
For the schooner *Pyoncere*	5,000
Eight smaller expeditions departing from Jamaica	30,000
Collected by General Sanguily	53,000

In addition to the mentioned sum, Cuban émigrés also underwrote the cost of sustaining the expeditions, their leaders while in the United States, and families in need.[2]

The Cuban community grew rapidly in the United States. By the time of the 1876 presidential elections, the July 27 edition of *El Pueblo,* of New York, placed the number of voting Cubans between 10,000 and 12,000, the majority of them living in New York and Florida.[3] The figures suggest that there were many more Cubans residing in the United States. Some did not have the required number of years to become citizens and vote, and some simply did not want to become citizens. The number of Cubans in the United States also fluctuated, however, as a result of the Zanjón Pact, which brought an end to the Ten Years War. Some émigrés accepted the pardon approved by the captain general of Cuba on March, 1877, and returned to the island.[4]

A detailed study of the failures of the Ten Years War is beyond the scope of this study, but Estévez provides some insights pertinent to our subject matter. The war fragmented the exile community into separatists, independents, and annexationists. The independents were further divided into two groups: those who supported Quesada, accused of squandering money raised for the revolution, and those who backed Aldama, criticized for not sending military help to Cuba. There were differences between workers and leaders. Other reasons included the U.S. government's decision, under Ulysses S. Grant, not to support the insurrection. Government officials believed that it was preferable to keep Cuba under Spanish control rather than to have one of the other European powers take over the island; the latter would have presented an even greater threat to the United States.

Cuban writers were among the first to migrate to the United States; they were at the forefront of their country's liberation movement. An overview of their histories shows a long tradition of Caribbean writings in the United States. Although the works have been read as literature of the author's country of origin, I propose that they also be studied by considering the context of their newly adopted homeland. These writers were influenced in one form or another by events taking place in the United States, which they also incorporated into their works.

José María Heredia was the first important Hispanic Caribbean writer forced into exile. A leader in the Orden de los Caballeros Racionales, a branch of the separatist society Soles y Rayos de Bolívar, Heredia was accused of participating in the conspiracy in 1823 and, with the help of friends, fled to Boston and lived in New York and Philadelphia. New York became Heredia's temporary home, allowing him to continue his literary career. Two years later, at the invitation of President Guadalupe Victoria, Heredia left for Mexico, a country similar to his own in its warm climate and the familiar Spanish language. However, before leaving New York, Heredia wrote and published his *Poesías* (1825), which placed him among the leading lyric and Romantic poets of Cuban and Spanish American literature. This collection includes his most important poem of the period, called "Niágara," a meditation on Niagara Falls that focuses on the poet's own passion and on the yearned-for palm trees of his native Cuba. En route to Mexico, Heredia wrote "Himno del desterrado" (anthem of the banished), a "hymn" about his country and his family but also about the detestable colonial condition in Cuba. "Himno del desterrado" became a source of inspiration to other Cubans living in exile.

Like Heredia, Félix Varela was also forced into exile in the first half of the nineteenth century. He was the first of many notable Cuban intellectuals to reside in the United States. With *Elenco* (1812), which served as a preliminary study of his four volume *Institutiones philosophiae eclecticae* (1812, 1813–14), Varela became the first Cuban to write on modern philosophy. He also wrote *Lecciones de filosofía* (1881) and *Miscelánea filosofía* (1819). But Varela was not only a philosopher; he was also a politician, novelist, teacher, and priest. As a delegate to the Spanish court he supported autonomy and later independence for Cuba, and opposed slavery at a time when the slave trade was a profitable enterprise. While in Spain he joined the Constitutionalists against Ferdinand VII. After signing a document against the monarch, Varela, with the help of the British, fled Spain and arrived in New York in December 1823. He subsequently lived in New York, Philadelphia, and St. Augustine, where he died in February 1853.

While living in the United States, Varela worked for Cuba's independence from Spain. He published *El Habanero* (1824–26), and with José Antonio Saco he founded *El mensajero* (1828–31). The views he promoted were much feared by Spain for their anticolonialist sentiments.

Although he was interested in political events unfolding in his native land, Varela was involved in activities in his adopted country. He resumed his religious practices in New York in 1824, served in various churches, was awarded the title of General Vicar of New York, and represented his diocese at important events. The Cuban humanist also founded two schools, one for Irish women and the other for children, and an asylum for orphans. Varela participated in the religious dialogue of the times and published *The Protestant Abridger and Annotator* (1830–31), *New York Weekly Register and Catholic Diary* (1833–36), *The Catholic Observer*

(1836–37), *The New York Catholic Register* (1839–41), and *The Catholic Expositor and Literary Magazine* (1841–43), among other newspapers. During this period he also published in two volumes *Cartas a Elpidio sobre la impiedad, la superstición y el fanatismo en sus relaciones con la sociedad* (1835, 1838; *Letters to Elpidio,* 1989), outlining his religious beliefs. In 1841 he received a doctorate of theology from the Santa María Seminary in Baltimore, Maryland.

Varela was also a novelist and published *Jicoténcal* in 1826, considered the first historical novel in Spanish and the first written in the United States.[5] Though the novel is about Hernán Cortez's conquest of Mexico and includes passages from Antonio de Solís's *Historia de la conquista de Méjico,* it also develops the love triangle between Teutila, Jicoténcal, and Diego de Ordaz, but also between Teutila, de Ordaz, and Doña Marina. The novel came to the attention of a U.S. readership and was reviewed in 1827 by the poet William Cullen Bryant in his *United States Review and Literary Gazette.* Varela also translated Jefferson's *Manual of Parliamentary Practices* and Humphrey Davy's *Chemistry Applied to Agriculture.*

Other Cuban activists soon followed Heredia. Cirilo Villaverde was forced into exile. He was a member of Domingo del Monte's literary circle and had produced a considerable body of literature before leaving Cuba. But in the 1840s Villaverde abandoned novelistic writings and became a political activist in the separatist movement. By 1847 he was a conspirator in the Club de la Habana, a group of well-to-do Cubans who desired separation of Cuba from Spain and annexation to the United States. Many of its members promoted this political solution to preserve slavery in Cuba, but others like Villaverde admired the democratic life of the northern states. Some simply preferred annexation to Spain's continual domination over the island. While in Cuba, Villaverde had joined Gen. Narciso López in a failed uprising against the colonial government. López fled to the United States, and Villaverde was captured and jailed on October 20, 1848. After a few months of detention, Villaverde escaped, reached Florida in April 1849, and became one of the first notable Latin American narrators to seek political asylum in New York. In 1882 he completed and published in that city the definitive edition of his antislavery novel *Cecilia Valdés* (trans. 1935, 1962). One of the most important works of nineteenth-century Latin American literature, the novel would not have been written had Villaverde stayed in Cuba, where slavery was an integral part of the Spanish colonial system.

Like most writers in exile, Villaverde's life and literary production can be divided into two parts: his formative years in Cuba, where he published most of his fiction, including two early versions of his *Cecilia Valdés,* and exile in the United States, where he wrote political essays and completed the definitive version of the novel. His later writings include a posthumous homage to Gen. Narciso López, who was captured and executed in Cuba in 1851. The manuscript was published under the title *General López, the Cuban Patriot* in New York, in 1850. He also drafted a response to José Antonio Saco's independence ideas, which he entitled *El señor Saco con respecto a la revolución de Cuba* and published in New York in 1852. In addition, Villaverde contributed articles to many magazines and newspapers and collaborated in the separatist magazine *La Verdad*, becoming its editor in 1853. That same year he founded and published the weekly *El Independiente* in New Orleans. Villaverde returned to New York in 1860 and established three publications: *La América, Frank Leslie's Magazine,* and *El Avisador Hispano Americano.* He was also co-editor of *La Habana* from 1858 to 1860, editor of *La Ilustración Americana* from 1865 to 1873, *El Espejo* from 1874 to 1894, and *El Tribunal Cubano* in 1878.

At the outset of the Cuban Ten Years War, Villaverde renewed his interest in politics, with a slightly different but significant change. Rather than supporting the annexation of Cuba to the United States, he now favored Saco's position, seeking total independence of the island. In a document addressed to Gen. Carlos Manuel de Céspedes, entitled *La revolución de Cuba vista desde New York* (1869), Villaverde warns the Cuban patriot of the U.S. intention not to help the rebel forces. Villaverde supported Céspedes and other rebels, and he explicitly embraced the antislavery cause. Because of his efforts, the Constituent Convention of the Guáimaro Assembly, of April 12, 1869, made a provision for the emancipation of slaves in Cuba. Although Villaverde lived to see the liberation of slaves in 1886, he did not witness the events that would lead to the independence of his country.

A combination of Villaverde's separation from Cuba, his political concerns, literary freedom, and the events unfolding in the United States, in particular the emancipation of slaves in 1865, encouraged him to rewrite his most important novel. The last version of *Cecilia Valdés* is a denunciation of slavery and the Spanish colonial government. Villaverde situates the main action between 1823 and 1832, that is, within the historical context of the corrupt administration of Gen. Francisco Vives. But Villaverde also reminds his readers of the Ladder Conspiracy of 1844 in which hundreds of free blacks and slaves, including artists and writers, were put to death. Villaverde was certainly influenced by the outcome of slavery in the United States, and the United States also provided Villaverde with the type of environment he needed to express his antislavery position. He incorporates his antislavery ideals into his novel, especially at the end, when the black character Pimienta kills the white Leonardo Gamboa, escapes, and is never caught.[6]

José Martí is certainly Cuba's most important literary and political exile. After his second expulsion from Cuba and except for brief periods, Martí resided in New York from 1880 to 1895. Like other intellectuals in exile, Martí continued to write, publishing the chronicles "Cartas de Nueva York; o, escenas norteamericanas" in *La Opinión Nacional* of Caracas, *La Nación* of Buenos Aires, *El Partido Liberal* of Mexico, and *La América* of New York, from 1881 to 1891. Martí also wrote for other New York papers, such as the *Hour* and the *Sun*. In New York, Martí expressed his political beliefs and made plans for Cuban independence. In 1892, he became a delegate to the Partido Revolucionario Cubano. He held other political positions, including consul of Argentina and Paraguay and representative of Uruguay to the American International Monetary Commission in Washington, D.C. In 1894, Martí completed the Plan de Fernandina, which outlined the invasion of Cuba in three expeditions, to be coordinated with internal uprisings.

A prolific writer, Martí's most important literary works were written and published in New York; they included his poetry, *Ismaelillo* (1882) and *Versos sencillos* (1891), the essay "Nuestra América" (1891; "Our America," 1953), and the novel *Amistad funesta* (1885), and, from 1878 to 1882, he wrote many of the poems included in his posthumous *Versos libres* (1913). With *Ismaelillo*, which contains fifteen brief poems dedicated to his son, and his preface to Juan Antonio Bonalde's *El poema de Niágara*, Martí initiated *modernismo* in Spanish America, a literary movement later associated with the Nicaraguan poet Rubén Darío. Martí's poetry came into fruition with his *Versos sencillos*, a sincere expression of emotions related to his homeland, nature, and mankind. His *Versos libres*, particularly "Amor de ciudad grande," referring to New York City, represents a period of transition and confusion in which he highlights content over form. These poems describe the strength and energy that pour from the poet's pen, and they convey their messages through universal symbols. Unlike *Versos libres, Versos sencillos* is filled with simplicity and sincerity, with love and reflection about past and friends. Two other collections, *Versos de amor* and *Flores del destierro*, published posthumously in 1930 and 1933, respectively, correspond to the period of *Versos libres*. Martí's presence in the United States allowed him to carry out his political ideas and to understand his adopted homeland. In his much publicized essay "Nuestra América," Martí warns the nations south of the border about their powerful neighbor to the north. The political and literary writings of Martí, Heredia, and Villaverde were profoundly influenced by their exile to the United States.

New York was also a haven for Puerto Rican activists. By the time Martí arrived in New York, Eugenio María de Hostos had already left his mark there, having lived in the city twice, in 1870 and 1874. He would return later in 1898, where Julio J. Henna and Manuel Zeno Gandía publish *The Case of Porto Rico* (sic) (1899), a document in defense of Puerto Rican independence. Although they did not coincide in New York, Hostos and Martí shared the same revolutionary spirit and belonged to the same

Partido Revolucionario Cubano. In New York, Hostos was the unofficial editor of *La Revolución* of the Comité Republicano Puertorriqueño and called on Puerto Ricans to work for independence. Noting the division among those who supported independence and those who favored annexation, he nevertheless wrote a manifesto calling for all Puerto Ricans to join the fight for independence. Later he became a leader among workers of the newly formed Club de Artesanos and promoted his ideas against annexation. Hostos's political ideas are gathered in his *Diario* (1939).

In New York, Martí met many Puerto Rican intellectuals by attending meetings of La Literaria, a Hispanic American literary society. Among those he met there was Francisco Gonzalo (Pachín) Marín. During this period of his exile, Pachín Marín wrote a series of articles about New York, published the newspaper *El Postillón*, and under the influence of Bécquer and also Martí, wrote his *Romances* (1892). Like Martí, Pachín Marín worked for independence; he participated in the Liga de Artesanos, was secretary of the Club Pinos Nuevos, and in Cuba gave his life for Cuban independence.

The theme of New York, important in later Puerto Rican migration literature, was already visible in the works of Manuel Zeno Gandía, one of Puerto Rico's best-known authors. North Americans are present throughout his works, but New York City becomes his main concern in an inconclusive work *Nueva York*, the fifth of a series of chronicles entitled *Crónicas de un mundo enfermo*, about the Puerto Rican migration to the United States. Needless to say, this work had a profound impact on future generations of writers who developed the theme of migration in Puerto Rican literature.

II

In the twentieth century, Cubans continued to flee political persecution. The Machado dictatorship caused the exile of two of Cuba's most important narrators, Lino Novás Calvo and Alejo Carpentier. Unlike their nineteenth-century counterparts, they lived in Europe rather than in the United States: Novás Calvo traveled to Madrid as a correspondent for *Orbe*, whose owners also published *El Diario de la Marina*, and after being detained by Machado's henchmen Carpentier fled to Paris, where he contributed to the surrealist movement and even participated in its disintegration.[7] During the same period, Nicolás Guillén lived in Cuba but also traveled abroad. He made two brief but important trips to the United States that influenced some of his poetry. The first was a train ride across the United States, from Mexico to Canada in 1937, after which he went to Spain; the second was a two-week excursion to New York before leaving for Moscow. Guillén was familiar with the racial situation in the United States, but he gained insight from his conversations with North Americans such as Lindem Henry and Lulu B. White, both of whom Guillén met as a delegate to the Congress of Peace in 1949. It was in his travels to the United States that he was able to confirm what he had already known. In an article "De Nueva York a Moscú pasando por París," published in *Bohemia* in 1949, Guillén describes impressions that would not fade easily from his memory.[8] He writes about the Harlem of luxurious cabarets but also of the misery under which many blacks lived. Although "Elegía a Emmett Till" was not written until 1956, it captures a part of the Americana Guillén experienced on his visits to the United States. Similar to Neruda's interrogation of the Wilkamayu river or Heredia's questioning of Niagara Falls, Guillén speaks to the mighty Mississippi about the death of the black boy. His experience also served him when writing future poems, including one about black activist Angela Davis.

Batista's dictatorship, from 1952 to 1958, produced a small number of young voluntary exile writers to the United States. Developing authors such as Roberto Fernández Retamar, Edmundo Desnoes, Pablo Armando Fernández, and Ambrosio Fornet lived and worked in New York, where they furthered their literary careers. For example, Pablo Armando Fernández's second book of poems, *Nuevos poemas,* with an introduction by Eugenio Florit, was published in New York in 1956; Desnoes was the editor of *Visión,* from 1956 to 1960; and Fernández Retamar was a visiting assistant professor at Yale University in 1957. That same year, Fornet was a student at New York University. Of the post–World War II period, Eugenio Florit is perhaps the best-known writer to occupy a position at a major university in the United States. He arrived in New York in 1940 to work for the Cuban Consulate, and in 1945 he joined the faculty at Barnard College of Columbia University. Florit promoted Spanish American literature with anthologies and works of scholarship and with his own poetry, which he wrote but did not publish in the United States. Unlike the poetry written in Cuba by members of *Orígenes* (1944–1956), Florit's poems are devoid of rhetoric and seek to capture the essence of poetic language. One of his best poems, "Los poetas solos de Manhattan," is dedicated to New York. This period includes his *Conversación a mi padre* (1949), *Asonante final y otros poemas* (1950), and *Siete poemas* (1960).

If the younger exiles returned to Cuba after Fidel Castro's victory to work in the construction of a new society, the same event also produced another wave of exiles, mainly to San Juan, Miami, and New York City, but also to other cities throughout the United States. Every Cuban writer living during the time of the Castro government would be affected in one way or another by its politics. Novás Calvo became the first and most important writer to leave Castro's Cuba; he sought asylum in the Colombian Embassy in 1960, traveled to New York City, and in 1967 joined the faculty at Syracuse University. He taught there until he suffered a stroke in 1973, from which he never recovered.[9]

Novás Calvo acquired literary prominence during the 1930s and 1940s with the novel *El negrero* (1933) and the collections of stories *La luna nona y otros cuentos* (1942) and *Cayo canas* (1946). In exile, Novás Calvo continued to write in the United States and, like Villaverde, he used his literary and political freedom to denounce events in Cuba. Of the first six stories he published in *Bohemia Libre*, from 1960 to 1963, five narrate events in contemporary Cuba.

In 1970 Novás Calvo published *Maneras de contar*, the only collection of short stories from his exile period. Of the eighteen stories, thirteen of them were written in the United States and relate events in the revolution; the other five were taken from his earlier collections and include "La noche de Ramón Yendía" (1942; "The Dark Night of Ramón Yendía," 1954) and "Aquella noche salieron los muertos" (1932; "That Night," 1963), two stories that date back to the Machado years. Novás Calvo's first exile stories are flawed, but he regained the mastery noted in his earlier tales after coming to terms with his exile condition. In this second period, Novás Calvo deemphasized the antirevolutionary theme of his exile years and returned to earlier concerns. In spite of his renewed efforts to write fiction, Novás Calvo was unable to reach the level of recognition he had known prior to 1959. As a writer, Novás Calvo's reputation was hindered by historical events. He wrote antirevolutionary stories at a time in which the Cuban government enjoyed wide support among intellectuals in Europe, Latin America, and even in the United States, a support that began to wane with the Padilla affair of 1971, one year after the publication of *Maneras de contar*.[10]

Perhaps one of Novás Calvo's important contributions to Cuban exile literature written in the United States is contained in "Un bum" and "La noche en que Juan tumbó a Pedro," both stories written in 1964 and with plots that develop not in Cuba but in New York. They narrate the cruel reality exiles must face in the United States, one that Novás Calvo elaborated from personal experiences. The theme of Cubans as foreigners has been repeated by younger Cuban exiles, in particular, in the works of those who were either born or raised in the United States.

Although Novás Calvo made an effort to keep his craft alive, other exile writers of his generation were less fortunate. Distinguished writers such as Lydia Cabrera, who left Cuba in 1962 and is known for her treatment of Afro-Cuban themes; Enrique Labrador Ruiz, who abandoned the island in 1970 and is known for his imaginative *novelas gaseiformes*; and Carlos Montenegro, who sought refuge in 1959 and is remembered for his prison narratives have faded into literary oblivion.

After 1959, few younger writers left Cuba. Of those who published in the early years of the revolution and wrote for *Lunes de Revolución*, edited by Guillermo Cabrera Infante (the literary supplement of *Revolución*, the official newspaper of the July 26 Movement), Matías Montes Huidobro has remained active. A professor at the University of Hawaii, he has written literary criticism and continues to write plays such as *Ojos para no ver* (1979), which describes Castro as a violent and enraged dictator. Other exile writers such as José Sánchez-Boudy have been active in promoting an anti-Castro literature.

In 1980 another wave of exiles, popularly known as the Marielitos, left Cuba during the Mariel boatlift. Established writers who had achieved recognition in revolutionary Cuba also sought asylum during this period. They included Heberto Padilla, José Triana, César Leante, Reinaldo Arenas, and Antonio Benítez Rojo. In comparison to the quantity of literature they produced in Cuba, these exile writers have published little in their respective genres. Economic imperatives have forced them to devote themselves to other intellectual work, such as publishing and teaching. Of these writers, Arenas, Padilla, and Benítez Rojo resettled in the United States. Benítez Rojo has reedited works previously published in Cuba and has shifted his interest from fiction to criticism. He published *La isla que se repite* (1989; *The Repeating Island*, 1992), a postmodern approach to Caribbean culture, in which he develops the scientific ideas associated with chaos theory and applies them to literature. He argues that within the complexity of that sociocultural region, order and disorder coexist. He focuses his study on the plantation system, which he deems as central for understanding the Caribbean. The plantation, he explains, has affected all aspects of life and is repeated in the various islands and other part of Latin America. *La isla que se repite* is a book that will find a place among such great works as Fernando Ortiz's *Contrapunteo cubano del tábaco y el azúcar* (1940; *Cuban Counterpoint: Tobacco and Sugar*, 1947), Ramiro Guerra's *Azúcar y publación en las Antillas* (1927; *Sugar and Society in the Caribbean*, 1964), and Manuel Moreno Fraginals's *El ingenio* (1978; *The Sugar Mill*, 1976).

Padilla, a poet, published *En mi jardín pastan los héroes* (1981; *Heroes Are Grazing in My Garden*, 1984), a novel written in and smuggled out of Cuba. While in the United States, he wrote *La mala memoria* (1989; *Self-Portrait of the Other*, 1990), a testimonial pertaining to events surrounding the Padilla affair in which he states for the record his version of the unfolding of political events in Cuba. Padilla and his wife, Belkis Cuza Malé, gave much of their time to editing *Linden Lane Magazine*, based in New Jersey, which publishes the works of exile writers.

Reinaldo Arenas, who after contracting the AIDS virus committed suicide, was the only writer from this group who remained productive, and his works have placed him among the leading narrators of Latin American literature. After his arrival, Arenas founded the magazine and publishing house Mariel, and he published a novel he had written in Cuba, *Otra vez el mar* (1982; *Farewell to the Sea*, 1986). His works in exile included the long poem *El central* (1981; 1984); a play, *Persecución: cinco piezas de teatro experimental* (1986); the collections of essays *Necesidad de libertad: testimonio de un intelectual disidente* (1986) and *Un plebiscito a Fidel Castro* (1990); and two novels, *Arturo, la estrella más brillante* (1984) and *La loma del ángel* (1987; *Graveyard of the Angels*, 1987). Like many Cuban exile writers, Arenas was critical of the Castro government. His political position was most explicit in *Necesidad de libertad*. Before his death, Arenas published two other works of fiction: *El portero* (1989; *The Doorman*, 1991), which takes place in New York and describes the protagonist's life in the city, and *Viaje a la Habana* (1990), which gathers three novelettes, each about a Cuban exile who returns to the island. He also published two collections of poems, *Voluntad de vivir manifestándose* (1989), in which he collects poems written in the last two decades, and *Leprosorio: trilogía poética* (1990). When he died, he left five unpublished manuscripts; the novels *El asalto* (1990; *Assault*, 1994), *El color del verano* (1991), and *Adiós a mamá* (1995); a collection of short stories, *Final de un cuento* (1991); and an autobiography, *Antes que anochezca* (1992; *Before Night Falls*, 1993), a scathing denunciation of the Castro government in which the author refers to his literary talents and homosexual lifestyle.

Arenas's *La loma del ángel* was conceived in exile, and it rewrites Villaverde's *Cecilia Valdés*. The life and works of the first author recall those of the second. Villaverde and Arenas each opposed their respective governments when they lived in Cuba. For their political beliefs, both Arenas and Villaverde were imprisoned in Cuban jails and escaped from the island, seeking refuge in the United States. Arenas completed his novel almost one century after Villaverde published the definitive version of *Cecilia Valdés*. Finally, both Arenas and Villaverde died in New York.

Of importance to Arenas's exile literature is *El portero*, a novel that takes place in New York, specifically in a private apartment building in an upscale Manhattan neighborhood. The protagonist, Juan (based on the life of his friend Lázaro), is a Cuban refugee who arrived in New York as a result of the Mariel boatlift and finds a job as a doorman. Part 1 of the novel describes the people Juan meets on a daily basis; part 2 centers on the pets and other animals who are aware of Juan's plight and talk to him about theirs. Influenced by Aesop, Fedro, Jean La Fontaine, and Spain's Félix María Samaniego, Arenas's animals describe their own experience and persecution to Juan. Like Juan, they are prisoners of men, in general, and their owners, in particular, and conspire with Juan to gain their independence.

Arenas's novel is a denunciation of the social and political conditions in Cuba that caused him, the doorman, and others to flee from the island. In Cuba, the doorman "lived seventeen years in hunger and humiliation under the Communist system and had fled on a boat."[11] In addition, the novel is a coming to terms with Arenas's exile condition in a foreign land.

Antes que anochezca, whose title refers to the author's need to write before the evening arrives, is arguably Arenas's best work. Arenas recounts his life in revolutionary Cuba from the perspective of death; he was on his deathbed when he wrote his autobiography and committed suicide shortly after completing it. Death is ever present, from the opening paragraph to the end.

Arenas's life, as presented in this work, represents an attack on the Castro government. The government objected to his writing, sexual orientation, and political beliefs, and Arenas used the same weapons to denounce the injustices to which he and many other Cubans were subjected. The detailed homosexual experiences are a way of desensitizing the reader to their fears about the issue of homosexuality but also of defying Cuban policy and culture. Arenas challenges the Cuban authorities by suggesting that all Cubans are homosexuals. From a Cuban cultural point of view, only the passive partner in a homosexual relationship is considered to be gay; the active partner is regarded to be exercising his rights as a man. Arenas looks at this relationship from a North American perspective and reveals that everyone in Cuba has had some form of homosexual encounter, including members of Castro's police and military force who feel they are machos but in reality are no different from him. In Cuba, Arenas is considered to be a marginal writer. But outside of the island Arenas's work elevates him to canonical stature.

III

Cuban literature written in the United States is distinctly different from Puerto Rican literature written on the mainland insofar as Cubans, with few exceptions, write about events and situations on the island. Puerto Rican literature written in the United States describes the lives of Puerto Ricans who migrated to New York. This essential difference has a historical basis. In the post-Castro period, Cubans migrated to the United States mainly for political reasons and viewed their exile as transitory. Their presence in the United States afforded them a political and literary freedom denied to them in their own country. Puerto Ricans traveled to the United States mainly for economic opportunities. The U.S. government's attempt to make Puerto Rico the showcase of the Caribbean and industrialize the island caused a decline in the Puerto Rican agricultural economy and forced many to leave the rural areas for better-paying jobs in the city. Operation Bootstrap displaced farmworkers from the countryside to San

Juan and from there to New York City. The Puerto Rican rags-to-riches dream turned into a nightmare, as a large portion of New York's Puerto Rican population was either unemployed or assumed the lowest-paying jobs. Puerto Rican writers witnessed and some even experienced the migratory phenomenon created, first by the Jones Act and second by the congressional decision of 1952, making Puerto Rico a Free Associated State.

The large migratory waves to the United States gave the Puerto Rican community a sense of permanence necessary for the development of a literature of migration. Therefore, Puerto Rican literature in the United States can be divided into two categories: The first is composed by island writers who visited but did not stay in the United States and is written in Spanish and published abroad. The second, which is more recent, is written by Puerto Ricans either born or raised in the United States. Because most of these writers lived in New York City during the 1960s and 1970s, they identified themselves with the city and called themselves Puerto Rican New Yorkers or Nuyoricans, an identity that gave meaning to their artistic and literary expressions. Although this term is still relevant today for some writers, it does not speak to the experiences of Puerto Rican writers born or raised in other parts of the United States. Regardless of whether they now live in or outside the city, members of this second group write mainly in English and publish in the United States. One similarity between the visiting and the permanent groups is that they both write about the Puerto Rican experience in New York. They share a common background with the other Hispanics born and raised in the United States, and as part of this larger group they are also known as Latinos.[12]

Hispanic Caribbean narrative written in the United States acquires an important dimension when considered part of the Puerto Rican writers of the Generación del Cuarenta (the Generation of the Forties), that is, those who began to publish after Operation Bootstrap. Many of them short-story writers, they testify to the effects of Operation Bootstrap on those who were adversely affected by the "Puerto Rican Miracle"—the U.S. effort to industrialize the island. Taken from society's lower socioeconomic levels, the characters are poor, uneducated, and marginalized; those who were supposed to benefit from the economic changes became society's victims. For them, pain, suffering, and personal tragedies are an integral part of their migratory experience.

Many of the stories reveal the reasons Puerto Ricans left their farms and villages for the city. The theme of displacement is best captured by René Marqués's *La carreta* (1951–52; *The Oxcart*, 1969), a play about a family who abandoned the countryside for the slums of San Juan and ultimately for the ghettos of New York City. But after tragedy strikes the family, the survivors return home. The theme of Marqués's play is explored later by other writers. Although it is difficult to state categorically that these authors wrote in the United States, we do know that they, like the Puerto Rican immigrants before them, traveled frequently to New York.

José Luis González was one of the first to write about the displacement of Puerto Ricans. In his third collection of short stories *El hombre en la calle* (1948), he outlines the Puerto Rican tragedy and signals a new trend in the short story, moving away from rural to urban themes represented by San Juan but also New York City. González's *En este lado* (1954), continues the theme of Puerto Rican migration, this time focusing more on the immigration from San Juan to New York. As he reveals "this side" of the Puerto Rican experience, González shows a keener awareness of society and race in and outside of Puerto Rico, including events occurring in Mexico and in South Korea during the Korean War.

González's first story about New York was published in his *En Nueva York y otras desgracias* (1973). In the title story, written in 1948, his protagonist, Marcelino Pérez, experiences a series of misfortunes from the moment his boat docks in New York harbor, some due to chance and unpredictable circumstances but others to his own ignorance. Like many of González's characters, Marcelino is a desperate man; despite his ill health, he abandons his bed to rob an elderly woman who happens to be Puerto Rican. But when he hears her speak Spanish, he does not go through with the crime. Himself a victim of circumstances, Marcelino retains a sense of national dignity and does not add to the suffering of his own people.

Many of González's ideas are gathered in *Paisa* (1950), a narrative version of Marqués's *La carreta,* in which he describes the same migratory pattern and moral and physical destruction of the protagonist present in the play. In New York, the story's protagonist, Andrés, is discriminated against and has no other alternative but to turn to a life of crime. In its narrative structure, *Paisa* is González's most experimental story about New York. Two narrations, one present and the other past, come together with the police's shooting of Andrés. The ending departs from *La carreta* but is similar to his stories "En Nueva York" and "El pasaje"; for the protagonist, there is no possible return to Puerto Rico, so he remains in the United States. Through another character, Perucho, González proposes that political action is the only solution to the Puerto Rican dilemma in the United States.

Language is important for authors writing about New York, and González captures an authentic dialect with varying success. His "En Nueva York" reveals a lack of familiarity with some linguistic aspects of the Puerto Rican experience abroad. For example, the narrator, who describes events in a flawless Spanish, reports the temperature in centigrade rather than in fahrenheit and, as Marcelino gets ready to assault a woman, he moves from house to house instead of from one building to another. Also, except for a scattering of Spanglish words, his uneducated characters speak standard Spanish. However, González is more successful in his reproduction of Nuyorican speech in "La noche que volvimos a ser gente," from *Mambrú se fue a la guerra* (1972), which describes the blackout of New York in 1965.

Of the writers of the Generación del Cuarenta, Pedro Juan Soto has been most preoccupied by the Puerto Rican presence in New York and with authenticity has recorded the speech of the poor or working-class Puerto Rican as well as the phenomenon of mixing Spanish and English. Soto writes from personal experiences, having lived nine years in the Bronx, from 1946 to 1954, and spending much of his time in Spanish Harlem. *Spiks* (1956), whose title is a pejorative term used to describe Puerto Ricans in the United States, contains Soto's best stories. The stories of *Spiks* reflect the same migratory pattern and issues the author was exposed to as a child, often contrasting life on the mainland with that of New York City. His "Los inocentes" and "La cautiva" describe the change between old and new values, echoing a conflict experienced by many immigrants. However, Soto's work suggests that unlike other immigrant groups Puerto Ricans are tragic figures. For sociopolitical reasons, their integration into the U.S. mainstream has been more difficult.

Although Soto resides in Puerto Rico, and on occasion travels to New York (Soto, who grew up in the Bronx, waited thirteen years before returning to New York, and from 1970 to 1971 taught at the State University of New York at Buffalo), he writes about Nuyoricans and pays homage to them in his *Ardiente suelo, fría estación* (1961). The novel is realistic insofar as it captures the problems experienced by many Puerto Ricans who returned to their native Puerto Rico during the 1960s and 1970s (in part as a result of the racial awareness brought about by the civil rights and Black Power movements and by a heightened sense of Puerto Rican nationalism). Puerto Rico symbolized the origin, but much to the dismay of Nuyoricans they were not accepted by Puerto Ricans on the island and were treated as North Americans; many Nuyoricans endured being considered foreigners because they did not share a common language and culture with the islanders. Similarly, *Ardiente suelo*'s protagonist, Eduardo Marín, is confronted with Puerto Rican chauvinism; to them he is an outsider. The frustrations Eduardo experiences on the island recall those same feelings he confronted in New York; he is an outcast both in New York and in Puerto Rico. In the end, he decides to return to the mainland, to a more familiar situation where he can assert his own individuality. His older brother remains in Puerto Rico, thus alluding to the separation of the Puerto Rican family. The themes of alienation and separation are repeated in subsequent Nuyorican writings, but unlike Soto's characters, those in the newer works highlight the Puerto Rican experience in the United States.

Unlike in *Spiks*, in *Ardiente suelo, fría estación* Soto's characters are better educated and speak standard Spanish and English. However, only

seldom do they code-switch or re-create language to show the imposition
and predominance of one culture over the other. The linguistic differences
between *Spiks* and *Ardiente suelo, fría estación* can be attributed not only
to the level of education of Soto's characters, but to Soto's distance from
the mainland. Perhaps Soto also wanted to appeal to a broader Spanish-
speaking audience; the novel was not published in Puerto Rico but in
Mexico.

Like *Ardiente suelo, fría estación,* Emilio Díaz Valcárcel's *Harlem
todos los días* (1987; *Hot Soles in Harlem,* 1993), a work that brings the
experimentation of the Boom novel—prevalent in his *Figuraciones en el
mes de marzo* (1972; *Schemes in the Month of March,* 1979)—to the theme
of Puerto Ricans in New York, continues the concern of migration so evident in the works of his generation. In *Harlem todos los días,* Díaz
Valcárcel underscores the anguish experienced by the poor, but also the difficult life of his counterparts; those with the resources exploit the less fortunate. Regardless of the social or economic differences, all are victims of
the New York environment. In this nationalistic novel, Díaz Valcárcel is
critical of the colonial status under which Puerto Ricans live. But like
other island-dwelling writers, Díaz Valcárcel is not able to capture effectively the linguistic complexity of Nuyorican speech. (The theme of the
two cultures coming together, this time on the island, is continued in his
Mi mamá me ama, 1981.)

IV

The reproduction of the Nuyorican dialect is best achieved in the
works of Nuyorican authors who are at the vanguard of a Puerto Rican or
Hispanic Caribbean ethnic literature in the United States, that is, a Latino
literature that questions, while at the same time accepts, its North
American environment. Sandra María Esteves, Miguel Algarín, and others
write in English and have published their works in the United States.
Unlike island Puerto Ricans who visit the United States and write for a
broad Spanish American audience, Nuyorican authors explore in detail the
lives and condition of Puerto Ricans who live in New York. These younger
writers use the language of the barrio to describe life in the ghetto. In this
regard, Nuyorican narrative is not directly influenced by Spanish American
literary currents, such as the literature of the Boom or post-Boom periods,
but by U.S. society and literature, in particular, the literature written by
African Americans; for example, some share common characteristics with
Claude Brown's *Manchild in the Promised Land* (1965). In general,
Nuyorican literature has no obvious model; rather, it emerges from individual reactions to the socioeconomic conditions experienced by Puerto
Ricans in the United States.

Unfortunately, Latino works still go unrecognized by many scholars
and critics of Spanish American literature. And, although Puerto Rican

writers in the United States celebrate their counterparts on the island, the appreciation is not reciprocal; many of the Nuyorican writers are unknown to the island public. This is so, as Soto has pointed out in his novel, because Nuyoricans are not considered authentic Puerto Ricans. Alienation on the island and mainland is also a concern many Nuyorican writers have and explore in their works.

Among Nuyorican narratives, Piri Thomas's *Down These Mean Streets* (1967) is already a classic. However, Thomas's book was not the first; it recalls other autobiographical works by Puerto Ricans in New York, in particular Pedro Juan Labarthe's *The Son of Two Nations: The Private Life of a Columbia Student* (1931), but is thematically closer to Jesús Colón's *A Puerto Rican in New York and Other Sketches* (1961). Both works were written and published in the United States, but they did not have the impact Thomas's autobiography has had on a Nuyorican- and English-speaking public. And only after the publication of Thomas's book are these earlier works receiving attention from critics and readers alike.

Labarthe's and Colón's books provide a framework for understanding works that were to follow. With their autobiographies two patterns emerged: First, *A Puerto Rican in New York* conveys the hostility with which Puerto Ricans are treated in New York, thus continuing the themes of the writers of the Generación del Cuarenta. Second, *The Son of Two Nations* reflects the lives of immigrants in general; the United States represents an opportunity for the characters to improve their social and economic positions. The first pattern is critical of the American dream; the other accepts it.

The difference in perspective can be attributed to the years in which the works were published. Labarthe published his novel shortly after the Great Depression, when many immigrants, regardless of their place of origin, were struggling to survive in American society. Puerto Ricans were one more group that had to overcome the same conditions as other groups. Colón's book profited from a different historical setting, marked by political awareness associated with cigar workers and other union activists, the detainment of Nationalist leaders such as Lolita Lebrón and Albizu Campos, the failure of the Tydings bill in 1943 to grant Puerto Rico independence, the implementation of Operation Bootstrap, and the prominence of the civil rights movement, particularly during the decade of the fifties.

Colón's collection of sketches, some of which first appeared in the *Daily Worker* and *Mainstream,* describe the assault of American society on Puerto Ricans, including the author who, because of his dark skin, was often mistaken for a black American. However, the book is also a testament of Colón's political beliefs and his support for the betterment of Puerto Ricans on the island through independence.

In contrast, Labarthe's book is a reflection of the good will and faith of North Americans and of the character's own intelligence. Labarthe's formative years were influenced by his aristocratic and pro-independence father and his humble and pro-American mother. The father's abandonment of the mother, among other reasons, brought Labarthe closer to his mother's ideology; they traveled to the United States not for economic reasons but in search of a better education. In the United States, Labarthe and his mother worked hard and with the help of friends, ambition, and a bit of opportunism, the author was able to transcend his condition and attain the "American dream."

Certainly Thomas's *Down These Mean Streets* is the best-known work to describe the Puerto Rican experience in New York during and after the Depression. Unlike Colón and Labarthe, Thomas was born in New York and had no direct connection with the island. Thomas was raised in El Barrio, and his life mirrors that of many Nuyoricans who lacked either economic opportunities or a political ideology and were susceptible to drugs, gangs, and crime. Thomas's life represents the United States at its worst; he is the product of a society that has destroyed him and his self-worth. *Down These Means Streets* allows the reader a window through which to see poverty, prejudice, racism, and discrimination experienced by many Latinos who have no other choice but to live in the ghetto. Examining the book from a different point of view, one realizes that as an author Thomas is a success story; he has transcended his economic and social conditions and has become an esteemed writer within the North American context.

Thomas's subsequent books develop aspects of his life already seen in *Down These Mean Streets. Savior, Savior, Hold My Hand* (1972) is a continuation of *Down These Mean Streets* and, therefore, of Thomas's life. Here Thomas looks to the Pentecostal Church for salvation, and his conversion is precipitated by his aunt and by Nita, his future wife. In the end, Thomas's rebellion against institutions results in his separation from Nita. *Seven Long Times* (1974) describes in more detail the chapter on prison of *Down These Mean Streets*, providing accounts of Thomas's life in Comstock. He presents prison as a home, a family of sorts, and a way of life for those who have difficulty in adjusting to the outside world.

Thomas's autobiography has opened the door for the writing and publishing of works by other Puerto Ricans living in the United States. Of particular historical value is *Memorias de Bernardo Vega* (1977; *Memoirs of Bernardo Vega: A Contribution to the History of the Puerto Rican Community in New York*, 1984). Vega wrote his autobiography in 1947, but César Andreu Iglesias did not edit and publish it until thirty years later. Although Vega intended to document the lives of Puerto Ricans in New York, neither he nor Andreu Iglesias thought that the time was right to publish it while the author was alive. Vega's autobiography offers a chronology of one century, from the American Civil War to the post–World

War II period. This is accomplished through a series of flashbacks narrated first by a fictitious Tío Antonio, who migrated to New York in 1847, and second by Vega himself, who traveled to the same city in 1916. The useful historical information offered by Vega, which includes statistics, interviews, and newspaper clippings, traces the origins of the Puerto Rican independence movement from the nineteenth century to the present. Antonio recalls the role played by intellectuals and workers living in New York, the center of Cuban and Puerto Rican independence movements. With his own experience, Vega shows that in the twentieth century the independent spirit was kept alive by the unionist activities of cigar makers. The workers have been at the forefront of the independence movement, though Vega sees marked differences between the Puerto Rican Nationalist and Socialist parties. Vega is concerned with preserving Puerto Rican nationalism and identity.

Other works that recall *Down These Mean Streets* are Manuel Manrique's *Una isla en Harlem* (1965), Lefty Barreto's *Nobody's Hero* (1976), and Nick Cruz's *Run Baby Run* (1968). Like Thomas's work, they are in large part autobiographical accounts of Puerto Ricans who turned to a life of crime and violence. However, Richard Ruiz's *The Hungry American* (1978) and Humberto Cintrón's *Frankie Cristo* (1972) follow more closely the pattern set by Labarthe's *The Son of Two Nations* and describe those who grew up in the ghetto and believed in the American dream. For Ruiz, New York is just a place to rest before embarking on travel to other parts of the United States. Ruiz's life prefigures Labarthe's: both authors were born in Puerto Rico, their families had a difficult time making ends meet on the island, they left hoping to improve their lives, and they succeed in making it out of the New York ghetto. Like Labarthe, who earned an M.A. at Columbia University, Cintrón valued education and completed his M.A. at the University of California.

If Thomas's experience provided a disturbing view of a United States in which violence, drugs, crime, and illicit sex were commonplace, the experience of women was much different. In this regard, Nicholasa Mohr, one of the first Puerto Rican woman to publish fiction in English, represents still another side of the Nuyorican perspective. An artist turned writer, she has been very active, publishing three novels, *Nilda* (1973), *Felita* (1979), and *Going Home* (1986); three collections of short stories, *El Bronx Remembered* (1975), *In Nueva York* (1977), *Ritual of Survival: A Woman's Portfolio* (1985); and a memoir, *In My Own Words: Growing Up inside the Sanctuary of My Imagination* (1994). Mohr's narratives appeal to a broader, English-speaking audience and have received awards such as the *New York Times* Outstanding Book of the Year, Library Journal Best Book of the Year, the American Book Award. Because of the simplicity of her language, images, and metaphors, and for marketing purposes, Mohr's books have been unjustly classified as children's literature. According to Mohr, only *Felita* was written for children.

Written from a child's or adolescent's perspective, her works offer a balanced view of reality, describing both positive and negative experiences. Many of Mohr's stories contain autobiographical references, particularly *Nilda* and *Felita*. For example, in *Nilda* she describes her brother's involvement in crime and drugs and in *Felita* the prejudice her family encounters when they move from a crowded multiracial neighborhood to a white one and back again. The child narrator is advantageous to Mohr, allowing her to describe the same ghetto Piri Thomas lived in, not with anger and hatred but with objectivity and innocence, tenderness and compassion unknown in his works and those of her male counterparts. Instead of providing the political or social commentaries of an adult narrator, she offers description of everyday life: the broken-down buildings, the roaches, the lack of food, and the loss of innocence are part of the narrative background. Mohr's works embody a new direction for Nuyorican narrators, away from the violence and assimilation and toward a more balanced view of Puerto Ricans in the United States.

Of the Puerto Rican American writers, Mohr, as well as Miguel Algarín, Tato Laviera, and Miguel Piñero, have been outspoken about reappropriating Puerto Rican identity and in their criticism of the treatment Nuyoricans receive when returning to Puerto Rico. Mohr demystifies the Puerto Rican paradise and accepts New York and the United States as her permanent home. The return to Puerto Rico is the theme of *Going Home*. Like Eduardo in Soto's *Ardiente suelo, fría estación*, Felita experiences difficulty in accepting the island's culture. Mohr contrasts the values of the mainland with those of the island and shows the difference between the treatment of men and of women. Felita misses New York and returns "home" to her native city. Mainstream Puerto Rican writers living on the island are also concerned about the question of identity. For instance, Luis Rafael Sánchez's story "La guagua aérea" (1994; "The flying bus," 1987) illustrates the daily air shuttles between San Juan and New York, or *allá* and *acá*, and how frequent migratory travel underscores the enigma of Puerto Rican identity. (Sánchez himself has become a frequent traveler since his appointment to a faculty position at the City College of New York, but he still maintains close ties to the island.)

Just as the narrative genre has played a prominent role in depicting the life of Puerto Ricans in the United States, Nuyorican poetry, although recent, is also popular and has reached large audiences in centers like The Nuyorican Poets Cafe, El Caney, and The New Rican Village. Puerto Rican poetry written in the United States can be traced to the works of William Carlos Williams, as suggested by Julio Marzán's *The Spanish American Roots of William Carlos Williams* (1994), but also to Julia de Burgos, who lived in New York from 1942 to 1953 and wrote about the city that occupied an important place in her life; this influence is particularly evident in her posthumous *El mar y tú, otros poemas* (1954). Moreover, her *Antología poética* contains fourteen poems written in New York, though others have been found. Like the island writers who traveled to New York, Burgos wrote about the political situation in her native Puerto Rico in such poems as "Una canción a Albizu Campos," "23 de septiembre," and "De Betances a Albizu." Toward the end of her life, she wrote in English about New York in "Welfare Island" and "The Sun in Welfare Island," where she died. It would, however, be left to another group of poets to displace the attention Burgos gave to Puerto Rico and develop further the ideas contained in the poems she dedicated to life in New York.

Puerto Rican poetry in the United States acquired a bilingual dimension with Jaime Carrero and his *Jet neorriqueño-Neo-Rican Jetliner* (1964), the first work to introduce the term *Neo-Rican*, which later gave coherence and identity to a group of younger writers. Carrero has also brought to poetry the theme of migration prevalent in the works of the writers of the Generación del Cuarenta. Carrero's poetry is taken one step further by Nuyorican poets, who are mainly concerned with the presence of Puerto Ricans in New York. Of this group, Pedro Pietri is its best exponent. A writer of plays, narratives, and poetry, Pietri is best known for his *Puerto Rican Obituary* (1973); the title poem was first published in *Palante: Young Lords Party*, in 1971, and was known to Latinos in New York City many years before. A descriptive as well as symbolic poem, "Puerto Rican Obituary" is the single most important poem in Nuyorican literature. Juan, Miguel, Milagros, Olga, and Manuel are familiar figures; they worked hard and believed in the American dream, which they could not attain. By mirroring the conditions under which the characters lived, the poetic voice condemns them for abandoning their roots and culture. According to the poem, the cycle can be broken if Puerto Ricans develop a sense of national pride and identity. Written in spoken (street) language, which for Pietri includes mixing some Spanish and English, this and other poems are closer to an oral tradition and are meant to be performed or read aloud. Language expresses pride, unity, and identity among Nuyoricans, thus allowing for a rejection of the pressures to assimilate into a "standard" language or way of life. Pietri continues the theme of his best-known work in poems such as "The Broken English Dream," where he shows that contrary to making the gains they sought, Puerto Ricans lost what little they had when they traveled to the United States, including their identity and pride.

The standards set by Pietri are matched by Tato Laviera, also a playwright and poet. In poetry, Laviera has published *La Carreta Made a U-Turn* (1979), *Enclave* (1981), *AmeRícan* (1985), and *Mainstream Ethics* (1988). Laviera's first book rewrites the ending of Marqués's play, but rather than returning to Puerto Rico, he chooses New York as the final destination; it is no lost paradise to which Puerto Ricans return, but a newfound reality: an acceptance of the same reality they had always known. By not completing the full circle, Laviera speaks about his own migratory process; he was born in Puerto Rico and raised in New York City. The poems reveal that despite the difficult life Puerto Ricans must endure in this country, they have undergone a change; although they still identify symbolically with the motherland, they are no longer her children and in reality can never go back. This observation is due to a noticeable predominance of English over Spanish. But, ironically, Laviera ends his book with a series of poems in Spanish, suggesting that the problem of identity need not be linguistic, but one of preference. Cultural elements such as those expressed in Afro-Caribbean culture are revered; they allow for an identification with others struggling in the ghetto, in particular African Americans. In effect, Puerto Ricans have set the groundwork for the creation of a Latino Caribbean culture within the North American context.

Laviera has the gift of assuming many voices, including the street junkie, the woman, and even the Statue of Liberty. But he is most effective when taking on the voice of a fetus about to be born on Christmas day. Drawing on religious symbolism, "Jesús Papote" is an epic poem about the Puerto Rican experience in the United States. This other Christ figure is born not of a sacred and divine virgin but of a heroine addict who has numerous lovers. The fetus's struggle for survival begins in the womb; he was forced to be a man before he became a child.

Another writer highly deserving of attention is Víctor Hernández Cruz, who serves as a bridge between Nuyorican writers and those who were born or raised outside the city. He attended school in New York City, has lived in California, and now resides in Puerto Rico. He was influenced by his environment, the poets of the Beat Generation, and also by William Carlos Williams. Hernández Cruz began to write at an early age and published *Papo Got His Gun* (1966), *Snaps* (1969), *Mainland* (1973), *Tropicalization* (1976), *By Lingual Wholes* (1982), *Rhythm, Content and Flavor* (1989), *Red Beans* (1991), and *Panoramas* (1997). Also noteworthy are Julio Marzán and Martín Espada. Marzán has published *Translations without Originals* (1986), and Espada's contributions include *The Immigrant's Iceboy's Bolero* (1982), *Trumpets from the Islands of Their Eviction* (1987), and *Rebellion is the Circle of a Lover's Hands* (1990).

The woman's perspective among poets is growing and is best represented by Sandra María Esteves, who counts among her publications *Yerba Buena* (1980), *Tropical Rains: A Bilingual Downpour* (1984), and *Bluestown Mockingbird Mambo* (1990). Esteves and other female poets belong to the tradition initiated by Burgos, but also by the women's movement in the United States. The female perspective is different from that of the male counterpart insofar as it challenges the Hispanic male dominant culture. Esteves acknowledges Burgos's importance in "A Julia y a mí" and recognizes the poet's strengths and failures. In her best poem, "My Name is Maria Christina," Esteves expresses pride in being a Puerto Rican woman from El Barrio. She accepts her traditional role as provider and child bearer and adds a new one as creator of different values. Moreover, she rejects the denigrating aspects of her culture. As a female Christ, Christina is origin and strength, elements necessary for the survival of Puerto Rican identity.

Luz María Umpierre—a recognized poet with works such as *En el país de las maravillas* (1972), *Una puertorriqueña en Penna* (1979), *Y otras desgracias / And Other Misfortunes* (1985), and *The Margarita Poems* (1987)— has been critical of Esteves's view of women, believing that she did not go far enough. Umpierre counters Esteves's "My Name Is Maria Christina" with her own "In Response," in which the poetic voice denies being María Cristina and, unlike her, is a totally liberated woman. Esteves continues the dialogue with "So Your Name Isn't María Cristina," which recognizes that the poetic voice of her previous poem was in the process of development. Though Esteves's and Umpierre's poems pertain to Puerto Rican culture, the poets' awareness comes from the North American environment, in general, and the woman's movement, in particular.

Puerto Rican identity is certainly important, but some of the poets are beginning to go beyond the familiar themes and include wider concerns. In the case of Laviera, he finds common ground with other Caribbean groups like Jamaicans and Chicanos. The attempt to enter the mainstream is exemplified by Algarín who has published *Mongo Affair* (1978), *On Call* (1980), *Body Bee Calling from the 21st Century* (1980), and *Time's Now* (1985). Algarín began to branch out and look for common ground among the different cultures as early as his second book, which includes his poems "Buddha" and "Balance," representing aspects of Asian culture and religion. His next book is more concerned with sex and the last one with love.

Among the Puerto Rican writers living and writing outside of New York City, Judith Ortiz Cofer's work is of particular interest. She is a poet and novelist and, along with Mohr, one of the few woman narrators writing in English. She has published three books of poems, *Latin Women Pray* (1980), *Peregrina* (1986), and *Terms of Survival* (1987); one book of memoirs, *Silent Dancing* (1990); one novel, *The Line of the Sun* (1989); and a collection of prose and poetry, *The Latin Deli* (1993). Most recently, she has published a book for young adults, *An Island Like You* (1995). Ortiz Cofer was born in Puerto Rico and raised in the United States; after her father joined the navy, the family moved often and lived in different cities. Her work touches upon some of the themes of other Nuyorican writers, but she expresses them from a less marginal perspective, in a language that is more polished and mainstream. Unlike the other writers, Ortiz Cofer is not concerned about the linguistic phenomenon caused by the coming together of Spanish and English nor about the clashing of the two cultures. Many of her poems are of a personal nature, often describing her innermost thoughts, vivid experiences, and members of her family. Poems such as "Housepainter," "Moonlight Performance," "Woman Watching Sunset," and "The Mule" are written with a keen insight into the subject and are composed with much thoughtfulness and mastery over her expressions, but they show no sign of her Puerto Rican or ethnic background. Other poems, such as "Visiting La Abuela," "The Gusano of Puerto Rico," and "Latin Women Pray," suggest a certain Hispanic thematics, but though they contain Hispanic names and references to the island, they are written in standard English. Only in a handful of poems does she venture away from English and incorporate a few words of standard Spanish such as *la leche* in "Pueblo Waking" and the vendor's call *frutas y viandas* in "The Fruit Vendor." Even though she chooses not to use her Spanish, Ortiz Cofer is certainly aware of her parents' language; she can use the poetic voice to teach it to others as she reveals in "Lesson One: I Would Sing." Ortiz Cofer's poem is concerned with translation and bilingualism, but is certainly aware of the power of Spanish verbs and tenses, which are antithetical to their less expressive English equivalents. This poem is about marginal people who speak a language and therefore live in a culture of hope. The last line of the poem is an affirmation of her Hispanic heritage and a desire to teach others the beauty she has found in Spanish language and culture.

Ortiz Cofer's *The Line of the Sun* is an autobiographical novel of sorts and narrates elements of the history of three generations of Marisol Santa Luz Vivente's family. Marisol, the granddaughter, is Puerto Rican by birth but raised in the United States after her parents migrate in the 1950s. The novel is divided into two thematic parts: The first pertains to the Puerto Rican village where her father and uncle grew up, and it describes rituals and traditions of the island and her uncle Guzmán's mischievous life. The second part takes place in El Building in New Jersey and in New York City, places where she experiences the harsh reality of living on the mainland. A comparison between the two parts shows that the poverty her family endured on the island resembles that of the mainland. Marisol suffers from an identity crisis created by living earlier in the Village of Salud, Puerto Rico, and later in Paterson, New Jersey, but also from her father's desire to become Americanized and her mother's knowledge of Puerto Rico and letters about Guzmán. Writing takes on a therapeutic purpose: it is a way of staying in touch with her Puerto Rican heritage while she lives in the United States.

Silent Dancing discusses the foundation of Puerto Rican culture, as conveyed by the protagonist's grandmother, and how it affects and controls the protagonist's life when she moves from the island to New Jersey. The island is associated with her maternal lineage and the mainland with her father, where they lived when he was not at sea with the U.S. Navy. Striving to reconcile both sides of her identity is, so to speak, the protagonist's dance between two cultures. Esmeralda Santiago is another writer whose words are receiving attention from the mainstream reader. She has published *When I was Puerto Rican* (1993) and *Américas Dream* (1996), which refer to aspects of her life in both Puerto Rico and the United States.

Like poetry and narrative, the Nuyorican theater is rapidly gaining in popularity with the emergence of such performing groups as the Puerto Rican Playwrights and Actors Workshops, Teatro Cuatro, El Teatro Ambulante, and Aquarius Theater. This genre is particularly important to the contemporary Puerto Rican and Latino communities because it re-creates the familiar difficulties and disappointments of life in the United States, thus providing an appealing art form for both first-time and experienced theatergoers.

Hispanic drama written in the United States has a long history that dates back to the nineteenth century; but in recent times Puerto Rican theater can be traced to Fernando Sierra Berdecía's *Esta noche juega el joker* (1939), a play about the cultural differences between the island and the mainland and the adjustments Puerto Ricans must undergo in New York. It received standing ovations from the public when performed at the Club Artístico del Casino de Puerto Rico and outside the island. Berdecía's tradition was continued by Manuel Méndez Ballester with *Encrucijada* (1958) and Jaime Carrero with *Caja de caudales F M* (1978). But Nuyorican theater is best represented by Pedro Pietri, Tato Laviera, and in particular Miguel Piñero, who was also known as a poet, with his play *Short Eyes* (1974). Like Mohr's stories, Piñero's play has met with great success, receiving the New York Drama Critics Circle Award and the Obie (Off-Broadway) for the year 1973 to 1974, produced by Joseph Papp at Lincoln Center, and earning laudatory reviews by magazines and newspapers such as the *New York Times*, the *Daily News*, and *Newsweek*, among others. The play received its strongest endorsement, by Hollywood, when it was made into a full-length motion picture under the same name. Piñero's play recalls the prison theme prevalent in Thomas's *Down These Mean Streets* and *Seven Long Times*. The play reduces the tensions in society to their basic premise, to the racial and ethnic discrimination blacks and Puerto Ricans in and outside prison must endure. In prison language (which recalls that of the barrios and ghettos), "short eyes" refers to a child molester, the most heinous crime of all. Prison life is a mirror of society in that it has a set of racial problems and a system of justice. However, it is also an inversion of society because the traditional and prejudicial understanding of good and bad are not relevant: the crime is committed not by a black or a Hispanic but by a white, the black and Puerto Rican prisoners in their overwhelming numbers are in power, and homosexuality plays an important role in prison life. As in society, prison in the play is ineffective for correcting behavior.

V

As chroniclers of an ethnic culture that is Puerto Rican and North American, Puerto Rican writers in the United States have provided a framework for other recent Hispanic Caribbean authors who write about their lives and experiences in the same North American environment. As Cubans come to terms with the permanent nature of their exile condition, many authors are writing about Cuban American themes. They describe the problems that affect the Cuban American community, even though this community is not homogeneous regarding its political views toward Cuba.

With the broad legal and political use of the term *Hispanic*, Cuban Americans as well as other Hispanic groups have taken advantage of opportunities created by the sacrifices Puerto Rican Americans and other dark-skinned groups have borne, and these groups have made a small amount of headway within North American culture. Whether North American culture can distinguish between the different Hispanic groups or whether it is more convenient for political and statistical purposes to lump them all together, recent Cuban Americans have profited from the changes brought about by the efforts attributed mainly to the Young Lords and other members of the Puerto Rican community.

It is still early to identify Cuban American figures who will leave a lasting mark, but some literary patterns are emerging. Cuban American narrators write in Spanish and in English. Those who use Spanish bring aspects of contemporary Spanish American literature into their works. Those who use English follow the same traditions as those writing in Spanish and also adhere to North American literary trends: the adopted language suggests an assimilation of sorts, whereas the continued use of the Spanish vernacular represents an attempt to preserve Cuban or Hispanic identity. Although some authors write in Spanish, an increasing number of them are writing in English. Some go a step further and capture the influence one language has over the other. These writers are at the forefront of developing a Latino intercultural literature.

In narrative, the theme of the coming together of the two languages and cultures is highlighted by Raquel Puig Zaldívar's "Nothing in Our Hands but Age." In this amusing yet tragic story, Puig Zaldívar unites two generations of Cuban exiles, one represented by a teacher educated in the United States and the other by an elderly exiled couple who must return to school and learn English to revalidate their degrees. The story is about freedom, pride, and perseverance. Similarly, Roberto Fernández's *La vida es un special* (1981), which pertains to Cuban exiles living in Miami, underscores the lack of communication between the younger generation that wants to assimilate into mainstream society, and the adults, who do not speak English and desire to preserve the original culture. In language, the harsh reality is represented by the coming together of Spanish, English, and Spanglish. Fernández's *La montaña rusa* (1985), influenced by the Spanish American novel of the Boom period, expands on the themes of the first work, depicts the life of Cuban Americans in Miami, and is critical of their sexual and anticommunist obsessions as well as liberal ideas. Most recently he published *Raining Backwards* (1988) and *Holy Radishes* (1995), novels that gather aspects of Cuban culture within the North American environment. In Elías Miguel Muñoz's *Los viajes de Orlando Cachumbambé* (1984), the author uses contemporary techniques to describe a Cuban exile narrator-protagonist who seesaws between two cultures as his mixture of Spanish and English suggests. Muñoz moves closer to North American culture in his *Crazy Love* (1989), whose title refers to a song by the American pop figure Paul Anka. The novel is written in English and highlights the convergence of the two cultures. By contrast, in María del Carmen Boza's story "Etruscans," reference to Cuba and Miami are part of the protagonist's past; Cuban culture can hardly be discerned, as the protagonist visits a farm in rural Pennsylvania. The story relates to school, friendship, pride, and honesty.

Cuban American writers, like their established exile counterparts, write about Cuba and exile. For example, Pablo Medina, who wrote *Pork Rind and Cuban Songs* (1975) and *Arching into the Afterlife* (1991), also published *Exiled Memories: A Cuban Childhood* (1990), an autobiographical account in which the protagonist recollects the first twelve years of his life, including his experiences in pre- and postrevolutionary Cuba, and those after his arrival in New York in 1960. Above all, the book is a collective memory of personal experiences, but it also comprises family customs and traditions that allow the protagonist to narrate events in the nineteenth and twentieth centuries. The book is a nostalgic account of the past and is accompanied by illustrations of Medina and his family. In Damián Fernández's short story "Litany," the protagonist lives in Cuba; he is not a part of mainstream life and does not participate in Cuban revolutionary society. In Roberto Fernández's "La encadenada," the characters find it difficult to overcome their exile condition.

The exile experience is also a theme among the younger writers of the "Mariel Generation." Virgil Suárez, the author of *Latin Jazz* (1989), *Welcome to the Oasis and Other Stories* (1992), *Havana Thursday* (1995), and *Going Under* (1996), also published *The Cutters* (1991), which describes a Cuban exile's worst nightmare. Julián Campos, waiting at the

Havana Airport to leave the island and join his family in the United States, is detained by the Cuban security police. Because of the departure of his family five years earlier and his desire to leave the island, Julián is forced to join the Communist youth and do additional voluntary work cutting sugarcane. The time of the narration is 1969, one year before the completion of the failed 10-million-ton sugar harvest. In the end Julián's situation is desperate, and he escapes from the island-prison and arrives in Miami. Two other writers of the Mariel Generation worth noting are Roberto Valero and Miguel Correa.

The representation of two cultures, two languages, and two countries in Cuban American narrative is also reflected in poetry. In *Cimarrón* (1979), Ricardo Alonso is disappointed with the United States but also knows that he is a stranger to the island. In *Sorting Metaphors* (1983), Ricardo Pau-Llosa looks at Miami with a distant critical eye. In her "Para Ana Velfort," of *Palabras juntan revolución* (1981), Lourdes Casal is caught between two worlds: the poetic voice refers to New York as her *patria chica*, even though she recognizes that she was not born there. But Casal's major contribution to the Cuban American community lies in her leadership as a founder of *Areíto*, the periodical that broke away from the monolithic view of the exile community and helped set the foundation for the creation of the first contingent of the Brigada Antonio Maceo, composed of fifty-five sons and daughters of Cuban exiles who returned to the motherland in December 1977. This last event was instrumental in setting the groundwork for "the Dialogue" between the exile community and the Cuban government and for the reunification of the Cuban family. In Cuba, members of *Areíto* published *Contra viento y marea* (1978), a collection of their experiences before and after exile.

The two most important Cuban American poets are Octavio Armand and José Kozer, whose works can be understood as responding to the problematics of contemporary Latin American writing. Armand's poetry includes *Horizonte no es siempre lejanía* (1970), *Cómo escribir con erizo* (1979), *Biografía para feacios (1977–79)* (1980), *Superficies* (1980), *With Dusk* (1984), and *Refractions* (1994). Armand's works are difficult to classify; he attempts to bridge the gap between poetry and prose, at times bordering on one or the other or even a combination of both. His works reveal a preoccupation with the word; not satisfied with its old referents, he desires to attribute to it more than what their tired meanings offer. Other concerns include the physical, psychological, and emotional estrangements in which the body, his and that of the text, plays an important role. In *Biografía para feacios* Armand searches for and escapes to where he is because there is no "other side."

Other poets go beyond the Cuban American experience. Kozer's most recent works include *La rueca de los semblantes* (1980), *Jarrón de las abreviaturas* (1980), *Bajo este cien* (1983), *La garza sin sombras* (1985), *El carrillón de los muertos* (1987), and *Carece de causa* (1988). The creativity in language noted in Armand's poetry is also present in Kozer's works except that in the case of the latter, it becomes an eternal quest for answers to questions that have no solutions. The poem becomes an unending search for identity and meaning. He tries to put together a puzzle in which he is just another piece: that of a Cuban Jew in an adopted New York environment. Some of Kozer's poems include Yiddish words with cultural and political referents, thus adding a multicultural dimension to his tropes. For example, in "Kafka" Kozer writes about physical isolation and mental escape and makes references to Prague and Lima. In "Julio" the poetic voice describes with nostalgia a past in which childhood and his grandmother were central elements. In an insightful essay on Kozer's works, "Noción de José Kozer," the critic (and poet) Gustavo Pérez Firmat highlights the use of various languages with their multiple referents and studies the grammatical function of parentheses in the poems.[13]

Cuban American theater is beginning to make inroads in the United States. Of the playwrights, Dolores Prida stands out as a premier writer. She has already written and produced the plays of *Beautiful Señoritas and Other Plays* (1991), which includes *Beautiful Señoritas* (1977), *Coser y cantar: A One-Act Bilingual Fantasy for Two Women* (1981), *Savings* (1985), *Pantallas* (1986), and *Botánica* (1990). *Beautiful Señoritas*, performed many years before it was published in 1991, deserves special attention. The play is influenced by the woman's movement in the United States and is an attempt to address the issue of Cuban or Hispanic women within the North American context.

Although writers such as Armand, Kozer, and Prida are gaining in popularity, other Cuban American writers are known only in small circles, mainly within the Cuban and Hispanic communities in the United States. Perhaps the exception is Oscar Hijuelos and his *The Mambo Kings Play Songs of Love* (1989), which was published by a major publisher, Farrar Straus Giroux, and earned him a Pulitzer Prize in 1990. Hijuelos had already published *Our House in the Last World* (1984), which pertains to the experiences of his family, who traveled to the United States in the 1940s, and *The Fourteen Sisters of Emilio Montez O'Brien* (1993) and *Mr. Ives' Christmas* (1995); but it was *The Mambo Kings* that made him the star figure of Cuban American writers. Reviewed by all major newspapers and magazines and turned into a motion picture, the novel, set in 1949, narrates the journey of two Cuban musicians, César and Néstor Castillo, who leave Havana and with hard work become musical celebrities of the mambo in New York. After his failed affair with María, Néstor devotes his life to her memory and writes twenty-two versions of "Beautiful María of My Soul." Music makes the protagonists famous during a period in which Latin Music was leaving its mark in the United States; they even appear on the *I Love Lucy* show and play in Desi Arnaz's Tropicana Club. In Margo

Jefferson's words: "Hijuelos is writing music of the heart, not the heart of flesh and blood that stops beating, 'but this other heart filled with light and music . . . a world of pure affection, before torment, before loss, before awareness.'"[14] With *The Mambo Kings*, Hijuelos has made the transition from Cuban American to mainstream North American literature.

Like Hijuelos, Cristina García is another Cuban American writer to arrive forcefully on the national scene. She announced her arrival with her first novel, *Dreaming in Cuban*, about the protagonist's life in New York and her return trip to Havana during the events surrounding the takeover of the Peruvian Embassy, which led to the Mariel boatlift. García has released a second novel, *The Agüero Sisters* (1997), which highlights the lives of the two sisters separated in childhood but reunited as adults. One lived in Cuba and the other in New York.

VI

Dominicans are the most recent group of Hispanic Caribbean authors to write in the United States. The Dominican Republic and its writers have been affected by two important events: the end of the Trujillo dictatorship and the U.S. invasion. In the Dominican Republic, these two events motivated a Dominican literature obsessed with narrating life under the dictatorship and during the U.S. occupation. The same events opened the door for a new wave of Caribbean immigrants to the United States, increasing in numbers in the decade of the seventies. Only in the decade of the eighties has a Dominican literature written in the United States emerged.

Dominican authors writing in the United States are mainly poets, and their works resemble those of first-generation migrants who write in Spanish and publish in their country of origin. Their presence in the United States has given them greater freedom to continue the Dominican literary tradition abroad. Some writers are merging their native culture with that of their adopted country to form a synthesis of the two. Magazines and anthologies have given publicity to these authors and helped create an interested public. Magazines that have featured Dominican work include *Letras e imágenes* (1981–82), *Inquietudes* (1981–82), *Punto 7 Review* (1985–), and *Alcance* (1983–). Unfortunately, as can be seen here, some of the magazines have had limited circulation. Of the anthologies, we should mention Franklin Gutiérrez's *Espiga del siglo* (1984), *Niveles del imán* (1983), and *Voces del exilio* (1986); Daisy Cocco de Filippis's and Emma Jane Robinett's *Poems of Exile and Other Concerns/Poemas del exilio y de otras inquietudes* (1988); and Cocco de Felippis and Franklin Gutiérrez's *Historias de Washington Heights y otros rincones del mundo/Stories from Washington Heights and Other Corners of the World* (1994).

Like other Hispanic Caribbean authors, Dominican writers are beginning to show the influence of North American culture in their works.

Leandro Morales writes about death in "Coplas para la muerte de mi madre" and about the French dramatist Artaud in "Antonin Artaud," a theme also repeated by Alexis Gómez Rosa in "Cédula métrica"; but in "Cielo pragmático" and "Una y otra vez me preguntaron," Gómez Rosa diverges from Dominican themes, describing the cemeteries of Newark and New York's Central Park, respectively. The search for an identity created by living abroad is present in English in Julia Álvarez's *Homecoming* (1984). She and Chiqui Vicioso also offer a female perspective in Dominican poetry. The loss of identity is a concern of Franklin Gutiérrez in his poetry collection *Helen* (1986); the title poem is about a woman whose transformation is evident in her name change from the Spanish Helena to the English Helen. The reality of living in New York and searching for the American dream is best captured by Guillermo Francisco Gutiérrez in *Condado con candado* (1986). The despair created by exile is present in the works of Tomás Rivera Martínez and Héctor Rivera. African American awareness of race and racism is another important influence on Dominican authors. Norberto James Rolling looks at the issues of race in the Dominican Republic and brings into focus an African Caribbean tradition. Chiqui Vicioso recognizes and defends the Haitian influence on Dominican culture.

Race is also the concern of Miguel A. Vázquez, one of the first Dominican narrators to write in the United States. His *Mejorar la raza* (1977) is a coming to terms with the racial prejudice of Hispanic Caribbean culture that promotes the betterment of blacks by "whitening" their skin color. Although the novel takes place in the Dominican Republic, the United States is mentioned briefly. The true focus, however, is on the matter of race.

Viriato Sención lives in New York and has already become a major Dominican writer. He has published *Los que falsificaron la firma de Dios* (1992; *They Forged the Signature of God*, 1995), which received the National Novel Prize in the Dominican Republic, an award granted by the Secretaría de Estado de Educación, Bellas Artes y Cultos. The novel uncovers the complicity between the church and state during and after the Trujillo dictatorship. Sención has also published a collection of short stories, *La enana Celania y otros cuentos* (1994).

Of the Dominican writers, Julia Álvarez has already found a place among her better-known Latino counterparts with her novel *How the Garcia Girls Lost Their Accents* (1991). Like Mohr and Ortiz Cofer, who write about their family and childhood memories, Álvarez also describes the dynamic relationships that exist between her mother, father, and their four daughters. Like other immigrants and exiles, she too tries to understand their arrival from the Dominican Republic to the United States at the age of ten and the pressures to assimilate and maintain her own identity.

The duality is also reflected in her writing style, in which she brings to English her knowledge of Spanish. Álvarez brings Dominican issues to the attention of a North American reader. *In the Time of the Butterflies* (1994), an account of the Mirabal sisters and their fight against the Trujillo dictatorship, shares the same structure as *How the Garcia Girls Lost Their Accents*. Both deal with Dominican themes and narrate the lives of four sisters during the Trujillo years, each of the sisters provides her own perspective, and one of them serves as the writer's alter ego. *In the Time of the Butterflies* was not only a project for Álvarez to reacquaint herself with Dominican history, but in the writing of the novel and taking on the voices of the sisters, she actively participates against Trujillo, whose government was responsible for her family's exile to the United States. Álvarez has also published *Yo* (1997), based on the character of Yolanda of her first novel.

Most recently, Junot Díaz's *Drown* (1996), a collection of short stories about Dominicans back home and on the continent, has made him a recognized writer almost overnight. Like Cristina García, he had published little before his first major work. He has also published *Negocios cuentos* (1997), which continues the themes of his first book.

It will only be a matter of time before other Dominican authors follow the path initiated by Puerto Rican American and Cuban American writers who use the adopted language to write about the Hispanic experience in New York and in other Spanish-speaking cities. Some writers, Morales, Álvarez, Gutiérrez, Rivera, and Gómez Rosa, for example, are already publishing in the United States.

Latino Caribbean literature written in the United States forms an integral part of a Spanish American literature of exile and migration. As the conditions of authors living in the United States become more permanent, their literature will include more images about Hispanic life in North American cities. Similarly, as the younger authors continue to express themselves in English, their works will become a part of a Hispanic American ethnic literature that describes the life of Latinos in the United States. Writers such as Nicholasa Mohr, María del Carmen Boza, Judith Ortiz Cofer, and Oscar Hijuelos are beginning to reflect the metaphorical dance between Hispanic Caribbean tradition and a North American context.

TWO

Puerto Rican American Poetry
Street Rhythms and Voices of the People

Another petal reaches

into the past, to Puerto Rico
when my mother was a child bathing in a small

river and splashing water up on
the yucca leaves to see them roll back pearls.
—William Carlos Williams

We want control of our communities by our people and programs to guarantee that all institutions serve the needs of our
people. People's control of police, health services, church,
schools, housing, transportation and welfare are needed. We
want an end to attacks on our land by urban renewal, highway
destruction, and university corporations. LAND BELONGS TO
ALL THE PEOPLE!
  —Point 6 of Thirteen-Point Program, the Young Lords Party

I

CARIBBEAN migration to the United States, for either economic
or political reasons, has had a profound impact on the experience
of all immigrants. This is especially true of Puerto Ricans, whose
country was transformed from a Spanish colony to a U.S. one.
During the late nineteenth and early twentieth centuries, Puerto Ricans
were already a visible presence in the United States. However, they and
other Hispanics were not always welcomed, and some were forced to abandon their culture and adjust to that of the dominant environment.

In *Divided Borders: Essays on Puerto Rican Identity* (1983), Juan Flores
identifies four moments in the Nuyorican ethnic consciousness, derived
from his reading of poetry.[1] I will outline them in the manner in which he
offers them, though he warns the reader that they should not be considered

in chronological order. The first is characterized by hostility Puerto Ricans face on a day-to-day basis, due to prejudice, bias, and discrimination. They view the dominant culture as denying them the opportunity afforded to other citizens. The second refers to a spiritual and psychological return to an idealized image of Puerto Rico. This return to the origin does not take into account the economic reality of why these immigrants left the island. They look to the island to recover a lost past that includes the African and indigenous foundations of Puerto Rican culture, not the elite, but the popular one, of the poor and working class. The third is an acceptance of the New York environment, which allows Puerto Ricans to insert themselves into the life of New York City and, consequently, an understanding of dominant and popular cultures. This is done, however, without abandoning an awakened island consciousness. In fact, it is the latter that leads to a renewed relation with the city. This category has a linguistic component of Spanish, but it also includes bilingualism. Moreover, there is an identification with Afro-Caribbean traditions. The fourth is distinguised by a branching out and interaction with the city's nondominant cultures, such as African American, Latin American, and Caribbean, a concept Flores associates with J. M. Blaut.[2] This approach, of course, does not imply assimilation or abandonment of national culture. Rather, it is a collective interaction.

Flores's four categories set the stage for a meaningful dialogue on Nuyorican identity. Though Flores does not say so, these categories should not be considered static, but dynamic. Because some overlap among them exists, it is conceivable for a poem or a sense of consciousness to move from one category to the other. For the writer, fluidity depends on the stage of his work at which he finds himself. Although some writers will only focus on one particular theme or possess a particular consciousness, others may show a certain development that will allow them to transgress the limitations or definition of any one category. More likely than not, it is possible that a poem or a writer will possess two or more of the categories.

Flores only refers to Nuyorican poetry and consciousness and does not consider the mind-set of Puerto Ricans living outside the five boroughs of New York City, in such places as Florida, Illinois, Connecticut, California, or Georgia. Although Puerto Ricans who live outside New York City are in the minority, they also represent an important and growing component of Puerto Rican American consciousness. Some have already constructed another poetic perspective that incorporates aspects of Flores's categories, but also goes beyond them. Noting differences in some of these non–New York groups, we come to realize that differences occur even if we limit our observations to Nuyorican poetry. Miguel Algarín and Bob Holman's anthology *Aloud: Voices From the Nuyorican Poets Cafe* (1994), contains poems that fit into Flores's four categories and others that do not. In fact,

Algarín and some of the poets represented in his anthology have found complicity with North American poetry, writers, such as Bob Holman, and promoters, such as Marc Smith, in and outside New York City.[3]

Some North American writers have become an integral part of the Nuyorican Poets Cafe; similarly, North American culture and politics have also been instrumental in the development of Nuyorican poetry in particular and Puerto Rican American poetry in general. I am referring to the contributions made by the women's movement in creating a sense of consciousness among both Puerto Rican male and female writers, leading them to challenge traditional Hispanic culture, as we shall see later. The gay and lesbian movement has also had a smaller, but nevertheless signficant, impact on writers as well.

Mainstream North American culture has certainly influenced Puerto Rican writers. This influence, as well as the intersection between North American and Hispanic or Puerto Rican culture, is evident in the works of William Carlos Williams, one of the great poets of U.S. literature. Williams's upholding of his Hispanic identity is the premise of Julio Marzán's *The Spanish American Roots of William Carlos Williams* (1994). According to Marzán, William Carlos Williams lived a dual existence, between the Anglo William and Puerto Rican Carlos; he inherited his identity from a Puerto Rican mother and a British father reared in the Spanish Caribbean. In his introduction Marzán sets the groundwork for his study:

> The household, at least during Williams' childhood, was predominantly Spanish-speaking, a setting that created a backdrop to a very common upbringing in this society: William Carlos grew up bicultural. This implicitly signifies that, like any child of immigrants or from a minority culture in the United States, Williams grew up aware of living in a society that devalued the foreign culture he received at home, imposing on him the life-informing quest to reconcile his cultures.[4]

Williams knew that if he wanted to be a successful mainstream writer, he would have to immerse himself in U.S. society and culture. Though Williams moved into the Anglo sphere, he was not able or willing to deny the Carlos side of his persona.

With this book, Marzán attempts to correct the misperceptions about Williams as an exclusively U.S. writer, to include his Hispanic side. Marzán's study uncovers different dimensions of William Carlos Williams's life, from the complex figures that William and Carlos represented, to his mother and father's influences on his life. Writers instrumental in Williams's development included Hilda Doolittle, Wallace Stevens, and Ezra Pound, who gave Williams the first two of four volumes

of *Poesías selectas castellanas,* which helped the evolving author to translate Carlos's culture into his own works. Furthermore, Williams was
inspired by Spanish poets—in particular Luis de Góngora y Argote,
Francisco de Quevedo y Villegas, Juan Ruiz (the Archpriest of Hita), and
Federico García Lorca—and Spanish American ones, like José Martí and
Luis Palés Matos. In chapter 7, "Conversation on the 'Weather,'" Marzán
discusses the importance of Williams as a North American but also as an
ethnic writer, in the sense that the North American literary canon is "a
compendium of a great ethnic literature."[5]

Marzán does a metareading of Williams's writings and recovers the
"Carlos" that was always present. The Hispanic side of Williams is evident
in works such as *The Autobiography, Yes, Mrs. Williams, Kora, Al Que
Quiere, The Tempers,* and poems such as "All the Fancy Things," "Eve,"
"Against the Weather," "El Hombre," and "The Open Window," which
uncover Hispanic culture and the Carlos within the William. Marzán uses
his knowledge of Spanish and Hispanic culture to decode Williams's works.
For example, in "The Ordeal" he shows that "our fellow" is "a pun on the
Spanish *falo,* 'phallus'" and that "disman" is a play on the Spanish *desma-
nar,* "an archaic word, one of whose meanings is 'to remove something
from use, to separate.'"[6]

Given the nature of his study, Marzán cannot help but take issue with
other scholarly works written about Williams, which emphasize the Anglo-
American identity and thereby undermine or downplay Carlos's Hispanic
culture. Marzán corrects well-regarded research, like Rod Townley's *The
Early Poetry of William Carlos Williams* (1975), Paul Mariani's *William
Carlos Williams: A New World Naked* (1981), Ann Fisher-Wirth's *William
Carlos Williams and Autobiography: The Woods of His Own Nature*
(1989), James E. Breslin's *William Carlos Williams: An American Artist*
(1985), and Kerry Driscoll's *William Carlos Williams and the Maternal
Muse* (1987). These and other studies show in their shortcomings that
scholarship is not objective; rather, it is based on cultural interpretations.

Marzán studies Williams's family to understand what affect his parents
may have had on his development. William George was an Englishman
who grew up in the Spanish Caribbean and was culturally mixed. Even
though Williams paints his father in "Adam" as a cold northerner, he did
marry a Puerto Rican. He worked with Williams on translations of Spanish
American writers like Rafael Arévalo Martínez, José Santos Chocano, Juan
Julián Lastra, Leopoldo Díaz, and José Asunción Silva. Furthermore,
Williams's father preferred to speak Spanish at home, and he traveled frequently to Spanish-speaking countries.

Williams was certainly influenced by his mother and her culture. As
he did with his father, Williams also translated Spanish literature with his
mother; Quevedo's *El perro y la calentura* stands out as a notable example.

Williams's suppression of Spanish, Marzán tells us, was a way of becoming independent from his mother and his father. His father's death coincided with a significant change in the poet's writing style. At that point, the poet distanced himself from the formality associated with this figure and from Spanish and Spanish literature, interests that later reemerged when Williams began to support the Republican forces in the Spanish Civil War. One oversight in Marzán's study is that he dedicates more than an entire chapter to Williams's mother, whereas the same importance in space is not afforded to his father, who even pointed out typographical errors in Williams' Spanish.

In spite of Marzán's attempt to amend the record, I wonder if he wanted to make Williams more Puerto Rican or Spanish American than Williams himself wanted to be. The book's title, where only the Spanish American roots are suggested, gives evidence to support this suspicion. In addition, Marzán's convincing study illustrates that just as Williams looked to Spanish America he also looked to Spain. Would not the word *Hispanic* be more appropriate because it encompasses the Spanish-speaking worlds on both sides of the Atlantic?

The Spanish American Roots of William Carlos Williams also alludes to the Spanish American roots of Julio Marzán and is therefore a personal study. Marzán is a scholar, poet, and narrator of considerable merit, and the research for his book has given meaning to his own Hispanic heritage within the U.S. environment. Like Flores's work on Nuyorican writers, Marzán's book will also provide an important avenue of identity for other Puerto Ricans and Latino writers born or raised in the United States and whose writings attempt to mediate between the two cultures.

Marzán's study is controversial because it questions accepted and dominant notions about Williams. However, it is not so much that Williams hid Carlos but that critics refused to give due credit to his Hispanic side. The Carlos within the Williams has always existed, and with this book, Williams no longer has to stir in his grave; he can now rest in peace.

William Carlos Williams is an important symbol for younger Puerto Rican poets writing in the United States. This holds true particularly in the case of Víctor Hernández Cruz, who found that Williams's works have a way of expressing the immediacy of the moment.[7] The inspiration of Williams's work is a spiritual and physical part of Hernández Cruz's poetry. In *Aloud: Voices from the Nuyorican Poets Cafe,* Algarín and Holman reproduce Hernández Cruz's "An Essay On William Carlos Williams," a poem written in a style and language that recalls the master poet's work.

> I love the quality of the
> spoken thought
> As it happens immediately

uttered into the air
Not held inside and rolled
around for some properly
schemed moment
Not sent to circulate a cane
field
Or on a stroll that would include
the desert and Mecca
Spoken while it happens
Direct and pure
As the art of salutation
of mountain campesinos come to
the plaza
The grasp of the handshake upon
encounter and departure
As gesture unveiling the occult
behind the wooden boards of
your old house
Remarks show no hesitation
to be expressed
The tongue itself carries
the mind
Pure and sure
Sudden and direct
like the appearance
of a green mountain
Overlooking a town.[8]

In recollection of some of Williams's poems, Hernández Cruz also includes references to Puerto Rican and Hispanic landscapes and culture.

If Williams can be considered a precursor for Puerto Rican and Latino writers who attempt to navigate between Hispanic and North American cultures on the continent, a different and more defining pattern emerges in the second half of the twentieth century with Puerto Rican poets also born or raised in the United States. Nuyorican poetry is a testament of the lives of the Puerto Rican community in New York, from the moment Operation Bootstrap was implemented and large numbers of Puerto Ricans were forced to leave the island and seek a better life in the United States. Whereas some writers look to William Carlos Williams for inspiration, others find it in Julia de Burgos, who lived and died in New York City. Burgos's works are an important source of motivation for male and female writers.[9] The revolutionary and defiant actions of Albizu Campos, Oscar Collazo, Lolita Lebrón, Ángel Figueroa, and other nationalist leaders have also had a major impact on mainland writers.

The poetry of Nuyorican writers is closely related to events that unfolded during the decades of the sixties and seventies in New York City and tied especially to the Young Lords Party. Similar to the Black Panthers, the Weathermen Underground, and other militant groups of the period, the Young Lords Party was a self-proclaimed revolutionary organization that engaged in social, education, political, and health programs. Members of the party became visible and outspoken leaders of the Latino communities mainly on the East Coast of the United States.

A Puerto Rican nationalist organization with an international outlook, the Young Lords Party brought unity and pride to many Latinos who had either rejected their Hispanic heritage and wanted to assimilate into North American society or were isolated from the dominant culture. They followed the teachings of Campos, as well as those of contemporary revolutionary leaders Fidel Castro and Che Guevara. Their discipline, philosophy, and attire—they were known for their black berets—recall those of Castro's rebel army who had defeated the Batista dictatorship and seized power in January 1959. At that time, Castro and other Cuban leaders served as a source of inspiration for anyone seeking to fight oppression.

The activities of the Young Lords Party follow in the tradition of nineteenth-century Puerto Rican organizations such as the Dos Antillas, affiliated with the Partido Revolucionario Cubano, whose members were both Puerto Rican and Cuban. Dos Antillas and other organizations were founded in New York and conspired against the Spanish government to obtain Cuban and Puerto Rican independence.

In the twentieth century the Young Lords Party recalled the actions of other groups that pressed for better conditions for Puerto Ricans and other Latinos living in New York, such as La Escuela Francisco Ferrer y Guardia, the Puerto Rican division of the Socialist Party, the Asociación Nacionalista, El Club Eugenio María de Hostos, el Comité Pro–Puerto Rico, La Asociación Pro-independencia de Puerto Rico, and El Congreso Pro-independencia de Puerto Rico, among others. Prior to World War II and Operation Bootstrap, El Barrio was often the center of political activities. When General Franco's air force bombarded Madrid in the summer of 1936, thousands of Puerto Ricans marched in the streets to protest the Fascist attack. Other demonstrations included support for Albizu Campos and Puerto Rican independence.[10] Like many socialist and communist groups of the first half of the twentieth century and other radical organizations of the anti-Vietnam era, the Young Lords considered the U.S. government a repressive force against Africans, Native Americans, Chicanos, and, of course, Puerto Ricans. The Lords observed a relationship between the oppressed condition of these minority groups in the United States and that of people in other countries, for example, in the developing world. The Young Lords, however, had a more tangible struggle: Puerto Rico continued to be a colony of the United States, and Puerto Ricans were reduced to a colonial existence on the mainland.[11]

The Young Lords Party began in 1970 as the New York chapter of the Young Lords Organization, a Puerto Rican youth group based in Chicago. In 1969 the Young Lords Organization had entered into a Rainbow Coalition with the Black Panthers and the Young Patriots Organization, a white group, and they worked together for the mutual benefit of the people they represented. In New York, the Young Lords Organization incorporated other smaller activist groups, including the prominent Sociedad de Albizu Campos.[12]

The Young Lords Organization united college students and members of the community and brought to El Barrio and other Puerto Rican and Hispanic communities in New York a sense of pride and identity that had previously existed among cigar makers like Bernardo Vega and Jesús Colón during the early part of the twentieth century. They initiated Free Breakfast and Lead Poison Detection programs, which rapidly became popular with the Hispanic communities, thereby demonstrating a concern heretofore unseen among government or private agencies. The group's notoriety came on December 28, 1969, when the Young Lords took over a Methodist Church, located on the corner of 111th Street and Lexington Avenue, which had been oblivious to the needs of the Puerto Rican and Hispanic community. They renamed it the People's Church, and for the next eleven days the Lords provided a series of activities, which they believed would benefit the community, including daily breakfast, free clothing, a school, political education, free health, a day care center, and evening entertainment. Soon the ideas and activities of the Young Lords Organization spread to Newark and the Bronx, where branch offices opened in October 1969 and April 1970 respectively. Other chapters included those in Philadelphia and Bridgeport and two in Puerto Rico. In addition, the organization published the newspaper *Palante, the Voice of the Young Lord Organization—East Coast*, on May 8, 1969, and founded a New York radio program in March of the following year.

With the increased activity in New York and vicinity and the lack of direction from Chicago, the East Coast Chapter leadership separated from the main organization and changed its name to Young Lords Party, thus emphasizing its political mission. The party became involved in political and social issues of concern to all Hispanics, and in which they were the most affected group. Attention was given to health care issues, such as those addressed by Hispanics working in Gouverneur Hospital, on the Lower East Side, and Lincoln Hospital, in the South Bronx. Young Lord demonstrations ranged from protest against the murder of Julio Roldán, a Lord accused of committing suicide while under police custody, to their commemoration of the Ponce Massacre of 1937.

The Young Lords Party exerted a strong influence on all Latinos, women and men, young and old, students and dropouts, gang members and law-abiding citizens, workers, welfare recipients, and the unemployed alike. The party articulated eloquently the needs and feelings of Latinos living in the United States and channeled their dissatisfaction into a political movement. Equally important, the Lords uncovered a common disdain among city officials toward Hispanics. Hispanics and Latinos realized that they were isolated and marginal to society and understood the need to unite in order to achieve respect and dignity in the metropolis as well as to liberate Puerto Rico.

Puerto Ricans in U.S. cities have been stereotyped as emotional, hot-tempered, knife or weapon carriers, gang members, and criminals, often operating outside of the law. The Young Lords appropriated these images and interpreted them along political lines. Using extralegal tactics and defying the authorities became other acceptable methods of combat. As a political party, the Lords worked within the legal system, but as a revolutionary organization they carried guns and used any means necessary to achieve their intended goal.

The Young Lords observed an inequality within the system of government and justice that kept large numbers of Latinos and blacks living in slums, unemployed, or in prison. For the Lords, prisoners were not criminals, but victims of a legal system that discriminated against them: in essence, they were considered political prisoners. Inmates also identified with the Young Lords and viewed their incarceration from a sociopolitical perspective. The Young Lords' interest in prisoners is described in the following manner:

> We first got involved in the prisons struggle when the prisons in New York City first got taken by the inmates. Many of the sisters and brothers in jail had come from the streets we had worked in, and had read *Palante,* or were reading smuggled copies. In October of 1970, an organization that arose from the prison rebellions came from the concentration camps to become a section of the Young Lords Party. This was the Inmates Liberation Front (ILF).[13]

The Latino communities developed respect for a group of young brave men and women willing to risk everything, including their lives, to denounce the injustices to which Latinos were exposed. Many supported the cause of the Young Lords, if not by demonstrating with them, then by sharing and promoting the organization's ideas. This was the case with those Latinos who began to look to art to express their ideas and feelings, from Nuyorican poets to those who composed, played, and sang salsa music.

Nuyorican poetry developed in the decade of the sixties, concurrently with the civil rights movement, the Black Panthers, the Young Lords, and other organizations promoting black and Puerto Rican pride. This was particularly the case among people living in the inner cities of the eastern part of the United States, where the inequalities were most evident. The poetry expresses issues similar to those addressed by the leadership of organizations that denounce the deplorable conditions of Puerto Ricans and other Hispanics and Latinos living in New York City. It emerges from the conditions in the barrios and ghettos and reflects the reality of the people. The Nuyorican poet became the prophet of the Hispanic and Latino communities; the poems capture the voices of the people, their outlook on life, their feelings about themselves and each other, and their hardships. Unlike Rubén Darío's *modernismo* poetry, which was written for a minority and which celebrated aesthetic values, Nuyorican poets write for a majority and provide a coherent understanding of the marginal and isolated conditions under which their neighbors live. The poetry comes from the street and is expressed in the language of the street, at times in Spanish, at times in English, but also in Spanglish. In his book, Flores aptly studies the dimension of Puerto Rican language in literature and culture.[14]

Pedro Pietri, one of the early Nuyorican poets, was a member of the Young Lords Party and his "Puerto Rican Obituary," recited throughout New York and vicinity, was first published in *The Palante: Young Lords Party*.[15] The poem appears immediately after the introduction and sets the tone for what will follow. It addresses the same community the Young Lords were helping, and it chronicles the lives of Puerto Ricans living in New York City who were dedicated to working hard to obtain the American dream. Pietri's poem became a model for other poets and helped to define the poetic style known as Nuyorican poetry.

Pietri, who dresses in black and carries a black attaché case with the inscription RIP, recites his poems in a manner that recalls both the medieval troubadours and the rhythmic and repetitive discourses of soapbox politicians and street preachers. His poems are meant to be read out loud; the author has emphasized key words and images and insists on creating acoustic and visual tropes familiar to his audience. He relies on commonplace situations and experiences and portrays them with distinct humor, captivating his public and obliging individuals to look into a mirror and laugh at others as well as themselves.

In the "Puerto Rican Obituary," the poetic voice begins by referring to five recent Puerto Rican immigrants, three men and two women, who have much in common. In the first stanza the poetic personae remain nameless, and Pietri uses the third-person-plural pronoun, *they*, to identify them. The use of the pronoun suggests both anonymity within the dominant society and a general representation, alluding to any and everyone. These individuals, who are symbolic of a larger group of people, were model workers; they worked hard, played by society's rules, never took time off or even objected to their working conditions. In spite of their dedication, they were unable to improve their lives.

> They worked
> They worked
> and they died
> They died broke
> They died owing
> They died never knowing
> What the front entrance
> Of the first national bank
>   looks like.[16]

The repetition of the verbs *worked* and *died* is important in the poem. Pietri takes two diametrically opposed concepts and brings them together to explain the lives of his characters. Under other circumstances work leads to prosperity, but for Puerto Rican immigrants, work leads to death. In the quoted stanza the word *work* appears six times and *died* four times; in the next one, the word *died* is used six times along with *kill*, repeated three times. The tone of the poem's rhythmic and repetitive words underscores the foundation of the Puerto Rican experience, based on related concepts like *work, death,* and *kill.* Death is perhaps the most salient metaphor of the poem.

In the second stanza *they* are revealed to the reader: Juan / Miguel / Milagros / Olga / Manuel. Unfortunately, they and people like them will die and continue to die. The only thing they win or inherit and pass on to their children is not the fruits of their labor, but their debts. By believing in the American dream, Pietri's characters grasped onto the false hope of succeeding in American society, represented elsewhere in the poem by the insurmountable odds of winning the lottery. Mainstream U.S. society is officially closed to them and they are only objects to be taken advantage of, indicated by the grocery store owner who "sold them make-believe steaks / and bullet-proof rice and beans."[17]

The characters abandon their sense of origin and identity to reach the American dream and, therefore, commit a physical and spiritual suicide. In fact, they were dead well before they died: they rejected their own identity to accept one that had already been denied to them. Death continues to be ever present.

> Juan
> died waiting for his number
>   to hit

Miguel
Died waiting for the welfare
    check
To come and go and come
    again
Milagros
Died waiting for her ten
    children
To grow up and work
So she could quit working
Olga
Died waiting for a five
    dollar raise
Manuel
Died waiting for his
    supervisor to drop dead
so that he could get a
    promotion.[18]

Juan, Miguel, Milagros, Olga, and Manuel all died waiting to achieve what they perceived to be reasonable and attainable goals but, within the context of the society in which they live, are beyond their reach. Each hoped to move out of the ghetto and into the suburbs, signified in the poem by Queens, New York, where they could distance themselves from other Puerto Ricans and own a home in a white neighborhood. But their only ride outside of Spanish Harlem occurs after they die and are transported to the cemetery. Their desire to purchase land and property in Queens is fulfilled with the acquisition of their grave sites in Long Island Cemetery, the only plots of land available to them.

The false dreams of succeeding in North American society were created by rumors in Puerto Rico that depicted New York streets as being paved with gold and by television programs intended to appeal to mainstream Anglo-Americans. Situation comedies such as *My Three Sons, Ozzie and Harriet,* and *Leave it to Beaver* portrayed stable white families in a suburban setting, a life foreign to Latinos and African Americans living in urban environments. Nevertheless, this is the reward or dream everyone who worked hard expected to obtain, including Juan, Miguel, Milagros, Olga, and Manuel. Anglo-American culture, the poem warns, is antithetical to the Puerto Rican people and their way of life and will ultimately destroy both.

Pietri incorporates elements of Caribbean traditions Puerto Rican immigrants bring to the United States, thus alluding to the presence of

Hispanic culture in the United States, with some important transformations. Hispanic culture is present within the context of Afro-Caribbean religion, when relatives of the dead visit Sister López, a spiritualist. But rather than pay their traditional respect to the newly departed, they have come for financial rewards. They hope that the relatives in the other world will return and help them win the lottery. Pietri ridicules those who have lost their sense of Puerto Rican cultural values and who place those of Anglo-American society, namely money, above everything else. The characters even bargain with the dead: if the living win the lottery, they will comply with their family obligations "and we will visit your graves / on every legal holiday."[19] U.S. culture has altered the values of Puerto Rican immigrants, which they used to gain access to Anglo-American dominant society.

In stanza 15 the poem's tone undergoes a change. Pietri hints that all is not lost; on the contrary, after death there is redemption, associated with self-awareness, a theme on which he will insist toward the end of the poem, as we shall see later. Nevertheless, Pietri continues to underscore the marginal position of Puerto Ricans. North American society discriminates and Puerto Ricans hold the lowest-paid jobs and titles:

> Assistant, assistant, assistant,
>   assistant
> To the assistant, assistant
>   dishwasher[20]

Juan, Miguel, Milagros, Olga, and Manuel lived totally destructive lives. Not only were they destroyed by the system, but they also internalized the hatred and destruction and destroyed themselves and each other:

> Juan
> Died hating Miguel because
>   Miguel's
> Used car was in better
>   condition
> Than his used car
> Miguel
> Died hating Milagros because
>   Milagros
> Had a color television set
> And he could not afford one
>   yet
> Milagros
> Died hating Olga because

Olga
Made five dollars more on the
    same job

Olga
Died hating Manuel because
    Manuel
Had hit the numbers more
    times
Than she had hit the numbers
Manuel
Died hating all of them
Juan
Miguel
Milagros
Olga
Because they all spoke broken
    english
More fluently than he did[21]

Pietri underscores an acquired competitive attitude that leads each one to hate the other. Hating their own people consumes them, and they carry this emotion to their graves.

In stanza 20, Pietri refers to Juan, Miguel, Milagros, Olga, and Manuel's lack of identity, a subtext introduced at the outset of the poem; they felt that the only way they could make it was to deny who they were. Having accomplished that, they still did not succeed in being accepted by mainstream society. Their superhuman efforts were insufficient to overcome the discrimination in North American culture. Juan, Miguel, Milagros, Olga, and Manuel lost everything. They failed to obtain wealth and success, and they also abandoned their identity. But Pietri alludes to a possible redemption associated with rejecting North American values:

If only they
Had used the white
    supremacy bibles
For toilet paper purpose
And made their Latin Souls
The only religion of their race.[22]

Pietri's characters could have lived and died with a sense of pride in and respect for who they were; they are beautiful people, and this is the message of success.

Redemption is indeed possible. Toward the end of the poem, the tone changes and the word *died*, and others associated with death, are excluded. The ending continues with the repetition of words, but these are now adjectives of location in both English and Spanish, *where* and *aquí*, the latter one in Spanish, suggests Puerto Rico and Puerto Rican culture. More appropriately, the location is not physical, but mental, and refers to a state of mind in which you know who you are and what you stand for. The poetic voice proudly states: *Aquí* there is no hatred, but unity and spiritual camaraderie, and a sense of nationalism: "Aquí se habla español all the time." "Aquí you salute your flag first."[23]

The last stanza replicates Spanish words, and they increase in intensity not only with *Aquí* at the beginning of each line, but also in their synchronic structure: "Aquí qué pasa" and "Aquí to be called negrito y negrita." The use of Spanish represents the poetic voice's acceptance of a Hispanic identity within a North American environment. After all, the poem's final thoughts are written in Spanish and English: "Aquí to be called negrito y negrita / Means to be called love."[24] Hispanic and Puerto Rican identity is associated with pride, love, and power.

One may argue that in the "Puerto Rican Obituary" the Spanish element is undermined by the English contained in the last line. I should stress that the poetic voice is speaking to Latinos in New York, many of them second- and third-generation Hispanics who may understand the vernacular language of their parents but who feel more comfortable expressing themselves in the one of their adopted homeland. Language is an important issue, but the sense of identity, regardless of the language chosen to communicate, becomes the overwhelming concern of Pietri's "Puerto Rican Obituary."

The reader should observe that Pietri denies his characters a voice. Perhaps they did not deserve one, or they have nothing to say, or the poetic voice's familiarity with their lives was sufficient for him to provide a coherent picture of who they are. The poetic voice interprets and reinterprets the actions of the characters so the reader can understand them from one particular point of view. Just as the dominant society presents a homogeneous viewpoint as reality, Pietri does the same, but from the opposite point of view. From his other outlook, there is only one perspective; it explains the causes of death and recommends a means of redemption for the Puerto Rican and Latino communities. He excludes all other interpretations from the poem.

Pedro Pietri was a member of the Young Lords Party, but a more direct connection between Nuyorican poetry and the Lords organization is evident in the presence of Felipe Luciano. Originally a member of the Central Committee, Luciano was demoted to the position of cadre, and finally left the party. As a member of the Lords and even after, Luciano continued to

complement the party's actions; he worked with the community and promoted Puerto Rican identity and culture. A more recent Nuyorican poet,
Tato Laviera, acknowledges Luciano's importance within the Puerto Rican
community in his poem "felipe luciano i miss you in africa," which speaks
of the poet's admiration for Luciano's leadership during a trip the two made
to Africa.[25]

Felipe Luciano composed poems widely known during the late sixties
and early part of the seventies; one in particular was commented on and
recited by many but which has escaped anthologizers. Luciano's poem is
representative of the period in which the Young Lords Party participants
enjoyed their most influential years as leaders of the Puerto Rican community in New York, and it captures the mood of the period. Luciano entitled
his poem "Jíbaro/My Pretty Nigger," and he recited it at Sing Sing Prison
in a program with Eddie Palmieri; he recorded it in Palmieri's salsa record
album, *Eddie Palmieri Recorded Live at Sing Sing with Harlem River
Drive,* in 1972.

But Luciano had already recorded his poem on film, in the eighty-
minute motion picture *Right On! Poetry On Film. The Original Last
Poets,* directed by Herbert Danska and produced by Woodie King Jr. and
Danska, in 1968; and a record *Right On! The Original Last Poets,* released
the following year.[26]

Luciano was one of the original Last Poets, a group of young, innovative, and expressive African American and Afro–Puerto Rican poets. The
film is staged on a rooftop in the Lower East Side and is juxtaposed with
images from street scenes. Luciano, Gyland Kain, and David Nelson, in
order of appearance, celebrate blackness as a form of racial, cultural, and
sexual expression and also as a defiant discourse of difference directed
against the dominant white society. To the beat of two conga players, each
of the three poets recites in street language and with rhythm the pain, out-
rage, injustice, discrimination, and genocide perpetrated against black people. They propose violence and revolution as a means of ridding themselves
of the forces that oppress their people. The film and record include
Luciano's "Jíbaro/My Pretty Nigger," "Hey Now," and "Puerto Rican
Rhythms"; Kain's "Been Done Already, "Tell Me Brother," and "James
Brown"; and Nelson's "Die Nigga!," "Black Woman," and "Poetry is
Black." As a member of the Last Poets, Luciano established another connection between African American and Puerto Rican American literature,
politics, race, history, and culture. Like Pietri, Luciano was an important
influence on the development of Nuyorican poetry.

Puerto Ricans are also of African descent. The relations between the
two groups have been addressed by critics such as Flores, whose Chicano
friend Francisco observes the unity between Puerto Ricans and African
American culture in New York, and by Roberto Márquez's personal recol-

lection of James Baldwin.[27] Luciano brings together the African American and Latino or Afro–Puerto Rican modes of cultural expression together and prepares the groundwork for others to do the same.

As I mentioned, Luciano also recorded his poem with Palmieri, whose live performance at Sing Sing was not only a gesture to entertain a large African American and Latino audience but to show his solidarity with their culture and political struggle, recognizing the injustices to which many have been subjected. In 1980, Palmieri performed at the Cárcel Modelo of Bogotá, Colombia.

The image of protest in music is exemplified best by Willie Colón and his lead singer for eight years, Hector Lavoe, who sang about injustices in Puerto Rico and in other parts of Latin America. Rubén Blades, a candidate for the presidency of the Republic of Panama in 1992, is also known for his social and political message. For example, "Pedro Navaja" represents Blades's concern for the marginal elements of New York or any Caribbean city. Miguel Rondón clarifies the message in Blades's songs:

> What Blades did was simply to point out that subtle and very important bridge that unites the South Bronx with the Perla and with Petate; Navaja is the same person in all of the marginal areas of the Caribbean. He responds to all and he ends in the same place and salsa, as a popular art, ultimately gains an important dimension when it points to that bridge which many are quick in denying.[28]

Felipe Luciano's "Jíbaro/My Pretty Nigger" is a tribute to the image of the Puerto Rican *jíbaro*, the country bumpkin or hick, who became a symbol of Puerto Rico after Operation Bootstrap was put into effect. Prior to that period many Puerto Ricans would have dismissed the *jíbaro* figure as backward and ignorant, but for those now living abroad he became a representation of Puerto Rico and Puerto Rican identity and culture. Like Pietri's Juan, Miguel, Milagros, Olga, and Manuel, Luciano's *jíbaro* was a real and familiar image to Puerto Ricans living in New York. The *jíbaro* was someone they knew, if not as a member of the family, then as a neighbor; he was an authentic person with specific characteristics.

If Pietri's poem focuses exclusively on the lives of émigrés living in the United States, Luciano first reconstructs history, starting with Amerindian and African cultures and ending with events associated with Operation Bootstrap. Luciano composes his poem in standard Spanish and English and begins with Spanish as a way of recalling an origin, a previous time, defined by past culture and Puerto Rico. The Spanish segment of the poem was not part of the original composition, which Luciano recited in the film *Right On!* Rather, it was added to place the origin in a historic and linguistic context and meant to coincide with the language of the salsa singers. Luciano situates the *jíbaro* within his natural setting, the countryside, with references to sugarcane forests and Amerindian culture.

In the second stanza, Luciano changes to English, allowing him to remember the *jíbaro*, not only as a father and an ancestral figure belonging to the earth, the womb, as he has suggested in Spanish, but as a victim of the English language and North American culture. The manipulation of time, as well as men, have altered the natural course of events. The wind objects. Whereas the past was once "so simple," the present is complex and difficult to discern. It is also charged with images of destruction and decomposed objects.

> Fish smells and cane smells
> and fish smells and cane smells
> and tobacco and oppression
> make even God smell foul[29]

Luciano overlooks history to underscore present concerns. The oppression to which Luciano refers is not associated with an early historical moment defined by the encounter between Europe and the New World and the subsequent Spanish massacres of Amerindians and enslavement of Africans. Instead, he relates it to a more immediate history initiated by the U.S. government with Operation Bootstrap. Luciano does not consider the migration of Puerto Rican immigrants to the mainland as they considered it prior to their departure, that is, as an economic opportunity for the island's unemployed or underemployed; on the contrary, he looks at it from a perspective of knowing what transpired after they arrived on the mainland. According to Luciano, the migration was not voluntary; it was forced, as the *Marine Tiger* "vomited you on the harbor of a cold city to die." The *Marine Tiger* is not a poetic construct; rather, it refers to the name of a ship that soon became the symbol of the early migratory process. Bernardo Vega provides the following information about the ship:

> On July 2, 1946, the *Marine Tiger* set sail for our great city carrying a thousand Puerto Ricans. From then on that boat—which was hardly fit to carry passengers—carried one load of emigrants after another. The ship itself became part of a new Puerto Rican folklore, to such an extent, in fact, that the new arrivals to New York were referred to as "marine tigers." That month Pan American also inaugurated its first regular flights between San Juan and New York.[30]

Luciano uses the ship to illustrate that the migration would not have taken place, at least not in the numbers in which it did, had conditions on the island remained as they were before the U.S. decided to launch the experimental program to industrialize the island. But the interference of the U.S. government and the subsequent industrialization altered the Puerto Rican economy and produced the forced migration.

The migration underscores the difference between the past and the present, the island and the mainland. One is warm and sunny with sand and palm trees, the other is dark, cold, and barren. Once on the mainland, the speaker realizes that the United States is a powerful country, a power associated with the might of God, thus he accepts the present destiny as a divine right. This relationship allows the reader to understand why God smells foul; it is God himself who has betrayed the Puerto Rican people. Because the power of God is equated with the United States, which is also all-powerful, the government is also a representation of a new God.

As with Pietri's characters in "The Puerto Rican Obituary," the *jíbaro*, once on the mainland, attempts to assimilate into mainstream North American culture. The speaker searches for the *jíbaro* who hides but also leaves a trace and is present everywhere, manifested in synecdoches such as in

> the curve of your brow
> the slant of your baby's eyes
> the calf of your women dancing
> I dig you.

Equally important, the search for the other is also an examination of the self. Luciano's love for the *jíbaro* and the repetition at the end of the poem of the lines "I love you 'cause you're mine / and I'll never let you go" implies the successful conclusion of a search for and an acceptance of an identity, the *jíbaro* and the self. On the mainland, Puerto Rican identity cannot be the island but rather the metaphorical representation of the island and island culture in the presence of the *jíbaro*.

On more than one occasion Luciano uses the word *nigger*, which he borrows from African American speech and culture, to refer to the *jíbaro*. Although the word has a pejorative connotation when whites address blacks, it means the opposite when blacks and Latinos use it to refer to each other. In Luciano's poem, *nigger* is used as translation for the Spanish *negro*, which he also uses, but to show an affinity with African American culture as well. Within the context of Puerto Rican culture, it can be used with the same affection as *negro* or *negrito*, as Pietri indicates at the end of "Puerto Rican Obituary." For Luciano, the *jíbaro* is not exclusively an island image. He also defines him as part of the African American cultural component in the United States.

Unlike many other cities, New York provides the unique opportunity for the different ethnic groups and races to interact with each other, and this is especially evident between dark-skinned Puerto Ricans and African Americans, as we will see later in Piri Thomas's *Down These Mean Streets*. The affinity Puerto Ricans and African Americans feel for each other is based on social and economic oppression and racial identity, because many Puerto Ricans who traveled to the United States are dark-skinned. Therefore, the word *nigger* points to the intermingling of Latino and African American cultures, already reflected in the political cooperation between the Young Lords Party and the Black Panthers and other African American organizations. It also represents the common ground shared by the Last Poets. The articulation of the word *nigger* by Puerto Ricans and Latinos suggests that even though this and other words particular to African American speech had a specific historical origin, the use of such words also became an acceptable method of expression when sharing a common inner-city experience.

Luciano's derogatory reference to God and religion is a subtext present in the works of other Nuyorican poets. Puerto Ricans are Catholics, and the poets rely on their religious background even though they also feel abandoned by or marginal to God's creation. This is the case with Miguel Piñero, one of the most talented writers to come out of the New York ghetto environment, who passed away prematurely in 1988. Perhaps sensing his mortality, Piñero wrote "A Lower East Side Poem," a confessional and autobiographical composition, which also became his living will:

> A thief, a junkie I've been
> committed every known sin
> Jews and Gentiles . . . Bums and Men
> of style . . . run away child
> police shooting wild . . .
> mother's futile wails . . . pushers
> making sales . . . dope wheelers
> & cocaine dealers . . . smoking pot
> streets are hot & feed off those who bleed to death . . .
> all that's true
> all that's true
> all that's true
> but this ain't no lie
> when I ask that my ashes be scattered thru
> the Lower East Side.[31]

Piñero had accepted his destiny, for better or for worse, in New York, where he wanted to die. When that day arrived, his friends honored his wishes and scattered his ashes throughout the Lower East Side. Miguel Algarín provides us with a moving recollection of that day, as people walked, their numbers growing as they processed from Houston to 14th Street and from Second Avenue to Avenue D.[32]

The idea of accepting New York City instead of Puerto Rico as a place of origin is also present in Piñero's "This Is Not the Place Where I Was Born." The poem highlights the poet's return trip to the island, his place of birth. Unlike Luciano, he rejects it as the place of his spiritual and physical origin, as stated in the poem's title and repeated in the second line.

In the third line, Piñero recalls the paradisiacal images of Puerto Rico, which refer more to his mother's childhood memories than to the reality that forced her to abandon the island and travel to the United States:

> the shadows of her childhood recounted to me many times
> over welfare loan on crédito food from el bodeguero
> i tasted mango many years before the skin of the fruit
> ever reached my teeth.[33]

The last image suggests that the fruit of paradise, here a symbol of Puerto Rican culture, was passed on to him through the umbilical cord.

Piñero describes his place of birth in a paradigmatic structure, starting with the first-person pronoun:

> i was born on an island about 35 miles wide 100 miles long
> . . . .
> i was born in a village of that island where the police
> . . . .
> i was born in a barrio of the village on the island
> . . . .
> i was born on an island where to be puerto rican meant to be. . . .[34]

This vision of the past, implying peace and harmony, where Puerto Ricans are not a minority but brothers and sisters, is juxtaposed with a similar structure containing the word *no*, negating his place of birth: "no, i was not born here . . . / no, i was not born in the attitude and time of this place."[35] This paradigm suggests a different type of Puerto Rico. In contrast with the Puerto Rico of his mother's recollections or that revisited in Pietri's and Luciano's poems, this one is full of images of artificiality, discord, and battles:

> of pre-fabricated house/hotel redcap hustling people gypsy taxi cab
> fighters for fares to fajardo
> . . . .

> & foreigners scream that puertorriqueños are foreigners
> & have no right to claim any benefit on the birthport. . . .[36]

"This slave blessed land," repeated twice in the poem, indicates forced enslavement of Africans brought to the Caribbean islands. The line also intimates that Puerto Rico is a blessed land for all Puerto Ricans, as Piñero's mother believed. But "slave blessed land" is an oxymoron. How can slaves live in a blessed land? If it were truly blessed, they would no longer be slaves. Does this mean that though the land is blessed, slaves will continue to be slaves?

Piñero shows that, to the slave, the blessed land, which evokes bitter-sweet sensations, is "where nuyoricans come in search of spiritual identity." This is precisely the purpose of Piñero's journey and that of many other Nuyoricans, as we shall later see with other writers, who have been reared in an inhospitable New York City environment; they idealize Puerto Rico through their parents' memories. But once Piñero and other Nuyoricans return to the island, they are astonished by the treatment of their Puerto Rican brothers and sisters, and "are greeted with profanity."

This other Puerto Rico in many ways resembles the all-too-familiar Anglo-American environment Nuyoricans left behind. If the police of Piñero or his mother's childhood was a "servant or friend," this other

> in el condado area puerto rican under cover cop
> stop &arrest on the spot puerto ricans who shop for the flag
> that waves on the left—in souvenir stores—.[37]

Piñero proposes that Puerto Ricans, who are forced to come together in the North American environment and who feel nationalistic about their island, cannot express their Puerto Ricanness in Puerto Rico the way they do on the mainland. Unlike Nuyoricans, Puerto Ricans on the island adhere to different political ideologies. There, the Commonwealth and Statehood parties receive the majority of votes at the expense of the Independent and Socialist parties. According to Piñero, Puerto Ricans who live in New York and fight for the rights of their countrymen on the island go unnoticed or are unappreciated by islanders when returning "home."

> puertorriqueños cannot assemble displaying the emblem
> nuyoricans are fighting & dying for in newark, lower eastside
> south bronx where the fervor of being
> puertorriqueños is not just rafael hernández. . . .[38]

Piñero suggests that Puerto Ricans in New York are more Puerto Rican than those who reside on the island. In fact, there are similarities between wealthy North Americans and wealthy Puerto Ricans. Piñero also goes on the offensive against Cuban refugees who, because of their education and economic position in Cuba, have taken over some control of the island. According to Piñero, they also conspire with the ruling classes. In essence Piñero rejects the present Puerto Rico, an island he cannot recognize but whose conditions are familiar to what he has known on the mainland.

Piñero's poem is significant insofar as a return to Puerto Rico, whether physical or spiritual, is no longer an option, as Pietri suggests. For Piñero, the beginning and the end are situated in the Lower East Side. As he notes in the poem by the same name, this is the privileged space, which he welcomes and accepts with all its evils, "gambling, fighting and unnatural dying":

> There's no other place for me to be
> There's no other place that I can see
> There's no other town around that
> brings you up or keeps you down
>
> . . . .
> Lower East Side. . . .[39]

Piñero is well aware of the evils of the city, with its hustlers, freaks, and perverts. But he also recognizes that he is a part of the environment, a thief and junkie. The North American experience has marked him, and he in turn has accepted his destiny. This poem, as well as other compositions, have a notable absence of Spanish. Puerto Rico and island culture are not even a remote memory. Instead, they are replaced by speech more readily associated with those educated in the streets of New York City, one closely related to that spoken by African Americans.

In Piñero's "The Book of Genesis According to Saint Miguelito," the poetic voice parodies the Bible and provides the reader with his version of the origin of time, one that explains the present course of events in places familiar to the speaker. Just as God designed the world and Adam and Eve, he also was responsible for inventing the ghettos and slums. As in Luciano's world, Piñero's God is not merciful and caring but is evil and sinister. The fall does not take place after the completion of God's creation, the appearance of the Devil, and the ejection of Adam and Eve from Paradise; it was already present from the start. He narrates that "In the beginning / God created the ghettos & slums," decorated them with lead-based paint, and filled the streets with garbage.[40]

Piñero relies on what is familiar to him and his environment and attributes that knowledge to God and his creation. God is omnipotent; he has created evil and is also influenced by the malevolence of his own creation. The opposite is also true: God reproduces on earth what is familiar to him in heaven. Piñero humanizes God and attributes to him the same characteristics present in Piñero's own environment. In Piñero's creation, God is a slumlord but also a drug addict:

> On the third day
> God's nose was running
> & his jones was coming down and God
> in his all knowing wisdom
> he knew he was sick
> he needed a fix
> so God
> created the backyards of the ghettos
> & the alleys of the slums
> & heroin & cocaine
> and
> with his divine wisdom & grace
> God created hepatitis
> who begat lockjaw
> who begat malaria
> who begat degradation
> who begat
> GENOCIDE[41]

Piñero's drug-infested God, sick from his own addiction, is responsible for the misery of his people and the disease that afflicts them. An addicted God cannot perform good deeds; he is only capable of providing pain and sorrow. God rides in an illegal gypsy cab and creates different ethnic groups. They are also condemned to live his miseries in the form of social evils, such as capitalism, which begot racism, exploitation, male chauvinism, machismo, imperialism, colonialism, Wall Street, and foreign wars.

As the poem progresses, Piñero instills God with more qualities familiar to his environment. On the fifth day the people wanted an explanation for their exploited condition and demanded to know, in a letter to the editor, why God created evil. However, God felt compelled not to answer. On the seventh day God felt tired, called in sick, collected overtime pay, and vacationed in Puerto Rico. As God heads south he observes Satan "planting the learning trees of consciousness / around his ghetto edens,"[42] an image of incipient change and a challenge to God's control and authority. God holds a news conference to speak to his creation to make sure that he is still in control of them. Piñero's God is also a politician who measures his words carefully and maneuvers around delicate situations to present himself in a positive light.

The relationship between Piñero's God and the frailties of his own creation suggests that God is omnipotent and responsible for his own deeds.

Moreover, he is of this world. When rereading the poem, I find that this interpretation becomes clear from the outset: "Before the beginning / God created God."[43] There are similarities and differences between the first God and the second. The second God is made in the image of the first and is just as accountable for the creation. God begot God, and the second God created hepatitis, which begot a series of other diseases, and created capitalism, which begot a series of other social and economic evils. If the first God can be associated with heaven, the second one is closer to earth and perhaps of this world. Within the context of the time in which the poem was written, this other God represents the United States government, an institution with Godlike qualities. Like the nineteenth-century followers of Manifest Destiny, Piñero's government is believed to have inherited certain natural powers, which a superior being bestowed upon the country. Piñero takes that myth one step further and indicates that the U.S. government intentionally created ghetto conditions and consequently is responsible for all the evils contained therein. In fact, God is personified in President Richard Nixon. When speaking on the fifth day to the people, God repeats words associated with the former president's style of expression. In the poem, God says:

> My fellow subjects [read as "My fellow Americans"]
> let me make one thing perfectly clear
> by saying this about that
> NO . . . COMMENT![44]

What is troubling about Piñero's God is not that he is Richard Nixon, the only U.S. president forced to resign from office, but that he is bilingual; he speaks in English and Spanish, the language of his subjects. Certainly, God's people reflect his image and his creation; therefore, like his people he also speaks their language. God is familiar with a Hispanic environment and Puerto Rico as a tourist destination and a paradise.

The most disconcerting moment of the poem is contained in the final line when God articulates the Spanish word *vaya*, repeated twice in the poem—first used on the fourth day when God begets social evils and realizes that it was good. Vocalizing *vaya* presupposes God's knowledge of Spanish and familiarity with Hispanic culture, but also that he may well be Hispanic. *Vaya* can be interpreted in different ways. It could refer to mockery as in the expression *dar vaya a* (to make fun of). Because this and other poems were read out loud, in Spanish it is difficult to distinguish between the sound of an orthographic *y* and an *ll*. Thus, *vaya* could also be *valla*, which in Spanish refers to a wall or, figuratively, an obstacle. In addition, *vaya* is also the third-person-singular subjunctive form of the verb *ir*, "to go." The semantic displacement of this word more appropriately refers to the interjection *¡vaya!* meaning "there, its finished!" If we choose to privilege the latter interpretation of the word *vaya,* God is pleased with his actions; but he is only deluding himself. God is omnipotent over his creation, but the people do have a natural sense for what is right and petition his authority. Most important, he does not appear to have total or even partial control over Satan, who is planting the seeds of knowledge and rebellion.

Piñero has taken images familiar to his audience, the Bible and the ghetto, and has turned them upside down to show the evil associated with the omnipotent power of God, the U.S. government, Nixon, and perhaps any Latino leader working on behalf of the government, to control and exploit the people he is supposed to serve. Yet it is Satan, a marginal but important figure in the creation, who will be responsible for introducing change. The relationship between God and Satan, the powerful and the disenfranchised but rebellious, can be extended to that of the U.S. government and the Puerto Rican Nationalist Party, the Young Lord's Party, Puerto Rican prisoners, or any other group that challenges absolute hegemony to obtain rights denied to them. Likewise, Piñero is a version of his own satanic figure. He too is marginal and has his own version of the creation.

Piñero is not the only Nuyorican to use religion as a source of inspiration for his poems. Another poet to emerge out of the Nuyorican poetic movement, Tato Laviera, relies on his own religious training to understand life in the ghetto. As Piñero makes clear in his "A Lower East Side Poem," Laviera considers New York his home, as indicated by *La Carreta Made a U-Turn* (1979). Flores reads Laviera's first collection of poems alongside Marqués's play *La carreta* (1951–52; *The Oxcart,* 1969) and places it within the context of class and popular culture:

> Laviera's Puerto Rican roots lead neither to the folkloric *jíbaro,* content under the Commonwealth, nor to the glorified pantheon of the national elite—two sources of patriotic pride that are so prominent in Marqués and his works. Rather, going back to Puerto Rico evokes the popular culture of an Afro-Caribbean island, the birthplace of musical and poetic forms like *la bomba, la plena, la décima,* and *el seis.* It is a culture of the slave and peasant masses, the culture of a colonial people who have known not only misery and submission—and pious "decency"—but also joy, creativity and struggle. All these strains of subordinate indigenous expression are invoked and affirmed in *La Carreta Made a U-Turn.*[45]

If Piñero depends on the Old Testament for inspiration for his poem, Laviera relies on the New Testament, and his "Jesús Papote," of *Enclave* (1981), is without a doubt one of the cornerstones of this biblically based subgenre. Laviera's poem is a parody of the birth and death of Christ; his protagonist is a fetus conceived on Easter Sunday and born midnight on Christmas Eve. Papote is an important character for Laviera. He originally developed this character in the first poem he wrote, "Even Then He Knew," of *The Carreta Made a U-Turn,* which initiated his poetic career. In the early poem Laviera gave Papote specific qualities he would alter in the later one. In an interview with me, Laviera provides insight into the origin of his poetic interest and character. He discloses that on a day he was sick and stayed home from school, he looked out the window and saw a youngster sitting on a stoop. As he watched him periodically, he observed that the young man remained immobile, in the same location. The soon-to-be poet felt sorry for him; he prepared a snack and when he descended the stairs, the youngster was gone.[46] For Laviera, the youngster was a symbol, and the event inspired him to write his first poem in July 1966. The poem contains the lines

> Papote sat on the stoop
> of an abandoned building
> and he decided to go nowhere.[47]

Papote is a fixture in the ghetto scenery of garbage, unemployment, malnutrition, and music. He is trapped by his environment and represents the stagnation of Puerto Rican New Yorkers. In "Jesús Papote," Laviera combines the name of his first subject with the religious symbol of Christ; and the new character, Jesús Papote, plays a more active role in his survival and that of his people.

"Jesús Papote" is a Christ figure and the poem reconstructs the sacred birth of our Lord. There are similarities and differences between the biblical figure and Laviera's poetic voice. Christ was proclaimed the Savior; son of the virgin Mary, married to Joseph; conceived by the Holy Ghost; and delivered in a manger. Jesús Papote does not have an identity. He was not planned; his mother is a prostitute addicted to heroine, has had many lovers, and does not know who impregnated her. Unlike Mary, the prostitute gives birth on a cold winter day in an abandoned lot on the Lower East Side. The Archangel Gabriel did not announce the coming of Jesús Papote; rather, he was the answer to his grandmother's prayers. But like Christ, Jesús Papote is a special being; there is something mystical about him for those living in New York and "contemporary poets felt the spirit in the air."[48]

Christ was born in humble surroundings to reflect the condition of those in need of salvation. Likewise, Jesús Papote responds to the circumstances of the times. The message is clear: if Jesus were to return, he would be born in the ghetto, and his disciples would be Puerto Ricans, the new chosen people. Jesús Papote is a ghetto child and a victim of his social and economic circumstances:

> i was addicted i was beaten i was kicked i was punched
> i slept in empty cellars broken stairways i was infect-
> ed i was injected spermed with many relations
> i ran from police jails i was high every day of life.[49]

Laviera assumes the voice of the fetus in the womb and takes the read-er on a nine-month epic journey that culminates in Jesús Papote's birth: April, he is conceived on Easter Sunday; his mother has multiple partners, which makes it difficult to identify the father; he is the answer to his grandmother's prayers. May, his mother discovers she is pregnant and attempts to abort the fetus, first with pills and later by punching herself; she also has syphilis. June, she submits herself to treatment to detoxify her body, and she breaks the habit cold turkey. July, she goes to Puerto Rico, a symbol of origin, and she and the fetus travel throughout the island. Life is peaceful, harmony reigns, and the fetus begs her not to leave: "mamita don't go back give birth in island nativeness / tropical greetings nurturing don't go back don't / go back."[50] As in the title, *La Carreta Made a U-Turn*, the destiny of Nuyoricans is the harsh reality of a New York environment, not the idyllic and mythical Puerto Rico. September, she is back in New York and the dominant image now is struggle. October, she tries training programs; the fetus, also struggling against heroine addiction, has a relapse, and she fights the drug urge. November, the grandmother's prayers are not answered, the dominant theme is "death la muerte," and the mother barely survives. As in Pietri's poem, the repetition of death in both Spanish and English underscores that it is ever present and that superhuman efforts are needed to overcome it. December, the nine-month cycle is completed and Jesús Papote is ready to be born. It has been a difficult odyssey, struggling in a society that condones, rather than outlaws, destructive ghetto life and the arduous journey mother and son have undergone.

Both the fetus and the mother are survivors, and instead of the mother helping the fetus, she draws upon the fetus's strength for her own. Jesús Papote assumes an active role in the birth process and even instructs his mother on what to do:

> Mami Mami push push i'm coming out celestial barkings
> Mami Mami push i don't want to die she slept
> Mami Mami push i want to live she slept cough
> Mami Mami i have the ability to love cough cough
> Mami Mami fight with me again she slept she slept
> Mami Mami i'm coming out out out push push push push
> Mami Mami can you feel me can you hear me push push
> push push empuja empuja cough cough push push push
> empuja empuja Mami cough cough push push i am fighting

> i am fighting push push nature nature i have a will
> to live to denounce you nature i am fighting by myself
> your sweeping breasts your widowing backbone
> yearnings your howling cemetery steps your
> death-cold inhuman palms Mami Mami wake up
> this is my birthday little mornings king
> david sang cough cough cough push push
> why do I have to eulogize myself
> nobody is listening i am invisible
> why tell me why do i have to be
> the one the one to acclaim that:[51]

A conscious, intelligent being, the fetus tries to revive his mother from her addiction and instructs her to push. He does not want to die; he is a fighter and must fight from the very beginning, the womb, and will continue to fight and persist throughout his life.

The questions raised at the end of the stanza just quoted suggest that the fetus has been launched against his will into a leadership position. What follows is the development of the fetus's own voice and identity. His first words after birth are articulated in both Spanish and English, in the first-person plural, "We, nosotros." Jesús Papote is the voice of the Puerto Rican and Hispanic people, and for that matter of all the people who live in the ghetto, whether they speak one language or the other. Jesús Papote represents the past and the future, not only because Hispanics will be the largest minority in the early part of the next century, but because they are multiethnic and multiracial, bilingual, a synthesis or blending of the different cultures in the United States.

In my interview with Laviera he provides insight into Jesús Papote, who, like Christ, had to develop his own voice and was later crucified by society. Jesús Papote was crucified before he was born; his crucifixion began in the womb. Laviera explains the need to create an authentic voice for Puerto Rican New Yorkers:

> Yes, in the womb, so that in his birth, at least when he comes out, the voice would be heard. I was looking for a voice and he gave me a voice that I wish my people would listen to for once. In order for him to have qualified to be the voice, he had to go through an enormous struggle, so when he said that word, "Bendición," it was pure. His resurrection was coming into the world. He came as a hero who could at least speak to my people on something which I didn't find in anybody else. My Puerto Rican people do not have a hero—I couldn't find one. So, having crucified him in the womb and at the point of his birth (or at the moment of his death), my

people would say let's listen to this character. I was looking for an epic character whom my nation would hear, because my nation doesn't listen to characters. I think I succeeded in making him an epic figure, and that was my goal. He had to go through all those things so that everyone in my community could just lean back and hear this guy say "Bendición" and live. I guess his womb was his crucifixion and his birth was his resurrection.[52]

In "Jesús Papote" Tato Laviera relies on religious and cultural symbols. For example, in November Laviera refers to All Souls Day, a religious holiday more appropriately celebrated by Puerto Ricans than by Anglo-Americans. Laviera's poetic persona is born on Christmas Eve, the day Hispanics observe the birth of Christ by attending midnight mass, rather than on Christmas Day, when North Americans are more apt to celebrate the arrival of Santa Claus. Similarly, Jesús Papote asks for his blessing, another reference to a custom among Puerto Ricans. Before his blessing, he asks for permission, which resembles the request good spirits make, in a Spiritualist session, as it possesses the medium's body. Laviera's Jesús Papote makes the same supplication:

> with the permission of all the faiths of all beliefs
> with the permission of this land
> with the permission of the elders
> with the permission of english
> with the permission of my community
> with the permission of god:[53]

Like the biblical figure, Laviera's Jesus is also a redeemer and a savior. He understands his mother's condition, does not blame her, and is proud to be her son. Jesús Papote has come into the world to save his mother and other Puerto Ricans and Latinos. She draws from his strengths and liberates herself from her condition: she gets up, breaks the umbilical cord, and joins the celebration of the birth of Christ and her own Christ (Papote). The ringing of the bells is a celebration of Christmas in the pagan and religious sense of the word. They are the bells of Santa Claus but also of the church, where Jesús Papote is present for everyone to see.

As the interview indicates, Jesús Papote is the messiah for which Puerto Ricans have been waiting. He is not some mythical figure that only those indoctrinated into religion could understand in the abstract; he is born of the same conditions many living in the ghetto experience and understand. Jesús Papote speaks from his condition to theirs. It is important to emphasize that the struggle for survival does not originate at birth or after adolescence, but at the moment of conception; those living in poverty and in drug-infested neighborhoods have been marked and con-demned before they are born. Jesús Papote is a survivor who gives strength to his mother and to all who need help in overcoming the great odds against them. And like Jesús Papote, the poet has an obligation to develop a voice for his people. For Laviera and his character, it is not a question of something they want to do; rather it is something they must do—their mission is to save the Latino community.

Miguel Algarín is another Nuyorican poet. He and Piñero were the founders of the acclaimed Nuyorican Poets Cafe, frequented by both Latinos and Anglos. Like the poems of his counterparts, his "A Mongo Affair" is also critical of the U.S. government's treatment of Puerto Ricans both on the island and on the mainland. But whereas Piñero and Laviera's poems are charged with religious metaphors, Algarín relies on other tradi-tional social and cultural elements and is sexually explicit; the phallic is the dominant trope. The poem develops as a conversation in San Juan, between a dark-skinned Puerto Rican and the poetic *I*, who appears to be knowledgeable about the life of Puerto Ricans in New York. Like Felipe Luciano, Algarín criticizes the events surrounding Operation Bootstrap that gave way to the large migration of Puerto Ricans from the island to New York and promoted the myth of the American dream; that is, that Puerto Ricans would be better off on the mainland than if they remained on the island. The popular belief on the island indicates that those who migrate will improve their conditions; Puerto Ricans are eligible for wel-fare, a monthly check, health benefits, free rent, clothes, and dental work. The poetic *I* knows better and demythifies those expectations, uncovering the true cost of the help Puerto Ricans receive:

> I have to admit that he has been
> lied to, misled,
> that I know that all the goodies
> he named humiliate the receiver,
> that a man is demoralized
> when his woman and children
> beg for weekly checks
> that even the fucking a man does
> on a government bought mattress
> draws the blood from his cock
> cockless, sin espina dorsal,
> mongo—that's it![54]

Algarín's poem is full of anger and in his search for the right word to describe the humiliating experience, the poetic voice finds it in an unerect-ed penis, resulting in an unconsummated sexual encounter:

> a welfare fuck is a mongo affair!
> mongo means flojo
> mongo means bloodless
> mongo means soft
> mongo can not penetrate
> mongo can only tease
> but it can't tickle[55]

The idea of having forced or consensual sexual intercourse with a man who cannot achieve an erection is the ultimate humiliation for the victim. One has to be overly patient and even desperate to engage in such an act, always with the false expectation that the encounter could be realized, learning that it will always be fruitless. Just as Piñero used *vaya* to convey many meanings, Algarín explores the multiplicity of the word *mongo*. It refers to the welfare system, the disappearance of Taíno masculinity, Puerto Ricans living in North American ghettos, and those who put up with the demands placed on them, such as Pietri's Juan, Miguel, Milagros, Olga, and Manuel.

The poetic *I* addresses the unconvinced Afro–Puerto Rican, the one most likely to migrate to improve his condition, and implores him not to believe in the lies spread about life in the United States:

> viejo negro africano,
> Africa Puerto Rico
> sitting on department store entrances
> don't believe the deadly game
> of Northern cities paved with gold and plenty
> don't believe the fetching dream
> of life improvement in New York
> the only thing you'll find in Boston
> is a soft leather shoe up your ass.[56]

Algarín underscores the important African component of Puerto Rican culture, race, and identity. According to the speaker, the U.S. government's interest is limited to sending Puerto Ricans to fight in the frontlines and die in wars like Korea and Vietnam, where they are blown up into pieces:

> los intestinos
> las piernas
> los bichos mongos.[57]

Soldiers taken from the island, enlisted, and sent abroad resemble the forced Puerto Rican emigration from the island to the mainland. This type of departure, according to the speaker, has depopulated the island.

Moreover, Puerto Ricans are a minority on the mainland and on the island. While Puerto Ricans have left the island, U.S. businesses and culture have taken it over.

Toward the end, the hostile and angry tone of the poem changes. If the earlier stanzas convey pain and indignation, the latter one is full of faith and optimism. The speaker now focuses on the person he is addressing: the old Afro–Puerto Rican. When addressing him, the speaker is unmasked and reveals himself to be the poet, Miguel Algarín:

> I, yo, Miguel ¡Me oyes viejo!
> I, yo, Miguel
> el hijo de Maria Socorro y Miguel.[58]

Miguel, who like the old man is homeless, seeks his protection. In so doing, the old man acquires additional allegorical characteristics. As an old African and Puerto Rican man, he is a symbol of Puerto Rican culture and the fatherland. Algarín reappropriates the image of the *jíbaro* and attributes to him qualities associated with the African past, an emphasis José Luis González also insists upon in his essay "El país de cuatro pisos."[59] The old man is also a sign of hope, the recovery of the island, and a return to a time before North Americans traveled to Puerto Rico. In addition, he is a symbol of the Nationalist Party, perhaps the Young Lords Party as well, and he states: "nosotros los que estamos / preparados con las armas" (Those of us / who are prepared with arms).[60]

Spanish here represents a master code language with a message meant to be kept secret from Anglo-Americans. These two lines are a call to action, and to fight for a recovery of the homeland, even if it means dying in the process. This message gives Algarín hope and determination that there will be a solution to the Puerto Rican dilemma of being a people without a country they can call theirs. Though the man dies, the idea will live and flourish.

II

> Under capitalism, women have been oppressed by both society and our men. The doctrine of machismo has been used by men to take out their frustrations on wives, sisters, mothers, and children. Men must fight along with sisters in the struggle for economic and social equality and must recognize that sisters make up over half of the revolutionary army: sisters and brothers are equals fighting for our people. FORWARD SISTERS IN THE STRUGGLE!
> —Point 5 of Thirteen-Point Program and Platform,
> the Young Lords Party.

The Young Lords' struggle for the rights of Puerto Ricans and Hispanics had a profound impact on all the communities in New York, in particular the Spanish-speaking one. But the Lords were not free of the oppression inflicted upon their community. In many ways they embodied the ailments of the Puerto Rican people living in New York. Some were drug addicts, some were members of gangs, and a few had even served prison sentences. However, the Lords also fought hard to rid themselves of these ghetto trappings. They believed it was the sum of historical, social, racial, political, and economic factors that attempted to destroy their sense of identity and self-worth.

The Young Lords were articulate about the oppression of Puerto Ricans both on the island and on the mainland and of other Latin Americans experiencing similar conditions in their native country. But they also recognized the oppression inherent in Hispanic culture. Attention to this issue was most evident in the relations between the sexes within the organization. Just as the Lords instructed its members on political ideology, they also addressed the changing roles in society as perceived in revolutionary movements in Cuba, other Third World countries, and the women's liberation movement in the United States. Pablo "Yoruba" Guzmán and other Lords recognized the need to break the sexual stereotype: it was important for men to cry, and it was equally important for women to pick up guns and fight. In an essay in *Palante,* Yoruba (the name refers to the Nigerian tribe enslaved and taken to the Caribbean) acknowledges the contribution the women's movement has made in fighting sexism. He also points to the importance of the gay liberation struggle in rounding "out the individual."[61] Yoruba admits that it will be difficult for some members of the party to make the transition, but has faith that the Lords will be successful.

The female members of the Lords assumed the leadership for redefining gender-specific roles among party members; they objected to the traditional position to which Hispanic culture and community relegated women. Denise Oliver best articulates the opposition to machismo, which she views as a necessary step for women to take for full participation in the fight against oppression. Machismo is a behavior she associates with Hispanics, though she recognizes that it was not limited to them. Oliver writes: "Women have been brainwashed into believing that they are weak, that they are not fighters, that they are not capable of picking up guns—in fact, they're supposed to be afraid of guns, afraid of anything mechanical."[62] Although Oliver welcomes the ideas proposed by the women's liberation movement and supports revolutionary women's struggle against white oppressors, she also acknowledges that Hispanics in general and the Lords in particular have different views on certain issues, including the volatile and sensitive topic of abortion.

> For one thing, we feel we can't have a dogmatic position on abortion. It would be incorrect for us to either be completely in favor of

abortion or completely against it. You see, we're very much aware of how genocide is practiced on Puerto Rican people and all Third World people through birth control programs, population control programs, and abortion programs. We could certainly not support any kind of abortion program which meant that if you wanted to get your welfare check, you'd better have an abortion and not have any more kids—that if you wanted a government subsidy of some kind or food stamps you had to limit the amount of your children because you didn't get paid enough money in your job at the factory to be able to support more than a certain number.[63]

Oliver alludes to the forced sterilization program conducted throughout many areas in Latin America and the testing of the birth control pill in Puerto Rico that left a large portion of the female population sterile, information that circulated among politically active sectors of the Latino community. She does favor a society in which women can determine whether they want to have a child or an abortion and supports abortion as long as it is under community control. For her, forced abortion is a form of slavery she fears can be used as a weapon, a form of genocide, against the Puerto Rican people. Oliver accepts the current issues not from a U.S. perspective, but from a Hispanic cultural one, which is in transition. She takes issue against the women's liberation movement insofar as it separates men from women. Oliver is also aware that capitalism is divisive: it has separated blacks, whites, and Puerto Ricans, as well as men and women from each other. She does not view the Latino struggle in isolation; rather, she considers it to include the education of men. Although the eradication of machismo within the Lords was perceived to be a continuous process, Oliver believes that just as there is a liberated woman, there has to be a liberated man. The relationship between men and women that the Lords supported was based on ideas borrowed from the women's liberation movement and from socialist and communist societies, modified and applied to their own particular circumstances and historical period.

Oliver and other Puerto Rican American women were instrumental in defining the direction of the organization. Similarly, Nuyorican female poets form an integral part of Nuyorican expression and share the same history and social circumstances as their male counterparts. Their works voice concerns similar to those of the poets discussed earlier. For example, the tension between those Puerto Rican Americans who look upon the island as a paradise and those who recognize that it is also part of the cycle of exploitation is effectively communicated by Amina Muñoz in "Welcome to San Juan, Oldest City in the U.S," a poem dedicated to Antonia Martínez, who died fighting for Puerto Rican independence. The poem acknowledges that the island, which is full of McDonalds and where "unemployment has risen from 15% to 25%," no longer belongs to Puerto Ricans, but to the United States. This idea is also present in Algarín's poem. The speaker repeats in bold letters: "KEEP OFF— / U.S. PROPERTY it says."[64]

The women's unique contribution to Nuyorican or Latino poetry is evident in their struggle against the oppression of society and also in their liberation from the Hispanic male-dominated culture, as they attempt to balance Hispanic and U.S. cultures. The female perspective shows concern for their national, cultural, and gender identity and is varied in style and theme. Although some poets, like Sandra María Esteves, can be classified as part of the Nuyorican group, others cannot. For example, Judith Ortiz Cofer affirms her Puerto Ricanness, but in a manner distinct in style and language from others in the Nuyorican group. The individuality expressed by these poets is an important characteristic that carries over into an exploration of their inner feelings, thoughts, and sexuality.

The complex role Puerto Rican American women play in North American society is evident in the works of Sandra María Esteves. In poems such as "For Lolita Lebrón," "From Fanon," "For Fidel Castro," and "1st Poem for Cuba," she conveys the same concerns associated with the Young Lords.[65] Esteves identifies with the oppressed against the oppressor and recognizes the international character of the Puerto Rican and Latino struggle. In "1st Poem for Cuba," Esteves uses a collective *we* and brings unity to a common cause.

Esteves's poetry also is of a personal nature, addressing her development as a woman. This aspect of her work, which differentiates her voice from that of her male counterparts, will be the focus of my study. In "For Tito," Esteves celebrates her subject's macho tendencies and aggressiveness: the first line reads, "you, macho machete." Whereas Algarín writes in "Trampling" about the subjugation of women, about the male's arousal by the woman's resistance, resulting in

> you get it hard
> and make her
> eat meat totally[66]

Esteves appropriates the same male symbols and wields them with the same passion, but from the other point of view. The machete, a tool for cutting sugarcane, has been turned into a phallic symbol. The unity between Tito and the speaker is achieved through aggressive intercourse:

> you, macho soledad
> are a unique language
> the one filling my eyes with heat for you

growing and pounding
with all the desire
of your drum
pounding with my womb
planting seeds in the night[67]

The aggression is present with the image of pounding, used with a different intention by Algarín when he writes, "by pounding blows all over her body."[68] Esteves repeats the word twice, one time to refer to the man and the other time to the woman. Aggression is depicted as a seductive act with the penetration of the machete and the planting of seeds, both of which she welcomes. The first line of each stanza provides an explanation of macho, thus creating a synchronic structure—"you, macho machete" / "you, macho paciencia" / "you, macho soledad"[69]—in which any of the terms following *macho* can substitute for each other. Therefore, *macho machete* is equivalent to *macho paciencia* and *macho soledad,* and the first line of the quoted stanza can also be interpreted as "you, macho machete."

The union of Tito and the speaker results in a substitution of the "you, macho machete / paciencia / soledad" for "together," with the symbolic representation of the island and its culture in the ghetto. But the images with which the speaker chooses to portray the island are clearly phallic: "sugarcane" and "palm trees grow ripe" and are "rich with coconut milk."[70] Esteves has internalized the male values of Hispanic culture and accepted them as hers, then reproduced them in this poem.

Sexual imagery is also present in Rosario Morales's work. It may be problematic to celebrate macho culture within a North American environment. Nevertheless, in "Spring Fever" Morales also begins her poem by identifying with the other. Although "you" can be interpreted to refer to spring fever, it more appropriately refers to a partner. Whereas Esteves used tropes to suggest island culture, Morales relies on the same poetic devices to bring to mind another familiar environment, that of the mainland: "You're like a crocus, like a sugar maple."[71] Both women refer to their loneliness. Esteves resolves hers by uniting with the other. Morales, however, separates the *You* from the *I*. But the speaker's partner goes through cycles of warmth and frost, and she needs and constantly seeks warmth. At the end of the poem she is awaiting the sun's strong rays or for her partner to arrive. For Morales, the island's culture, represented by its climate, can be substituted for an intimate relationship with the other.

When reading "For Tito" and "Spring Fever" together, I am left to wonder whether the differences in the resolutions of the two poems suggest the changing times or the different cultures used to express them. The island culture produces unity and the North American one separation. In one culture Esteves has identified with her lover, in the other Morales has not. In "Spring Fever," the second-person pronoun expresses ambiguity and could refer to anyone. Nevertheless, both Esteves and Morales achieve fulfillment in their communion with the other.

The difference in voices or points of view between Morales's and Esteves's poems allude to a conflict the poets feel between their loyalty to Puerto Rican culture, whose tradition insists on the femininity of women and masculinity of men, and the acceptance of North American society, whose liberal sector calls for the equality of women. The tension derived from these two points of view is best expressed by Sandra María Esteves and Luz María Umpierre, in a poetic dialogue regarding the role of the Puerto Rican woman in the United States.

Esteves initiates the dialogue with "My Name Is Maria Christina", a poem of self-discovery and identity. The speaker proudly affirms who she is within the North American context: "I am a Puerto Rican woman born in el barrio."[72] By identifying herself in this manner, the speaker signals early on the type of transition between island and mainland cultures that she and many other immigrants undergo. Maria Christina recognizes the traditions inherited from her ancestors, but also the need to depart from them.

> I respect their ways
> inherited from our proud ancestors
> I do not tease them with eye catching clothes
> I do not sleep with their brothers and cousins
> although I've been told that this is a liberal society[73]

In that stanza, the speaker respects the old ways, but does not tease men or participate in incestuous relationships, illicit behaviors associated with island culture and also present in New York City. Although Maria Christina defines a new space within the North American environment, she still is tied to, and perhaps unwilling to break totally from, certain elements of Hispanic culture:

> I do not complain about cooking for my family
> because abuela taught me that woman is the master of fire
> I do not complain about nursing my children
> because I determine the direction of their values[74]

As a woman, she is content with playing a supportive role relative to men, yet she is also willing to change to improve her situation and that of her people. Esteves opens and closes her poem by repeating the lines "Our men . . . they call me negra because they love me / and in turn I teach them to be strong."[75] Here Esteves is careful to explain that *negra* should be read not in racial terms, as the word suggests, but understood within a Hispanic Caribbean cultural context of love and affection. Although the stanza is meant to describe a reciprocal and harmonious relationship between men and women, the speaker assumes a passive position. She mentions that men love her, but she does not refer to her own love for them. Is it implied, or is she satisfied to be an object of love? Instead, she teaches men to be strong. Teaching is presented as a virtue, but it is not clear if she has to teach men to be strong because she lacks the same strength and expects to be protected by them or because she is the source of strength that she will pass on to them. Certainly, the latter observation accords with the dominant interpretation of the poem.

In combining the past with the present, one culture with the other, Maria Christina emerges as origin of a new culture: "I am the mother of a new age of warriors."[76] In this regard, Maria Christina accepts her past but also recognizes her role in the new society. Maria Christina is also a religious symbol; her name, Mary, suggests the mother of Christ. Another religious interpretation emerges as well. Maria Christina is a child who carries great burdens: "I am the child of a race of slaves."[77] The word *child* alludes to a history of exploitation and another religious figure, the sacrificial Christ child who shoulders the sins of the world. Analogous to Tato Laviera's "Jesús Papote," who presents the Puerto Rican people living in the United States with a savior born into the same conditions as his people,[78] this poem offers the interpretation of Christina as the Christ child: her name is the feminine form of Christ. Christ was oppressed by the Romans; similarly, Maria Christina feels the present pain and oppression of life in the ghetto. Christina's children "o.d. under the stairway's shadow of shame."[79] And like Jesus of Nazareth, Maria Christina is a *teacher*, a word the speaker repeats six times in the poem.

In "My Name Is Maria Christina," the speaker desires to preserve aspects of Puerto Rican culture and at the same time accepts her new destiny in the United States. She is willing to work within the North American environment. As a mother and a teacher, she instructs her children on how to overcome the obstacles of oppression. She is born not in Puerto Rico, but in El Barrio, and this acceptance of her fate is further reflected in how Esteves uses the English spelling of Christina, with an *h*, rather than Spanish style.

Luz María Umpierre engages Esteves in a dialogue regarding Maria Christina's identity. Umpierre was familiar with Esteves's work. She studies aspects of Esteves's poetry in an essay "La ansiedad de la influencia en Sandra María Esteves y Marjorie Agosín" and identifies the level of anxiety in the works of those two poets.[80] In that essay, Umpierre relies on Harold Bloom's *The Anxiety of Influence* (1975) and analyzes the importance of Julia de Burgos for Esteves and Pablo Neruda and Nicanor Parra for Agosín.

In the case of Esteves, Umpierre compares poems written by de Burgos with Esteves's "A Julia y a mí," in which Esteves points out similarities and differences or misreadings in Bloomian terms. These are evident in particular with references to death. Umpierre observes that Esteves's reading of de Burgos is not as combative as De Burgos appears to be; however, this change allows her to transcend the position exemplified by de Burgos's words. In so doing, Esteves places herself within a tradition Burgos represented, and by writing about both of them, Umpierre does the same.

Umpierre also insists on a poetic dialogue with Esteves. In her "In Response," she even corrects "My Name Is Maria Christina" by presenting another version of the Puerto Rican woman not born in El Barrio: "My name is not María Cristina. / I am a Puerto Rican woman born in another barrio."[81] Umpierre takes some of the images used by Esteves and turns them upside down. Whereas Maria Christina mentions that Puerto Rican men call her "negra," Umpierre's speaker claims that the same men will recognize her aggression and determination and call her "pushie." In fact, Umpierre rebels against Puerto Rican culture, which she considers "shed down from macho-men ancestors."[82]

Umpierre's strongest objection to Hispanic culture is expressed in sexual terms; that is, she values her sexual liberation and doing what she pleases with her body, without being accountable to anyone. She repeats the idea of her emancipation throughout the poem. In the first stanza she states, "and I do fix the leaks in all faucets"; in the second, "I sleep around whenever it is possible"; and in the last, "and I do fix all leaks in my faucets." In her opposition to male dominant cultural signs, Umpierre takes her rebellion to the other extreme. Whereas Esteves looked to define a new space within Hispanic culture and may have put her own sexual desires aside to please men, Umpierre focuses exclusively on the speaker's sexual needs. She is willing to "sleep around whenever it is possible," and she does so within her marriage. The subtext to this action may be that her husband is a typical male chauvinist and has extramarital affairs; therefore, she reasons that if he can do it, so can she. But this conclusion is not clear. Although it is possible to propose that he is not loyal to her, the opposite may also be true; that is, that he is faithful to his marriage and in spite of this, she has sexual relations with others. If the former is true, then the speaker is looking for a degree of equality that she and other Puerto Rican women do not enjoy within their culture. However, if the latter is the case, then the speaker has appropriated the same male symbols she criticizes and accepted them as her own. Within that context, even if her husband were loyal to her, the speaker would be willing to exploit and abuse him. The poem favors this interpretation because she refers to her husband with the adjective *dearest*. Although some may argue that the term is used with irony, there is an identity of expressions she employs to describe the two men mentioned in the poem, her husband and father. The speaker claims that she does not need permission from her "dearest" husband "or kissing-loving papa." There is no irony in Umpierre's description of her father; rather, she mentions him with the same affection she attributes to her "dearest" husband. Evidently, Umpierre categorically labels all men the same. She has replaced the culture of "macho-men ancestors" with that of "feminist-women ancestors."

When Umpierre criticizes Esteves for writing a poem entrenched in Puerto Rican culture, the solution she has in mind is to reject Hispanic customs and embrace North American beliefs, represented by the values promoted by an extreme sector of the feminist movement. My reading should not be interpreted as derogatory and antifeminist; nor should it suggest that Puerto Rican culture, whether on the island or mainland, is static. Rather, my intention is to explore and contextualize the cultural symbols Umpierre uses. For example, the speaker is not socially conscious but appears to be self-centered, society and, for that matter, the world, revolving around her needs. This self-centeredness, which I associate not with Puerto Rican but with U.S. culture, can be traced to the industrial revolution and the breakup of the extended family. The attitude, which developed to an extreme after the sixties and in particular in the eighties, reflects the individual and "Me" generation and puts personal values above those of the community. The *we,* or *nosotros,* plural pronoun seen in Esteves is absent in Umpierre's composition. Instead, Umpierre employs frequently the first-person-singular pronoun, *I*—twenty-three times in a forty-one-line, seven-stanza poem. By comparison, Esteves reproduces the first-person-singular pronoun eighteen times in a twenty-nine line, seven-stanza poem. She also uses *our* twice and makes numerous references to other members of her family. Esteves appears to use the *I* more times per line than Umpierre, but there are important differences. Esteves uses the *I* five times in relation to teaching and another five times to distance herself from the stereotypical Latina. Although she does employ the first person, the emphasis is one of communion with her culture and others. In addition, children are mentioned, and they play an important part. With Umpierre, men are present to be accused or transcended, students are taught, and small children are noticeably absent. The emphasis is on "Me" and no one else. This is also expressed with the reiteration of the possessive adjective *my:*

> My eyes reflect myself
> the strengths that I am trying to attain
> the passions of a woman who at 35 is 70
> My soul reflects my past,
> my soul deflects the future.[83]

In her criticism of Maria Christina, a symbol of Puerto Rican culture, Umpierre emerges as a woman who affirms her own individuality and in so doing places her needs above those of her culture and others. In fact, there is no sense of otherness in the poem: they are not important; only the affirmation of the self achieves primacy.

The speaker in Umpierre's poem is fighting oppression, which suggests that María Cristina is oppressed. But is Umpierre addressing the same speaker that Esteves describes in her poem? Esteves's speaker is Maria Christina and not María Cristina; and her persona already alludes to the synthesis of Puerto Rican and North American cultures. When Umpierre writes about María Cristina, her correcting of Esteves's spelling of the first and last names signifies a character more entrenched in Hispanic culture. In any event, Maria Christina is oppressed, especially if we interpret her to be a symbolic representation of the Christ child and a savior of her people.

Umpierre's poetic voice identifies herself as "I am a Puerto Rican woman born in another barrio." What is puzzling here is that in her fight against the values imposed by traditional Hispanic culture, she accepts U.S. symbols and ideology. Umpierre's "response" to Esteves's poem reminds us of the aggressive outlook manifested in the way the United States conducts foreign policy toward many of its Latin American neighbors, as portrayed in the histories of Puerto Rico, Cuba, and the Dominican Republic. If María Cristina is a metaphorical representation of Puerto Rico and Puerto Rican culture, then Umpierre's response parallels the colonial relationship between colonizer and colonized. There is no attempt to create a third space, as Homi Bhabha does in *The Location of Culture*,[84] that could negate both Puerto Rican and North American cultures; rather, we are only given the choice to condemn one by embracing the other. However, I am left wondering, if Umpierre is "a Puerto Rican woman born in another barrio," where is that other barrio to which she alludes? Certainly, it cannot be the one located in East Harlem, in which Puerto Rican culture continues to thrive. Perhaps it is one in which whites also live, but more appropriately it is a figurative barrio that exists within the creation of her own individual Puerto Rican and Latino identity.

The acceptance of a North American value system, which to some degree undermines Umpierre's own Puerto Rican identity and sense of liberation, is explicit in the last line of the first and last stanzas, which speaks about her own sexual liberation: "and I do fix all leaks in my faucets." Because the speaker attempts to liberate herself from a past in which women did not perform mechanical tasks, fixing leaks may refer to her gaining independence through becoming a capable plumber. She does not need to depend on a man to help her repair household items. But the faucet is also an obvious allusion to her sexuality. Then, does the line in question indicate that her sexual liberation and exploits are above anything, including morality, religion, and politics? Does the shifting emphasis from "all faucets" of the first stanza to "all leaks in my faucets" insinuate that she will repair the leaks of the exploited and the exploiters? Again, is libidinal egoism above the values and ideologies of those who are leaking and whose leaks need to be fixed?

The shift from "all faucets" to "all leaks in my faucets" also questions a traditional-gender reading of the poem. An alternative to the traditional reading suggests that Umpierre has appropriated the male symbol for her own use. That is, in the first stanza she is able to stop the leaks from all faucets, which can be seen as an allusion to the female sex organ. In the last one, she is the one who has a faucet, which also leaks, but which she is able to control. An important shift takes place in the poem: the poem begins with an allusion to the female sex organ and concludes with a reference to the male organ, which is also hers. Umpierre takes her observation one step further and places into question gender identity. She questions the traditional male and female sex roles. As a woman with male organs, she also refers to lesbian identity. The comparison of the first and last lines helps to explain the speaker's reliance on and appropriation of conventionally male-dominant symbols.

Esteves continues the dialogue with Umpierre by composing "So Your Name Isn't María Cristina," rightfully dedicated to Umpierre. In this most recent response, Esteves internalizes the characteristics of her speaker and accepts Umpierre's criticism, as the Spanish spelling of María Cristina suggests. According to Esteves, María Cristina was a young and confused woman in search of identity: "Caught somewhere in between the casera traditions of Titi / Julia / and the progressive principles of a Young Lords cousin."[85] Esteves concedes that María Cristina lived in a haphazard manner, reacting to situations without any understanding of her vast cultural tradition.

In the third stanza, Esteves and María Cristina come together, for the poetic persona is also a poet: "María Cristina was naive when she wrote her first poem, / just beginning her metamorphosis."[86] In this autobiographical reference, Esteves and María Cristina have changed, and the poet-persona has grown up with respect to age and wisdom.

About halfway through the poem, Esteves speaks directly to Umpierre: "So your name isn't María Cristina." She looks to Umpierre, who is one year older than Esteves, as an older sister and teacher. Unlike the situation in her first poem, in this one the speaker is not a teacher, but a student with much to learn. Esteves even conveys a sense of admiration for Umpierre's fighting spirit and independence. But though María Cristina has learned from her older sister and changed, Esteves is reluctant to rid herself completely of the past, preferring to combine the two:

> Now she can build her own house
> as well as sew, cook, wash, have babies,
> even if her name hasn't changed.[87]

The first line refers to Umpierre's independence and her ability to fix her own faucet. Similarly, Esteves can build her own house. But within the context of the next two lines, building a house also means taking on the responsibility of being head of the household, as she also balances other activities associated with the home. The lines just cited acquire importance because they are repeated in the next-to-last stanza; however, Esteves modifies them and suppresses the second line, the one outlining the traditional and cultural tasks of women: "Now she can build her own house, / even though her name hasn't changed."

If I were to insist that Esteves's characterization of women is problematic, I would suggest that the reader is left with the impression that the missing line, with its assertion of traditional female tastes and the importance of pleasing men, has not totally disappeared. It has been displaced to other poems in the collection, and evident in the book's title. *Bluestown Mockingbird Mambo* serves as an apt name for the collection, but in particular it points to two poems whose titles also invoke the same two musical compositions. The first word of the title, *Bluestown*, suggests African American culture and thus applies especially to "Black Notes and 'You Do Something to Me'"; the third one is *Mambo*, a musical composition that originated in the Spanish Caribbean, and its importance is most salient in "Mambo Love Poem." "Black Notes and 'You Do Something to Me,'" is a Hispanicized celebration of African American culture and music, represented by jazz and, more appropriately, Latin Jazz. Esteves concludes her rhythmic poem in the following manner:

> Jazz
> How I love your sweet soul sounds.
> Yeah,
> how I love how you love me.
> Yeah, how I love that deep black thang . . .
> . . . "You do so well" . . .[88]

Jazz is a style of music, and from this perspective the poem's signifiers convey the rhythms of the music it signifies. The poem mentions the names of jazz musicians, and it reproduces the fast and slow alternations known to this musical composition. But Jazz is also a prosopopoeia that represents two people making love. The poem alludes to the male organ as an integral part of that relationship. This is evident in the suggestive title, "Black Notes and 'You Do Something to Me,'" and in the first line "Jazz—jazzy jass juice," which not only underscores the music in the poem but contains the word "ass" and "juice," connoting intercourse and the culmination of the sex act. The fast rhythm, most evident at the end of the first stanza, also recalls the state of sexual excitation of the poetic voice. This is then followed by the culmination of the sex act, and, in the last stanza, by a restful state associated with the end of the same act. The poem conveys the different rhythms associated with lovemaking:

> Those multifarious dimensional openings
> playin' loud—soft—hard—cold—slow—'n—suavecito black.
> Playin' it runnin'—jumpin'—cookin'—greasin'—'n—smokin'
> black.[89]

In fact, the poem can be read as an exultation of black lovemaking.

The second poem, "Mambo Love Poem," is another version of Esteves's "For Tito," included in the same anthology that contains "My Name Is Maria Christina," and describes the lovemaking between Carlos and Rebecca:

> Rebecca y Carlos become one
> like two birds flying through the open sky,
> in mambo cha-cha to celebrate their joy,
> their feet no longer touching the ground.[90]

Rebecca and Carlos's lovemaking is placed within the context of Afro-Caribbean culture and religion. The mambo is related to the rumba, which has its origin in Afro-Cuban religions, as indicated in her poem "Rumba Amiga, Amiga," of the same collection.

Looking more closely at each stanza's first line in "Mambo Love Poem," we notice that the man is given primary importance in the relationship. The first lines, respectively, of each of the poem's five stanzas are as follows: "Carlos y Rebecca dance across the floor," "Carlos y Rebecca move," "Rebecca y Carlos glide across the floor," "They forget their pain in this land of joy," and "They dance." Notice that in the first two stanzas, Esteves places Carlos first or on top of Rebecca, in the third she changes the order and places Rebecca first or on top of Carlos, and in the final two stanzas they merge into the plural *They*, a pronoun that invokes the unity already seen in "For Tito" and "My Name Is Maria Christina." But whereas the fourth stanza contains "Rebecca y Carlos," as shown in the earlier four-line quote, it is embedded in the stanza and is not given the significance afforded to the first line of each stanza. I want to stress that even though "Mambo Love Poem" and "Black Notes and 'You Do Something to Me'" are sexually explicit, from Umpierre's viewpoint neither one incorporates the transformation and growth Esteves claims María Cristina has undergone. In each poem, Esteves reveals that she is dependent on the male symbol for her self-expression. The following discussion will also touch on this element in "So Your Name Isn't María Cristina."

I will now explore further the title *Bluestown Mockingbird Mambo.* Evidently, it incorporates the emotions and sadness associated with the African American musical composition known as the blues and the happiness and fast pace of the mambo. However, Esteves brings together Bluestown, the mockingbird, and mambo. As we know, the mockingbird is native of the southern part of the United States. In this respect, the blues of the South is complemented by the mockingbird of the same region. But the mockingbird is known for its ability to imitate or mimic the notes of other birds, which suggests that this collection of poems, in particular "So Your Name Isn't María Cristina," has a certain element of imitation or repetition. Imitation here implies copying the "original" or the "model," perhaps without any real understanding of what it is saying. Moreover, mockingbird also contains the word *mock,* a way of making fun of or ridiculing someone. This interpretation could also be read into "So Your Name Isn't María Cristina," especially if you combine it with the book's cover, which shows a slim and sexy young woman with her hands on her waist, holding up her skirt, and revealing her legs and portions of her thighs in a provocative manner. The emphasis of this insert on the book's cover is not the person but the body; the woman's head has been cropped from the photograph and we cannot see her face. It is obvious that the insert emphasizes the feminine and is sexually evocative. Although the photograph depicts a woman ready to dance the mambo, I submit that she could be a representation of Esteves's María Cristina. What is more difficult to answer is whether the photograph is of the original Maria Christina or the new María Cristina, the one who has grown and changed. Even if we were to concede that it refers to María Cristina, she has not totally abandoned her past. For this reason the line "as well as sew, cook, wash, have babies," which alludes to her first poem and is present in the second one, though suppressed from its penultimate stanza, continues to be echoed in the collection.

This current perspective allows me to revisit my first interpretation of "My Name Is Maria Christina." If my observation is correct that Esteves's *Bluestown Mockingbird Mambo* contains an element of mockery directed at Umpierre and that the cover art underscores feminine qualities, then María Cristina has not evolved to the level she claims to have reached in the poem "So Your Name Isn't María Cristina." Consequently, is it possible that Umpierre found a significance in Esteves's poem that we overlooked? Or, if my reading was correct, was Umpierre guided by extraliterary and biographical concerns? Was she apprised about aspects of Esteves's life not contained in "My Name Is Maria Christina" but which she put into her own rendition "In Response," which could be subtitled "My Name Isn't María Cristina"? In either case, Umpierre may have been justified in overreacting to Maria Christina's overt or implied identity. If we look back to "My Name Is Maria Christina" from Umpierre's and my present point of view, then Esteves's persona may have also been "mocking" when she said that she did not tease men with her eye-catching clothes. This is certainly the case with the woman who appears on the cover of *Bluestown Mockingbird Mambo.* Is she not raising her skirt seductively? If so, is Esteves imitating Umpierre in "So Your Name Isn't María Cristina" to be politically correct, contrary to her real feelings?

From another perspective, María Cristina attempts to draw from two different cultures. What Esteves may have conceded in her most recent poem to Umpierre as María Cristina's confusion, may very well be fortitude. Seen in this light, María Cristina's ability to draw from both Hispanic and North American cultures is not weakness but strength. This idea is also evident in the book's title, as it combines two different types of music: blues and mambo, one associated with African Americans and North American culture, the other with U.S. Hispanic communities. Moreover, the two compositions are opposites; the blues is sad and slow, the mambo is lively, danced with many movements, at a faster beat. Nevertheless, they do underscore a dance between two cultures.

The synthesis of the two cultures is apparent in a comparison of Esteves's essays with her poetry. In an article entitled "The Feminist Viewpoint in the Poetry of Puerto Rican Women in the United States" (1987), she reviews briefly Puerto Rican female poets and gives publicity to their works, highlighting their political and feminist discourse. In the essay she traces the change in the consciousness of Puerto Rican women in the United States to Julia de Burgos and Lolita Lebrón and dedicates one paragraph to Luz María Umpierre. What is striking about the essay is that by the time it was published in 1987, Esteves was familiar with a feminist discourse that she accepted also as her own. Toward the end she writes:

No longer are women traditional symbols of passive resistance to male domination. No longer are women content to be slave workers or cheap laborers. The modern woman is making a vital and active contribution to participate in the politics of her destiny; and the Puerto Rican woman is a very real part of that movement.[91]

The essay was written seven years after Esteves published "My Name Is Maria Christina," two years after "In Response," and three years before "So Your Name Isn't María Cristina." With this in mind, it is difficult to understand why in the second poem Esteves apologizes for writing "My Name Is

Maria Christina" and thanks Umpierre for showing her what she had already known, at least as early as when Esteves wrote her essay on feminist poetry.

What "My Name Is Maria Christina" and "So Your Name Isn't María Cristina" show is an internal struggle that Esteves, Umpierre, and perhaps other Latina Caribbean writers undergo when trying to maintain their Latina identity in the United States. The tension emerges as they embrace a Hispanic culture that is familiar to them and which they call theirs, and a North American one that is also familiar to them, but which they do not consider theirs. However, this other culture is attractive to them, as Umpierre has shown, insofar as it supports the liberation of women and promotes women's equality. This important dilemma is viewed in a binary manner: if you accept U.S. culture, then you must reject Puerto Rican traditions; but if you accept Puerto Rican traditions, you are not a supporter of women's rights as defined within the U.S. context. Both Esteves and Umpierre overlook the dynamic inner workings of culture; Puerto Rican culture, whether on the island or on the continent, is constantly changing, and evolving with time. The same occurs with U.S. culture: as Latinos contribute with their presence to mainstream society, the dominant culture will appropriate increasing aspects of the Latino one as its own. This is the case with U.S. critics who rely on Latino or Chicano or Xicanismo discourse as a way of understanding society. With their poetic dialogue, Esteves and Umpierre foresee the coming together or dance between the two cultures and the mediation that must take place when dancing in the same geographic space.

Luz María Umpierre depends on the feminist discourse to question Hispanic culture, and she rebels against the male-dominant society in her brief, powerful poem "Rubbish." Here she reacts against the laws and conventions of the dominant culture, regardless of how sensible they may be. Her cultural rebellion is directed against even the most mundane acts: waiting in line to get the bus, walking on the right-hand side of the street, talking softly, not littering, taking a number and waiting your turn, parking the car close to the sidewalk and away from the fire hydrant, and walking fast. Umpierre ends her poem with

> I b-e-g yul paldon, escuismi
> am sorri pero yo soy latina
> y no sopolto su RUBBISH.[92]

Umpierre's rebellion is not related to a problem of comprehending a different language, which she alludes to with the interference of her Spanish, but to the fact that she is *Latina*, a term synonymous with rejecting all that is mainstream culture. Umpierre's rebellion is also a linguistic one. Although she expresses herself in standard Spanish and English, in the last stanza she begins by Hispanicizing English, then switches to Spanish, and finishes with a mixture of both: "y no sopolto [soporto] su RUBBISH," a euphemism that could be understood in either language.

If Esteves and Umpierre strive to define María Cristina's identity within the context of either the Hispanic or North American cultures, Rosario Morales sees it from a different perspective. For Morales, "My Revolution" is a personal one, neither tailor-made nor in fashion, but ongoing and long-lasting. It is not limited to blue- or white-collar work, in or outside of the house, but encompasses both extremes and all the gradations in between. It includes political and daily occurrences:

> I can wear it in the fields
> I can wear it to go dancing
>> do the dishes
>> do the laundry
>> see the movie
>> do the marching[93]

It is a personal revolution that embraces doing traditional household chores, as Esteves underscored; yet it is not limited to them. Morales continues:

> My revolution is not cut from a pattern, I designed it.

> It's home made and handcrafted
> It's got seams to let out
>> and hems to let down
>>> tucks to take in
>>>> darts to take out.[94]

Morales breaks from the constrictors of the past to propose her own method of thinking and acting. This idea is also incorporated into the structure of the poem. The first stanza contains two alternating voices. The first voice is the poet's voice, and the second, in parentheses, is a more traditional one, which commands her to act. When Morales opens the poem with "My revolution is not starched and ironed," the other voice states: "(Stand over the ironing board, wield the hot iron)." This second voice may also belong to Morales's subconscious, for she has also internalized elements of a traditional culture. But it is clear that the parentheses are intended not only to separate this voice from her present beliefs, but to restrict and contain it. After the first stanza, the second voice disappears and the speaker is free to explore what she believes to be her own revolution.

III

Although Puerto Rican American poetry has been associated mainly with the Nuyorican writers and has focused on the plight of Puerto Ricans in New York, there are other Puerto Rican American writers who write beyond the inner-city experience. Some poems express the same emotions, hatred, and violence familiar in much Nuyorican writing and others do not. Some writers even mix styles, choosing to be aggressive in some writings and not in others. On the whole, they prefer to use a more conventional language common among mainstream North American poets. Rosario and Aurora Levins Morales, mother and daughter, in their "Ending Poem" write about the complexity of being Puerto Rican. If in the "Puerto Rican Obituary" Pedro Pietri refers to the lack of identity of Juan, Miguel, Milagros, Olga, and Manuel, then Morales and Levins Morales show that they are indeed Puerto Ricans and much more. Whereas Pietri's characters accepted the myths imposed upon them by the dominant society, those of Morales and Levins Morales reject any preconceived category and search for their own definition of who they are. Esteves and Umpierre write within the Hispanic and North American cultures, respectively; Morales and Levins Morales, in contrast, write in the "Ending Poem":

> I am what I am.
> *A child of the Americas.*
> A light-skinned mestiza of the Caribbean.
> *A child of many diaspora, born into this continent at a crossroads.*
> I am Puerto Rican. I am U.S. American.
> *I am New York Manhattan and the Bronx.*
> A mountain-born, country-bred, homegrown jíbara child,
> *up from the shtetl, a California Puerto Rican Jew*
> A product of the New York ghettos I have never known.
> *I am an immigrant*
> and the daughter and granddaughter of immigrants.[95]

The poetic *I* is both singular and plural. It recognizes the past, but it is not tied to it:

> I am not African
> *African waters the roots of my tree, but I cannot return.*
>
> I am not Taína.
> *I am a late leaf of that ancient tree,*
> and my roots reach into the soil of two Americas.
> *Taíno is in me, but there in no way back.*
>
> I am not European, though I have dreamt of those cities[96]

And they come to a closure or a conclusion to the search of their own identity and affirm: "I am a child of many mothers. / . . . *Born at a crossroads.*"[97] They do not question which one they should choose; instead, they choose all because they physically carry all within them, and all are a part of them. This is evident also in the plurality of motherhood; both speakers represent more than one womb or origin. They are two, but more important they are also one. *They* and *we* and *I* are united at the end "And we are whole."

The poem contains the same alternating structure present in "My Revolution." It may have been composed by combining two separate poems, one written by the mother and the other by the daughter. The structure also represents two perspectives on the same issue (the roman type corresponds to the mother and the italics to the daughter). By bringing the two perspectives together, the reader profits from a much richer understanding of what it means to be Puerto Rican. Puerto Rican can mean island-born and of a Hispanic tradition, but it can also mean North American, Jewish, inner-city, country, or poor; Puerto Ricans have African, Amerindian, and European roots, without necessarily being exclusively from one of those places. In essence being Puerto Rican entails embodying the cultural complexity evident throughout the New World.

There are other Puerto Rican American poets who are concerned about a plurality of themes that transcend the ghetto; they compose their poems using a less hostile and more mainstream language. This is also the case of Julio Marzán, who lives in New York but does not write in the style known to Nuyorican poets. Just as Williams translated the Carlos within him, Marzán does the same as he suggests in the title of his first book of poems, *Translations without Originals*, which evokes the poet's bilingual and multicultural facets. Some of his poems contain images of Hispanic culture: flamboyants, yucca plants, mangos, the Spanish fortress. Others are of the North American society: the porter, the boiler, and a junkie. All are mediated by a standard English language and culture to express his thoughts.

Marzán's "Sunday Morning in Old San Juan" is a nostalgic and romantic re-creation of the Puerto Rican capital. If Puerto Rican writers of the Generación del Cuarenta used the city to describe the migratory process to the United States, Marzán's speaker, like Algarín's and Piñero's, returns to San Juan; he basks in its sunlight and beauty, and describes a city that appeals to the senses. But whereas the Nuyorican poets express themselves with anger, Marzán's tone and images are different. Certainly, there are elements that provide a contrast to life in the North, such as "the transparent warmth" and the colors produced by the sunlight; and the Spanish fortress and wrought-iron balconies allude to a different historical development.

One ingredient of the poem's appeal to the senses lies in the speaker's concentration on the chromatic spectrum: the yellow, of the "Egg of morning"; the blue, repeated five times, of the sea and sky; the "Flame-orange" of the flamboyants; the "red-orange" of the rain; and the violet of the hyacinths, all of which together produce a rainbow of colors. The emphasis on the color blue recalls Rubén Darío and his book, *Azul* (1888), which gave coherence to the *modernista* movement. Although *modernismo* borrowed from the French symbolist and Parnassian movements, it refocused the tropes to create the first poetic tradition originating in Spanish America. From a *modernista* perspective, San Juan is described as an exotic city of delight and tranquility that is suspended in time, suggested by the absence of punctuation, as the poetic *I* and the *you* are an integral part of the scenery and ensemble of colors.

Although colors are an important motif in the poem, they are not the only images that appeal to the senses: smell, taste, touch, hearing are also stimulated. The speaker mentions the "scent of hyacinths" in addition to pointing out their color. The morning egg can be interpreted as the yellow of the sun, but also as a breakfast dish, thus pleasing to the taste buds. The tactile—the feeling of the wind blowing—and the auditory—the sounds produced by the breeze, the trees, and the rain—are replicated in the poem by "Flame-orange flamboyants," "Blowing these flaming / Flamboyants in its breeze," and "In the red-orange rain."[98]

In his "Sunday Morning in Old San Juan," Marzán captures a moment in time in the city when migration began and to which many return, if not physically then psychologically. Víctor Hernández Cruz uses a similar theme but a different setting when he encapsulates a moment from the past, of innocence, expectation, and tranquility, in a busy New York City environment. Hernández Cruz best represents a mixture of the two poetic styles we have outlined, and he provides a transition from one to the other. He lived in New York City and knows firsthand what it means to be a Latino in that city. However, he also lived in California, where he was exposed to a different cultural reality. Currently, he resides in Aguas Buenas, Puerto Rico, and is becoming familiar with the culture of his past. Hernández Cruz's poetry is presently undergoing a change, and his environment continues to play an important part. While he lived in New York, Hernández Cruz was influenced by Puerto Rican sounds, by William Carlos Williams, and by the coming together of the cultures:

I was raised in New York with English and Spanish spoken in my barrio. In my family there were traces of Hispanic traditions, such as poetry readings. That's why my first effort in English consisted of trying to write décimas—what a ridiculous thing! It is difficult to find rhythms in that vertical language, with Germanic roots. I continued to read contemporary poetry. I came across the poetry of William Carlos Williams and my poetic voice found a way to express the present, the place where I stood. In reading the North American I was also reading the Puerto Rican; I read everything I could find in New York. Reading is part of writing, if you are a cultured poet; all those readings helped me to express my duality, the stereophonic I felt inside.[99]

Music is essential for Hernández Cruz and "Going Uptown to Visit Miriam" combines sounds and images of the New York City environment and a secret the speaker possesses. It takes the reader on a subway ride from one extreme of the island of Manhattan to the other, from lower Manhattan to the northernmost part, as the train makes local and express stops:

> the train pulls in & out
> the white walls   dark-
> ness   white walls   dark-
> ness.[100]

The subway ride provides a glimpse of the changing faces of the city and its people, made evident by the train stops; some women get off at 42nd Street to change for the West Side line, while others get off at 59th Street to shop in department stores. For the speaker, the train riders are silly, caricatures of people who are superficial and whom he will never get to know. Although the train is full of riders, whose faces constantly change, they do not speak to one another. The lack of communication, which under different circumstances may have referred to alienation, conveys silence and the speaker's own secretive destination. He repeats: "but no one knows where i am / going to take this train."[101] All the passengers guard their own destinations. Their secrets stimulate the poet's imagination and make him wonder where everyone else is going:

> ladies looking up i
> wonder where they going
> the dentist   pick up
> husband pick up wife
> pick up kids
> pick up ?   grass?
> to library   to museum
> to laundromat   to school[102]

The speaker's destination is kept not only from the train passengers but also from Sonia, perhaps another girlfriend who lives in Miriam's neighborhood and whom he does not want to meet or see.

The structure of Hernández Cruz's poetry suits his concerns. It recalls the experimental style of the vanguard movements at the turn of the century as well as that employed by the Beat generation. "Going Uptown to Visit Miriam," is devoid of uppercase letters, except for the last stanza, and punctuation. The repetitions and spacing between words reproduce the smooth and jerky train ride as the speaker travels uptown, seen in rhythmic line pairs such as "to take this train / to take this train," "to visit miriam / to visit miriam," "taking this train / to visit miriam." I want also to point out that in the lines cited, taking the train and visiting Miriam have their own separate stanzas and represent two different and independent thoughts. However, in the last stanza, they come together. The unity between the train and Miriam, the means and the end, is also present in the contraction *i'm* in the last stanza, "But no one knows where i'm taking / this train," in which the speaker substitutes the word *going* for *taking*, a change that takes him closer to his goal. The substitution also makes the expression more concise and direct. He now prefers "taking this train" over "going to take this train," to visit Miriam. The poetic voice's language is less choppy, reflecting a shift from a local to an express track, and more fluid as he reaches his goal. Like Dante's ascent into paradise, the poetic voice has gone from one extreme of the island to the other, to be received by Miriam, his Beatriz.

The syntactic unity seen at the end of the poem refers to his oneness with Miriam. It also suggests another type of coming together, between Spanish and English, North American and Hispanic cultures. It is important to note that in the line "pick up ?grass?" the question mark has been placed closer to grass than to the verb *pick up*, different from the way it would normally appear in English. This observation responds to the logic of my cross-cultural interpretation, since someone could be riding the subway to pick up someone else and to pick up grass, a euphemism for marijuana. However, it would also make sense if we read the line as a Spanish construction. In Spanish a question starts with an upside-down question mark and ends with a right-side-up question mark placed at the end of the sentence. In the absence of a typewriter or computer with Spanish letters, it is common to place a right-side-up question mark at the beginning of the sentence. Thus the speaker asks with Spanish intonation if someone is going to pick up grass.

The right-side-up question mark at the beginning of the word *grass* points to another construction that could have come from Spanish. In describing the stops where the women exit the train and station, the speaker states:

at 42 to change for the
westside line   or off
59 for the department store.[103]

In New York, these streets are written and pronounced 42nd and 59th, but in Spanish they are simply written and pronounced "la 42" and "la 59." It is evident that the speaker dropped the Spanish article but retained the Spanish transcription. In the aforementioned interview Hernández Cruz refers to his use of language:

> There is an aspect of my use of language which is not directly or consciously controlled by me. As I was a child of the migration who went with the Spanish language inwardly intact into a storm of English and a blizzard of buildings—both languages developed a strange relationship with each other, so that while my head could be in Spanish cadence I am writing physically with the English language. This contrast between English and Spanish and even between rural-ness and urban-ness gives a special air and vitality not just to my poetry but to much of the Chicano and Puerto Rican literature of the U.S. . . . These layers of history and linguistics reside now in my work—as I said as a manifestation that is unconscious in operation and as criteria of my aesthetic.[104]

Hernández Cruz's poem is about his secretive relationship with Miriam and also about the Hispanic and North American cultures coexisting in the same person and city.

In "Three Days/out of Franklin," Hernández Cruz takes the reader to another uptown location. In this poem, the speaker is absent from Franklin High School, located on the Upper East Side of Manhattan, considered one of the roughest schools in New York City. Although it is possible to propose that the speaker did not attend school because it may have been a three-day weekend or because he decided not to go to school, it is also likely that he was suspended for the same period of time. The poem describes what takes place in the life of the speaker during his absence. Certainly, there is some antagonism between the speaker and authority figures, such as the ones in his school. This is evident when he watches a program of cowboys and Indians, and sides with the underdogs. In the program, the cowboys are portrayed as the "good" guys and the Indians as "bad." But from the speaker's point of view, the Indians are the good guys and the winners:

saw the indians
on t.v.

> & in my mind
> & heart
> they kick
> the white man
> in the ass[105]

The poem lists the speaker's activities during the three days, days that run together and whose beginning and end are only decipherable by "night/morning." Time as a point of spatial reference is not important. The speaker's inability to distinguish clearly between one day and another may be due to the influence of drugs, as indicated by "got high." Although getting high is important for the poetic voice, it is not the only thing the narrator does. Even though he is out of school, learning does take place. The words *got high* are repeated three times, but only during the first day, and they are not mentioned on the second or third days. Equally important is that he reads three times, twice on the first day and once on the second. Most meaningful, as an indication of the development of his consciousness, is the word *wrote*, which also appears three times. But unlike the word *read*, it is present once on the first day and twice on the second. The number three is important because it reflects the number of days absent from school. Other repeated words are *beautiful* and *soul;* they are combined in the opening line, "the soul is a beautiful thing." The word *soul* appears four times and the word *beautiful*, three. The poem ends in the following manner:

> three days
> with myself
> & the world
> soul is beautiful
> thing
> the smell of
> everything
> ahead
> the earth
> & all the people /
> > victor hernández cruz
> > exiled from franklin
> > december 14 to 19[106]

The ending of the poem brings the words *soul* and *beautiful* together and clarifies that the four recurrences of *soul* suggest another reiteration, that writing is "repeated" four times and is also present on the third day. While the speaker was "exiled" from school, he composed the poem under discussion. Each day he wrote, once on the first day and twice on the second, as indicated by the word *wrote,* and he completed the poem on the third day.

Another contrast, between what occurs inside and outside of school, highlights that school does not automatically produce learning. The opposite is also true: education does exist outside of school. The speaker may not have learned much in school, and this may have been the reason for the suspension, which he expresses in political terms when he identifies with the Indians against the white man. While he was away from school, the speaker did learn about himself, represented by word *soul* as in "the soul is a beautiful thing." The number of repetitions, present or implied, of the words *soul* and *writing* point to their relationship. For the speaker, writing is a way of learning about and understanding the beauty of the soul or the self, an expression the speaker uses to open and close the poem.

Although Hernández Cruz entitles his poem "Three Days/out of Franklin," the signature line at the bottom suggests that there were five: "exiled from franklin / december 14 to 19." Nevertheless, we can assume that there were three days of missed school, from Wednesday to Friday, and that the other two days were Saturday and Sunday. So the learning process did take place when he was supposed to be in school; he then rested Saturday and Sunday, or used that time to polish the poem. My reading acquires a religious tone as well, similar to the one contained in Genesis, where the Lord worked for six days and then rested on the Sabbath. The number three in the poem's title is also of religious importance. Like Christ, the poetic voice resurrects on the third day and emerges a new person, full of renewed life, with his own creation, represented by the poem.

I would like to comment on the structure of the poem. As in "Going Uptown to Visit Miriam," the formality associated with uppercase letters, punctuation, and a "traditional" education is also absent here. Rather, like the three days, the ideas flow together. The poem has a syntactic, but mainly diachronic, importance, because many lines have only one word. Whereas a word in a syntactic structure allows it to be read within the environment of the line, a one-word, self-sufficient line forces the reader to take into account the previous as well as the following lines. In addition, this structure requires readers to slow down their reading in order to pay close attention to each word line. The structure could be read in political terms, as suggested by the word *exile,* thus alluding not to an equality indicated by synchronic syntactic elements, but to a hierarchy or a diachrony. Moreover, the emphasis on diachrony, the lack of punctuation, and the use of images common to the speaker's surroundings exist in binary opposition to the poetry, structure, and grammar taught by a rigid school system that demands conformity and denies the individuality and freedom the persona finds in his poems. Rebellion from the mainstream produces a different type of learning, as valid or more valid than the traditional one.

The political, personal, and educational differences present in "Going Uptown to Visit Miriam" and "Three Days/out of Franklin" are communicated in cultural terms in "The Physics of Ochun." The two cultures come together in New York City, represented by the scientists of Columbia University and by the González family. The two occupy the same space when the scientists go to Mrs. González's apartment and collect the tears of the Virgin de la Caridad del Cobre, the patron saint of Cuba, whose Yoruba name is Ochún. Upon examining the tears in a laboratory setting, they read the word *Jehovah*. The scientific instruments indicate that the miracle is not a part of the scientists' or the González's imagination, but a confirmed, verifiable, and proven reality.

The scientists witness the supernatural a second time when they and Mrs. González climb a staircase that had grown from her window. The transformation that Mrs. González and her daughter experienced, "We got hair permanents / and our nails manicured,"[107] verifies their experiences, which is also confirmed by the scientists and their scientific method:

> The scientist with the test tube
> saw it get full of a white liquid
> The scientist with the air bag
> felt it change into a chunk of metal
> The scientist with the writing pad
> saw a language appear on it backwards
> printing faster than a computer[108]

The poem refers to how people from different cultures observe and approach a "magic" reality, always interpreting it from their own cultural perspective. The scientists who represent civilization, reason, logic, Western thought, and objectivity are taken aback when confronted with a supernatural situation foreign to their culture but which they can observe and measure. Mrs. González, born into Puerto Rican or Cuban culture, is more willing to accept the phenomenon. What is clear is that Ochún's world is as real as that of the scientist; Mrs. González and the scientists observe the same transformations. When looking into the microscope, they see the word JEHOVAH. But if the water the Virgin produces is sacred and pure, that used by the scientists is not: "They sent for a bottle of Scotch."

There are other supernatural events. A staircase goes from the window to the sky, which they climb because a

> long white rope had come out
> of their belly buttons and some-
> thing was pulling them up.[109]

Although the white rope recalls the seed and tree of "Jack and the Bean Stalk," the umbilical cord is a natural lifeline to the Almighty. Mrs.

González and her neighbors have a spiritual connection absent in those who lack faith and demand proof. If Mrs. González and her daughter believe in the miracles of Ochún as a representation of the supernatural, so does their neighbor Concepción, who finds a piece of paper one of the scientists dropped into her pot of red beans, the staple of Puerto Rican cuisine. Concepción's relationship with her physician ("He thought it was the imprint / of flower petals / so even and bold in lilac / ink")[110] mirrors that of Mrs. González and the scientists. The note appearing on the scientist's writing pad coincides with Concepción's dream that she is pregnant; she informs her physician that she will see him in nine months and proceeds to finish her cooking. Concepción, whose name reflects the process of conception she is experiencing, possesses knowledge; she knows how to interpret events, whereas her doctor, who is better educated than she, does not. For those who do or do not believe, the world of Ochún is also valid and scientific, as the title of the poem reveals.

Like the other poems written by Hernández Cruz, the "Physics of Ochun" underscores the differences between Hispanic culture and North American society. One represents the mainstream, formality, science, reason, education, conformity; and the other informality, spontaneity, "ignorance," "superstition," and "lack of education." In postcolonial terms, one is the center and the other the periphery. The world of Hispanic culture, as the scientists find out and as the physician will soon discover, is as real and perhaps even more real than any other.

Judith Ortiz Cofer's poetry is distinctly different from that of the other Nuyorican poets described so far. Although there does not appear to be any question about her own Puerto Rican identity, she is not as preoccupied with the exploitation of the Puerto Rican masses who traveled to the United States, as she is with writing about more personal concerns. Her language is standard English and does not include the mixing of Spanish and English common in the works of other Puerto Rican American poets. When she does incorporate Spanish words, they are used in a standard and conventional manner.

"The Idea of Islands" is composed as an interview in which the speaker refers to Puerto Rico and the Caribbean as her place of birth; she also talks about Atlanta, which for her has been transformed into a port city. When asked about her place of birth, the poetic voice first takes us to Atlanta and then to her island. Ortiz Cofer relies on images associated with Caribbean culture and landscape and uses them to describe this southern city. There are historical events that unite the southeastern part of the United States and the Caribbean. During the mid-nineteenth century, the Knights of the Golden Circle selected Havana as the center of a circle whose circumference encompassed the Caribbean islands and the agricultural south. The area contained in the circle supported and promoted slavery.[111] In a similar manner Ortiz Cofer considers Atlanta as part of the Caribbean and a metaphorical island. But there are clear and significant differences between the real and the metaphorical island; one is associated with paradise and the other with life after the Fall:

> Since you ask, things were simpler
> on the island. Food and shelter
> were never the problem. Most days,
> a hat and a watchful eye were all
> one needed for protection, the climate being
> rarely inclement. Fruit could be plucked
> from trees languishing under the weight
> of their own fecundity. The thick sea
> spewed out fish that crawled into the pots
> of women whose main occupation was to dress
> each other's manes with scarlet hibiscus,
> which as you may know, blooms
> without restraint in the tropics.[112]

Ortiz Cofer's island is the biblical paradise Adam and Eve inhabited before Satan's appearance. Unlike Adam Eve, who want to remain there and who after the Fall desire to return, the speaker wishes to escape. If Adam and Eve were happy in paradise, the speaker is not content with having everything handed to her. She is different from the others, more ambitious, overdressed, and she has no desire to eat mangos three times a day. Whereas Adam and Eve were ejected from the Garden of Eden because they ate from the forbidden tree of knowledge, Ortiz Cofer is ready to leave on her own. Unlike the Nuyorican writers who resent having been forced to abandon the island and denounce their mistreatment on the mainland, Ortiz Cofer sits by the beach, guarding a fire, and waits for someone to go ashore and rescue her from "paradise."

The poem is written from the present, in which the speaker looks back and compares the island with the mainland. She distances herself from the past because the present is where she feels comfortable and belongs. The Caribbean is her place of birth, but not the place where she wants to spend the rest of her life. Within the Caribbean image of Atlanta that she prefers, the city's bright lights are like stars and the

> the traffic ebbs and rises like the tides
> and in a crowd,
> everyone is an island.[113]

Adam and Eve were ejected from paradise and human nature is associated with a desire to return to a lost paradise, as Henri Baudet has explained in

Paradise on Earth: Some Thoughts on European Images of Non-European Man (1965).[114] Ortiz Cofer prefers Defoes's resolution, a rescue of Robinson Crusoe and a return to civilization. To her, it is not the physical island that is important, but the metaphorical one, the island you carry within.

As a Puerto Rican poet writing in the United States, Ortiz Cofer has come to terms with her past and present, a resolution that allows her to compose poems about daily life. Having lived outside New York City, her references go beyond the social and political spheres characteristic of Nuyorican poets and appeal to a broad sector of mainland readers. She does not express the same concerns seen in the works of Esteves and Umpierre, of sexual liberation and oppression, and when she does touch upon similar themes they are described in a language that separates her from the other Latina writers and brings her closer to the style used by mainstream North American poets. Furthermore, her ontological concerns differ from theirs. "They Never Grew Old" is about a cousin in a sanitarium. If she were one of the New York poets, she would have commented on the institution as an oppressive element of society that dehumanizes individuals and isolates them from their people and culture. Like Hernández Cruz's secretiveness about Miriam, Ortiz Cofer concentrates on the guarded secret of those present and absent. She describes the family meeting from a distance, as an innocent child, an observer not privy to her relative's innermost secrets.

The subject of the poem, like the relatives everyone has but no one talks about, for "Every family had one," was separated from the family and seen only occasionally. In many instances, such relatives are "put away to die and forgotten." However, this pale- and frail-looking member of the family, whose "coffee cup at her side would later / be discarded, the chair she floated on—she seemed / to have no volume or weight—would be scrubbed,"[115] is also a human being and feels love and passion. The speaker looks beyond the physical characteristics of the cousin and people like her, and she concentrates on their inner beauty. She tells a story she has heard about two young people who escaped from the sanitarium to be together. The speaker identifies with the girl who wants to help them, and not with the "townspeople scandalized / that the ill should want to make love"[116] and who could not understand them or embrace the sacrificial and romantic meaning of love. The escapees are not recluses; they are two people willing to give up their lives to be together.

As in "The Idea of Islands," Ortiz Cofer asserts her individuality. She is different from her relatives, and at the end of the poem she accepts what they fear and reject:

> I too wanted to live in *a very clean place*,
> where fragile as a pale pink rosebud I would sit
> among my many satin pillows and wait for the man with whom
> I would never grow old, to rescue me from a dull life.

> Death and love once again confused
> by one too young to see the difference.[117]

As a child, the speaker is not interested in social commentary on sanitariums, their reasons for existing, or even the family trauma of having to find permanent refuge for one of their own; instead, she concentrates on the innocent and romantic notion of love. Love, I venture to say, is something the speaker would find in any situation. The sanitarium becomes one more manifestation of the voice speaking to her from within.

For Ortiz Cofer, love is also a guarded secret, perhaps equivalent to the one kept about a relative in a sanitarium. It is also equivalent to the secret Hernández Cruz wrote about in "Going Uptown to Visit Miriam." But Ortiz Cofer's concept of love is distinct from the one described by Umpierre when referring to a Latina woman from another barrio. Although both Ortiz Cofer and Umpierre accept aspects of North American culture to express themselves, they do so from different points of view. The former draws from a more conventional tradition, and the latter from a rebellious one.

THREE

Puerto Ricans in New York
Memoirs of Bernardo Vega and
Piri Thomas's *Down These Mean Streets*

The problem with beginning is one of those problems that, if allowed to, will confront one with equal intensity on a practical and on a theoretical level. Every writer knows that the choice of a beginning for what he will write is crucial not only because it determines much of what follows but also because a work's beginning is, practically speaking, the main entrance to what it offers. Moreover, in retrospect we can regard a beginning as the point at which, in a given work, the writer departs from all other works; a beginning immediately establishes relationships with works already existing, relationships of either continuity or antagonism or some mixture of both. But the moment we start to detail the feature of a beginning—a moment likely to occur in examining many sorts of writers—we necessarily make certain special distinctions. Is a beginning the same as an origin? Is the beginning of a given work its real beginning, or is there some other, secret point that more authentically starts the work off? . . . Thus between the word *beginning* and the word *origin* lies a constantly changing system of meanings, most of them of course making first one then the other word convey greater priority, importance, explanatory power. As consistently as possible, I use *beginning* as having the most active meaning, and *origin* the more passive one: thus "X *is the origin of* Y," while "The beginning A *leads to* B."
—Edward Said, *Beginnings*

I

PUERTO Rico and Puerto Ricans have been the subject of numerous studies, but very little is known about Puerto Rican Americans living in New York City, whose presence can be traced to the early part of the nineteenth century. As with other Caribbean people of the period, in particular Cubans, Puerto Ricans traveled to the United States for economic and political reasons, transforming New York into a city in which Caribbean culture and identity developed and flourished.

Memorias de Bernardo Vega (1977; *Memoirs of Bernardo Vega*, 1984) is an autobiographical account of Bernardo Vega (1885–1965), a Puerto Rican who emigrated to New York in 1916. The work documents life in the city before and after his arrival, up until 1947, the year the U.S. Congress allowed Puerto Ricans on the island to elect their own governor. Vega's memoirs contain information about ethnic and cultural groups excluded from many official histories of the United States, Latin America, and the Caribbean. Vega is conscious of his attempt to challenge a homogeneous discourse and inscribe Puerto Ricans and other Hispanics into history. *Memorias de Bernardo Vega* is obsessed with origins and the need to document the beginnings of a Hispanic Caribbean community in the United States. To this end, Vega registers the names of countless individuals living in New York, the names of Puerto Rican organizations, the year in which they were founded, and their leaders. In particular, Vega highlights the history of Puerto Rican and other Hispanic tobacco workers and the continuity of their efforts to attain Cuban and Puerto Rican independence from Spain, in the nineteenth century, and Puerto Rican independence from the United States, in the twentieth century.

Vega chronicles the demographic changes in Harlem, as the neighborhood was transformed from a Jewish community to a Puerto Rican one. He informs the reader that the León family arrived in New York in 1904 and that they were among the first Puerto Rican families to live in Harlem, which at the beginning of the century housed approximately 150 Puerto Rican families. After Brooklyn, and especially the district near the navy yard, Harlem housed the second-largest Puerto Rican community in New York. By the time Vega arrived in New York in 1916, Hispanics numbered 16,000, of which 6,000 were Puerto Ricans. Of these, 60 percent were tobacco workers. Vega also provides details that would be of interest to Puerto Ricans currently residing in New York, such as the name of the first Catholic church to offer religious services in Spanish and the year the first *piraguas* (snow cones) were sold.

To complete the record, *Memorias de Bernardo Vega* also denounces the persistent discrimination Puerto Ricans and other Hispanics encountered when making the mainland their home. Vega's prose demystifyies, often challenging conventional history. Vega directs his strongest attack at a popular and admired first lady, Eleanor Roosevelt. The author reveals that after a trip to Puerto Rico in April 1934, Mrs. Roosevelt, speaking to the Women's Trade Union League, underscored the misery she found on the island and the high number of cases of tuberculosis among Puerto Ricans there and in New York, a comment that resulted in increased discrimination.

Certainly, during the period in question Puerto Ricans living both on the island and in New York had one of the highest tuberculosis mortality rates in the world. It was higher in urban than in rural areas, among blacks than among whites, and among women than among men.[1] Tuberculosis, Lawrence Chenault argues, is a sensitive measure of the health of any given group. It is a disease related to the economic position and standard of living of its victims. Chenault provides the following observation:

> The main factors entering into the explanation of the existence of the disease and the high mortality rate among the group here would be the fact that so many Puerto Ricans are infected before they leave the island and the fact that in New York they continue to live under extremely crowded conditions, so that the disease rapidly spreads among these people whose poor economic status gives them insufficient vitality to resist it.[2]

Another explanation for the high rate of tuberculosis among Puerto Ricans pertained to the changes in climate the immigrants withstood, from the tropics to the harsh New York winters. Regardless of the understanding doctors and the general public had of the disease when Mrs. Roosevelt spoke to the Women's Trade Union League, her comments had an adverse impact on the Puerto Rican community in New York, placing many jobs in jeopardy, particularly restaurants and cafeteria workers and female domestics and baby-sitters.

Although Puerto Ricans have held a variety of jobs in New York, Vega appears to dedicate a significant portion of his memoirs to cigar makers of Puerto Rican and other Hispanic groups. Vega was not only gathering information about a dying craft; he was making a political statement: cigar makers represented an ideological and political position. In *Contrapunteo cubano del tabaco y el azúcar* (1940; *Cuban Counterpoint: Tobacco and Sugar,* 1947) written in the same decade Vega was collecting data for his book, Fernando Ortiz shows that both tobacco and sugar influenced cultural development in Cuba.[3] According to Ortiz, tobacco and sugar are opposites: one is native and the other foreign, one is dark and the other white, one male and the other female. The farming of sugar requires large parcels of land and is administered by a monopoly and a central organization. Unlike sugar, tobacco relies on individualism, local control, and small plantations.

The tasks of growing tobacco and making cigars correspond to distinct political positions. Ortiz tells us that tobacco workers participated in the fight to make Cuba independent from Spain. *Memorias de Bernardo Vega* complements *Contrapunteo cubano del tabaco y el azúcar* insofar as Vega's work provides information about the lives of Puerto Rican cigar makers who migrated to New York and supported nineteenth-century leaders such as José Martí of Cuba and Eugenio María de Hostos and Emeterio Betances of Puerto Rico. New York became a Caribbean-like home that offered a haven for political and economic exiles to organize and carry on their fight for independence. In the twentieth century, cigar makers continued to champion what they felt were just causes. Puerto Ricans joined the French forces during World War I, the Lincoln Brigade during the Spanish Civil War, and the U.S. forces during World War II.

Vega's memoirs document nearly a century of the Puerto Rican experience in New York City. Beginning in 1857 with the arrival of his uncle Antonio, the memoirs recount the history of Vega's family, highlighting his grandfather's escape from Spain to America and Antonio's reasons for traveling to the United States. Vega reconstructs events of the past and offers a personal view of well-known figures of the period who lived in New York, such as Martí, Hostos, Betances, Pachín Marín, Arturo Schomburg, and others.

The chronology continues in 1916, the year Vega arrived in New York and met his fictitious uncle, who, after lengthy conversations with the author, died, which allowed the nephew to narrate his own experiences. This section of the memoirs indicates that as more Puerto Ricans made New York their home, they transformed some areas of the city into Puerto Rican communities. Vega's memoirs end on a mixed note. He is disappointed with the U.S. Congress's unwillingness to grant Puerto Rico independence, but he is encouraged by Henry Wallace's decision to become the presidential candidate of the Progressive Party.

Vega's choosing to describe the history of Puerto Ricans in New York was innovative, but the structure of his memoirs and the concerns expressed therein resemble those of other writers documenting for the first time a particular historical aspect of their lives. In this respect, there is an uncanny relationship between Vega's memoirs and Domingo Faustino Sarmiento's *Recuerdos de provincia,* published in 1850.[4] Like Vega, Sarmiento was obsessed with origins, and he divided his book into two parts. The first part narrates the arrival of Sarmiento's family to the southern section of South America during the colonial period and the family's contribution to the history of that region. The second half begins with Sarmiento's birth in 1811, one year after the proclamation of the Republic of Argentina in 1810, and strives to inscribe the author into a modern history of Argentina; he is a symbolic representation of the new republic. As with Vega and his uncle, Sarmiento and his family are witnesses of and contributors to the unfolding of events.[5]

If we read *Memorias* and *Recuerdos* together, they suggest a remarkable similarity between the two writers. Sarmiento began his formal education in 1816. Vega initiated his own education when he arrived in New York one century later. Both men were owners of weekly newspapers: Sarmiento edited *El Zonda* and Vega the *Gráfico,* and as journalists they used their skills to promote and defend their ideas. Sarmiento wrote to denounce

Facundo Quiroga and Juan Manuel Rosas; Vega criticized the Roosevelts and Puerto Ricans like Santiago Iglesias, for his conservative position within the Socialist Party. The earlier author supported the Unitarian Bernardino Rivadavia, president of the Unión de Provincias de la Plata; the later one the Socialist Vito Marcantonio, a congressman, and Henry Wallace, candidate to the U.S. presidency. More important, both men were influenced by their uncles: José Eufrasio de Quiroga Sarmiento taught the young Sarmiento how to read; and priest José de Oro became the boy's mentor, instructing him to love liberty and his country. Like Sarmiento's uncles, Vega's uncle Antonio uncovers for his nephew the history of the family and, as well, that of Puerto Ricans and cigar makers in New York. Although it is difficult to determine whether Vega read Sarmiento, there is an intertextual relationship between their works, as each author documents a critical moment in history. In addition, one text can be read in terms of the other.

Sarmiento and Vega responded to the times and the societies in which they lived: both writers were concerned about political and economic conditions of the countries they wrote about and looked to education and immigration as possible remedies; both texts are designed to educate; and each writer discusses an inevitable immigration policy that determines the number of individuals traveling from Europe to America, in one case, and from Puerto Rico to the United States, in the other. Finally, through their writing of history Sarmiento and Vega illustrate that they privilege their family origins and will continue to do so.

Vega is conscious of rescuing from the margins of history the lives and traditions of Puerto Ricans in New York. However, his concern for history and origins is meaningful not as an initiation of a process, but as an outcome of one; that is, after the process has had time to unfold and gain importance. Like literary modernity, an origin can only be understood in relation to history and other origins.[6] While I agree with Edward Said that beginnings are important, as my chapter epigraph indicates, I also contend that "endings" and the present are equally meaningful for understanding the text.[7] As an autobiographical text, *Memorias de Bernardo Vega* is more than a chronological reconstruction of the lives of Puerto Ricans in New York; rather, it is a looking back in order to compare the past to the present. Just as the text is divided into two, between Vega and his uncle, the narration reproduces two origins, one initiated by Antonio and the other by Vega. *Memorias de Bernardo Vega* commemorates the past. For Eugene Vance, commemoration is "any gesture, ritualized or not, whose end is to recover, in the name of a collectivity, some being or event either anterior in time or outside of time in order to fecundate, animate, or make meaningful a moment in the present."[8] Although Vance recognizes that the past is significant for the present, it is also true that the anterior time must be read in a way that makes it coincide with the later period. In other words, the present determines how we read or commemorate the past, and in so doing, it rearranges and at times alters the past in order to justify itself.

In *Memorias de Bernardo Vega,* the past is only purposeful in relation to the present, and the present time of writing is reflected in the past, where certain themes are recurrent. In Vega's narration there is no chronological progression from Antonio to his nephew. On the contrary, Antonio serves as a mechanism for the author to restate the present in the past. Vega's narration replicates Antonio's voice, and his desire to document the history of Puerto Ricans in New York is echoed in Vega's writing of his memoirs. The personal discrimination one experiences in New York recalls the same hostile feelings the other endures; the newspaper attacks against the Puerto Rican community in one period are also evident in the other; and the fight for Puerto Rican independence in the nineteenth century refers to the one continued one century later.[9]

If the present is imposed on the past or the past is read in such a way as to coincide with the present, then the origin of Vega's text cannot be found at the beginning of the memoirs; that is, when Vega arrived in New York or at the start of the chronology, when Antonio reached the same city. More accurately, the beginning is at the end of the text, perhaps in 1947, the date of the last chapter, or in 1955, when Vega wrote the prologue. The origin can also be placed in 1965, when Andreu Iglesias edited the manuscript and prepared it for publication, as I will discuss later. An overview of the period in which Vega was completing his memoirs may help in understanding the concerns the author expresses when writing the history of Puerto Ricans in New York.

In the decade of the forties, Puerto Rico experienced a degree of modern economic development. Governor Rexford Guy Tugwell, the last North American governor (1940–44), encouraged the industrialization of the island, and Operation Bootstrap was soon put into effect. The Administration for Economic Development saw in Puerto Rico an "adequate industrial climate" and recommended tax incentives for U.S. corporations to build plants on the island. The Administration for Economic Development restated the advantages to U.S. businessmen in their pamphlet *Advantages of Plant Location in Puerto Rico* (1967): "The availability of labor, the lower production costs, the tremendous savings in an atmosphere of excellent conditions and services—all within the control of the Federal Government of the United States—make Puerto Rico a unique opportunity for industrial investment."[10]

Operation Bootstrap aimed to make Puerto Rico a showcase of the Caribbean, a model for other developing countries. However, it had the opposite effect; it changed the Puerto Rican economy, displacing farmers from the countryside to better-paying jobs in San Juan. But unemployment was high in the city, and many Puerto Ricans were forced to travel further north looking for work. The literature of Puerto Rican migration is abundant and of particular concern to the writers of the Generación del Cuarenta; René Marqués's *La carreta* (1951–52; *The Oxcart*, 1969) is a notable contribution.[11]

Puerto Rican migration was compounded when the Partido Popular Democrático of Luis Muñoz Marín passed the Land Law of 1944. The law essentially divided large estates and redistributed land to farmers. Even though the distribution of land was not carried out in its entirety, those peasants who did obtain land soon found it difficult to compete with imports from the United States. The result was the progressive deterioration of agriculture in Puerto Rico and the mass exodus of its peasant population.[12]

The year Vega completed the last entry of his memoirs was the same year U.S. immigration policy changed, making it easier for Puerto Ricans to travel to the mainland. Law 89 (of May 9) eliminated travel restrictions imposed by Law 19, of 1919, and later amended by Law 54, of 1936.[13] The change in law allowed for what was then termed "one of the greatest exoduses of population recorded by history."[14]

After World War II, there was an unprecedented movement of Puerto Ricans to the United States. Demographer José Luis Vázquez Calzada has pointed out that between 1898 and 1944, approximately 90,000 Puerto Ricans migrated to the United States. However, in the decade of the forties, more than 150,000 Puerto Ricans left the island and the number continued to increase in subsequent decades. In the decade of the fifties more than 400,000 Puerto Ricans left the island. Calzada adds that if we take into account the total number of emigrants and the children they would have had on the island, between 1940 and 1960 Puerto Rico lost more than 1 million people.[15] Vega provides his own statistics about the rapid immigration that occurred when he was writing his memoirs:

> The census reflects clearly this huge increase in Puerto Rican emigration to the United States. The figures show 1,904 persons arriving from Puerto Rico in 1940, 988 in the following year, and 1,837 in 1942. From that point on, the number skyrocketed: 2,599 in 1943; 7,548 in 1944; 14,704 in 1945; 21,531 in 1946; and by April 1947, in those first four months alone, 26,000 Puerto Ricans landed in New York. . . . Added to that, 60,000 Puerto Rican children were born in New York in the seven years between 1940 and 1947. (227)

If Sarmiento looked to European immigration as a way of "civilizing" Buenos Aires and Argentina, Vega saw a clear distinction between the

Puerto Ricans who migrated to New York in the late nineteenth and early twentieth centuries and those who left the island in the decade of the forties and in particular after World War II.[16] The first were skilled cigar makers, who commanded decent wages and, according to Vega, belonged to the most illustrious sector of the working class. For Vega, the cigar factories were like university centers. They employed morning and afternoon readers and it was not uncommon for cigar makers to be familiar with the works not only of more literary authors like Victor Hugo, Gustave Flaubert, Benito Pérez Galdós, Maxim Gorky, and Leo Tolstoy, but also the more politically minded Charles Darwin, Friedrich Engels, Karl Marx, and Mikhail Bakunin. At times the topics of discussion pertained to socialism and anarchism and, during the World War II period, they concerned imperialism and pacifism. Those readings and discussions were not unique to the tobacco factories in New York. They had started in Cuba in 1864, and with the emigration of tobacco workers, they were introduced in Spanish-speaking tobacco factories in the United States around 1869.

Vega compares the present with the past. Unlike the immigrants who arrived during the periods in which Antonio and Vega traveled to the United States, many of the Puerto Ricans who migrated in the decade of the forties were unskilled workers. There were agricultural workers who began to migrate after the U.S. occupation of Puerto Rico in the late nineteenth and early twentieth century. But these Puerto Ricans were recruited to cut sugarcane in Hawaii, as well as in Cuba, Panama, the Dominican Republic, and Mexico.[17] Those who migrated to New York during the same period were, according to Vega, skilled tobacco workers. However, with the introduction of machines in the decade of the twenties, the tobacco industry underwent a change, forcing many factories in New York to reduce their demands for workers. Surprisingly enough, Vega himself promoted the machines. As an arbiter of the newly founded Amalgamated Tobacco Workers Industry, composed of Jews, Italians, and Hispanics, he mediated between workers and owners, and at times was unsuccessful in convincing fellow workers of the implications associated with the tranformation of the industry. After what appeared to be senseless battles, Vega resigned his job and joined the army of the unemployed.

The decline in jobs for tobacco workers signaled a period in which many Puerto Ricans worked illegally in *chinchales* (small tobacco vendor's stalls), and even more Puerto Rican immigrants arrived in New York. Some of them filled unskilled positions and worked in barbershops and restaurants. Unlike cigar makers, they lacked political awareness and convictions; they were more concerned with their social lives. By the time Vega drafted his memoirs, there were numerous splits in the Puerto Rican community: some joined the traditional Democratic and Republican parties, others, like Vega, joined the Fusionist Party, and still others belonged to organizations that argued back and forth the status of the island; that is, whether Puerto Rico should be independent, a state, or a commonweath state. Vega differed with the newly arrived Puerto Ricans, who preferred to socialize and party over becoming involved in the politics of the times. On more than one occasion he objected to the culture of the new immigrants, who celebrated an increasing number of dances and social club activities that often irritated neighbors of other nationalities:

> Those boisterous Puerto Rican parties would often disturb neighbors of other nationalities, which led to some serious conflicts and unpleasant quarrels.
> And there were some less innocent events as well. In the more spacious apartments in Harlem some people threw parties on Saturdays and Sundays that weren't just family parties, but full-scale dances with cover charge and all. And once you were in they'd take you for whatever else you had, for drinks and tidbits. Which is not the least of the shameful things that went on.
> There was none of that in the homes of the *tabaqueros.* [18]

From this perspective, Vega's memoirs are a means of comparing the large wave of recently arrived Puerto Ricans, many of whom were uneducated, with those employed as skilled cigar makers. The recent immigrants were changing the face of New York and the impression tobacco workers had established in their neighborhoods. In addition to documenting the change in the immigrants' social makeup, the memoirs are a nostalgic narration in which Vega recovers and, in his writings relives, the past of tobacco workers and their commitment to political change.

Vega's initial project, documenting the history of cigar makers and inserting himself within the same historical discourse, is undermined by the fact that the author of the memoirs only worked as a cigar maker for a short period. Although Vega tells us that he was a cigar maker back in his native Cayey, in New York, Vega held odd jobs and worked as a cigar maker for a only a brief time in the factory El Morito. Vega does not reveal the length of time he worked at El Morito, though we can deduce that it was for no more than two years; by 1918, Vega was married and had a child, could not make ends meet, and was forced to leave El Morito and take a job as a life insurance agent. Although Vega held a variety of jobs, he continued to identify with tobacco workers.

Vega worked as a newspaper editor and journalist for as long as he did making cigars. As a member of the Amalgamated Tobacco Workers Industry, Vega was one of four editors of the organization's newspaper,

The Tobacco Worker, published in Spanish and English. Moreover, he became the owner of the weekly *Gráfico,* which he published between 1927 and 1929.

If Vega was a cigar maker but also a newspaper man, why did he choose to dedicate more space to tobacco than to journalism? Certainly, he was qualified to write a history of the origins of the newspaper industry among Hispanics and Puerto Ricans in New York. Vega was well aware that by 1869 Hostos had become a collaborator of *La Revolución,* a publication of the Puerto Rican Republican Committee in New York, edited by Enrique Piñeiro, and that on June 20, 1874, the Puerto Rican patriot edited and administered the short-lived *La Voz de Puerto Rico,* the first Puerto Rican newspaper published in New York.[19] Vega could have transformed his uncle Antonio into a journalist and highlighted a continuity between his uncle and himself or made a comparison between journalism during the time in which Vega was writing his memoirs and the past. However, Vega downplayed this aspect of his life, preferring to underscore his involvement with tobacco workers. Because he wanted to emphasize the activism associated with these workers, writing about journalism would have been contrary to his overall project. Generally speaking, journalists are perceived to be intellectuals who, for the most part, prefer to observe and contemplate events rather than act and risk their lives. This perception is widely accepted, even though Hostos and Martí, for example, were journalists and men of action. Vega's memoirs would not have had the same interest or impact had he decided to write about the history of journalism.

In spite of his effort to portray himself as a tobacco worker, Vega was a newspaper man. His memoirs could not have been written by a tobacco worker who by nature, according to Vega, would have chosen action over words. Not just a recollection of the past, they are carefully researched and include a conglomeration of other texts. The work is a collection of interviews; letters; articles; fragments of a personal diary; conversations; selections from *The Communist Manifesto,* Hostos's *Diary,* and Flor Baerga's *Memorias;* statistical information; and oral history, stories that had been told to him.

There is certainly a close relationship between Vega's book and the weekly *Gráfico.* A study of that publication will help us to understand better the period Vega refers to in the text. Vega bought the Spanish weekly *Gráfico,* the "Semanario defensor de la Raza Hispana," soon after it was released. Located originally at 108 West 115th Street in New York, *Gráfico* began publication on Sunday, February 27, 1927, under Editor Ramón La Villa and Managing Editor Alberto O'Farrill. *Gráfico*'s mission was to publicize injustices committed against Hispanics, regardless of national origin. The magazine covered local and international news, sports, arts, and literature and had social and gossip columns. Under

Vega's leadership, *Gráfico* continued the social and educational projects started by La Villa.

In comparing *Memorias* and *Gráfico,* I noticed discrepancies regarding dates and ownership of the weekly. Although Vega states that he bought *Gráfico* from Ramón La Villa on March 20, 1927, Vega does not appear as editor of the weekly until July 24, 1927. From its inception until July 17, 1927, the magazine continued under La Villa, when it changed publishers, not to Vega but to Adolfo Rodríguez, the proprietor and editor. Other members of the staff at that point, when the address changed to 62 East 112th Street, included Ramón La Villa, managing editor, and Alberto O'Farrill, assistant to the publisher. Under Rodríguez's direction, the weekly underwent two important changes. The format changed from a magazine to that of a newspaper, and the price was reduced from five to two cents.

The July 24 issue is the first one that lists Vega as president and editor and Ramón La Villa as secretary and manager, and it was published at 27 West 111th Street. Under Vega, the design changed again; that is, from a newspaper back to a magazine, with another important difference: the editorials were written in both Spanish and English, an affirmation of the magazine's commitment to being the voice of the people. The use of both languages was intended to appeal to a wider audience and recalls the linguistic format of the *Tobacco Worker,* which Vega had coedited seven years before. In addition, Vega raised the price of the weekly back to five cents.

Gráfico evolved according to the owners' philosophy. One clear indication of change is contained in the weekly's subtitle. Under La Villa, the weekly was known as the "Semanario Defensor de la Raza Hispana" (weekly defender of the Hispanic race); under Rodríguez the "Semanario Defensa de la Colonia Hispano Americana"; and under Vega the "Semanario Defensor de la Raza." Vega dropped the "Hispano" from the original title, thus alluding to a wider concern that perhaps went beyond Hispanics and included race.[20] He may have been influenced by José Vasconcelos's *La raza cósmica* (the cosmic race), published in 1925, or by the emphasis on race in the United States.

The changes were evident in the magazine's subtitles and on the first page, where the picture of a well-known person was often reproduced. Under Vega's initial direction, the pictures included those of distinguished figures, such as Professor J. M. La Calle (August 7), Dr. Marcelo Gutiérrez (August 14), and Dr. C. M. de Castro (September 4). However, the issue of September 18, in which Pilar Arcos is present on the cover, is subtitled "Semanario Defensor de la Raza," whereas the following one, of September 25, in which Lois Morán appears, is subtitled "Semanario Satírico, Cómico, Literario." *Gráfico* continued its mission to inform the Hispanic community, but the subtitle clearly suggests a new direction, one that included more entertainment. Although it is difficult to ascertain the reason for the change, it may be related to a reorganization of Vega's staff. The September 11 issue indicates that Ramón La Villa was replaced by René Borgia, the new assistant to the editor. The presence of Borgia coincides with the appearance of female artists on the cover. Likewise, it is during that second period that we observe an increase in the number of North American and European women on the front page, many of them actresses of Universal Studios and other theater and film companies.

The change in subtitles from La Villa's "Semanario Defensor de la Raza Hispana," to Rodríguez's "Semanario Defensor de la Colonia Hispano Americana," to Vega's "Semanario Defensor de la Raza" (July 24), to "Semanario Satírico, Cómico, Literario" (September 25), to no subtitle (May 6, 1928), and finally to "Semanario Ilustrado" (November 11) moves the weekly away from an exclusively Hispanic and political publication to one of more general appeal. In this last period the magazine was published by Gráfico Publishing Company, at 83 Pearl Street, no longer with Borgia but with José Matiengo as business manager, and the format changed to that of a newspaper. If there is a relationship between the memoirs and the weekly, then the text should also reflect a wide appeal, even though Vega wrote his memoirs some twenty years after he sold his magazine.

From a broader perspective, Vega's memoirs in *Memorias de Bernardo Vega* suggest that members of the Puerto Rican and other Hispanic communities in New York did not live in isolation but participated in and contributed to the politics of the times. Non-Hispanics, in turn, contributed to the Puerto Rican cause. To this end, Vega dedicated at least one chapter to the efforts of Vito Marcantonio, the congressman from District 20, and narrates important aspects of his biography. Marcantonio, whose career spans from 1934 to beyond the time of the writing—the memoirs state that he was last elected in 1946—was, according to Vega, the "Champion of the Poor." Marcantonio becomes a dominant figure toward the end of Vega's memoirs. Vega provides a firsthand account of Marcantonio's commitment to all poor people but above all to Puerto Ricans. On more than one occasion, Marcantonio made Puerto Rican independence his own cause.

Marcantonio was a progressive congressman from the East Harlem Congressional District, then a heavily Italian American community that repeatedly sent him to Congress, from 1934 to 1950, with the exception of one term. Marcantonio championed the poor regardless of ethnic origin, often taking unpopular positions, including the cause of Puerto Rican independence. Salvatore J. LaGumina defines Marcantonio's constituency in the following manner:

> A most remarkable thing is that his constituents, Italians, Puerto Ricans, and Negroes, voted for him even though the vast majority of them did not subscribe to his political ideology. Perhaps they

saw him as a people's politician, as the spokesman for the down-trodden, attempting to secure for them the promises of American democracy, and were thus inclined to overlook or ignore his controversial position and negative aspects of ethnicity and of the imperfections and, hopefully, of the ameliorative capacity and mobility of American society.[21]

Marcantonio's close relationship with the Puerto Rican community is best described in Gerald Meyer's *Vito Marcantonio: Radical Politician, 1902-1954* (1989), which devotes an entire chapter to "Marcantonio and El Barrio."[22] Meyer, who relies on Vega's memoirs and Jesús Colón's sketches as sources for his book, recognizes the shifting demographic conditions in Italian East Harlem, which began to change as Puerto Ricans moved into the area. As the years went by, Marcantonio depended on his growing Puerto Rican constituency for reelection and also made their concerns his own. Marcantonio was the most important advocate Puerto Ricans had in Congress. He was even more instrumental and effective on legislative matters than Puerto Rico's own resident commissioner. For example, on May 6, 1936, Marcantonio introduced the first of four bills that granted independence for Puerto Rico and demanded that the U.S. government assume responsibility in rehabilitating the island's disastrous economy. He is credited for passing legislation that included Puerto Ricans in the 1939 extension of the Social Security Act and the 1942 bill that granted U.S. citizenship to all Puerto Ricans born on the island. Moreover, he argued in the House on eight separate occasions, between 1939 and 1940, for a minimum hourly wage of twenty-five cents for Puerto Rican workers on the island, accusing the government of protecting mainland companies who underpaid them; and in a 1946 speech to Congress, he defended the reinstatement of Spanish as Puerto Rico's language of instruction.

Marcantonio had many enemies, and they became stronger as the American Labor Movement and the Socialist and Communist parties, which supported him, began to decline in influence. Magazines and newspapers such as the *American Magazine* and the *Daily Mirror* attacked Marcantonio for creating slums, for breeding communism, and for bringing Puerto Ricans to New York to ensure his reelection.[23] Marcantonio's enemies also included Puerto Ricans. During his 1949 mayoral campaign, then Governor Muñoz Marín asked Puerto Ricans to distance themselves from a candidate who supported a leftist ideology; and Felisa Rincón de Gautier, the first woman mayor of San Juan, traveled to New York to campaign against Marcantonio.

Marcantonio defended Pedro Albizu Campos, the leader of the Puerto Rican Nationalist Party, convicted of conspiring to overthrow the U.S. government. He did so in spite of pressure from the Department of State's

Division of Territories and Island Possessions, exchanging strong words with its head, Ernest Grueining. Marcantonio also attacked Blanton Winship, appointed governor of Puerto Rico, and was instrumental in having President Roosevelt dismiss him. Equally important, Marcantonio fought for Puerto Ricans in New York. For example, in 1939 he defended Puerto Rican children who were discriminated against on the basis of an I.Q. test, which placed them in an inferior position regarding other children. The test did not take into account the linguistic, social, economic, and environmental factors affecting the performance of the children.[24]

Even after he left office Marcantonio continued to fight for his beliefs. He expounded his philosophy in a column he wrote for the New York *Daily Compass*. As a lawyer he used his skills to defend W. E. B. DuBois and many Hollywood stars fighting the House Committee on Un-American Activities, and he led the battle to obtain clemency for Oscar Collazo, a Puerto Rican national who attempted to assassinate President Truman.[25]

Vega narrates Marcantonio's political biography with great thoroughness, but he does so at the expense of those of distinguished Puerto Ricans who were making their mark during the same period, such as Oscar García Rivera, who in November 1937, with the help of the American Labor Party, became the first Puerto Rican to win a major office in the United States, and Clemente Soto Vélez, one of Marcantonio's key lieutenants, who with Albizu Campos was accused of violence against the U.S. government.[26] The most significant exclusion pertains to information about Don Pedro Albizu Campos, who became a visible figure in the United States. Campos had studied in the Northeast and obtained degrees from the University of Vermont and Harvard, and he later became a symbol of Puerto Rican independence. However, Vega mentions Campos briefly and only in reference to other figures and events. Although he spent most of his life in Puerto Rico, Albizu Campos's activities were followed closely by his countrymen both on and outside of the island. Campos dedicated his life to liberating the colony of Puerto Rico from the United States. In April 1939 he and other Puerto Rican nationals were arrested and sentenced to sixteen years in an Atlanta prison for conspiring against the U.S. government, recruiting soldiers for an armed struggle, and attempting to overthrow the government on the island. Campos received support from many organizations, such as the Partido Nacionalista de Puerto Rico, La Liga Norteamericana Contra la Guerra y el Fascismo, La Orden Internacional de Trabajadores, La Defensa Internacional del Trabajador, the Communist Party, the Communist Youth League, and the organizations of Lower Harlem. As we have mentioned, Vito Marcantonio was Campos's legal counsel. And when Campos suffered a heart attack, the Puerto Rican patriot was transferred from the Atlanta prison to Columbus Hospital in New York, where, after his release from medical supervision, he completed a reduced sentence in New York in 1947.[27]

If Vega wanted to narrate life among Puerto Ricans in New York, he made a serious omission by not dedicating more space to the popular figure of Albizu Campos and the support he received among Puerto Ricans and other Hispanics in New York. Neither did he document two later, unprecedented events that sent shock waves throughout the Puerto Rican and Hispanic communities in the United States. The first one refers to Oscar Collazo and Griselio Torresola, who together on November 1, 1950, attempted to kill President Truman while he was residing temporarily at Blair House. In the failed attack, Torresola died and Collazo was fatally wounded. As with the reaction to Campos's imprisonment, Puerto Ricans and Hispanic organizations in New York united in Collazo's defense. The journalist Luisa Quintero organized the Comité Pro–Oscar Collazo. It and other organizations from Latin America lobbied effectively, and President Truman commuted Collazo's death penalty to life in prison. Certainly Vega knew about the event and the efforts of the Comité Pro–Oscar Collazo. Luisa Quintero appears twice in the memoirs and is cited extensively. She is first mentioned for writing in the *Diario* against the opposition to the Tyding Bill, whose passage would have made Puerto Rico independent; then for attacking the *New York Times*, which blamed Puerto Ricans for their economic problems, after receiving forty-six years of help from the United States. Furthermore, Oscar Collazo was a registered member of the American Labor Party, and his political adversary James G. Donavan used the volatile incident to tie Marcantonio to the assassination and communism and defeat him in the congressional elections.[28]

The second incident relates to the strong support the Puerto Rican community in New York gave Puerto Rican nationals Lolita Lebrón, Andrés Figueroa Cordero, Rafael Cancel Miranda, and Irving Flores, who on March 1, 1954 staged an armed attack on the House of Representatives and wounded five congressmen. All of the assailants lived in New York. This action led to another government raid against Albizu Campos in Puerto Rico that resulted in his arrest. As in the case of Collazo, there was international support for the Puerto Rican nationalists, including from Mexican writers like José Vasconcelos, who embraced Puerto Rican nationals demanding the independence of Puerto Rico and who considered Campos "the last of the Liberators of America."

As the previous discussion illustrates, in spite of his attempt to write the history of Puerto Ricans in New York, Vega did not provide elaborate descriptions of Albizu Campos nor did he interrupt his silence and pick up his pen to narrate the strong support given by the New York Puerto Rican community to Puerto Rican nationals. We should keep in mind that Vega does not conclude the memoirs in 1947, the date of the last entry, but in

1955, when he completes the introduction, and so he could have mentioned those salient events. Perhaps Vega wanted to highlight a different viewpoint of the independence movement, not the nationalist but the socialist, which was closer to the political position held by tobacco workers and continued by Marcantonio. However, it is conceivable that Marcantonio defended with enthusiasm the nationalist cause because most of the Puerto Ricans in New York, unlike their counterparts on the island, favored Puerto Rican independence. On the mainland Puerto Ricans felt a more intense and immediate discrimination, which they channeled into their opposition to the U.S. government and endorsement for Puerto Rican independence. Unlike the Puerto Rican nationalist movement, the socialist one had broader appeal and included North American backers. Certainly, the socialist discourse is an important element of the memoirs, increasing in intensity toward the end of the book.[29]

Even though both Vega and Campos supported Puerto Rican independence, they differed in how to obtain it. Despite his awareness that Campos made important contributions to Hispanic communities in the United States, Vega purposefully omitted any homage to Campos because of their different ideologies. The Nationalist Party was founded in September 1922, under the leadership of José Coll y Cuchi and others, but in 1930, under Albizu Campos, it became more combative and revolutionary, embracing armed insurrection. Vega, as a Puerto Rican living in New York, favored Puerto Rican independence, but unlike Campos, he was committed to working from within. Vega was tired of and frustrated by the lack of unity among the various Puerto Rican organizations and even underwent a period of apathy and dissillusionment.

Vega continued to support Puerto Rican independence, but because of the continual division among Puerto Ricans, he did not join any one of them and instead endorsed them all. Vega was one of the few Puerto Ricans who attended Santiago Iglesias's funeral; he also participated in the celebration of the election of 1944, which brought the Partido Popular Democrático, under Muñoz Marín, to power. Writing in his diary entry dated November 4, 1954, Vega notes that the division of the Confederación General de Trabajadores is imminent: "No reconciliation is possible! I'm afraid that from here on in, the labor movement in Puerto Rico is going to turn into a can of worms" (224).

Toward the end of writing the memoirs, Vega found meaning in fighting fascism in Europe and discrimination against Puerto Ricans in New York, as promulgated by the *World-Telegram*. To this end, he joined the governing board of the newly formed Convención Pro Puerto Rico, and became a member of the editorial board of *Liberación*. However, on a return trip to Puerto Rico, Vega was accused of being a member of the Communist Party and those on the island objected to his representing them at the Convention. Disillusioned, Vega resigned. This final aspect of the memoirs inadvertently underscores not Vega the tobacco worker, but Vega the writer of the memoirs; that is, Vega the intellectual and journalist.

In his introduction to *Memorias de Bernardo Vega,* César Andreu Iglesias provides a few details about Vega's life after he completed the manuscript. Vega became the national director of the Hispanic division of the committee to elect Henry Wallace and, after an unsuccessful campaign, Vega moved back to his native Puerto Rico. Back on the island Vega continued to be active in politics and joined the Partido Independentista Puertorriqueño (PIP), founded in October 1946, which favored a Puerto Rican socialist republic. Later, he became a member of the Movimiento Pro Independencia (MPI), founded in 1959, which favored a nonpartisan and antielectorate program. The MPI had broken ranks with the PIP and, under the leadership of Juan Mari Bras, became the Partido Socialista Puertorriqueño. The MPI favored independence for Puerto Rico and promoted a program of social justice. In 1961, toward the end of his life, Vega became secretary of the Organización de la Misión Nacional. While in Puerto Rico, he must have been aware of the imprisonment of Albizu Campos and the delicate state of Campos's health. Both Vega and Campos died a few months apart: Campos in April 1965 and Vega in June of the same year.

A close reading of the memoirs indicates that in spite of Vega's exhaustive research and conscious or unconscious omissions, he may have made some mistakes. For example, Vega states that the Guerra Chiquita in Cuba ended in 1875, but more correctly it took place from 1878 to 1880. If this and other historical inaccuracies are oversights by Vega, then how do we come to terms with more serious errors about the author's own life, information of personal interest to him? Vega tells us that he acquired *Gráfico* on March 20, 1927 instead of on July 24, as mentioned earlier. But more critical is the year Vega was born. Vega writes that he arrived in New York in 1916 at the age of thirty, thus insinuating that he was born not in 1885, as we have deduced from Andreu Iglesias's introduction and from Vega's own diary, but in 1886. Was the change in birth date a conscious effort on the part of Vega to have his birth share the same date as a historic moment; that is, to the emancipation of slaves in Cuba, a change that would have coincided with his and his uncle's convictions? Was it Vega's intention in part to create a fictional narration, as Andreu Iglesias tells us, or does it point more appropriately to the intervention of the editor himself?

We know that Andreu Iglesias edited and published Vega's memoirs. If not for him, Vega's text would have been lost to history. A reading of other autobiographies and testimonial works about the lives of marginal members of society, such as Juan Francisco Manzano's *Autobiografía* (1937;

"Life of the Negro Poet," 1840), Miguel Barnet's edition of Esteban Montejo's *Biografía de un cimarrón* (1966; *Autobiography of a Runaway Slave*, 1968), and Elizabeth Burgos's edition of *Me llamo Rigoberta Menchú y así me nació la conciencia* (1983; *I, Rigoberta Menchú: An Indian Woman in Guatemala*, 1984), shows that in each instance the editor intervenes in order to document an aspect of history previously unavailable. But, in so doing, the editors change and reshape the document to conform to their own personal and sociopolitical convictions.

The slave Manzano complied with Domingo del Monte's request that he write his autobiography to denounce the slavery system. The Cuban critic gave Anselmo Suárez y Romero the slave's manuscript, which contained numerous grammatical mistakes. Suárez y Romero not only corrected and made the autobiography presentable to members of the del Monte literary circle, but he altered the events to make it a stronger denunciation against slavery than what the slave had intended. A copy of Suárez y Romero's version of the autobiography was given to the British abolitionist Richard Madden to include in an antislavery portfolio to be presented before the Antislavery Society in London. Madden published the autobiography, some of Manzano's poems, two of his own, and interviews with del Monte under the title *Poems by a Slave in the Island of Cuba* in London, 1840.[30]

In their interviews with Esteban Montejo and Rigoberta Menchú, both Barnet and Burgos guide and even control their informant's discourse by posing questions that organize the interviewees' thoughts. Additionally, they edit the informants' responses to conform to their own anthropological and political preoccupations. For Barnet, Montejo represented an opportunity to learn about the runaway slave communities in the mountains of Cuba, and so he may have focused his questioning in that area. Moreover, while transcribing the interviews, Barnet underscored Montejo's independent and revolutionary position so that it would coincide more closely with events in the Cuban Revolution. Barnet also ends *Biografía de un cimarrón* after the U.S. intervention in the island and the establishment of the Republic of Cuba to allude to another historical time, the Cuban Revolution and Castro's success in making Cuba an independent nation.[31]

Similarly, for Burgos Menchú became a means of uncovering the secrets of the Mayan culture. Although Burgos, in her introduction, tells the reader that she did not intervene in Menchú's discourse, the critic structured and later rearranged her interview with the informant to coincide with her own beliefs. Burgos suppressed and altered some information. A comparison between the epigraphs taken from the interview and their reproduction in the text illustrates that Burgos indeed intervened in Menchú's discourse. Furthermore, Burgos divides Menchú's ideas into fixed categories as defined by the chapter headings, whereas the informant's own discourse may have been more fluid. Just as the bosses and masters of Manzano, Montejo, and Menchú attempted to control them, their lives continued to be dominated by their editors.

Memorias de Bernardo Vega has also been altered. Andreu Iglesias read an early version of Vega's manuscript, which ends in 1947; but Vega completed the text in 1955, when he wrote his prologue, "Advertencia a los lectores" (a word to the readers). Vega gave the manuscript to his friend Andreu Iglesias, who recognized its value and recommended that Vega eliminate fictitious elements in the work and change the narration from third to first person, modifications the author rejected. Vega's death in 1965 inspired Andreu Iglesias to edit and publish the manuscript. Ten years later, Andreu Iglesias completed his editorial task. The book was finally published in 1977, twelve years after Vega's death.

Andreu Iglesias altered the manuscript to reflect the advice he had once given Vega. His primary concern was to separate fact from fiction. Therefore, he eliminated Vega's prologue, which identified the fictional characters, and replaced it with his own, and he changed the narrative point of view from third to first person, thus accentuating the autobiographical and testimonial nature of the memoirs. In essence Andreu Iglesias has provided the reader with a version, his version, of Vega's memoirs, one that conforms closely to his editorial changes and his own personal, artistic, and political interests.

Other questions about Iglesias's participation in the manuscript can be raised. For example, did Vega divide the book into twenty-nine chapters or was this done by Andreu Iglesias? And who provided the title headings? And which came first, the chapter headings or the chapter divisions? Were the titles created to fit the chapter divisions, or was the book divided to fit the titles? A brief analysis of the chapter headings will show that when reference is made to the narrator, he is mentioned in the third person. For example, in chapter 1, "De su pueblito de Cayey a San Juan y de cómo Bernardo llegó a Nueva York sin reloj" (From his hometown Cayey to San Juan, and how Bernardo arrived in New York without a watch) indicates that the author does not identify himself as "I" but as the other.[32] A similar comment applies to chapter 5, "Una experiencia amorosa y otros incidentes que dan sustancia a esta verídica historia" (An amorous experience and other incidents that lend substance to his truthful tale), again suggesting that the love encounter is not with the first-person narrator, but with the "you" protagonist. Does this perspective correspond to Vega's desire to write a manuscript in the third person as he had suggested to Andreu Iglesias or to the editor's synopsis of what the chapters contain? However, the title of chapter 6, "Ascendencia de los Vega en América, con algo de mitología y mucho de historia" (The Vega ancestry in America, a wealth of history with a touch of myth), more clearly indicates not the author's handwriting, but the editor's own signature. Had Vega provided the title, he would not have told the reader that what he had written was both fictitious and historical, information that would have appeared in "Advertencia a los lectores," which Iglesias suppressed. Let us remember that Vega wanted to write a fictional narration about Puerto Ricans in the United States, and it was Iglesias who instructed the author to change it to a first-person narration and eliminate the "mythological" elements. The separation of history and fiction, as the chapter title indicates, points more to Iglesias's own intervention in the text than to the author's commentary about his own work. With the chapter title, Iglesias discloses to the reader that he left the text as the author intended, but warns the reader of the mixture of fact and fiction. Moreover, the title of chapter 6 implies that Iglesias did not intervene there as directly as he may have done in other chapters, thus possibly allowing Vega's text to stand closer to the way the author wrote it.

I have tried to show that the chapter headings refer to Andreu Iglesias's reading of the chapters more than to Vega's own comments. The same observation can be made of the last chapter, entitled "Un capítulo inconcluso y su lección no escrita: siempre es más interesante vivir que escribir" (An unfinished chapter with an unwritten moral: it is always more interesting to live than to write). More likely than not, the inconclusive title was provided by the editor, who felt that the last page warranted some kind of categorization. I suspect that had Vega conceived it as inconclusive, in the ten years that elapsed between writing the manuscript and the introduction, he would have finished it. Let us note that the chronology, which Vega painstakingly constructs, is disrupted in the unfinished chapter. Chapter 29 refers to the events of August 5, 1947, in which Congress granted Puerto Ricans the right to choose their own governor, and of November 12, in which Rafael Pérez Marchand and Antonio Ayuso Valdivieso traveled to New York to protest Puerto Rico's colonial status before the United Nations. However, the previous chapter had already referred to events that unfolded on November 1, the date Vega and other Puerto Ricans living in New York demonstrated before the headquarters of the *World-Telegram,* a protest attended by Congressman Vito Marcantonio and by City Councilman and African American leader of the United States Communist Party Ben Davis. Interestingly enough, the chapter does not end there but after Vega traveled to Puerto Rico as delegate of the Convención Pro Puerto Rico. The question remains, did the trip take place before or after Pérez Marchand and Ayuso Valdivieso's visit to New York?

Andreu Iglesias changed parts of the memoirs and, in effect, offered the reader a partial reading of the manuscript and of Vega's own life. Andreu Iglesias conditions the public to read the manuscript from his point of view, his recollection of Vega as the tobacco worker. After the author's death, Andreu Iglesias wrote and published Vega's obituary in the newspaper *El Imparcial.* By entitling Vega's obituary "El último tabaquero" and reproducing it in its entirety in his prologue, Andreu Iglesias is underscoring above all Vega's work as a cigar maker. However, the obituary was not motivated by a reading of the manuscript, but by extraliterary concerns. Andreu Iglesias stresses tobacco in the obituary because "on the afternoon when he died in his home in the Santiago Iglesias housing development in San Juan, Bernardo Vega was rolling his last cigar" (xvii).

In the same obituary, Andreu Iglesias, one of the founding members of the Congreso Pro Independencia (1943)—and who himself sought Puerto Rican sovereignty and friendship with the people of the United States— underscores Vega's relationship with the socialist Santiago Iglesias, even though, unlike Santiago Iglesias, Vega fought against colonialism and for independence. Andreu Iglesias may have emphasized the relationship between Santiago Iglesias and Vega because the young Vega was initiated under his leadership or because Vega lived in the neighborhood that honored the socialist leader. In any case, Vega was critical of Santiago Iglesias.

Iglesias's decision to publish the manuscript ten years after Vega's death responds to concerns of the time in which he completed his editorial work and prologue. Like Vega, Andreu Iglesias may have been concerned with Puerto Rican immigration, during and after Johnson's Great Society, when an alarming number of Puerto Ricans continued to leave the island and seek employment in the United States. From the time Vega completed his introduction to the time Andreu Iglesias wrote his, the Puerto Rican population in the United States grew from 301,375, in 1950, to 1,548,000, in 1974, most residing in New York.[33] Unlike when Vega migrated to the United States, only a reduced number of Puerto Ricans over sixteen years of age were employed as artisans. In 1970, about 41,210 men and 2,990 women worked in that capacity. In the same year, the majority of Puerto Ricans found jobs as factory and service workers: 133,778 men and 63,904 women. In addition, there were a high number of office workers: 27,703 men and 36,349 women.[34] Two years after the employment statistics were made available, the unemployment records of Puerto Ricans, in relation to the general population of the United States, were released and proved equally revealing: in 1972, of the employable population between the ages of sixteen and sixty-four, the official figure shows that 6.2 percent of the general population was unemployed in comparison to 12.6 percent of the Puerto Rican community; the adjusted figure is even higher, 33.0 percent, which takes into account the work force for the entire nation.[35]

The large number of Puerto Ricans living in New York, and the increasing number of Puerto Ricans returning from the United States, particularly from New York, to Puerto Rico, may have encouraged Andreu Iglesias to publish Vega's document. In 1972 and 1973 there was a negative migration to the United States, –34,015 and –20,948, respectively.[36]

Between 1970 and 1974, the negative migration and the number of Puerto Ricans returning to their country of origin indeed brought more awareness to island Puerto Ricans about the conditions of their counterparts living in the United States. The reverse migration accentuated the cultural and linguistic differences between Puerto Ricans on the island and those living on the continent, thus making the Puerto Rican migration a problem for all Puerto Ricans.[37]

A reading of the prologue and the manuscript shows that Andreu Iglesias was a biased rather than an objective reader of the memoirs. His editorial work coincides more closely with his own recollection of Vega; thus in editing the manuscript he presents the reader not with the text Vega wrote, but the text he wanted Vega to write and, consequently, the person he wanted Vega to be. In other words, Andreu Iglesias does not provide us with the historical Vega, but with a re-creation of him. From another perspective, however, Andreu Iglesias's intervention is a positive response to Vega's own desire to introduce fictitious elements into the narration. The changes the editor made in Vega's life also produce a textual and personal reality, and reflect the controls, changes, and compromises Vega and other Puerto Ricans must undergo when adjusting to the culture of New York. The book, which combines Vega's and Iglesia's efforts, embodies the same mediations and negotiations its narration attempts to portray.

Memorias de Bernardo Vega captures the spirit of the migration of Caribbean people who traveled frequently among the islands and also of those who migrated from the Caribbean to Caribbean-influenced cities in the United States, in both cases sharing each others' cultures. During the time Vega wrote his memoirs, the migration signaled the coming together of the cultures and history of Puerto Ricans and North Americans. That the memoirs end when Vega joins the Wallace campaign reinforces this convergence.

As a text, *Memorias de Bernardo Vega* has allowed me to understand that just as the presence of Puerto Ricans and other Hispanics in the United States can be traced to the nineteenth century, so too can the origins of Puerto Rican and other Hispanic Caribbean literatures. In addition, Vega's memoirs are a part of the literary tradition that unifies two cultures and sets the groundwork for other Latino Carribean literatures created in the United States and written in Spanish, English, and Spanglish. The literature of Puerto Rican writers in the United States form part of the canon of Hispanic and U.S. literatures; it is indeed a product of both.

II

The Latin, Black, Indian and Asian people inside the u.s. are colonies fighting for liberation. We know that washington, wall

street, and city hall will try to make our nationalism into racism;
but Puerto Ricans are of all colors and we resist racism. Millions
of poor white people are rising up to demand freedom and we support them. These are the ones in the u.s. that are stepped on by
the rulers and the government. We each organize our people, but
our fights are the same against oppression and we will defeat it
together. POWER TO ALL OPPRESSED PEOPLE!

—Point 4 of Thirteen-Point Program and Platform, the Young
Lords Party.

In his memoirs, Bernardo Vega uncovers details about the lives of
Puerto Ricans living in New York during the first half of the twentieth century. As a cigar maker, journalist, and leader within the Puerto Rican and
North American communities, Vega worked hard to make the United
States a more hospitable place for Hispanics. But the memoirs describe
only one segment of the Puerto Rican community living in New York,
mainly those who arrived knowing a particular craft, in Vega's case that of
a cigar maker. Vega's narration is incomplete insofar as he does not provide
insight into the lives of unskilled Puerto Rican immigrants, some of whom
were dark-skinned, experienced racism, and identified with African
Americans, thus bringing the Puerto Rican or Hispanic and African
American communities together.[38]

Memorias de Bernardo Vega decouples political and racial issues.
Perhaps Vega believed that developing the theme of race would detract from
political concerns; perhaps as a Marxist or socialist he considered all matters subordinate to those of class struggle; or perhaps Vega, who at the
beginning of his memoirs identifies himself as white, knew little about race
matters and how they relate to the African American community and so
did not feel qualified to elaborate on them. Vega emphasizes his phenotype:

> I was a white, a peasant from the highlands (a *jíbaro*), and there
> was that waxen pallor to my face so typical of country folk. I had a
> round face with high cheekbones, a wide, flat nose, and small blue
> eyes. As for my lips, well I'd say they were rather sensual, and I
> had strong, straight teeth. I had a full head of clear chestnut hair,
> and, in contrast to the roundness of my face, I had square jaws. All
> in all, I suppose I was rather ugly, though there were women
> around who thought otherwise. (3)

After this description, Vega points out that while living in New York he
was mistaken for a "Polish Jew, or a Tartar, or even a Japanese," which
explains why Vega was able to move among the various ethnic groups in
the city. Juan Flores places the emphasis of the mentioned passages on the

"humanity" Vega learned from his parents, which drew him to others.[39] But it is also clear that Vega was not treated as if he were an African American or an Afro–Puerto Rican.

In his prologue to the memoirs, Iglesias tries to separate the Puerto Rican community from the issue of race; for example, he informs the reader that Puerto Ricans, compared to other groups, were not as preoccupied with racial differences. The prologue also stresses that Puerto Ricans were different from other foreigners and that early tobacco workers were unlike the more recent immigrants. As the manuscript points out, cigar makers were active in the politics of Cuba, Puerto Rico, and the United States.

In contrast, the issue of race within North American literature is a constant in works written by African Americans and made evident by contemporary critics such as Henry Louis Gates and Houston Baker, two scholars whose works have received much attention. There is also a large body of fiction and criticism about blacks, slavery, and race in Latin American literature.[40] However, little is known about black Puerto Ricans and other Latinos living in the United States, though the contributions made by Puerto Rican Arturo Schomburg to both Hispanic and African American communities are receiving increasing attention.[41] Jesús Colón's *A Puerto Rican in New York and Other Sketches* (1961) is one of the few works to underscore the racial and cultural discrimination black Puerto Rican immigrants experienced in the early to mid-twentieth century.[42] A close look at his work will help to discern the problematics of race within the context of the Puerto Rican community in the United States.

Colón's dark skin made him more predisposed than Vega to understanding and discussing the racial attitudes in the United States, and race appears as a subtext throughout his sketches. Even so, Colón is ambivalent about the significance of race. It is difficult to determine if the stories in *A Puerto Rican in New York and Other Sketches* embody a development in Colón's thinking. The book seems to have been organized chronologically but also thematically.[43] The sketches that describe race matters are present from the beginning and appear to increase in number toward the end. I would like to look more closely at these sketches in the order in which they appear. In "On the Docks It Was Cold," Mr. Clark, an African American foreman, teaches Colón the trade. Although Colón liked him, and Mr. Clark may have been from the Caribbean, Colón's relationship with him was defined by work and not by race. Similarly, in "Kiplin and I," he talks about when others in the employment office complained about the difficulty "Negroes and Puerto Ricans" have in finding a decent place to live and about being the first to lose their jobs, Colón always remembered Kipling's poem "If." "Kiplin and I" shows how he learned to persist and remain under control, thus separating himself from the actions of those who would be more emotional and easily provoked in his situation.

Another series of sketches do, however, suggest the theme of race. In "Carmencita," about his mother-in-law's trip to the United States, Colón provides her and therefore the reader with an interpretation of events associated with racial hatred. He informs her that "Negroes" did not have the same rights as whites and were not served at the Radio City Cafe. Colón continues:

> Joe and I sat down with Carmencita to explain that there was something greater than nationality and so-called 'race'—and that is the conscious feelings and understanding of belonging to a class that unites us regardless of color and nationality, without belittling the contributions and positive qualities of our particular nationality.[44]

Despite the racism he describes in the Radio City Cafe, Colón rejects race as a factor for understanding discrimination in the United States. Like Vega, Colón was a socialist and he had joined the party in 1923. He reiterates the same interpretation in the last sketch, "A Puerto Rican in New York," and states that Puerto Rican sugar planters have more in common with rich North American investors than they do with the Puerto Rican masses they exploit, a rationale that led him and Vega to support North Americans like Vito Marcantonio.

In his foreword to *A Puerto Rican in New York*, Flores refers to how immigrants like Colón gained heightened social awareness:

> Like Colón and Vega, the majority of those *tabaqueros* and other workers who migrated in the early decades ended up staying in New York, as their nagging hope to return to the Island drifted ever further into the future. The critical convictions many of them had gained in childhood from the social struggles back home were only reinforced by the long lives of hardship and resistance they were to endure in the land of opportunity. In New York they came to understand even more clearly the international dimension of the struggle against that very system of imperialism which held their beloved Puerto Rico in direct colonial bondage, the same system that was ultimately responsible for their own "decision" to leave their homeland behind.[45]

In spite of the explicit assertions of class over race, Colón is concerned about being black and recognizes that others interpret events along racial and national lines. This is evident in "Little Things Are Big," in which he struggles internally between assisting in the middle of the night a white woman, with children and luggage, descend into the subway, and doing nothing, so as not to run the risk of having his actions misinterpreted by her. More important, in the following sketch, "The Mother, the Young Daughter, Myself and All of Us," Colón cannot help but accept that race and not class is an issue. He recounts how, when he was drinking coffee at a counter, and a client's daughter refused to sit next to Colón because he was a "nigger." The subtext of race as a dominant element over class is by no means an isolated case. It is also present in sketches like "Greetings from Washington," which includes a description of a patriotic Puerto Rican veteran of World War I who was outraged that a restaurant owner served whites but not "Negro girls." The sentiment is present as well in a sketch about Puerto Rican teachers who were separated and classified by the color of their skin, whites sleeping in hotels and blacks in dormitories at Howard University. In "Grandma, Please Don't Come!" Colón admits that in the United States people will object to hearing Spanish and threaten or beat the speaker. He writes to his grandmother, "It has been done, you know. People have been killed because they are heard speaking Spanish."[46]

Although Colón adheres to the position of the Socialist Party and accepts the class division between workers and owners, this premise is undermined when he also recognizes the significance of race. But it would be left to another Puerto Rican to interpret events solely from a racial perspective.[47] Piri Thomas's *Down These Mean Streets* (1967) narrates the same period of the Great Depression that *Memorias de Bernardo Vega* and *A Puerto Rican in New York and Other Sketches* depict. However, Thomas reveals a different side of the Puerto Rican experience in the United States than the one portrayed by Vega and Colón: the life of a dark-skinned and unskilled laborer who was not ideologically or politically committed to the groups to which Vega and Colón subscribed.

The migratory process of Piri Thomas's family was the same as Vega and Colón's and as that of other Puerto Ricans leaving the island prior to the events associated with Operation Bootstrap in the late forties and fifties. Vega traveled before Puerto Ricans were granted citizenship in 1917; Colón, who was from the same town, Cayey, left in 1918. The Thomases traveled to New York a decade later, in time for Piri to be born in 1928. Vega and Colón were trained in the craft of cigar making, and Vega arrived in New York with a letter certifying him as a member of the Puerto Rican Local of the Unión Internacional de Tabaqueros A.F.L. Others, like the Thomases, abandoned the island after World War I, hoping to improve their condition and benefit from the prosperity the United States enjoyed before the stock market crashed in 1929. During that period many Puerto Ricans were subjected to racial and national prejudice, especially as the numbers of dark-skinned Puerto Ricans increased. In his studies on Puerto Rican migration, Lawrence R. Chenault points out that in 1930, two years after Thomas was born, about 21 percent of the total 52,774 Puerto Ricans residing in the United States were classified as "colored."[48] He also describes how Puerto Ricans were discriminated against on the basis of the color of their skin:

> There is often discrimination against the Puerto Rican worker on the basis of color. . . . The entire group is sometimes referred to by Americans as "colored." One instance of their troublesome problem for the Puerto Rican came about a few years ago when a large religious organization in New York is said to have classified all of the Puerto Rican applicants in its employment division as "colored." Another agency which supplies domestic help reported that it is not unusual, when a woman calls by telephone to inquire about obtaining a Puerto Rican worker and is asked whether she prefers a white or colored Puerto Rican, for the woman to reply that, since she has asked for a Puerto Rican, of course she wants a colored person.[49]

Gerald Meyer adds that in the postwar period the "colored" population of El Barrio, in East Harlem, was as high as 43 percent, a ratio much higher than that of the island or other Puerto Rican communities on the mainland; the Bronx, for instance, reported 23 percent. Meyer explains that black Puerto Ricans were reluctant to move out of El Barrio for fear of being treated like African Americans and that the educational level of nonwhite Puerto Ricans was lower than that of white Puerto Ricans, who earned more than their dark-skinned countrymen.[50]

Puerto Ricans were not welcomed in the United States. The language barrier and cultural differences forced many who arrived in the 1930s to reside in Manhattan; the lower and eastern sections of Harlem; and Brooklyn, along the waterfront from the navy yard south to Gowanus Canal, two areas where a disproportionate number of the dark-skinned Puerto Ricans lived. Chenault adds that "outside of Manhattan and Brooklyn, the proportion of white Puerto Ricans is much greater than in these boroughs."[51] They had no choice but to live in deplorable conditions, in old buildings in need of repairs, many without any heat; that is, in blocks and neighborhoods other immigrants had abandoned and considered uninhabitable. Chenault summarizes the housing conditions as follows:

> The Puerto Ricans in the Harlem section are provided with poorer housing facilities than many of the other groups in the city. As a whole, these facilities are below the average in Manhattan. . . .
> The character of the housing in the Brooklyn area is less favorable than that of the area in Harlem. Practically all of the buildings are old, and a large proportion of the family quarters do not have

baths and private indoor toilets. Unsatisfactory conditions and standards are also indicated by the low rentals paid by the majority of the families.

On account of their poverty, the Puerto Ricans in the Harlem and Brooklyn areas often occupy the more unfavorable quarters. The conditions under which the colored Puerto Rican family lives, especially in the Brooklyn area, are in many cases wretched. Unsanitary conditions are frequently found among these very poor families both in the Harlem and Brooklyn areas.[52]

Within U.S. society Puerto Ricans were considered the other, as Pliny the Elder has explained in his studies of non-European people.[53]

The strengths and weaknesses of Puerto Rican identity are reflected in the reasons for migrating. Their sense of identity is tied to keeping alive the dream of returning to the island and its culture. It is also influenced by acceptance or rejection by the dominant culture.[54] Unfortunately, not everyone made the journey back as soon as expected; it would be many decades before Puerto Ricans returned to the island in large numbers, and that did not happen until the decade of the seventies.[55] Many had no other choice but to stay. The cold and inhospitable New York environment made Puerto Ricans idealize the island, often forgetting the reasons for abandoning their place of birth. Piri Thomas's mother described the island in biblical terms, a paradise, "Moses' land of milk and honey." Mrs. Thomas, who emigrated to New York before the U.S. involvement in World War II, did not share with Piri her recollections of the island living conditions at the time she deserted her familiar surroundings. Rather, she chose to share a nostalgia associated with her childhood, augmented by the impossibility of recovering the idyllic years of the past.

Although Vega, Colón, and Thomas highlight the lives of Puerto Ricans in New York, they do so with important differences. As I mentioned, Vega and Colón were cigar makers and their works feature a skilled sector of the Puerto Rican community. Vega wrote his work in Spanish and it was published in Puerto Rico; it was intended to appeal mainly to island and other Hispanic readers, and secondarily to first-generation Puerto Rican migrants. Both Colón and Thomas wrote in English, and they therefore address a U.S. audience. They highlight the discrimination they feel as dark-skinned Puerto Ricans during the periods they narrate. Whereas Vega and Colón record their stories in formal Spanish and English respectively, Thomas, who unlike them was born in the United States, describes his life in a nonstandard language, which mixes Spanish with English and produces a unique combination that reflects the coming together of the two cultures he represents.[56] Thomas's use of street language is another sign of solidarity with a particular segment of the urban Puerto Rican and black populations, and it alludes to his alienation from North American society.

Puerto Ricans in general were the object of discrimination, but race added another dimension of prejudice to the experience of dark-skinned Puerto Ricans. Unlike Vega, who was discriminated against for being Hispanic, and like Colón, Piri Thomas had the burden of dealing with his Hispanic heritage and the color of his skin, at a time before the civil rights movement had gained momentum. North Americans treated dark-skinned Puerto Ricans and other Hispanics as if they were African Americans, many times ignoring cultural, linguistic, and historical differences. Because of this, dark-skinned Latinos gravitated toward African American culture and heritage and some even accepted it as their own. African Americans welcomed dark-skinned Latinos into their communities and viewed them as suffering from the same oppressive conditions they were enduring. In *Down These Mean Streets*, Piri Thomas confronts his identity crisis, provoked by a society that offered him citizenship, but did not grant him the rights and privileges associated with his status.

Down These Mean Streets is an autobiographical account of Piri Thomas, a dark-skinned Puerto Rican who was born and raised in Spanish Harlem during the decades of the thirties, forties, and fifties, the time in which Bernardo Vega observed a transition in the waves of Puerto Rican immigrants coming to New York. Thomas's experiencing of an identity crisis distinguishes him from Vega. Born in the United States, he considered himself Puerto Rican, an identity kept alive by his immediate family and his mother's dream of one day returning to the island.

Thomas is Puerto Rican, but within the North American context he is considered black. The romantic vision of Puerto Rico is contrasted with the harsh reality of living in a racially charged New York environment. From a sociological point of view, the autobiography explains the racial conflicts of the times, inflicted upon the protagonist by a racist society that measures the value of an individual on the basis of skin color. It also describes his attempt to survive and eventually overcome the odds against him. The autobiography reflects the racial attitude of the time of the narration, throughout all aspects of society: schools, jobs, streets, prisons, and home life.

Discrimination is present from Thomas's earliest recollections, when he first moved into a white neighborhood, became aware of race, and searched for his identity within the African American community. But for Thomas, the issue is not simply black and white; his work reflects the complexity of race relations in various U.S. communities. Just as Vega pointed out the unity and the fragmentation within the Hispanic community, Thomas notes that similar divisions are also present among African American people. Of the characters in *Down These Mean Streets*, Brew, proud of the color of his skin, accepts Piri as a black; Alayce, Brew's girlfriend, influenced by attitudes of the dominant society, internalizes her own racial inferiority; Andrew, with one-eighth black blood, negates his identity and prefers that of whites or Hispanics; and the black Muslims capitalize on everyone's frustration and preach racial hatred against whites.

The polarity of the black-white conflict is best expressed by Brew, in one of the most powerful scenes in the autobiography, when he explains to Alayce and Piri his reasons for leaving the South, the center of racial discrimination and tension at that time. Brew, who was taught by his mother to stay out of trouble and respect whites, was challenged by two whites who wanted to rape him: "Fine, fine. Jus' take your pants down an' we jus' do a li'l corn-holin' with you-all." After a scuffle, in which Brew gets the upper hand, he humiliates the whites by demanding they repeat after him:

> "Say, *A black man's better'n a white man.*" He sat there lookin' at me funny-like. Ah raised the rock an' said, "Say it!"
>
> "A-black-man-is-is-bet . . . *You goddamn black bastard! I won't say it, yu goddamn nigger!*"
>
> Brew stood there and his hands slowly let go of an imaginary rock. "Ah dropped that fuckin' rock dead on his mouth and watched him spit out blood an' teeth, an' then Ah went home an' tole Momma what I done, an' next thing Ah was in a car with mah Uncle Stevens drivin' like hell ovah the state line an' on a train to New Yowk. That was three years ago."[57]

With this moving description, Thomas alludes to the history of slavery and the postslavery period, in which blacks are still treated as slaves or animals. The request made by the two whites represents a symbolic rape of African American people and culture and was meant to humiliate Brew in the most profound way. Brew's response is one of rebellion and self-defense, an attempt to preserve his pride and self-respect.

In the United States, blacks have been condemned to suffer. God, Thomas feels, has abandoned African Americans. While Brew tells his story, Piri stares at a crucifix on the wall and Christ seems indifferent to Brew's story in particular and race discrimination in the United States in general. Although Brew's story pertains to the South, the problems of race are also present in the North; such issues permeate the book.

Tense race relations are inherent in society at large. They occur also in Piri's own family, thus reflecting issues that affect the racial complexity of the Puerto Rican people. Whereas the same issues may have been dormant back on the island, on the mainland they gather momentum and even influence the inner workings of the Puerto Rican family. In his sketch "Greetings From Washington," Colón describes Rosa and her white daughter, María, who lives with friends in the nation's capital. Every time Rosa visits her only daughter, María does not take her to the apartment but meets her in some public location.[58]

Like Rosa and María, Piri's family is also divided: he and his father are dark-skinned; his mother, two brothers, and sister are white. However, Piri is isolated. He feels his father rejects his own color and discriminates against him and that his brothers do not understand his isolation and conflicts. His brother José comes from a dark-skinned parent, yet he refuses to associate with blacks, insisting that Puerto Ricans are different from African Americans, whom he probably perceives to be inferior. The family prefers to assimilate into the North American system, and the father avoids his own racial struggle.

> "I ain't got one colored friend," he added, "at least not one American Negro friend. Only dark ones I got are Puerto Ricans or Cubans. I'm not a stupid man. I saw the look of white people on me when I was a young man, when I walked into a place where a dark skin wasn't supposed to be. I noticed how a cold rejection turned into an indifferent acceptance when they heard my exaggerated accent. I can remember the time when I made my accent heavier, to make me more of a Puerto Rican than the most Puerto Rican there ever was. I wanted a value on me, son. But I never changed my name. It was always James Thomas. Sometimes I was asked how come, if I was Puerto Rican, I had James Thomas for a name." (153)

Mr. Thomas replies that his father was a proud North American, an ancestry the son now rejects.

Like all Caribbean countries, Puerto Rico had a slave population, but race issues were complicated by the attitudes manifested by the North Americans present on the island after 1898, attitudes certainly reflective of the situation on the mainland. Mr. Thomas's reluctance to be classified as an African American may be a way of preserving his Puerto Rican identity that corresponds to his generation and reflects his immigrant status. Mr. Thomas belonged to Vega and Colón's age group, and they were first-generation immigrants. Like Mr. Thomas, both Vega and Colón wanted to decouple the national and race issues. Unlike them, Piri Thomas accepts his father's national identity, but he does not reject the racial classification of African Americans.

From an autobiographical standpoint, *Down These Mean Streets* portrays the life of a youngster who rebelled against society and against a family he believed ignored him. Thomas's identity crisis is centered on what he perceives to be his family's rejection, and later his hatred manifests itself against mainstream U.S. society. More likely than not, family discord resulted from societal pressures imposed on Puerto Ricans by the dominant culture. U.S. attitudes toward race are present throughout all levels of society and even intrude upon and destroy the sanctity of the family unit. Racial prejudice is divisive; it turns family members against each other: Mr. Thomas rejected his father and Piri does the same with his own. However, unlike his father, Piri seeks refuge in African American culture. He does so to defy society and his father's beliefs, and also to show racial solidarity with blacks. More important, African Americans and blacks in general represent a counterdiscourse to the discourse of power. Thomas's rejection of mainstream culture allows him to align himself with everything contrary to what society symbolizes. He is the quintessential outlaw: he is Jesse James, Bonny and Clyde, Dillinger, Al Capone, but also the Native American, the African American, and the Latino. African Americans and their culture are the symbolic antitheses of the North American white power structure. In the autobiography, Piri rejects all that a conformist society demands. He belongs to neighborhood gangs, enters a life of crime, and indulges in drugs, marijuana and heroine, which lead to more serious crimes: armed robbery and attempted murder.

The autobiography explains and justifies Thomas's life from his own point of view. He challenges conventional "wisdom" and statistics that highlight the high number of burglaries, homicides, and assaults committed by Puerto Ricans in New York, and he blames the dominant white society.[59] Piri Thomas is a product and a victim of a New York City environment, one which condemns him and other Latinos and African Americans to fail, providing few if any avenues of escape. Throughout the text, blacks and Puerto Ricans occupy the lowest socioeconomic levels of North American society.

Racism is an issue that has determined the course of Piri's life and that of many other African Americans and Latinos, and it is one the author continues to insist on throughout this and other works. In his most recent book, *Seven Long Times* (1974) Thomas expands on the chapter in *Down These Mean Streets* that describes an armed robbery attempt and his subsequent prison sentence, and he articulates the same racial concern at the end, in the epilogue, as he awaits the decision of the parole board, in September 1955. He thinks to himself:

> I committed the crime, I pulled those stickups. I'd stand up to that. But who's going to stand up and admit it was this country's racial and economic inequalities that forced so many of us to the brink of insanity, making our anger and frustration so great that we literally blew ourselves over the precipice into deep, dark whirlpools of drugs and crime? Racism was my mind and anger was my heart, and I fought in the only way I figured was left open to me.[60]

I believe that Piri Thomas is sincere in his assessment of race relations in the United States. His statement provides insight into the life of someone condemned by a society that judges in order ultimately to remove him from his community. After his incarceration, Thomas devotes his efforts to helping other inmates.

Thomas's armed robbery led to a six-year imprisonment. He and two other friends robbed at gunpoint a Manhattan club. The incident became newsworthy and was reported with varying information by the New York City papers of that period. The robbery was covered from the day it occurred, Saturday, to Tuesday of the following week, and it was mentioned at the annual installation of officers of the Detective Endowment Association in the Hotel Astor.[61] The Sports Extra edition of the *New York Journal-American* of February 25, 1950, had the most complete description of the robbery. This and other editions of the day placed the event on the front page. The Wall Street and Sports Extra editions of that paper had it under the title "Dope-Mad Thugs Peril 250 Guests." Because the Sports Extra edition provides a detailed account of the robbery and is slightly different from the other versions and from the one Piri provides, I have decided to reproduce it in its entirety as follows:

A band of professional gunmen, who had been on a marijuana-liquor jag, tried to hold up a jammed Greenwich Village night club—the Moroccan Village, at 23 W. 8th st.—at 3:45 a.m. today.

In a matter of seconds the basement club became a cell of terror and panic as two detectives, who had been talking to the owner and had a premonition of an impending "heist," shot it out with the bandits.

The holdup began when one of the robbers mounted the stage, shoved a woman entertainer aside, grabbed the microphone and announced: "This is a stickup" and then, lying, "I've got six others with me."

Five persons, one detective, the bandit leader, an entertainer and two customers were wounded. Two other gunmen were captured as well as a fourth man identified as a member of the mob.

ADMIT 50 HOLDUPS.

Police said they admitted 50 stickups in the last three years.

Men and women screamed and dived under tables, or stood rigid with fear against the walls, as guns blazed in the smoky fetid interior of the club, lighted dimly to further the illusion of gaiety.

Some customers were trampled by others in the plunging, screaming rush for safety. When the shooting was over the place was a shambles.

Tables and chairs were overturned. Band instruments were strewn about. Little pools of blood were on the shiny surface of the floor.

At least three gunmen and possibly four hopped up by marijuana cigarettes and emboldened by liquor, took part in the attempted holdup.

WOUNDED IN HOSPITAL.

The casualties, all in St. Vincent's Hospital, are:

DETECTIVE JOHN O'NEILL, of the Mercer st. station, bullet wound in right thigh.

PETER THOMAS, 20, alias James Ford and Pedro Gonzales [sic] of 107 E. 104th st., bandit leader, gunshot wound in stomach, critical condition.

PAUL KNIPS, 33, of Fords, N.J., near Perth Amboy, a customer, shot in left chest and right arm when he tried to seize Thomas' gun.

(An earlier and erroneous police report identified Knips as one of the robbers. This was quickly corrected when it was established he was a heroic customer who went to the aid of detectives. Knips is in serious condition.)

ENTERTAINER SHOT.

JOHN MAHONEY, 52, of 201 E. 39th st. an entertainer with the stage name of Jean Evel, shot in right leg.

BOBBY DELL, 36, of 209 Lexington ave., a customer, shot in left arm and left hip.

Captured after they had stolen a taxicab and had been cornered near Cooper Square were:

JOHN SHELB, 29, of 240 E. 634 st.

WILLIAM WARRELL, 27, of 2319 Geary, Philadelphia.

Arrested at his home on information from the prisoners was CLAUDIO DIAZ, 22, of 109 E. 634th st.

Deputy Inspector John McGarty said Diaz had been scheduled to take part in the robbery but had become "ill." Diaz was considerably sicker today.

250 PACKED IN CLUB.

Near noon another handcuffed man was brought into the Mercer st. station. He was not identified, but police said he had been implicated in other robberies of the gang.

In today's stickup they got nothing but trouble; not a dollar, not a piece of jewelry.

There were an estimated 250 persons, including 17 entertainers, packed into the club. It is entered down a flight of seven steps and through heavy swinging doors. The doors give on to a lobby, back of which is the hatcheck counter.

At the right is the bar and at the left a long, narrow room, faced at the rear by the entertainment platform.

In what passes for the dining room, the lights shine dimly through opaque colored glass and there are spotlights on the walls to be turned on entertainers and customers.

In detailing the plan and operation of the stickup, detectives said Thomas, Shelb and Morrell met yesterday afternoon in the Times Square area.

GUNS IN BAGS.

They smoked a few marijuana reefers and then as evening came, they went to Harlem where they visited some bars.

At 11:45 p.m. they entered the Moroccan Village.

Grotesquely, they carried a woman's red leather overnight bag in which were four loaded revolvers.

They left their coats, hats and the bag with the hatcheck girl, Virginia Toy, of 86 W. 12th st. and went to a table.

They sat through the first show, drinking steadily. They had paid for two rounds of drinks and owed for 10 more, when Detectives O'Neill and Thomas Tyrell, of the Mercer st. station dropped in the course of their rounds.

SLEUTHS SUSPICIOUS.

The detectives stood at the far end of the bar talking with Allen Bono, of 11 E. 11th st., owner of the club.

The behavior of the three men at the table aroused the suspicion of O'Neill and Tyrell.

The men kept getting up and sitting down. They were nervous. They weren't paying much attention to the show. Besides, they were running up a sizable tab.

"Things don't look right," said O'Neill quietly to Bono. "This looks like a heist."

"Better get your money."

Bono spoke to his cashier, George Archangel, who handed over $1,000 from the cash drawer. Bono took it and put it in the safe in his office.

DISTRIBUTED GUNS.

As this was going on, one of the gunmen, probably Thomas,

sauntered to the hatcheck girl and got the overnight case. He took it to the table and secretly distributed guns to Shelb and Morrell.

The last show was drawing to a close. Blackie Dennis, diminutive woman entertainer, dressed in a man's dinner jacket, was singing in the microphone. About ten men and women entertainers and a six-man orchestra were with her on the platform.

Shelb suddenly jumped on the stage, fired a shot in the ceiling, seized the microphone and shouted:

"This is a stickup. Put your jewelry, purses and money on the tables. I've got six others with me."

DETECTIVES OPEN FIRE.

Morrell, gun in hand, was standing just below him on the floor. Thomas was at the other end of the room, toward the street.

O'Neill and Thomas fired virtually simultaneously. The bandit was hit in the stomach and the detective in the leg. Another bullet from the bandit's gun went wild.

O'Neill slumped to the floor and crawled into the kitchen.

Knips, who was seated at a nearby table with two friends, grabbed the gun from Thomas, but not before he had been shot twice.

Tyrell was shooting now, advancing toward the other two bandits in the dining room.

The other two gunmen returned the fire and the place in an instant was filled with panic.

Thomas staggered out of the club, lurched up the stairs, brushed past the 82-year-old doorman, Benjamin Boykin, of 226 Thompson st., and flagged a passing taxicab by almost throwing himself in front of it.

The cab, driven by Samuel Byalick, of 90 Amsterdam ave., was carrying a man and a woman.

Thomas opened the door, half crawled in and shoved his gun against the back of the driver.

"Go ahead or I'll Kill you," he ordered.

BOTH KICK BANDIT.

It was a wild, bizarre ride. Both the man and woman were punching and kicking Thomas, who still managed to hold his gun against the driver.

The cabbie drove to W. Broadway and Bleecker st., where he found what he had been looking for, a police radio car. He signaled with his lights and horn, jammed on the brakes and threw himself on the floor.

The tonneau door of the cab opened and the male passenger and Thomas rolled onto the street, locked together.

Patrolmen Martin Kirby and William Bond of the Mercer st. station ran over.

"Be careful, this guy has a gun," Byalick shouted, pointing to Thomas.

The policemen wrenched the two struggling men apart and seized Thomas, still holding his gun. They took him back to the club. The man and the woman passenger disappeared, unidentified.

In the meantime, Shelb and Warrell had run from the club to a taxicab parked a few feet away.

They pointed their guns at the driver, Max Hollander, of 240 Grand st., Brooklyn, and ordered him out of the front seat.

CABBIES CHASE GUNMEN.

The Gunmen crowded into the front seat with Shelb at the wheel and sped east on 8th st., crossing 5th ave.

Hollander yelled to another cabbie, got into the second cab and started in pursuit.

The fleeing cab drove through a red light. The cab was cut off by a radio patrol car in which were Patrolman Michael Tobin and Alfred Strickert, of the Mercer st. station.

They seized Shelb and Warrell.

On the rear seat they found a .25 calibre and .45 calibre automatic and a .38 calibre revolver.

By this time radio cars had arrived at the club. One customer gave police a description of a 1938 Buick which earlier had been parked near the club. The car was found in front of 65th ave.[62]

Although there are important differences between the novel and the preceding newspaper citation, there are others among the various editions of the *New York Journal-American*. A comparision of the newspaper accounts of the robbery helps to explain how the information developed and, most signficiant, how Hispanics or Latinos were treated by the media. A close reading of these newspapers will show the literary liberties journalists incorporated into their writings, a theme that also relates to the factual or fictional elements in journalism and in Thomas's own writings.

Of particular interest is the description of Thomas's escape. As the Sports Extra edition indicates, Thomas had been shot in the stomach and staggered out of the club. He climbed into a cab and fought with the passengers. The Wall Street Special Edition of the *New York Journal-American* reports it as "Thomas staggered out, flagged a taxicab and crawled in. A man and a woman were passengers and the man started hitting him.

"At West Broadway and Bleecker st. the male passenger and Thomas rolled to the pavement as the cabbie signalled a radio car. Thomas was seized."[63] The Night Edition offered its readers yet another account of the holdup. Unlike the others, it identifies Thomas as James Ford, age twenty-two, and denies any struggle with the passengers in the cab:

> Dashing east on 8th st., he stepped in front of a taxicab headed south on 5th ave., drew his gun and told the occupants of the rear—a man and his wife—to:
> "Move over, keep quiet and you won't be hurt."

> FLASHES LIGHTS.
> When he told the driver of the cab to drive south through Washington Sq.
> The driver did as the gunman said.
> But as he drove he flashed his headlights at every car he thought might contain police.
> The blinking lights caught the attention of two radio patrolmen who swung in front of the cab and got out, revolvers in hand.
> The wounded bandit gave up without a struggle and was taken to St. Vincent's Hospital.[64]

There are similarities and differences among the three editions of the *New York Journal-American*, but the Sports Extra went beyond just reporting the facts, as the Wall Street and Night editions attempted to do. It is possible that by the time of publication there was additional information that could have been included in the Sports Extra. But does this information really provide more details about the robbery? Or does it help attain a literary quality absent in the others? Or is there another purpose, to dehumanize the assailants and ridicule them before the public? Certainly, the Sports Extra overemphasizes the group's drug and alcohol consumption. This is present thoughout the article, and the word *dope* also appears in the headline. The emphasis is gratuitous, especially when taking into account that there was a shootout and more than one person was wounded. The Sports Extra even gives significance to a woman's red leather bag the bandits used to carry their weapon, information not corroborated by the other editions, nor by Thomas's own account. Because the bandits were robbing a gay nightclub, did the journalist allow his interpretation to be clouded by dominant North American interpretations of the other? Moreover, the fourth participant, who is not Claudio Díaz, alluded to in the Sports Extra, becomes a fifth participant in the Night Edition.

Thomas's narration follows closely the events reported in the newspapers and, they may have even served him as meaningful sources for remembering the past, with some important differences. In his autobiography, Thomas omits any reference to having shot Paul Knips, who in the newspaper reports tried to wrestle the gun from him and whom he allegedly shot, or any allusion to a fifth accomplice. He does, however, recall a drunken woman who approached him and whom he assaulted before being shot by the undercover officer. He also recalls a man who knocked him down but whom he did not shoot. The discrepancies can be explained in the following manner: it is possible that Thomas does not remember all of the events narrated in the newspapers or he wanted to underscore the inaccuracies reported by the media, denying he had shot Knips, thus suggesting that either his buddies or the police did.

It is reasonable to propose that the autobiography reproduces the events of the robbery not only because they were part of Thomas's life, but because he wanted to privilege one interpretation and correct inaccuracies reported by the newspapers. From Thomas's perspective, his autobiographical account is more factual than those offered by the articles. For example, Thomas admits to being high but states that he and his buddies did not have a "red woman's bag"; rather, Billy had checked a "little black box," which contained three .38s and one .45 caliber gun. However, according to the *Journal-American* Sports Extra edition, Shelb and Warrell were apprehended with one .35, one .45, and one .25 caliber revolvers. An initial question is: Did Thomas recollect properly something so familiar to him? If he did, where did the .25 caliber revolver come from? Did Shelb or Warrell hide it from the rest of the gang members? Did the reporter mistake a .38 for a .25 gun? Or did the police plant the .25 weapon?

Thomas's description of his getaway coincides most closely with the Night Edition. In his narration, Thomas reports carjacking a cab with two passengers; the woman was hysterical and the man sat next to him. He denies any scuffle with the passengers. When the cab stopped, Thomas claims that he stumbled out. However, he does admit that the cab driver grabbed him and that Thomas hit him and was about to shoot, but realized he had dropped his gun. Then, Thomas recounts, he walked up to the police car and tried to shoot the officer with his finger, believing he still had the gun in his hand. From an observer's point of view, these events can be interpreted as Thomas's surrender.

There are other discrepancies between Thomas's work and the newspaper accounts and among the different editions that describe the same event. The Wall Street and Sports Extra editions and the *New York Journal-American* Sunday edition, which by now had removed the event from the front page, claimed Thomas was twenty years old; the latest-news edition of the Monday paper reported it as twenty-five.[65] But if he was born in 1928 and the robbery took place in 1950, then the age should have been recorded not as twenty or twenty-five, but twenty-two. In the same editions, Piri Thomas is identified as Peter Thomas, James Ford, and Pedro Conzales [*sic*]; his address is given as 107 East 104th Street; and he is marked as the bandit leader. The Sunday edition corrects the Sports Extra and Wall Street editions and claims that there were four suspects, which included Claudio Díaz, an accomplice who did not participate due to an illness, and the Night Edition identifies two of the gunmen as James Ford, 22, and Paul Knips, 33.

The *New York Times* of February 26, 1950, which places the crowd at one hundred, corrects inaccuracies of the *New York Journal-American* and, like the Night Edition, reports Thomas's age as twenty-two. However, it introduces other inconsistencies, identifying him not as Piri or Peter Thomas, but as Pedro Gonzales and giving his address as 115 East 104th Street.[66] The Sunday and Monday editions of the *New York Journal-American* confirm the name reported by *The New York Times*, but they continue to give his address as 107 E. 104th Street. The Sunday edition disregards the description of the escape as reported in the Night Edition, and it reiterates what had been publicized in the Wall Street and Sports Extra, that Thomas and the man fought in the cab. The Night Edition and *The New York Times* article concur; they do not report a struggle in the cab. Like the Monday edition of the *New York Journal-American*, *The New York Times*'s article further clarifies that five rather than four were booked: John Shelb, William Warrell, and Pedro Gonzales, who participated in the holdup; Claudio Díaz, who was ill; "and William J. Smith, 28, of 342 East Eighty-fifth Street, who was charged with the hold-up several weeks ago of a bar and grill at 81 University Place."[67] William Smith does not appear in any of the other newspaper articles or in Thomas's narration. By the time Monday arrived, the robbery was no longer a significant event. Newspapers did not provide a description of the chase, though the latest-news and afternoon editions continued to emphasize the use of marijuana and liquor. Furthermore, Pedro González, fighting for his life in the hospital, gained more coverage than his partners and was accused of shooting four persons.

The additional inconsistencies suggest that Thomas altered his information, was misunderstood by aggressive reporters, or was simply mistaken for someone else, as Smith's accusation suggests. It is also possible that the police were eager to solve the crime, blamed Piri for everyone who was shot, and accused Smith of a robbery he did not commit. It appears that some reporters exaggerated their descriptions of the robbery, embellished their reports, and added a literary quality to their narrations. In this regard, Thomas's account competes with the official accounts and resorts to narrative strategies to overcome the failings of the published versions of the same events.

An intertextual reading of Thomas's robbery and incarceration produces still other discrepancies that must be understood within the same frame of reasoning I have outlined. In *Down These Mean Streets*, Thomas reports that he was incarcerated for six years and was released when he was twenty-eight, on November 28; if we calculate based on his having been twenty-two years old and committing the crime on February 25, 1950, the year of release should have been 1956. But his book about prison is entitled *Seven Long Times*, suggesting that he was in jail seven years. Considering the information Thomas divulges in the epilogue, he sat before the parole board in September 1955 and was released from Comstock in October of the same year. If we insert that year into our calculations, he only served five years and seven months.

The shift in dates and identity responds to the picaresque nature of Thomas's narration, or for that matter of any other autobiography, as the protagonist moves through the city and the country, wearing different masks, learning from different people and situations, and justifying his actions. It also refers to his identity crisis: he is the English Peter Thomas and James Ford and the Spanish Pedro Gonzales, or the fictitious Pedro Conzales, but also the Spanish and English Piri Thomas. The identity crisis is evident in *Down These Mean Streets*, as I have attempted to show, but the shifts in nomenclature were already present from the time he was born. In his essay "A Neorican in Puerto Rico: Or Coming Home," the author states that at birth he was supposed to have been named Juan Pedro Tomás Montañez but that he later discovered that his birth certificate reported his name as John Thomas, which made him question whether the change was made by the hospital or his parents.[68] His decision not to use John or Juan arises more directly from a personal rebellion against his father (whose name was also Juan) than to a rejection of an assimilationist campaign. However, Thomas's shifting identities in the texts to which I have referred also allude to a desire to distance himself from the past. Whereas he may have been James, John, or Juan, Ford or González, he is now Piri Thomas. The change indicates a rewriting of his life from the point of view of having to come to terms with his own past and identity; it represents a conversion from the person he was to an acceptance of the person he is, as we shall see later.

Thomas's description of life in prison symbolizes his fall and reveals still another aspect of the lives of Puerto Ricans and African Americans who have been condemned, this time by the North American legal system. In *Down These Mean Streets* there is a close relationship between life in New York City and life inside prison. Prison is a microcosm of North American society, certainly a more intense and perhaps more deformed or "accurate" version of it. Life on the inside recalls life in the barrio. The majority of prisoners are Latinos and African Americans. Just as in the outside world, they congregate in their own groups and the white guards are the authority figures who hold all the power. Prison has its regulations, but as in the ghetto, the prisoners within the confines of their restricted lives make their own rules, which at times even rival those concocted and administered by policymakers. Drugs and violence are present, and prisoners have sexual relations and marry among themselves. In this sense, they continue to challenge the system by creating an environment that provides some outlets for their own particular needs. And as in the streets, one's reputation, or having heart, becomes the single most important way of maintaining pride, the only recourse after everything else has been taken away.

Thomas's incarceration is the subject of *Seven Long Times*, which describes in more detail his life in prison and those with whom he associated during that period of his life. Both autobiographical accounts raise the issue of the effectiveness of inmate incarceration and rehabilitation. The subject is first present in *Down These Mean Streets* when Thomas, who has served four years, comes up before the parole board for the first time. Drugs, weapons, violence, abuses, and more serious crimes continue to be part of the prisoner's life. Thomas has not been rehabilitated by his prison experience and refuses to allow the system to change him; even if it meant serving the entire fifteen years, he has decided he is not going to crack.

In *Seven Long Times*, Thomas pays particular attention to his rehabilitation. In a chapter entitled "Is You Rehabilitated Yet?" Thomas recalls the time he came before the parole board and no one was interested in his rehabilitation; the members of the board were more concerned with trying him a second time. As a reaction and a form of therapy, Piri composes two letters, one mentally and the other in print: the first is an honest and angry response and the other is more diplomatic in its presentation. In the mental letter to Mr. Alfred R. Loos, chairman of the parole board, Piri expresses his belief that no one on the board is really interested in what he has accomplished. He believes that prisons are not intended to rehabilitate inmates but to punish them for what they have done. He even questions if it is possible to reeducate someone in an environment full of hatred and injustice. In fact, he asserts, prisons serve to intensify the criminality of prisoners so, when they leave prison, they are monsters. He even welcomes parole board members to live with the prisoners so they will have firsthand experience for making decisions. It is not by accident that Thomas's description of what takes place behind bars recalls another prison, the ghetto.

In the second letter, Thomas is a changed man and talks about his rehabilitation. He allows himself to get close to Reverend Winch, the prison's chaplain, studies and graduates as a brick mason, receives his high school equivalency diploma, and takes up the hobby of guitar playing. He also wants Mr. Loos to understand the context for his actions, his environment and the pressures placed on someone trying to belong. He ends the letter by referring to his good church-going family and his own religious beliefs.[69]

Although Thomas did participate in prison reform and obtained a Bible correspondence course certificate on January 4, 1951, a high school equivalency diploma in 1952, and a certificate for bricklaying on November 18, 1952, in *Down These Mean Streets* he presents himself to be an unchanged person.[70] The change that does take place is in his presentation. Thomas did learn to reproduce the discourse of the parole board and others in power and repeat what they wanted him to say, while still harboring hatred, as he indicates in the letter he composed but did not send. The composition of the mental letter, which is transcribed in the text, attempts to convince Mr. Loos or anyone else in power of the reality of prison life. The hatred Thomas harbors toward the prison, the guards, and the parole board was already present well before he was confined to Comstock. He had been conditioned to despise authority figures. Therefore, his hatred and criminal behavior could have resulted from social, economic, or genetic factors. But his aggression, and that of many other inmates, can best be understood as political and directed against North American culture and the institutions that promote it. It is an attack on the symbols that reinforce oppression. Five and one-half years into his sentence, and a few weeks before his second parole board hearing, Piri is still loyal to his prison inmates and considers his prison family thicker than blood. They are not only his symbolic family; they are victims of the same society that has consistently and historically discriminated against him. He even has to struggle within himself about whether or not to participate in the prison uprising.[71] Thomas's decision is made for him when the guards escort him to the cell, removing him from potential violence and allowing him to save face.

When Thomas comes up before the board for the second time and after almost six years, he is allowed to go home because he has been "rehabilitated." But he questions whether this is true. When the officials mention that he will be allowed to leave in spite of a few infractions, Thomas thinks to himself, "Yeah, a few, not counting the couple of million I never got caught on." His attitude shows that as a prisoner he mastered the prison game, similar to the one he had already learned in El Barrio, that in the presence of guards and prison officials, inmates must show and tell them what they want to see and hear. Certainly, he is not totally rehabilitated. He returns to his home, El Barrio, and soon thereafter revisits the life he once knew:

> The first rule I broke was the one about not fucking broads who weren't your wife. I shacked up with one of the homeliest broads I ever had seen, but she looked great after my long fast. Having

broken one rule, I found it easier to break another, and soon I was drinking again. Then I started smoking pot. This went on for some weeks.[72]

Piri Thomas's narration does show signs of a change, not so much because of any rehabilitation program designed for prisoners and which awarded him certificates, but because of his own personal commitment to alter his life. Thomas continues:

Then, one morning, after a wild, all night pot party, I crept into Tia's apartment and dug myself in the mirror. What I saw shook me up. My eyes were red from smoke and my face was strained from the effort of trying to be cool. I saw myself as I had been six years ago, hustling, whoring, and hating, heading toward the same long years and the hard bit. I didn't want to go that route; I didn't want to go dig that past scene again. (321)

Down These Mean Streets explains Thomas's downfall and his resurrection. Thomas's rehabilitation may have arguably begun in prison, but it was completed sometime after the end of the narration and before the act of writing. We should keep in mind that Thomas writes from a rehabilitated point of view. After his release and the conclusion of the narration Thomas worked with street gangs in Spanish Harlem, and in Puerto Rico he developed a program for drug addicts. In his appendix 1 to *Seven Long Times*, Thomas quotes statistics that show that only 10 percent of the prison population is "hard-core" and the other 90 percent can be rehabilitated. By the time he completed his prison sentence, there were only a handful of organizations that could help the inmate with his transition into society. In the appendix 2 he provides a list of organizations, publications, and special programs for former prisoners.[73]

Thomas's rehabilitation is more clearly understood as a religious or spiritual conversion. The narration explains it as an acceptance, while in prison, of the Black Muslim religion, perhaps the best organized prisoner group in prison, offering the inmates a way of understanding their conditions and gaining a sense of worth. Thomas never forgot the lessons of his teacher Muhammad, who said: "'No matter a man's color or race, he has a need of dignity and he'll go anywhere, become anything, or do anything to get it—anything'" (297). But even the Muslim religion, which stimulates Thomas's desire to learn and to explore knowledge, is secondary to Christianity, to which he had been exposed as a child—Thomas tells the reader that his mother was a Seventh-Day Adventist. Thomas's rediscovery of God is certainly an important factor in his transition to a better life. As was mentioned earlier, he completed a Bible correspondence course in prison, and religion is the subject of his second book *Savior, Savior, Hold My Hand* (1972).

The autobiography could only have been written after Thomas's conversion, and the act of writing is a symbolic representation of that change. If we read the autobiography from this perspective, we find that Thomas's self-awareness is incorporated into the narration and is evident from the start. It is apparent when he and Brew travel down south to understand the origin of race relations in the United States. Piri's journey of self-discovery mirrors Dante's own descent into hell and Brew is his Virgil, his guide, though with some important changes. Virgil guides Dante through the inferno and purgatory, and upon on entering paradise, Dante receives his recompense in Beatrice. Thomas's experience begins in purgatory, the barrio, and descends into hell, and his Beatrice is a prostitute.

Thomas's voyage of self-discovery through the writing of his autobiography is expressed in two different but related incidents, and each one reflects the person Piri Thomas became after his conversion. The first takes place in the physical center of the book with regard to number of pages and chapters. In chapter 18 (of thirty-five), entitled "Barroom Sociology," Thomas and Brew meet Gerald Andrew West, from Pennsylvania, who like Piri has traveled south to study race relations in the United States and gathers information to write a book. Gerald, who is a mixture of races and ethnic groups, including white and black, does not feel black, and he attempts to impose his own feelings on the research he is conducting. He proposes to show that in spite of slavery, blacks are working with whites to improve their relations. Although Brew and Piri oppose Gerald's integrationist ideas, there are similarities between Gerald and Piri, and one appears to be a copy of the other. Gerald is of mixed race but claims that he looks Hispanic and even identifies himself as one. In some way, Gerald mirrors Piri's own identity crisis and may be a manifestation of Piri's alter ego:

> "I believe the Negro has the burden of his black skin," Gerald continued. He was in focus now. "And I believe the white man has the burden of his white skin. But people like me have the burden of both. It's pretty funny, Mr. Johnson. The white man is perfectly willing for people like me to be Negroes. In fact, he insists upon it. Yet, the Negro won't let us be white. In fact he forbids it. Perhaps I was a bit maudlin in describing what I was looking for in the southern Negro, and this may have set you against me. But I would like you to know that if, because of genetic interbreeding, I cannot truly identify with white or black, I have the right to identify with whatever race or nationality approximates my emotional feelings and physical characteristics. If I feel comfortable being of Spanish

extraction, then that's what I'll be. You might very well feel the same way, were you in my place."

Piri continues the narration and identifies with Gerald's conflicts. As Gerald talks, Piri contemplates: "I was thinking that Gerald had problems something like mine. Except that he was a Negro trying to make Puerto Rican and I was a Puerto Rican trying to make Negro" (176–77).

Later in the chapter, Piri opens up to Brew in a way that recalls Gerald's concerns: "I still can't help feeling both paddy and Negro. The weight feels even on both sides even if both sides wanna feel uneven. Goddammit, I wish I could be like one of those lizards that change colors. When I'd be with Negroes, I'd be a stone Negro, and with paddies, I'd be stone paddy" (180). Thomas's shift in names is a way of transforming himself from who he is to someone else and back again. Gerald's research on blacks will be transformed into the book Thomas will write, the autobiography that explains and resolves Piri's identity crisis.

The second episode, referred to earlier under the section on Thomas's conversion, is a physical journey into a Dante-like inferno, this time to the southern regions of the United States. In their voyage, Piri and Brew descend from Norfolk to Mobile, where Brew, whose experience allows him to introduce Piri to this part of the country, mysteriously and conveniently disappears from the autobiography but remains in spirit. Thomas has learned from Brew but has also become independent of him. Dante no longer needs his Virgil. In Texas, the southernmost region of this journey, Piri finds a perverted form of his Beatrice in a brothel, a kind of paradise. Piri's communion is not one of harmony but of defiance; he wants to let the white woman, and consequently everyone else there know, that she had sex with a black.

Thomas continues to insist on the idea of dissent. He returns to Norfolk and embarks on a second voyage further south than Texas, this time to the West Indies. In so doing, Thomas shifts the action to another geographic location, the Caribbean, where slavery had a strong hold in some islands well after the institution was abolished in the United States. Equally important, his use of that setting alludes to the fact that race issues are widespread and transcend the boundaries of the U.S. mainland. As he travels to the Caribbean, Thomas enters a symbolic hell in the bowels of a ship, where he works first as a coal fireman and then as a coal supplier. On the ship Thomas also defends himself against a Swede but hesitates to and does not go through with killing him. He looks to a West Indian messman, Isaac, for some advice. Isaac, who serves as a Virgil in Brew's absence, accuses Thomas of being a coward. Isaac recalls Abraham's Isaac, who understands God's work and escapes his father's sacrifice. The biblical Isaac is embodied in the Isaac of his namesake. He teaches Piri another valuable lesson:

I think you're yellow not because you didn't kill him but because you didn't want to kill him. You'll learn, boy, this is a hard life for a black or brown man. I'm black, you're brown. Unless you're willing to kill at the exact moment you have to, you'll be a pussy bumper for the rest of your life. You got to have the heart not only to spare life but to take it. You can only spare it now, but maybe you'll learn. I don't mean you're yellow in heart, just in instinct. (191)

While on his seven-month voyage through Europe and the rest of the Americas, Piri learns over and over the same lesson: blacks are treated as inferior. In the postslavery period, they and other racial and ethnic minorities must stand up to the injustices perpetrated against them; they must demand, be ready to fight, and claim their position in society. In the narration, Piri contextualizes and therefore prepares the reader for the violence in which he will participate. Isaac's advice comes in handy when Piri confronts his father and consciously decides to walk away from a fight with him and spare his life. It is also relevant when he robs the used-car dealer and knows that he must beat him almost to death. He again follows Isaac's advice by shooting a police officer when he, Billy, and Danny rob the nightclub. The advice also proves useful when Thomas is in jail and has to survive a five- to fifteen-year sentence.

Isaac further influences Piri when Piri leaves prison and writes his autobiography as a literature of protest. The theme and the literary style continue to challenge conventions. As I have stated, Piri Thomas's autobiography was written after his conversion; writing serves as a way of reflecting upon his past experiences, but also contains his salvation. Like Dante he must descend into hell, the South, in order to come to terms with the past but also the present race relations in the United States. Piri's physical and metaphorical descent reveals that hell is not in the South nor is paradise in Puerto Rico. Hell, purgatory, and paradise occupy the same space: they are all present in El Barrio, and wherever he is; they are also an integral part of his own psychic and spiritual being. Therefore, from a rehabilitated point of view, Piri's racial frustrations and his outspoken hatred toward whites have been resolved and transcended.

In the narration the emphasis on racial discourse is undermined and counterbalanced by the unfolding of a series of events that are present from the outset of the autobiography through to the end. These events appear as a diachronic line and represent a subtext in the work. Piri's narration is not one-sided; it portrays another aspect of whites and alludes to possible harmony between whites and blacks, as Gerald had expressed. Gerald explains the intent of his book to his newfound friends: "I want to write that despite their burdens they [blacks] are working with the white man toward a productive relationship" (170). This other perspective is an integral part of Piri's conversion and the act of writing his autobiography. Certainly, there is ample evidence of this in the text.

Another, further reading of *Down These Mean Streets* discloses that Thomas's autobiography is not about racial segregation but about racial harmony. Although this type of reading resembles Vega's and Colón's positions, the premise is different. Vega's and Colón's ideas are based on a preconceived ideology, Thomas derives his from personal experience. For example, when Piri fights with Rocky, the older Italians in the neighborhood come to Piri's aid, demanding that the Italian kids leave him alone; in this situation the adults are not racist but concerned individuals, at the expense of criticizing one of their own and supporting a Latino of dark complexion. Moreover, when Piri fights with one of Rocky's friends, Tony throws a handful of gravel in his eyes; the reader is exposed to anger and fear, but also tenderness on the part of Rocky who, in spite of racial and ethnic animosity, wishes for Piri to get better. And just as Piri fights against whites, he also defends himself against the Jolly Rogers, the rival Puerto Rican gang.

Other events show that Thomas rejects a categorical understanding of the black and white races, where one is inherently good and the other bad, favoring instead a balanced view that includes good and bad people. Piri's rejection by the white girl in a Long Island school is counterposed by his white girlfriend, with whom he sleeps, and by his sexual encounter in a crowded New York City subway, where he and a white woman press against each other, practically making love, which results in his having an orgasm. The one negative experience with a white woman is offset by two positive ones.

A view more balanced between whites and blacks is also evident when Thomas and Louis team up with Billy and Danny in armed robbery. Although Piri is suspicious of the two whites, the group's decisions are democratic and not based on race. Ironically, however, it is Louis, his Puerto Rican all-time buddy who, after the failed robbery, betrays him in order to save his own skin; Billy, Danny, and Piri are loyal to each other and are sentenced to prison. Of equal significance is the way some officers treat him. The person most helpful to Piri is Casey, a white prison guard, a symbol of white authority. On more than one occasion, Casey saves him from a longer jail term. And when Piri leaves prison, the officers who transport him to the Bronx County Tombs treat him as a human being, with trust and respect. Equally telling is that if he believes that God is right, he is willing to accept God as white.

Although Thomas succeeds in overcoming the odds against him and arrives at a resolution regarding his identity crisis, the autobiography ends on a chilling and prophetic note. Life in the ghetto will continue to get worse and claim more victims, including members of the younger generation. The youngster Piri shares a cell with in the Tombs, who is awaiting sentencing for armed robbery, is a more dramatic version of what Piri was. Just as Gerald reflects Piri's identity crisis, the youngster also underscores the narrator's social, economic, and political concerns. He is an exaggerated copy of Piri: they are both Puerto Ricans who wounded police officers and were in turn wounded by them; Piri did time in prison and so will his younger counterpart who has begun his life of crime at an early age. Piri recognizes the similarity and says to himself: "*This kid shot a cop and got shot; I shot a cop and got shot. What's happened to me is going to happen to him. He's going to do time, maybe a lot*" (315). The kid shot the cop, and he wounded the youngster four times. Piri notes that indeed the situation has gotten worse.

The idea of a deteriorating ghetto is highlighted in the final scene of Piri's autobiography, his encounter with Carlito, a neighborhood boy from his past; the youngster is now a heroine addict with an expensive daily habit. Like the early Piri, and many other addicts, he fools himself into thinking that he is in control and will overcome his addiction. The situation is certainly worse: the heroin that Carlito is consuming is inferior and is rotting his body; chances are that he may not even live long. Carlito is a symbol of the future of Puerto Rican New Yorkers, and by extension all ghetto youths. In the final scene, Piri walks away from Carlito, his past, and moves to a higher plane, the second floor of his apartment building, a metaphoric transcendence of his own past condition.

By writing *Down These Mean Streets,* Thomas looks back to his past. In so doing he offers the reader a clear picture of life for many dark-skinned Latinos living in the ghettos and explains to himself and others the person he used to be. The narration contains a sense both of doom and hope. The act of writing is a sign of salvation, as represented contextually by the author's own life. Thomas is the most accomplished Puerto Rican American writer in the United States. By revisiting his own life, Thomas provides a solution derived from his own fall and salvation. He finds that society must rehabilitate itself and eradicate the structures of prejudice and discrimination that force Latinos into a life of crime. Likewise, he makes plain that individuals cannot wait for society to change; they have an obligation to take charge of their own lives and rehabilitate themselves.

FOUR

Cuban American Poetry
The Cuban American Divide

> ¡Me espanta la ciudad! Toda está llena
> De copas por vaciar, o huecas copas.
> ¡Tengo miedo ¡ay de mí! de que este vino
> Tósigo sea, y en mis venas luego
> Cual duende vengador los dientes clave!
> ¡Tengo sed; mas de un vino que ni la tierra
> No se sabe beber! ¡No he padecido
> Bastante aún, para romper el muro
> Que me aparta ¡oh dolor! de mi viñedo!
> ¡Tomad vosotros, catadores ruines
> De vinillos humanos, esos vasos
> Donde el jugo de lirio a grandes sorbos
> Sin compasión y sin temor se bebe!
> ¡Tomad! ¡Yo soy honrado, y tengo miedo!
>
> —José Martí, "Amor de ciudad grande"

I

THE overwhelming proportion of the Cuban American community in the United States lives in Miami and supports the U.S. embargo of Cuba and the overthrow of the Castro government. But not all Cuban Americans think alike, especially among the children of Cuban exiles born or raised and educated in the United States. In the decades of the sixties and seventies, groups of young Cuban Americans who favored a more balanced U.S. policy toward Cuba began to emerge independently of each other. The Cuban American groups were formed at the time the civil rights and antiwar movements were well under way. In 1967 a group of Cuban Americans from the Northeast began meeting informally in Union City, New Jersey. Later known as La Cosa, they studied problems related to Cuba and the revolution. Another one, Juventud Cubana Socialista, began in Miami in 1970, spread to New York and Puerto Rico, and promoted Puerto Rican independence.[1]

The two most noteworthy Cuban American groups convened in the Northeast in 1973 around the periodicals *Joven Cuba* and *Areíto*. Both groups supported events in Cuba, but each one had a different mission; the first one worked with the Hispanic communities in the United States and the second one with university students and the so-called progressive sector of the Cuban exile community. Of all the Cuban American groups, Areíto was the most important one. Areíto grew at the expense of the other groups, drawing on their membership and other university students, from the Northeast to Florida and Puerto Rico.

As a group, Areíto began in New York City and in a short period reached prominence as representative of a new and different voice within what was then perceived to be a homogeneous exile community. This was particularly so during the years in which Lourdes Casal was its leader, and one of the editors of the magazine, up until her premature death in 1981.[2] Casal was an enthusiastic, charismatic, and hardworking organizer and the backbone of the group. The position Casal and other young Cuban Americans represented can be found in the pages of *Areíto*.[3]

The group was born at a time in which Chicanos, Puerto Ricans, African Americans, and Native Americans were accepting their own identity and demanding recognition. The recent Cuban exiles refused to give up their identity and assimilate into U.S. society; they believed their return to the island was imminent. However, the younger generation found meaning not only in their parents' plight but in the search undertaken by other minority groups. The members of Areíto questioned their parents' political position and supported daring and controversial activities, including normalized relations between Cuba and the United States, the independence of Puerto Rico, civil rights for U.S. minorities, a dialogue with the Cuban exile community, and Cuban American literature.

During the decades of the seventies and eighties *Areíto* became a forum for Cuban Americans and other Latinos living in the United States whose attitudes ranged from tolerance for and coexistence with Cuba to outright support of the Cuban Revolution. The magazine also published articles written by Cubans from the island and North Americans who believed in the same goals the editors wanted to achieve. For many, *Areíto* became an important source of information about events in Cuba that were either not covered by the news media in North America or were usually filtered through the perspective of the Cuban exile community. Similar to the objective of Cuba's Casa de las Américas and its journal, in the United States *Areíto* served to circumvent the cultural blockade that the U.S. government had imposed on Cuba, which had been in effect since Fidel Castro seized power. Members of Areíto became more active in promoting relations with the Castro government. They sponsored trips to Cuba, visits by Cubans to the United States, distribution of Cuban books, and travel to and from the island.

Areíto's position is evident in the pages of the magazine, and made explicit in an editorial entitled "Un recuento de nuestro primer año" ("a rememberance of our first year") (1975), assessing the first year of its publication.[4] The editorial mentions the common problems associated with any new publication, but it also recognizes the phenomenon the magazine represents. The magazine was born of a group of Cuban Americans growing up in the United States, who were in the process of reevaluating Cuban culture as well as North American and Cuban revolutionary societies. They viewed their situation not as an isolated case, but as a sociological and psychological process. Understanding the events in Cuba was considered to be a first step in coming to terms with their minority status in the United States, similar to those of Chicanos and Puerto Ricans, among others.

The editorial also refers to the first two published in *Areíto*. The first one indicated that Cuban American history and culture were determined by the Cuban Revolution. The Cuban Revolution was seen as a vehicle for understanding the group's identity in the United States, a country where, paradoxically, they did not find support for their ideas. The second dicussed the need to correct the distorted vision exiles have created of the Cuban Revolution. The publishers interpreted their position as ideological pluralism. They wanted to convey that the exile community was not homogeneous; the younger generation did not share the views of the older one, and they had not been traumatized by the past. The editorial ends by indicating that there would be more studies on the Cuban minority in the United States, to which the future of *Areíto* was tied.

The ideas of the Areíto group are also present in *Contra viento y marea* (1978) a collection of interviews by the sons and daughters of Cuban exiles. In this unprecedented work, members of the Areíto group, in a questionnaire, recalled their experiences as children in Cuba and as youngsters and adults in the United States; that is, before and after they emigrated, their impressions of the revolution and of life in exile.[5] As was expected, *Contra viento y marea* was received with enthusiasm in Cuba and awarded La Juventud en Nuestra América prize by Casa de las Américas, in 1978. Carlos Olivares Baró reviewed the book in *Areíto* and said the following:

> *Contra viento y marea*, of the *Areíto* group (recipient of the extraordinary prize La Juventud en Nuestra América, awarded by Casa de las Américas, 1978), is a sincere, precise and eloquent testimony of a unique phenomenon from within the Cuban exodus to the United States after 1959. The youngsters who left the country were still children or pre-adolescents. After a process of internal and objective struggle they arrived at a radical consciousness which ranged from liberal to Marxist in confessions, which

demonstrate their sympathy with the revolutionary Cuban process.

All emigration encompasses this phenomenon; that is, a return to the abandoned homeland. But what is astonishing is that the children of those who still oppose the Revolution they abandoned, radicalize their manner of thinking and see their motherland as something they should never have lost. They propose a more objective point of view and emphasize an acceptance of the Revolution without prejudice.

Areíto is a magazine published in New York. Its editors were members of the Brigada Antonio Maceo, which recently visited our country.

The magazine, the brigade, and the group have a common objective: to let it be known that not all Cubans who live outside of the island, especially in the United States, have a homogeneous and, of course, counterrevolutionary position with respect to our country and our process.

Contra viento y marea, from beginning to end dazzles because of the spontaneity of its testimonies. There is nothing prefabricated. Each interview uncovers a sincere and passionate revolutionary sentiment.

The book, structured in five chapters with an introduction and an appendix, reveals nostalgically the experiences of the precise moment of their departure from Cuba (I. Exit); the first years in the United States and the violent clash with the other culture (II. Prehistory of Radicalization); it outlines the events that led these youngsters to become radicalized, evident with Vietnam and the Civil Rights movements in the United States (III. History of Radicalization); the importance of our Revolution for them from a realistic and critical position (IV. The Revolution); in addition to giving us an unrestrained image of an ironic poetry of exile reality: Imaginary travel of Eighth Street or the return to Miami and its eighty worlds (V. Exile).

The book's appendix, with its statistical tables, chronology of events, and political documents, presents more objectively the phenomenon it reveals.

"Contra viento y marea" reminds us of a cinematographic documentary; on the one hand, the editor gives us a technical view of events; on the other, the informant, as a counterpoint, with his testimony supports the truth of that theoretical vision (cinematographic technique of documentaries).

Although the book is emotional and honest, tender and

instructive, at times with a poetic slice of biting irony, it is above all an important political document of our times. The book merited the prize it received in the Casa de Las Américas contest of 1978, as example of the extraordinary strength of the youth of our America.[6]

Cubans on the island were surprised and elated to uncover a group of Cuban Americans within the exile community who dared to question their parents' position toward the Cuban government and their reasons for leaving the island. The same group also represented a dissenting voice with regard to U.S. foreign policy toward the Castro government.

Members of Areíto wanted to witness for themselves the legacy of the revolution, and they petitioned the Cuban government to allow them to return to the island. The idea was first discussed in a meeting at the Instituto de Estudios Cubanos in Gainesville in 1974 and proposed formally to the Cuban government in 1976.[7] In December 1977 a group of fifty-five Cuban Americans, many of them members of the Areíto group, were granted permission to return to Cuba. The brigade spent twenty-one days becoming familiar with an island that was once a part of their childhood. Named after one of Cuba's nineteenth-century heroes, Antonio Maceo, the Brigada Antonio Maceo, or the *maceítos*, as the participants were affectionately called, experienced firsthand the revolutionary process: they worked in construction, traveled to the interior of the island, and explored the island from one end to the other, visiting schools, hospitals, and cultural centers. In Havana and elsewhere, they met with political and cultural leaders, including Castro, and were treated with the fanfare afforded to high-level dignitaries. In addition, the *maceítos* spent time with relatives and friends whom they had not seen since emigrating to the United States.[8]

The Antonio Maceo Brigade visit became headline news in Cuba. The activities were covered on a daily basis by newspaper and television reporters and followed closely by everyone on the island. The trip was, however, viewed with mixed feelings in the United States. Jesús Díaz and his film crew from the Instituto Cubano de Artes e Industrias Cinematográficos, Cuba's film organization, traveled with the members of the brigade and recorded their experiences in a documentary entitled *Cincuenta y cinco hermanos* (Fifty-five brothers and sisters) (1977). Like the brigade and *Contra viento y marea*, the documentary received much coverage in Cuba. Baró reviewed the film in his article "Sobrevivientes" for the Cuban magazine *Bohemia*, September 22, 1978, and the review was reproduced in *Areíto:*

> The victims of one of the most infamous campaigns against our nation—among the many of them—that of the "patria potestas," go

solemn with floral offerings to pay homage to the fallen in the criminal attack of Barbados, one of the most barbarous attacks, among
thousands, carried out by counterrevolutionaries against our country.

Using direct language, "Fifty-five Brothers and Sisters," the
cinematographic report by Jesús Díaz, captures the first visit to
Cuba by members of the Antonio Maceo Brigade, made up of
youngsters taken, while children, from Cuba to other lands, especially the United States.

Showing the most significant moments of the visit, such as
the meetings with leaders of the Revolution, with workers and
young technicians formed by the Revolution, Jesús Díaz develops
the two essential questions related to the visit: the explanation of
the lives of these youngsters in the interior of the monster, subjected to the violence of the capitalist system, their alienation and
rejection, as they are considered as an inferior race, their radicalization due to events such as the Vietnam War or the Civil Rights
Movement in the U.S.A., their conservation of the firm sentiment
of their nationality among many avatars (pure survivors); and the
reception, the understanding demonstrated by the people who
received them as one of their own almost twenty years after their
departure. These are the people who have aroused the admiration
and respect of the entire world and who show with pride their
accomplishments, above all the new man which it has been forg-
ing in twenty years of struggle and internationalism.

In full color the images gathered show the dazzling reunion
and the scenery, the nostalgic visit to the houses where they lived,
the neighborhoods, the strong family embraces, the total integration with workers in their voluntary work, their critical questions, doubts and, above all, burning desire to stay in their homeland. The counterpoint is also offered, the need for reflection and
analysis that that step represents, answers given, likewise, by the
young naval technician and leaders of the Revolution.

And upon their departure, they leave rejuvenated, committed
not to interrupt the new relationship, ready to fight to return in a
not too distant future, hopeful, because they don't march alone,
through lost roads: They are standing on the road which they will
be hard pressed to abandon.[9]

The visit of the Brigada Antonio Maceo to Cuba was not without personal risk to the participants. The activities of some of its members led to
violent clashes with those of the more reactionary and violent exile
groups.[10] Nevertheless, the *maceítos* helped to establish communication

between the Castro government and the more moderate members of the exile community. Nine months after the brigade's visit, Castro invited representatives of a broad sector of Cuban Americans and held a dialogue in Havana between them and members of his government. The success of these talks led to the government's decision to set the groundwork for the release of political prisoners and the reunification of the Cuban family. The time appeared to be ripe for such a risky undertaking. Castro had celebrated the First Congress of the Communist Party in 1975 and Jimmy Carter's presidency departed from that of previous administrations, offering a more open approach toward Cuba and Latin America.

In an article "Fidel Castro: invitación al diálogo" (Fidel Castro: Invitation to a Dialogue), Lourdes Casal describes the two major issues discussed in Havana: the release of political prisoners and the reunification of the Cuban family. The problem of political prisoners was divided into two main categories: the amnesty of political prisoners and the departure from the island of those prisoners who desired to leave.

The family issue comprised six parts: (1) Remedying two situations in order to reunite nuclear families: those who live in the United States and want to return to Cuba and those who live in Cuba and want to leave the island. (2) Family visits in both directions. (3) Permanent return of senior citizens to the island. (4) Other permanent returns. (5) Mailing of packages to families. (6) Monetary help and other assistance, which includes the visits of émigrés in general. According to Casal's summary, and evident in Castro's September 6 speech, Castro agreed to continue a series of conversations with representatives of the Cuban American community, excluding the leaders of counterrevolutionary factions.[11] It was clear that both groups had much to gain. On the one hand, the Cuban American community would travel to the island, visit and help relatives, and press for the release of political prisoners; on the other, the Cuban government would gain the hard currency the economy desperately needed, improve its public image among the exile community, and eventually influence public opinion and U.S. foreign policy. After the collapse of the Soviet Union, the Castro government has depended more than ever on Cuban Americans, and the hard currency they take or send to the island, to keep the economy afloat. However, the reunification of the family has created inequalities among Cuban nationals. Those with relatives abroad who returned to the island or sent money and goods have profited from their relations and have joined a new privileged class.

The success of the first contingent of the Brigada Antonio Maceo led to others, also formed by the sons and daughters of Cuban exiles. Many of the Cuban Americans who traveled to the island during the late seventies and eighties were enthusiastic about returning to the island they once knew. They seized the opportunity to visit with family members they had not seen in more than twenty years. But the enthusiasm wore off. Although the *maceítos* were shown the best that Cuba had to offer, including the health and educational accomplishments under Castro, family members and friends talked about the difficulties of life on the island that a short visit would otherwise not have uncovered. More important, some of the government supporters and administrators with whom the Cuban Americans established relationships during their visits began to seek exile. And once outside of the island, they painted a different picture of the revolution and their own complicity with the government. As time elapsed, a significant number of these early pioneers became disillusioned with the policies of the Castro government. Although the United States was responsible for Cuba's economic and political problems, so were Castro's failed policies. The problems in culture were already evident in 1961, with the censorship of Sabá Cabrera Infante and Orlando Jiménez Leal's *P.M.*, a short film about the nightlife of Afro-Cubans; the government officials accused the film of being counterrevolutionary. It was most obvious with the closing of *Lunes de Revolución*, the magazine edited by Guillermo Cabrera Infante. The act constituted a direct blow against Carlos Franqui, the editor of the newspaper *Revolución*, and supporters of the July 26 Movement. The problems continued with the closing of the private publishing house El Puente, whose members were accused of aestheticism and homosexuality, many sent to concentration camps known as Military Unit of Aid to Production (UMAP). They were also present in the events surrounding Heberto Padilla's controversial book of poems *Fuera del juego* (Outside of the Game) in 1968, his subsequent imprisonment, and his staged confession in 1971.[12]

The result of Castro's economic and social policies became particularly evident in 1980, with the failure of the announced 10-million-ton sugar harvest and events pertaining to the takeover of the Peruvian Embassy and to the opening up of the port of Mariel. The last two occurrences underscored a strong division among Cubans living on the island. Opponents of Castro's government cast a negative vote and left the island in large numbers. The exiles had a strong impact on those witnessing the events and their experiences would be recorded by Cuban American writers. Very few really fathomed the magnitude of the Cuban resistance to the Castro government. The more than 125,000 Cubans who departed showed those who had believed in the success of Castro's programs that in many respects the policies had failed, their lack of success particularly evident in the high number of young Cubans wanting to leave. It was easier to explain the emigration of older Cubans, who were reared under the capitalist system the Batista dictatorship represented. But many were surprised by the departure of those for whom the revolution had triumphed. The youth had become a symbol of the new Cuba.[13]

During this period Cuban writers also sought political exile. Some were known dissenters, like Padilla, but others appeared to be supporters of Castro's policies. As contributing editor to the "Hispanic Caribbean Section" of the Library of Congress's *Handbook of Latin American Studies* (1982), I referred to the defection of intellectuals as the most significant event of the biennium:

> The defection of six of Cuba's most important writers is the most significant event in recent years. Heberto Padilla (March 1980), Reinaldo Arenas (May 1980) and José Triana (December 1980) were granted exit visas by Cuban authorities. Antonio Benítez Rojo (May 1980) and César Leante (September 1981) sought political asylum while en route to conferences in Europe. That Leante and Benítez Rojo sought exile was most startling since they had no known political problems and held high level positions in the Ministry of Culture and Casa de las Américas, respectively. To this group, one must add Edmundo Desnoes, who has been in the U.S. since Sept. 1979. Unlike the others, however, Desnoes retains permission to stay from the Cuban Ministry of Culture. That dissatisfied writers are allowed to leave marks a significant departure from Cuban policy. The desperation of those who have left without permission has also become evident.[14]

Those who stayed to live in the United States would contribute to the tradition of Cuban writings abroad. Since I wrote that introductory paragraph to my review of fiction and nonfiction works, other Cuban intellectuals have abandoned the revolution, including one of its ardent supporters, Jesús Díaz.

The dissenting position of the younger Cuban Americans who once hailed the revolution should not be confused with that of their parents or other anticommunist and unconditional supporters of the U.S. embargo of the island. Unlike their parents, the sons and daughters of these Cuban Americans were influenced by events that had gained strength and popularity in the decade of the sixties, in particular the movements associated with the Vietnam War, women's liberation, and civil rights, which questioned to varying degrees the policies of the U.S. government and the nuances of North American culture. Although their current position may resemble those of their elders, the younger generation arrived at it from a totally different perspective.

Certainly, the Areíto group made important contributions to establishing a dialogue between Cubans living on the island and the mainland and to publicizing the Cuban American experience in the United States. A good number of Cuban Americans who supported Areíto went on to become leaders in their chosen professions. The members of Areíto as well as other younger Cuban Americans, regardless of their political orientation, either born or raised and educated in the United States, form part of an intermediate generation Rubén Rumbaut refers to as "1.5" which he defines as follows:

> Children who were born abroad but are being educated and come of age in the United States form what may be called the "1.5" (one-and-a-half) generation. These refugee youth must cope with two crisis-producing and identity-defining transitions: (1) adolescence and the task of managing the transition from childhood to adulthood, and (2) acculturation and the task of managing the transition from one sociocultural environment to another. The "first" generation of their parents, who are fully part of the "old" world, face only the latter; the "second" generation of children now being born and reared in the United States, who as such become fully part of the "new" world, will need to confront only the former. But members of the "1.5" generation form a distinctive cohort in that in many ways they are marginal to both the old and the new worlds, and are fully part of neither of them.[15]

Rumbaut is a member of the generation he studies and so is Gustavo Pérez Firmat, whose *Life on the Hyphen: The Cuban-American Way* (1994) is the most significant analysis of Cuban American culture and literature in the United States to concentrate on the contemporary period and the Miami experience. Although Rumbaut considers Cuban Americans as marginal to both worlds and belonging to neither one, Pérez Firmat looks at his peers from the opposite point of view: he argues that the same generation belongs to both sides of the Cuban American hyphen. That the members of Areíto attempted to define a Cuban American identity within the U.S. cultural environment supports this perspective.

Cuban Americans have made notable contributions to many facets of life in the United States, before and after the revolution, most evident in business, politics, music, art, sports, and scholarship. Outstanding individuals include Desi Arnaz, Xavier Cugat, Gloria Estefan, Bob Vila, José Canseco, and Oscar Hijuelos. Likewise, mambo and salsa are household words. Such influences are explored in *Life on the Hyphen:* Pérez Firmat begins his chronology during the decade of the thirties, when Desi Arnaz's celebrity made him the first Cuban American cultural symbol.

In *Life on the Hyphen,* Pérez Firmat proposes that Cuban American culture is shaped by forces he calls *traditional* and *translational.* The second one he associates with *traduttore* and *traditore* (translator and traitor), saluting Guillermo Cabrera Infante's allusional wordplay in his *Tres tristes tigres* (1967; *Three Trapped Tigers*, 1971). Pérez Firmat also relies on concepts he had already developed in *The Cuban Condition: Translation and Identity in Modern Cuban Literature* (1989), where Cuban culture and identity are viewed as transcultural and translational, developing concepts expressed by Fernando Ortiz's *Contrapunteo Cubano del tabaco y el azúcar* (1940; *Cuban Counterpoint: Tobacco and Sugar*, 1947).[16] With the new study, Pérez Firmat suggests that these ideas can also be applied to the Cuban American experience. For him, tradition and translation also mean bicultural. These concepts are expressed in terms of others, which include the "Desi Chain" (Desi as the initiator) and the "1.5" generation.

Pérez Firmat studies Cuban American images popular before the Castro takeover and from that moment to the present. For him, the *I Love Lucy* show is a notable contribution. Pérez Firmat walks the reader through what he regards to be important episodes of the television series *I Love Lucy*, which allow him to consider intercharacter dynamics and stage sets and to understand the workings of the show, but which also give insight into Desi Arnaz's character, Ricky Ricardo, as a hyphenated Cuban American. He also studies Desi Arnaz's memoirs, *A Book* (1976), and his contributions as an entertainer, not just merely as Lucille Ball's husband. Pérez Firmat completes his study of Arnaz by looking at the full-length films that prepared him for the role of Ricky Ricardo and others that attempted to ride on the popularity of the television show.

Pérez Firmat also reviews the history of the mambo, which had Cuban origins but gained recognition within the context of the Cuban American experience. He traces the mambo from its origins as a religious dance to its development into a secular dance, relying on the works of Fernando Ortiz and on articles published by the popular Cuban magazine *Bohemia*. The mambo went from Arcaño's "danzón de nuevo ritmo" to Pérez Prado's modifications with his North American type orchestra, and his recording of "Qué rico el mambo," which topped the pop charts and sold more than 600,000 copies. Pérez Firmat is correct in describing Pérez Prado as the greatest promotor of the mambo, but he was not the only one. Others considered kings include Machito (Frank Grillo) and the Puerto Rican Tito Puente.

In the contemporary period, he focuses on Latin music played in Miami as well as the unique blend of Cuban and pop music characteristic of that city. He considers various groups and their lyrics, paying particular attention to Hansel y Raúl, Willie Chirino, and the Miami Sound Machine. The first band typifies the traditional Miami sound, entrenched in the old Cuban values; the second is a mixture of Cuban and pop music; and the third moves back and forth between the two cultures. Like her counterparts, Gloria Estefan looks to the past but, unlike them, she is not tied to it.

For Pérez Firmat, Cuban American literature is represented by Oscar Hijuelos and José Kozer. With regard to Hijuelos's *Our House in the Last World* (1984) and *The Mambo Kings Play Songs of Love* (1989) Pérez Firmat considers the first novel autobiographical because the protagonist is forced to reject Spanish and accept North American culture. The second is a picaresque but also a way for the author to come to terms with the Cuban past. According to Pérez Firmat, it is written "'from' Cuba but 'toward' the United States."[17] Pérez Firmat considers Kozer the most important Cuban American poet. Kozer does not mention the United States in his works; he prefers to write about Cuba in a language that is not Cuban, one already contaminated by his exile condition. "His poems mingle idioms and vocabulary from all over the Spanish-speaking world."[18] As a reflection of his own condition, Kozer brings together elements that have their own unique context.

Each of Pérez Firmat's chapters is interspersed with brief notations he calls "mambos," a meditation on some personal aspect of the author's interaction with Miami's Cuban American culture. The "mambos" recall Cabrera Infante's vignettes in *Vista del amanecer en el trópico* (1974; *View of Dawn in the Tropics*, 1978) and they impart Pérez Firmat the writer and, with the last mambo, the poet. Like the Cuban master writer, Pérez Firmat is also known for his puns, of which there is no lack in his book.

With *Life on the Hyphen*, Pérez Firmat walks with success the "thin" (hyphenated) line between the Cuban and North American cultural divide and convincingly shows that there is a truly Cuban American culture. Younger Cuban Americans, like those of Pérez Firmat's generation, became "1.5" because when their parents arrived in the United States, they kept alive a Cuban way of life, which they planned to revert to upon their return to the island in what they thought would be the not-too-distant future. This feeling is captured by the title of Pérez Firmat's autobiography, *Next Year in Cuba: A Cuban Emigre's Coming of Age in America* (1995).[19] Furthermore, the Cuban migration took place in the decade of the sixties, when African Americans, Puerto Rican Americans, Chicanos, and Native Americans became proud of and vocal about expressing their own cultural identity. Members of the "1.5" generation who, under different historical circumstances, would have assimilated into the North American society, found meaning and identity in their parent's Hispanic culture. In some respects, Cuban Americans profited from the political and cultural ground gained by other "minority groups."

Contemporary Cuban American culture is not limited to the Miami experience. Many Cubans live in Miami, and there is a distinct Cuban American Miami culture. However, that culture does not translate to the experiences of Cuban Americans living in other parts of the United States, especially if we consider the experiences of Areíto members who made

New York City their home. Moreover, salsa played by Cuban Americans such as Rey Barreto is closer to the sounds produced by Puerto Rican musicians from New York than to Chirino's music.

Life on the Hyphen is not only a book about Cuban American culture; it also exemplifies the same tradition it studies. As well as writing about a generation that joins together the Cuba, of the past, and the United States, of the present, the author also addresses music, film, narrative, poetry, and his own writings. He does so in a language that is familiar to Pérez Firmat the critic and writer, one sprinkled with Spanish. Like Julio Marzán's *The Spanish American Roots of William Carlos Williams* (1994), Pérez Firmat's *Life on the Hyphen* is a very personal book that brings together the scholar and writer searching for his own space: "By recovering a long-standing tradition of Cuban American cultural achievement, I am looking for a way to make sense of my life as a Cuban American man in the post-Castro era, a time when I will no longer be able to rely on the structures of thought and feeling that I have used for three decades."[20]

Like Pérez Firmat, other Cuban American writers are searching for a space from which to write. This space is different from the one used by their Cuban exile counterparts educated in Cuba, even though the exiles, such as Arenas, Benítez Rojo, and Padilla, in the United States, also write from a perspective distinct from those who remained on the island, such as Miguel Barnet and Nancy Morejón, in Cuba. The Cuban American writers attempt to mediate between their parents' past in Cuba and the present culture of the United States.

Life on the Hyphen discusses the coherence of Cuban American culture. Cuban American magazines played an important role in giving a voice to this new generation of writers. *Areíto* was one of the first magazines in the United States to publish the works of Cuban Americans, and other Cuban American publications like *Linden Lane Magazine* (1980–), *Término* (1982–), *Unvailing Cuba* (1982–), and *Mariel* (1983–) soon followed. The most recent contribution to this list of publications is *Apuntes postmodernos: Una revista cubana de crítica: cultural, social, política, de las artes (A Cuban/American Review of Culture, Society, Politics, the Arts)*, edited by José A. Solís Silva. Other Hispanic American or Latino periodicals such as *Chiriquí, Américas Review,* and *Bilingual Review/Revista Bilingüe* also found it meaningful to publicize this sector of the Hispanic population living in the United States.

II

In 1988 another member of the "1.5" generation, Carolina Hospital, published *Cuban American Writers: Los Atrevidos* (1988), an anthology of poetry and prose works of members of the "1.5" generation of Cuban Americans who write in English. Some live in Miami but the vast majority reside in English-speaking communities. Although Hospital does not include the works of José Kozer and Octavio Armand, the two best Cuban American poets, she does give publicity to other writers who deserve to be recognized and whose works reflect generational concerns. Hospital characterizes the writers she anthologizes as follows:

> All of the writers in the anthology were born in Cuba; however, all left the island at a young age, some as young as 2 years old. Consequently, they have had to develop their talents within two cultural and linguistic worlds: a private one and a public one. Six of the writers live in very different areas of the United States: Wichita, Kansas; Buffalo, New York; Chapel Hill, North Carolina; Martinsburg, West Virginia; Alhambra, California and Tallahassee, Florida. Four live in New Jersey and two live in Miami. They are obviously dispersed, but what brings these writers together as a group is their willingness to go out on a limb and take risks linguistically and structurally, thus creatively.[21]

The dispersal to which Hospital alludes may be due to the writers' employment as professors at various colleges and universities thoughout the United States. Nevertheless, the works of Cuban American writers can be depicted as occupying a space in which the two cultures converge. Hospital adds:

> Even though we can point to specific cultural legacies, in reality all of these writers are affected by a mosaic of cultural traditions, as well as an underlying exile consciousness. The sense of severance and rupture, provoked by this exile consciousness, manifests itself at structural, rather than thematic, levels. The personas in the poems or the novels are trapped either by physical limitations in the environment or by their own inabilities to reconcile with their sense of alienation. Conflicts arise at all dimensions: linguistic, cultural and ideological. Oppositions predominate in the texts and it is from these tensions that emerges a daring creativity.[22]

I would like to look at a few of the works contained in Hospital's anthology, poems of writers who have chosen to express themselves in English.

Ricardo Pau-Llosa's poetry represents the tensions with which Cuban Americans live. Even though he has accepted his destiny in the United States, Cuba continues to be a haunting memory. His exile condition is revealed in tropes like dreams, the past, mirrors, and betrayal. Some of these images are gathered in "The Beauty of Treason," a composition that underscores an awareness of cultural readings, especially in a land where

different groups of people reside. In "The Beauty of Treason" images are
expressed in terms of the poet and the emperor, which allude to a historic
and literary tension between arms and letters, which Cervantes had already
written about in his masterwork *Don Quijote*.[23] The poem begins with the
certain death of a poet who, as a final act, wants to throw his poem, which
he considers of little importance, into the fire. The emperor misreads the
poet's intentions; he believes they are inspired by the future and love,
which the victim wanted to capture in words.

In the second stanza, the poet is moved by the emperor's words and
spares the text. We also learn that he is from another country, but has
adjusted well to his new environment:

> He had learned the music of the court
> and found it better than that of his own
> land, which he was now forgetting.[24]

In comparison to his previous life, the present one is more attractive. But
the past is also pleasant and to preserve his memory of it, the poet, like
Pau-Llosa, writes poetry. In so doing, he was "happy to confuse his dreams
for theirs."[25] The latter line suggests that from the poet's point of view,
there is a meeting ground between his dreams and those of the people of
the court. However, the poem ends with a startling revelation. The poet,
who was unable to completely extricate himself from the past, recorded it
in such detail that the emperor's army used the poem as a battle map in its
conquest of the poet's native land.

The poem divulges that there are at least two perspectives. One pertains to the poet, who writes and interprets events from his own "ambas-
sadorial" position. He sees much fruit in his adopted land, and is rapidly
forgetting his own. The other is that of the emperor; he doubts the poet's
loyalty and motivation, and he ultimately finds a utilitarian purpose in the
poem, which he uses in his conquest. Although the poem is self-sufficient
and outlives the poet, its interpretations serve two distinct purposes: for
the poet to recall the past and for the emperor to conquer other lands.

"The Beauty of Treason" raises a fundamental question: What kind of
treason did the poet commit? Was it abandoning his land of origin? This
interpretation can be substantiated because we are told that the poet
appreciated his new land more than his place of birth. Then, in spite of
his appreciation, is the treason associated with the act of remembrance;
that is, his inability to extricate completely the past from the present? In
this sense, treason, the reason for putting the poet to death, is associated
with the poet's desire to be true to himself. The act of betrayal is not of
his own making, but an interpretation that the emperor imposes on his
poem. According to the emperor, the poem is not an artistic composition;
it has a specific referent and use. The title of emperor indicates that he is

all-powerful and that only his interpretation, whether right or wrong, is allowed to exist.

My reading of the poem is at best problematic. We are told that the poet found life in the court much better than that of his homeland—which he was rapidly forgetting—because he had lived most of his life in a foreign land. In fact, he was happy to confuse his dreams for theirs. What is not clear is if his dreams refer to the past, which was less attractive in comparison to the present, or to the future. Was the poet's fledging memory capable of capturing with exactness the past, or do the dreams insinuate a different time and space? Likewise, are the dreams of those who live in the court of the past or of the future?

Because we have no reference to the past of the court, the poet's dreams may not be of the past of his country of origin, but of his future in the court. If this is so, the poet was not necessarily writing about his homeland, but rather about his dreams of the future of his adopted land. It now makes sense to me that it would be logical for the poet's dreams to be confused with those who live in the court. The poet had forgotten about his past and was writing about his adopted land. Whether there were more similarities than differences between his homeland and adopted country, is not as important as the emperor's inability to forget that the poet is a foreigner who cannot, regardless of the amount of time spent in the court or of his loyalty to the throne, be assimilated into the new country. If the poet is able to forget his past, the emperor cannot. From the emperor's perspective, the poet had to be a traitor. His poem could not be a metaphorical representation of reality, but a precise reconstruction of the enemy's land. The treason is not committed by the poet, who is true to his feelings, but by the emperor, who welcomed the poet only to mistrust and betray him at a later date. The poem points out similarities between the poet's homeland and the adopted country, making it easier for him to assimilate into the new culture and for the emperor to conquer the poet's native land. Because the poem presents at least two points of view, either the poet or the emperor could be considered to have committed treason.

Pau-Llosa's concern about life in North American society is repeated in "Terraces," which describes a recent stage in man's alienation in a postmodern society. The poetic voice outlines a typical morning in the life of a person living in a condominium, where everyone is compartmentalized and anonymous:

> Anonymously, each a notch
> in a switchboard of bronze glass
> and balconies in order rising
> to scrape the baroque,
> semitropical atmospheres
> with Malthusian mortgages.[26]

The subject of alienation is further reinforced when the persona of the poem is identified by the pronoun *you* and by the parts of her body. She lives on the twelfth floor, neither the highest nor the lowest one. Her presence on the terrace incites others above and below her, including the poetic voice, to go out on their terraces to observe her. She and her "admireres" are described in terms of blossoming flowers. This is particularly so with the persona of the poem, who is compared to an orchid of tropical America:

> your violet and darker violet
> caftan sailing up from you
> as you water your *Cattleyas* and *Oncidiums*,[27]

Regardless of what each resident may be doing or the reason for being on the terrace, they all reach unanimity when looking up at a passing plane. It is with the plane that the anonymity of the people in the poem acquires another meaning. They are products of a postmodern era, but are not content to be numbers, a cubicle on the terrace; they want to break from the pact, even if it means wishing others harm. The gazers hope for an airplane disaster so that they may be witnesses on the evening news:

> our faces on the evening news
> shattered with grief like the jet's
> windows, blossoming on TV sets
> the way we do on these terraces
> in clear sight of which the plane
> moves on and away,
> its smoke trails blazing into swans
> that will never nest on our cool floors.[28]

The poem ends reaffirming the theme of isolation, indicated by the distant plane. The anonymity continues; the plane did not blow up, thus denying the gazers an opportunity to be famous. The final lines of the poem suggest that within the society in which the poet lives, grief, or any other emotion, is associated not with the event that produces it, but with a mask one wears to elicit the desired outcome, in this case to break with isolation. Anonymous people profit from the grief of others.

The description of the woman and all the other condominium occupants as blossoming flowers on the terraces brings to mind various relationships. The blossoming is associated with the morning sun and the water that orchids receive, but it also applies to the connection between the people and their condos: the terraces represent their lifelines; that is, what gives them purpose and existence. Being indoors is associated with inactivity, sleeping, or death; and the terrace with the outdoors and life.

Pau-Llosa pairs the same word with the desired airplane tragedy. Just as the morning sun gives the anonymous people life so will the witnesses blossom on television from other people's tragedy.

Pau-Llosas's terrace refers to life in the United States, but the terrace is also described as a balcony, which may also be an allusion to the Spanish *balcón*, common in Caribbean homes, particularly Cuba. Unlike their North American counterparts, however, Cuban homes with balconies are not very high and the inhabitants of these buildings do not live in anonymity, nor do they face overwhelming mortgages. For the most part, they know and speak to their neighbors. There is no need for grief or profit from someone else's misfortune. The connection between life and culture on the island and that on the continent is further accentuated by the types of orchids seen on the terraces, which are also typical of Cuba. The anonymity of life on the terrace gains meaning when compared to the Cuban balcony and life on the island prior to the poet's exile.

Pau-Llosa's life has been affected by his exile condition, which to some degree has become an obsession. Although the past is important to his contemporaries, not all poets give it the same value and interpretation. Similarly, an individual poet may emphasize the issue more in some poems than in others. Pau-Llosa's position regarding his past and present is even more evident in "Exile," where the images of birds recall two different moments in his life. "Exile" draws a distinction between "these birds" and "those other birds." The first one refers to his present situation, where metaphorical birds fly in circles, without any direction, in a gray sky devoid of color and meaning. The second applies to his youth, the birds of the past described as vibrant, joyful, singing, and flying in lines; that is, in some specific direction. "Those other birds" signify the essence of life: "Each bird was a heart in the great / green heart of the tree."[29] The past is viewed with harmony created by the use of the pronoun *we* and the song of the thousands of birds.

Pau-Llosa concludes the poem with "Then we would have made the hours pure / with the hand, the kiss, the word."[30] The poem alludes to a lost paradise, where there was harmony not only between man and nature, but also between man and woman, man and poetry. In contrast, the harmony of the past is absent in the present location, where "these birds" fly. In spite of the poet's affirmation, it is not the nostalgic past or the lost paradise, but the infernal present that leads the poet to fill a void with the act of writing and composing "Exile." Whereas the past is viewed as creating a relationship between man and poetry, it is the present space that allows the poetry to become a reality. The past meant the absence of writing; the present creates a need to write about the past.

Like Pau-Llosa, Pablo Medina is also haunted by the past. Medina composes a poem entitled "The Exile," in which the persona of the poem, as in

Pau-Llosa's "Exile," journeys to an earlier time. The poetic voice travels to his place of origin, to an unkept house, with tall grass, silence because of the absence of people or dogs, and a moment where time is meaningless. The return could be a physical one in which the poet revisits the island; more likely than not, though, it takes place in his mind, the recollections of forgotten times expressed throught the images of the untended grass and the unkept house.

In the second stanza, the poetic voice's return is associated with memories brought back by the physical surroundings: the trees, the sugarcane fields, the smokehouse. In the third stanza a voice from the river speaks to the subject: "Will you be with me?" Although the subject does not answer, he clearly desires a communion with the voice, nature, and the past.

A communion with the past is not possible. In the fourth stanza, the subject picks up stones and throws them down the well. Although the subject may have performed this mechanical act in the past, in the present it acquires a different meaning. The stones represent the past and are described as "smelling of time." Throwing them down the well signifies the loss of that time, the inability to smell them anymore, because the rocks will never be recovered. In addition, once the rocks hit the well water they produce a different sound, distinct and in direct contrast with the one emanating from the river, asking the subject to return to the past. One sound is natural: it comes from the river; the other is not: it comes from a manmade well and is produced by man himself. In effect, the sound of the rocks falling in the well is meant to drown out the voice coming from the river. Whereas the Wilkamayu in Pablo Neruda's *Alturas de Macchu Picchu* (1945; *The Heights of Macchu Picchu*, 1966) and the Mississippi in Nicolás Guillén's "Elegía a Emmett Till" are interrogated by the poets because they are witnesses of the past, Medina distances himself from a voice that desires a communion with him. The poem ends with the following stanza:

> It made him smaller. He walked out the gate
> and closed it behind him, wiped the sweat from his
> eyes, felt his feet settling on the road.[31]

Here the subject realizes that the past must remain in the past. He must leave behind the physical space known to him; he closes the gate after he exits the property. However, this is not an easy decision for the subject, for the sweat from his eyes is really tears, caused by his desire to return to the past and the impossibility of doing so. Nevertheless, he is certain of his course of action, as he has his feet squarely planted on the road, one that will lead him in a different direction. The future direction is not important. What is clear is that he closes the gate behind him, thus coming to terms with his past. We should note that in order for the poetic voice to move forward, he must return to the past and confront it.

The obsession with exile seen in poems written by Pau-Llosa and Medina is further developed in the works of Elías Miguel Muñoz. Muñoz does not have a poem entitled "Exile," but he does inscribe in his poem "Returning" the same conditions experienced by Pau-Llosa and Medina. Like them, Muñoz situates his poem on the island and recalls the moment before exile. Although no one has said anything about a departure, the children have a positive impression of North America, represented by "And we all dreamed about apples / and mint-flavored chewing gum."[32] This perception may be due to the impact U.S. culture has had on Cubans from the time of the Spanish American War or of the Platt Amendment's incorporation in the Cuban Constitution of 1902, which gave the U.S. government the right to intervene in the island's internal affairs. Whereas some Cubans resented the North American presence on the island, Muñoz's children looked upon it favorably and were anxious to leave for the United States.

The rapidly approaching future is compared to the present or past. Culinary or cultural symbols, represented by rice and beans, the staple of the Cuban diet, are rejected for something else. But rice and black beans also have a racial connotation. Whereas *moros y cristianos* suggests a blending of the white rice and the black beans, the black beans and rice of which Muñoz writes are, under normal circumstances, placed separately on the plate. Unlike Puerto-Rican Americans who write about their solidarity with African Americans and show pride in their racial background, Muñoz of the past separates the white from the black.

The absence of eternal summer, dirt streets, and sugarcane is associated with "we would no longer have dark skin," of a past, or origin and backwardness, of *quimbumbia* and *yuca*, words derived from African and Amerindian languages, and mud puddles. What is not clear is if the children are preparing themselves for a racial condition they will encounter in the United States or if they are responding to the racial circumstances on the island in which African traditions are essential elements of Cuban culture. The race question is further alluded to in the final stanza, in which the "we" want to forget the "conga player's outfit." The conga drums are a typical Cuban instrument; they originated in Africa and are used in Afro-Cuban religion and culture brought to Cuba during slavery. The outfit may refer to the colorful shirts with puffed-up sleeves, typical of the rumba and mambo periods.

From the present, the future is expressed in the conditional tense, which indicates that the past will be erased:

> So we could sing, later,
> to a different beat.

So we could forget your
conga player's outfit.
So we could chew away
until we had no teeth.
So we could speak of the things
we lost,
things we never had.
So that later,
under the Northern skies,
we could begin to dream
about returning.[33]

The chewing gum and the act of chewing until you have no more teeth refer to a type of freedom in North American culture, even if it is harmful to the individual. But of interest are the last four lines of the poem, which convey a process in which the exile rejects the past in order to accept the future. This is evident if dreams refer to aspirations. Another interpretation, just as evident as the first one, is of dreaming about returning to the past, regardless of what that past actually represented during the moment in which one lived it. The poem alludes to a possible circumstance, proposed by the conditional, in which the poet finds himself in the United States but is also contemplating a return.

If the poem represents the return, its content is the rejection or distancing of the native in order to accept the foreign, followed by the same rejection seen in the home country but now applied to the adopted one, and concludes with the dream to return; this is to say that departing and returning are part of a hermetic process with repetitions and no end. The poet was already an exile before he actually became one. Equally important, if the speaker is in Cuba thinking about the United States and he anticipates that in the United States he will be thinking about Cuba, then he is not content wherever he finds himself; neither in Cuba nor in the United States.

It is also possible to read the title and the poem as the poetic voice's return to the mother country. Therefore the children contemplate returning (or going) to the United States, followed by a dream of returning to Cuba. This analysis allows us to understand why the poetic voice is familiar with North American culture and why he uses it as a point of comparison from which to read his experiences upon his return to the past. As a child, the poetic voice draws on analogies between the home and host countries known to the adult, which he had attributed to his own past. Unlike Medina's subject, who has his feet planted on the ground, Muñoz desires to be where he is not. In essence the poem contains the tension the exile experiences, one that distances the individual from but also returns the individual to the place of origin. For Muñoz, the exile experiences a life of real and imaginary displacements.

Among Cuban American writers, Pérez Firmat adds another dimension to the themes of exile and displacement, one that brings his work closer to those of Puerto Rican American poets. If Nuyorican writers such as Tato Laviera and Miguel Piñero no longer look to Puerto Rico as a paradise from which they were ejected, but consider the New York environment as their home, Judith Ortiz Cofer does the same with Atlanta, and Pérez Firmat adheres to the same tradition. In *Life on the Hyphen,* he posits not Cuba, but Miami as an origin that has been lost and to which he desires to return, if not physically then symbolically. This is the case with his poem "Chapel Hill," which features a geographic location he considers artificial and unnatural to his state of being. Here he holds his breath until he is "Carolina blue," figuratively submerged until holidays, when he returns to Miami for air.

Pérez Firmat combines the anger noted in the works of Felipe Luciano and the linguistic concerns of Laviera. In "Bilingual Blues," he views living simultaneously in Cuban and North American cultures a contradiction of sorts, and he expresses the dilemma in emotional terms. Using the Cuban culinary term *ajiaco,* known to Fernando Ortiz, Pérez Firmat writes:

> Soy un ajiaco de contradicciones
> I have mixed feelings about everything.
> Name your tema, I'll hedge:
> name your cerca, I'll straddle it
> like a cubano.[34]

According to Pérez Firmat, the Cuban American way is to straddle the fence. Living on the hyphen can be contradictory, debilitating, and even paralyzing; it also offers flexibility. As the first stanza explains, Pérez Firmat's contradictions allow him to state, but also reverse, his position. In the second stanza, he inverts the first two lines of the first stanza, thus balancing the other side of the hyphen, or of the Cuban American divide: "I have mixed feelings about everything. / Soy un ajiaco de contradicciones." The line that conveys his contradictions is repeated a third time, but it is embedded in the structure of the poem.

The defiance, frustration, and anger against the established norms, also present in the works of Luciano, is evident in

> You say tomato,
> I say tu madre;
> You say potato,
> I say Pototo.[35]

While making reference to a famous Broadway song, it is evident that Pérez Firmat's sense of living contradictions allows him to view reality from a different perspective. He does not follow in the footsteps of the majority, those who say "tomato" and "potato." Rather, he is willing to defy the majority. He frames this idea in cultural terms and prefers to say "tu madre" and "Pototo," the stage name of a well-known Cuban comedian. Within Hispanic culture, mentioning someone's mother in a derogatory manner is enough to provoke a fight. The mother is sacred; she represents an origin that must be preserved and protected. Yet at the same time origin and home are transitory and not defined by any particular geographic location, whether they be in Cuba or even Miami. Home, in the poem, is defined in sexual terms by the *hueco* (the hole) and the *cosa* (the thing) and by the communion with the other: "and if the cosa goes into the hueco, / consider yourself at home."[36] Sexual intercourse is a return to a physical and metaphorical origin, a concept Octavio Paz had addressed in his *Libertad bajo palabra*. The communion is with the other and not with a geographic location that creates origin; it gives life to the self and provides a family.

As a hodgepodge or mixture of things, Pérez Firmat is not sure whether he should express himself in Spanish or English, and so uses both languages to convey his inevitable "bilingual blues." Pérez Firmat's linguistic immobility recalls similar concerns expressed by Laviera, particularly in "My Graduation Speech." In a language familiar to Pérez Firmat, Laviera says:

> tengo las venas aculturadas
> escribo en spanlish
> abraham in español
> abraham in english
> tato in spanish
> "taro" in english
> tonto in both languages[37]

Laviera's acculturated veins is equivalent to Pérez Firmat's *ajiaco*. Laviera ends his poem in the following manner:

> hablo lo inglés matao
> hablo lo español matao
> no sé leer ninguno bien
> so it is, spanglish to matao
> what i digo
> > ¡ay, virgen, yo no sé hablar![38]

Although it is obvious that Laviera can compose poems in standard Spanish and English, his "My Graduation Speech" conveys that learning does not necessarily take place in school. Rather, schools are insensitive to the needs of Latinos with bilingual skills. More likely than not, learning takes place outside the classroom, as we have seen in Víctor Hernández Cruz's "Three Days/out of Franklin."

Both Laviera and Pérez Firmat end their poems in standard Spanish, suggesting that the Hispanic identity is still important and alive in their works. But in the second-to-last line of his poem, Pérez Firmat claims "que nadie nunca acoplará" (that there is no coming together). However, this denial, when viewed in light of his often successful blending of two worlds, can also be considered one of his many contradictions.

In Laviera and Pérez Firmat's poems, the two languages and cultures they represent collapse, mix, fuse, and emerge as a combination of the two. There is no negation or questioning of one culture over the other, to determine which is dominant and which is recessive, but an affirmation of the two. Both Spanish and English languages and cultures occupy the same time and space. Laviera and Pérez Firmat are on the verge of creating a new culture and language, not one that negates the native for the foreign, but one that combines Spanish and English, communicating their Latino reality within the North American context.

III

The female poets represented in Hospital's anthology belong to the same generation as Pau-Llosa, Medina, Muñoz, and Pérez Firmat. They have also suffered from the exile conditions and isolation their male counterparts write about, but without the same obsession that ties the male poets to the past. As a group, their poems show a willingness to put the past aside and start anew. In Berta Sánchez-Bello's "Thanksgiving," she looks back not to the past of Cuba, but to a period after she left the island. Thanksgiving is a time to reflect, to contemplate the present as well as the past. The poetic voice's "sedated" condition allows her to recall five events "in cinematographic / capsulized vignettes": a country setting in April, an old woman looking for spiritual salvation, water from a hotel sink in Madrid, wet pumps on a rainy day, and a Christmas tree in an attic in Jersey City.

Two locations are discernible in the images: Madrid and Jersey City. The other incidents are not located in any specific settings and could refer to places in the United States, Spain, or even Cuba. Within the context of the exile experience, Madrid may be a temporary stop on a journey of exile from her native Cuban countryside to New Jersey, the final destiny. With this in mind, it would not be unreasonable to read the vignettes as unfolding in a chronological order; that is, the two prior to her arrival in Madrid may refer to an earlier time in Cuba, which the poet has difficulty placing. Therefore, the poem describes a journey from Cuba, to Madrid, to New Jersey.

The physical journey coincides with a temporal one that includes April and November, spring and fall. But there is also another time, represented by the Christmas tree in the attic, that could refer to summer, because there is no need for a Christmas tree during the summer months, or to the coming holidays, as she thinks of the tree soon to be decorated. The Christmas tree also alludes to the holidays and winter. In any case, the poetic voice accepts the North American traditions, the celebration of Thanksgiving and the decoration of a Christmas tree, as part of her own.

In the second, and last, stanza, the poetic voice returns to the present and reaffirms her isolation in the following lines:

> Sitting on the couch
> totally incapable of writing
> a preamble to my own death:
> nobody would read it and besides
> it would ramble.[39]

The last stanza is also another vignette and takes place after she arrives in New Jersey and contemplates the Christmas tree in the attic. It should be read alongside the other vignettes. Death is a reference to the loneliness during a Thanksgiving afternoon, in which one should be in the company of friends and family, but the multitudes also cause isolation and metaphorical death. The rambling alludes to writing or thinking in a more or less concise and acceptable manner, represented by the cinematographic vignettes. The incapacity to write can be associated with the "sedated" state in which the poet finds herself. Death should not necessarily be read as a termination of life as we know it but as closure of a particular stage— as we have seen with the geographic displacements already undertaken by the poetic voice—and the beginning of another one. In addition, death can refer to a coming to terms with the past, as represented by the sequence of vignettes, to a conclusion of a search and an acceptance of the present. One vignette leads to another and all point to the poetic voice's transition up to the present.

In "Elizabeth, New Jersey," Sánchez-Bello develops the theme of the last one (or two) vignettes and captures a snapshot of her new environment, which she describes with love and affection. Unlike her male counterparts, it is Elizabeth, New Jersey, and not Havana or Cuba that has become part of her past. Whereas Medina, Pau-Llosa, and Muñoz must return to the past in order to come to terms with it, the women poets have already adapted to their new environment: "This, my beautiful city / remains the same."[40] Like Judith Ortiz Cofer's acceptance of Atlanta, Sánchez-Bello embraces the city of Elizabeth that she has grown to love, one with a permanence and distinctiveness regardless of the amount of time transpired. But unlike Ortiz Cofer's Atlanta, Elizabeth is origin.

Beauty is found not in an idyllic recollection but in one full of opposition: a pregnant blond, a would-be prostitute, and the five happy but unlucky bums, recovering perhaps from a hangover. The women shop, whereas the men have no where to go. However, what appears to be the bums' happiness is undermined by the inevitable consequences of their actions, for the bench they are on is located in a graveyard. The description of a fourteen-year-old Adenis (a symbolic Adonis?) jumping the tracks is followed by that of an ancient woman located on the third floor. In this latter comparison, we see temporal as well as spatial differences, referring to the different generations and perspectives.

Until the end the poem does not reveal any signs of Sánchez-Bello's Hispanic culture, and the poem could have been written by any North American poet who has lived in New Jersey. Only in the last three lines does the poet mention Cuban Americans and this, not as the center of the poem, but as part of the scenery the poet has been enumerating:

> At la Palmita
> The Cuban workermen
> never stop dreaming or swearing.[41]

In Sánchez-Bello's mind, Cubans are synonymous with eating (at la Palmita), working hard, dreaming of the past they left behind and always carry with them, and swearing. The poet clearly states that it is the "workermen" who never stop dreaming or swearing, and it is perhaps possible to see with the specific reference to men that these are important characteristics of the Cuban male exile culture. Contrary to their male counterparts, women have been able to reconcile their exile past and condition, with less difficulty than their male counterparts. The men are a fixture in the poem and the city. The poetic voice is mobile; she has left Elizabeth and has returned for a visit or to live.

The change in life that distances the female poets from the past is best expressed by Hospital's "Dear Tía." In a poem written as a letter, the poetic voice explains to her aunt in Cuba why she no longer writes to her. The years have indeed separated her from the past, which is present only in the given name the poetic voice and her aunt share, and a black and white photograph of her aunt's youth. The two sources of remembrance have been reduced to a singular memory.

> The pain comes not from nostalgia
> I do not miss your voice urging me in play,

your smile,
or your pride when others called you my mother.
I cannot close my eyes and feel your soft skin;
listen to your laughter;
smell the sweetness of your bath.
I write because I cannot remember at all.[42]

Cuba and the past at one time represented origin because the aunt was mistaken for her mother or she was like a mother to her. It is now a memory that cannot be recalled. In spite of having the name and photograph of her aunt, the only recollection is about another one that reminds her of the past that has been forgotten. The poet has lost the sensation of the past and is left with either fabricating a memory or searching elsewhere for inspiration.

Hospital's "Dear Tía" recalls Gertrudis Gómez de Avellaneda's "Al partir," and the nineteenth-century poem helps us to understand the one written one century later. In Gómez de Avellaneda's poem, the speaker is sad as she says farewell to her birthplace, Cuba, an island described as a pearl and a star, two precious items found in two extreme locations. As when Hospital was a child, Gómez de Avellaneda is leaving against her will, taken away from her childhood, childhood memories, and paradise, and launched into the outside world by a sailboat, which takes her to Spain. However, Gómez de Avellaneda is writing about Cuba at the moment of departure, and the island's name will always bring her comfort and happiness, whereas Hospital writes much farther away in time and space to her aunt, who is now a distant memory, a single black-and-white photograph, metonym of the past.

The poetic voice experiences pain, but the pain does not derive from the nostalgia for the past, in which the aunt had attained the status of the speaker's mother. Rather, the pain is caused by not experiencing the pain of remembering or forgetting. It comes from an absence of memory: "I write because I cannot remember at all." This last line suggests that the act of writing is a means of remembering the past, not as origin, because she cannot recall it, but as a (re)creation of it. The absence produces a necessity to fill it and thus launches the poetic voice into writing, into an activity to fill a void that cannot be filled. Gómez de Avellaneda's poem allows us to understand that Hospital's Tía is also a representation of Cuba; no longer the mother country, but a distant and forgotten aunt.

Sánchez-Bello's emphasis on the present and Hospital's inability to recollect a past that must be invented indicate that poets such as Pau-Llosa, Medina, and Muñoz are hostages of a memory they cannot extricate from their lives. In addition, their poems suggest that the same memory is not a reconstruction of the past but an invention fabricated in the present. This invention, according to Sánchez-Bello, is an integral part of the male exile experience. For Hospital, the act of writing preserves something that has disappeared and can no longer be recalled. Accepting the present implies forgetting the past; likewise, forgetting the past is a way of coming to terms with and accepting the present condition in the new environment.

The women's contribution to the development of a Cuban American voice is most evident in their emphasis on the present and not the past. They treat the same past with a certain indifference caused by the present. For the female poets, the present is a privileged space in which they accept North American culture. Like the Puerto Rican American women poets, such as Sandra María Esteves and Luz María Umpierre, who question the male dominant Hispanic culture, the Cuban American women writers find in the United States a freedom that allows them to explore their own sensuality and sexuality.

Members of the Areíto group drew upon the social and political movements in the United States to question U.S. policy toward Cuba and their parents' reaction to the Castro government. Similarly, the women poets have relied on the women's movement to undermine the traditional role of women in Hispanic society and their parents' cultural values. In fact, like North American women, Cuban American women poets challenge and rewrite the traditional role of Hispanic women within the Hispanic and North American contexts, using an abundance of sexual images and metaphors.

The title of Mercedes Limón's "Arrival," within the context of the Cuban American experience, may refer to the presence of an immigrant in a new land. But thematically the poem does not follow the same path Cuban American male poets would have developed. Limón's poem unfolds in a different direction and is transformed into a sexual and orgasmic act. It is not she but the other who arrives first:

> You arrive
> swallowing me whole
> squeezing my silence
> rising to my mouth.[43]

The *You* arrives to where the poetic voice is or resides. But the arrival touches upon the sensuality associated with a *plaisir,* and focuses on *jouissance,* the sexual act, which the poet describes as a welcomed aggression with images such as "swallowing," "squeezing," "savagery," and "claws."[44]

The arrival is a holistic experience, described in binary opposition of love and hate, creáte and kill. The *I* of the poetic voice and the *You* she encounters become one. The lines "You arrive / bound to matter / wrapped in your I," could be a manifestation of the other's ego. But the signifier *I* is a physical representation of an erect phallus, described by the line, of "stone and sling."[45] The *I* of the other, as subject pronoun and signifier, leads to the emergence and affirmation of the poetic voice. It is as if the male *I* brings to life the female *I*. That is, if the poem started with *You* it ends with total emphasis of and concentration on the pronoun *I*:

> I naked
> skin burning
> coarse and affectionate object
> travel through your whims
> through your biting edge
> and explode
> in the midst of furious panting
> hate
> and a violent and clammy
> sweat.[46]

The mention of *You arrive* four times in the poem is balanced or offset by the presence of a singular poetic voice, in her affirmation "I naked." The male signifier *I* is taken and reappropriated by the female, and redefined as her *I*. The male penetration is counterbalanced by the "I naked" who "travel through your whims / through your biting edge." In this poem, Limón is not interested only in the pleasures of the *You*. She concentrates on those of the *I*, followed to an explosive climax. Toward the end of the poem she too "arrives." It is not the man's but the woman's fluid that is present, first as "a sensual flood" and then culminating in "sweat."

In "Your Picture" Limón, contrary to the approach she takes in "Arrival," does provide the reader with a description of the poetic voice's partner as he appears now, which is different from the way he was before. At one time in the past he was an entity, a whole person. In the present he is not an individual but part of the whole. The fragmentation is present in the title and could be a reference to an actual photograph. Because it can only be reproduced in two dimensions, the picture offers a limited perspective of the subject. More likely than not, the description is also a subjective interpretation motivated by past and present experiences.

If love existed in the past, it is absent in the present. Rather than conjure up affection, the present invokes fear. The welcomed aggression and "sweat" in "Arrival" has been turned into brutality and "A fierce sweat runs down my back." Sexual intercourse is interpreted as pain, violence, and sacrifice—"You again crucified onto my loins"—perhaps caused by an altered state, "a proud pillpopping setback,"[47] which has changed dramatically the character of the person she once knew.

In spite of the change, the poetic voice still recognizes the same features that used to attract her: (vanishing) words and his physique, enhanced by his tan skin and an opened shirt that reveals part of his body. The difference between now and before is the poetic voice's current understanding of the shallowness of the person in the picture. Toward the end, the poem provides insight into the reason the person in the picture is hated. The mention of the physical is followed by violence:

> You have smeared your skin at every instant
> with a trail of vanished words
> with an open chested-body
> and a heart torn out
> in a numb grimace
> that once was a smile
> a taste of mint
> a violent abortion
> now hunger
> wounded word
> that never was poetry[48]

The reader encounters linguistic, but also conceptual, violence when trying to make sense of the last lines, beginning with the torn heart that could be associated with the person who has the "open chested-body." One reading is that either he or someone else tore his heart out; that is, hurt him and made him incapable of love. He once smiled but now has a numb grimace, indicating that the love was insincere, a deception the poetic voice now unmasks and rejects. However, it is possible that the torn heart is not his but that of another person he has dislodged and wears as a trophy also smeared on his skin. The latter interpretation gains currency when it is considered that the person is unmasked and that there is no reason for him to open his chest and pour his heart out unless it is a sign of sincerity. But the previous time—"that once was a smile / a taste of mint"—is also associated with "a violent abortion," which takes us back to a present time of "Now you are fear" and the last three lines of the stanza. The poem suggests that the abortion may have been metaphorical but also real and the origin of violence, the turning point of understanding the mixed metaphor of the real person in the picture who produced an absence, of hunger, in her. The picture and not the living person reveals the actual characteristics of the person who inflicted violence.

It is difficult to ascertain the identity of the person to whom the violence has been directed. If in "Arrival" we have the emergence of the poetic *I*, in "Your Picture" the same *I* has been suppressed and could therefore refer to someone else. But the *I* is implicitly present as the object of the violence, and the suppression of the pronoun should also be interpreted as part of the same violence that has erased or interred the identity of the *I*. It is this violence that leads to a denial of poetry itself.

Limón's poem "Now" contains elements from "Arrival" and "Your Picture." The poem refers to a picture of the other and the urgency of the present, described by the word *now*, both elements of "Your Picture." Imagery involving sweat also appears, as in "Arrival" and "Your Picture." In "Now," sweat is described on the face of the subject of the poem in a way similar to as if the face were captured by a photograph. Perhaps one poem alludes to the other; the same image is continued, and the "sunburnt skin" recalls "you wear the sun like makeup on your cheeks" of "Your Picture." In "Now," the subject is a worker, someone who "hacks out roads" with a "sickle and scythe." Although the sickle may be a reference to one of the symbols on the flag of the Soviet Union, it more appropriately refers to a worker, with

> onto the calloused heel
> that moves
> through the jungle.[49]

Like the first two poems, this poem can be given a sexual interpretation. The person who "hacks out roads" is also a "fleshcarver." I do not mean to say that the persona of the poem is a murderer or a cannibal, but rather someone who carves flesh by penetrating it. The worker is persistent and sweats profusely, starting at the face and descending down his thighs, foot, and calloused heel, moving through the jungle. Although one can read the "aged sweat" that "runs on the cracks of his face" as being the same as "the crude sweat / the rough sweat,"[50] it is also possible that they are different. The latter images may refer to a similar hard-working condition but this time associated with the genital area that produces the "sweat" that runs down his thighs. The title of the poem insists on the present and an act that produces the crude and rough sweat and *now* runs down his thigh. The sweat pertains to the past and the present; it is aged and it is fresh.

Sexual metaphors are also present in Iraida Iturralde's poems. "Elephant Ride" recalls a form of entertainment found in any amusement park, in which the poetic voice conveys to the reader the emotions associated with riding an animal whose walk causes the rider to sway back and forth. But the poem also alludes to the ride as a sexual experience with a large man, as conveyed by the elephant's trunk. "Up and open the legs spread dauntingly," referring to the mounting of the elephant, is also a preparation for engaging in sex. And the "—One thump, and yet another—" imitating the elephant walk, is the sound two bodies make during intercourse. Being on top of the elephant produces a pleasurable sensation, but so does the sex act, as the poetic voice situates herself in the upright position: "The arms sprawl writhing at each movement: / A gothic human concert,"[51] a reference to supreme ecstasy.

The male and female organs are both present: The phallic is revealed in

> The bodies tumble, tear through the curtain
> And then fall silently agape. One sagging muscle
> Is lured to erection, hugging warmly
> The sensuous summit: the erotic snapshot
> Of a tusk enclaved.[52]

The vulva is mentioned in relation to the trunk, another reference to the phallic:

> Nudging gently on
> The trunk, lest they should miss the ride
> Through the cherry-scented garden
> The nest where hedonists are fed, nipple-baiting
> To reap laurels, making up
> For time unspent.[53]

The ride, as expected, produces a climax, followed by the completion of intercourse: "The elephant pours out its mystic's soul / On their dismount." The rider has been brought to her climax which is described in the short, but brief second stanza:

> Psst. The ride is over.
> One thump. Another.
> Careful. I'm still wet.
> Don't make a splash.[54]

This stanza reveals the pleasantness of the ride, and the desire to remain in that state and ride again. But the poetic voice has to be awoken from ecstacy and brought back to reality. Similar to Limón's "Arrival," the communion with the other allows the poetic *I* to reveal itself. Limón's "I naked" is equivalent to Iturralde's "I'm still wet."

IV

There are two other anthologies of Cuban American poetry worth studying, *Poetas cubanos en Nueva York* (1988) and *Poetas cubanas en Nueva York/Cuban Women Poets in New York* (1991) both edited by Felipe Lázaro. In these two works Lázaro pays homage to New York, a city where Cubans continue to live and write; his portrayal of New York differs in the two anthologies. *Poetas cubanos en Nueva York* traces a tradition of Cuban exile poets who were deeply influenced by the northern metropolis, a tradition that began in the nineteenth century with José María Heredia's "Niágara" and José Martí's "Amor de ciudad grande," as I have indicated with the epigraph, and chronicles.

Lázaro resumes the chronology in the twentieth century with Eugenio Florit's "Los poetas solos de Manhattan" and after 1959 with works written in New York and Cuba by such poets as Reinaldo Arenas and Jorge Valls. As well as including these and other Cuban-born and -educated poets, Lázaro also incorporates those raised and educated in the United States, younger writers like Rafael Bordao, Alina Galliano, and Isabel Parera. The themes of the anthology vary widely and include poems that pertain to New York City, such as Antonio Giraudier's "Horarios de Nueva York" and Reinaldo García Ramos's "Por fin hacia Columbus Circle." Others, like those in Hospital's anthology, refer to exile. Representative are José Corrales's "Exiliado," in which the poetic voice experiences a fall and an uncertain future; Antonio Giraudier's "La Habana," in which the Cuban capital is viewed with nostalgia; Valls's "Yo quiero irme para mi casa, hijo," which describes the progressive loss of home, husband, and son that produces the mother's loneliness; and Alina Galliano's interconnected poems that affirm the impossibility of escaping from an island and question whether one can really return. Lázaro also includes a sample of José Kozer's work, who is without a doubt one of the leading poets living outside of Cuba.[55] But Lázaro's anthology also proceeds in the direction taken by Hospital's. A few of the poets underscore the coming together of Cuban and Anglo-American cultures. For instance, Walter de las Casas's "To Bob Fosse" is written in English, and José Corrales's "Exilio casi veinte años" and Emilio M. Mozo's "Love Is Not Enough" both contain a line in English. Like Hospital's anthology, Lázaro's includes a representative number of female poets. His anthology differs from Hospital's in that it was not compiled for a North American audience but rather to let the Hispanic-speaking reader in Spain and other countries know that there are Cuban poets in the United States writing in Spanish.

Unlike in his *Poetas cubanos en Nueva York* or even his *Poetas cubanos en España*, each of which gathers the works of Cuban poets in locations where they have congregated, in *Poetas cubanas en Nueva York/Cuban Women Poets in New York* Lázaro was influenced by criteria present in North American culture for his selection of writers and works. Certainly the existence of an anthology devoted exclusively to female poets is itself testimony to the strength of the women's movement in obtaining attention and recognition previously denied women as a group. But Lázaro could have compiled an anthology of female poets that, like his *Poetas cubanos en Nueva York*, traces the tradition of female writers to the nineteenth century and included well-known writers such as Gertrudis Gómez de Avellaneda and the Condesa de Merlín. He also could have edited a study of female poets born and educated on the island and now living in the United States, including poets like Belkis Cuza Malé. However, in *Poetas cubanas en Nueva York*, Lázaro accepts current trends and influences in criticism and pays close attention to the voice of Cuban American female poets raised and educated in the United States. Unlike his previous work, which included female poets of an earlier generation, such as Inés del Castillo, Arminda Valdés Ginebra, and Isel Rivero, he gathers younger ones like Magali Alabau, Alina Galliano, Lourdes Gil, Maya Islas, and Iraida Iturralde, though he excludes one of the youngest of the group, Isabel Parera. Lázaro presents their works in a bilingual anthology targeted at a readership that is Hispanic, but also proficient in English, and, most important, is North American. This brief anthology, as indicated in the book's subtitle, introduces the works of five poets born in Cuba but raised in the United States who continue to preserve their Spanish language and Cuban culture.

Poetas cubanas en Nueva York appeared four years after *Cuban American Writers*. Of the women writers gathered in Hospital's anthology, Lázaro includes Iraida Iturralde and Lourdes Gil, and he adds three others, Magali Alabau, Alina Galliano, and Maya Islas, which also belong to the same generation Hospital addresses. Though Lázaro's anthology is bilingual, the poets have chosen to write in a standard Spanish known to Spanish American writers, and all except for one have translated their works into English. The Spanish in this anthology is consistent with the other two Lázaro edited and with those of Spanish American poets writing for a Spanish-speaking audience. The English translation is also consistent with that of the works in Hospital's anthology. However, the title of Lázaro's anthology denies them what Pérez Firmat would call a hyphenated experience. Like *Poetas cubanos en Nueva York*, in *Poetas cubanas en Nueva York*, Lázaro chooses the preposition *en* and not *de* (in and not of), to suggests that above all they are Cubans living in New York and not Cuban Americans who belong to the same city.

The poems gathered in *Poetas cubanas en Nueva York* range widely from Iturralde's "From Your Eye to the Nest," which contains a swan, a symbol of Rubén Darío's *modernismo* movement, to Islas's "Text Based on a Painting by Ruth Hardinger," "Text Based on a Painting by Rudolf Stussi," and "Poetic Text Based on a Painting by Jesús Desangles," which attempt to reproduce in one medium what appears in another; and her "Havana 1" and "Havana 2," which could have been composed by someone writing from the island. In fact, as a prosopopoeia "Havana 1" recalls the same trope used in Nicolás Guillén's *El gran zoo* (1967). As was noted in the previous section with regard to the female poets, Islas's poems, which refer to Cuba and the past, are devoid of the nostalgia associated with the male poets of Hospital's and Lázaro's anthologies. I agree with Perla Ronzencvaig's introduction, which underscores the impact the exile experience has had on these female poets.[56] Whereas the male poets are obsessed with their exile condition, the female poets do not show any desire to underscore the past; Cuba per se is a vague memory. The past is revisited, but to uncover and understand events that have become meaningful in the present. I would like to look more closely at some of the works of the poets included in Lázaro's anthology but not in Hospital's collection. Whereas in Hospital's "Dear Tía," the poetic voice cannot recall the past or can only summon up a memory about a memory that used to exist, Magali Alabau writes, in an untitled poem:

> Cuba is a trunk bound with straps,
> full of the forbidden
> A box I don't open
> because from it, one by one, emerge
> evils.[57]

By situating Cuba in the past, Alabau is able to focus on her family and express an intimacy that includes sexual relations between her parents and her and her sister's own awakening. But even here the present is emphasized over the past. Throughout the poem, the island is portrayed as synonymous with destruction:

> My sister's toys
> were a dwarf and a broken island.
> Moving around the deserted island, the deaf mute
> episode.

And later: "The island is being eroded from the center."[58] Alabau is careful not to let external time, perhaps associated with the image of the island, affect her own particular time and space, represented by "this night":

> Banned from the outside world
> we shelter under the mosquito net and despite the smothering,
> the failing air, I'll sing to you your song.
> Outside the mosquito net there is the sun,
> says the song.
> Outside the mosquito net there is the sun
> and the forbidden garden.
> Inside, the large ugly monsters
> born of night and the cramped space.

Outside is not ours. What we see
when we stretch out our arms and sigh, runs away.
You and I are inside. We can touch each other.
We can sleep. Watch the insects attack.
We stroke the small night of a flimsy net.
Outside the sun is running away,
no matter how loud we sing, it goes running away.
Sister, let us accept this night.
Let us imagine a boat in this space, the sea,
an unbroken island.[59]

The mosquito net represents innocence, imagination, and the comfort of the womb; outside the net is the real world of pain and suffering.

There is no question that Alabau relies on past images to capture a moment of tenderness. Similarly, there should be no doubt that for her the island has been destroyed or no longer exists as it used to be or as it does for Medina, Pau-Llosa, and Muñoz. The island, for her, has been redefined and consists of much more than the past and, most important, it contains the present.

The sexual images associated with the discovery of the other and the self, noted in the works of the female poets discussed in Hospital's anthology, are also present in the works of other writers in Lazaro's anthology, as I indicated in Alabau's poem. In "Homage to the Virgins," Islas places women in a privileged space. She elevates them to the status of virgins, in the religious and biological sense of the word. In so doing, she negates her individuality not because of the presence of a man, but because she is part of a larger sphere, the universe of women. There is common ground in sisterhood: she and other women are different from men; they have in common their virginity. She writes

I belong to the universe
with my white uterus
containing a door
kept by an angel and his glance.
No one enters.[60]

The uterus is objectified and becomes an empowered space that holds the mysteries of pleasure and birth.

The purity of the "white uterus" is described as a door, guarded by an angel, perhaps an allusion to the angel guarding the door to Dante's paradise. Yet there is certainly a relationship between Islas's door and Dante's. Each possesses a secret. And after the completion of his journey, Dante will be rewarded with his Beatriz. In Islas's poem, only a special *he* is allowed to enter, perhaps a Moses figure, who will descend from the mountain and explain to others the miracle he has witnessed. But the *he* in the poem is multiple. It also can refer to a child, as the miracle of birth takes place, and, more appropriately, to he who has participated in the pleasure of the divine and shares his experiences with the world. But his neighbors will not understand because they have not participated in the same miracle he has.

Galliano consistently refers to the other in her poems. In each poem included in Lázaro's anthology, Galliano describes the relationship between the speaker and the other, in which the other is not always a male. The other, who is a means to an end of fulfillment, does not always have to be physically present, but is there for her own use. In "VIII" she writes:

> You crawl
> my throat
> caterpillar
> for the dream
> of my back;
> I don't know you
> nevertheless
> I invent
> your scent,
> I create you
> almost better
> than anyone;
> I keep you
> in the cabinets,
> under the table,
> by the window sill,
> in the fingernails,
> transforming
> the patterns
> of your face,
> I dissolve you
> while hiding myself
> away from you
> between the crystal
> and the voice
> in case
> I ever need you.[61]

Galliano's poem suggests at least two or three separate but interrelated interpretations. In the first, the *you* is a real person with whom the poetic voice has an intimate relationship. However, she is not totally satisfied with this individual and transforms him into someone he is not, someone who can meet her sexual needs. In the second interpretation, the *you* could be an individual but is more likely to be an object or an individual treated as an object. The poetic voice describes how she keeps the *you* in the cabinets or in other locations, ready for her use. It is also possible that there is no person or object present and that the poem is a fantasy of the poetic voice's imagination. The reader's inability to clearly identify the other indicates that the *you* is not really important. The focus of the poem is the *I* and her needs. Regardless of whether the *you* exists or not, there is no doubt that the poetic voice relies on her imagination to create or invent a situation that will be the most pleasurable to her. This observation suggests her needs cannot be satisfied in the real world, only in her imagination. The poem further illustrates that the poetic voice's psychological needs are more important than her physical ones.

If in "VIII" the *you* is undefined; in "XIV" the *you* is a woman to whom the poetic voice speaks in the third person. At the outset of the poem the poetic voice indicates that she is moved by the other's voice, described as "her shattered / mirrored voice."[62] The shattered mirror refers to the sharpness of the tone and words, which may damage, but also to their reflexive properties, in which the poet can recognize parts of herself or a fragmented image of her self.

The other's voice produces a reaction:

> I vanish
> into the night
> searching for words,[63]

launching the poetic voice into a quest for the other in the night, but also within the self. The other is a part of the poetic voice that cannot be extricated from the self:

> for I still
> preserve her fragance [*sic*]
> crawling within
> my fingers,
> fabricating textures
> for my mouth,[64]

The fragrance is a trace of the other's presence, and the fingers and mouth are the instruments of love that unite the two. The relationship is not one-sided, but mutual, because the other also seizes the poetic voice's flesh into her memory. Just as the speaker feels that she is affected by the other, she also believes that the other is influenced by her, for she is concerned about being engraved in the other's memory.

The equality between the two women is conveyed in terms of how each is affected by the other. This type of relationship is different from the one often developed between a man and a women, in which one is superior and the other subordinate. The identity and symmetry between the women expresses the desire to be recorded in the other's memory, but also with the open communication that exists:

> seeking for my embrace
> within that place
> in which life
> can resemble her eyes,
> where I know that
> I may dialogue
> with her kiss.[65]

The relationship described in "XIV" appears to be one of mutual consent and benefit for each of the two women, indicated in the visual communication, embraces, and kisses. But this relationship also recalls the one described in "VIII," not because this one may now suggest an affair between two women, but because the one under discussion also exists in the imagination. Although the poem alludes to a relationship that was real, it is now a part of the imagination. Hearing the shattered voice stimulates the speaker's recollection of the other and her belief that the other feels the same way as she does. But the relationship takes place in the memory:

> in that place
> where sometimes
> I perceive her,
> saturated
> by shadows,
> unfolding love
> behind the gesture.[66]

Puerto Rican American and Cuban American male poets differ from the female poets: whereas the men refer to their socioeconomic and migratory experiences, the women write about these themes but also express their innermost emotions. Living and writing in the United States has given female writers the freedom to distance themselves from and question the culture of their parents. In so doing they evolve as individuals without limitations other than those imposed by the language they use to express themselves. Poetry affords them the opportunity to look inward and write about their most sacred thoughts, a practice previously prohibited by a tradition that did not recognize their needs. The feelings with which they are in tune include their relationships with the other, allowing them to explore their own sexuality. And if the Nuyorican poets use a colloquial speech to reflect their socioeconomic and political condition, poets like Julio Marzán and Ortiz Cofer, who write in a standard language, come closest to their Cuban American counterparts. Their poetic images are expressed in the language of mainstream North American society.

FIVE

Master Codes of Cuban American Culture
Oscar Hijuelos's
The Mambo Kings Play Songs of Love
and Cristina García's
Dreaming in Cuban

Doing the last Lucy-Desi Comedy Hour was not easy. We knew it was the last time we would be Lucy and Ricky. As fate would have it, the very last scene in that story called for a long clinch and a kiss-and-make-up ending. As we got to it, we looked at each other, embraced and kissed. This was not just an ordinary kiss for a scene in a show. It was a kiss that would wrap up twenty years of love and friendship, triumphs and failures, ecstasy and sex, jealousy and regrets, heartbreaks and laughter . . . and tears. The only thing we were not able to hide was the tears.
After the kiss we just stood there looking at each other and licking the salt. Then Lucy said, "You're supposed to say 'cut.'" "I know. Cut, goddamn it!" I Love Lucy was never just a title.
—Desi Arnaz, *A Book.*

I

MUSIC has been an integral part of the lives of Hispanics who, because of adverse economic or political conditions in their homelands, travel to and reside in the United States. As an artistic expression it embraces the sounds, gestures, language, beliefs, and poetry—in short, the cultural fiber of a people whether living in their native or adopted countries. For economic, social, cultural, racial, or political reasons, Hispanics residing abroad recreate an environment familiar to them, and music becomes a main pillar of immigrant life. Music is also a master code of their cultural experience abroad. It is a link with the homeland that reinforces cultural identity and slows or even redefines the immigrant's process of integration. But neither the immigrant's music nor the mother culture can be perpetuated in a vacuum. On the contrary, they interact with other forces present in the new locale.

The coming together of Latino Caribbean and Anglo-American people is a metaphorical dance between two cultures. For some, the dominant culture leads and the other follows; for others, the recessive one becomes assertive. However, both listen and dance to the same tune in the same geographic space. Although critics may argue about which culture has the greater impact at any given historical moment, there is no question that one affects the other and that neither remains the same.

Oscar Hijuelos's *The Mambo Kings Play Songs of Love* (1989) best represents the dance between two cultures in both its literal and metaphorical meanings. The novel highlights the lives of the Castillo brothers, who, responding to the historical circumstances under the Grau San Martín (1944–48) and Prío Socarás (1948–52) administrations, leave their family in Oriente to better their musical careers in Havana. The introduction of the "talkies" led to the disbandment of theater orchestras, sending musicians to look for jobs in the popular nightclubs. However, because such a large number of talented artists were applying for a few positions, many were forced to seek employment abroad. Like other musicians who left the countryside and went to Havana, the Castillo brothers did not stay in the capital city; in 1949 they abandoned the island and migrated to New York, another city with a strong tradition of Caribbean culture. In his work, Hijuelos traces the lives of the Castillo brothers and the history of the mambo, and documents the contribution many Puerto Rican and Cuban musicians made to the development of Latin or Latino music in the United States.

The Mambo Kings Play Songs of Love follows a long-standing Hispanic tradition of incorporating music into literature. In the contemporary period, Alejo Carpentier was the best-known writer to study music, as illustrated by his painstaking research of *La música en Cuba* (1946).[1] Carpentier also relied on his studies of music to write fiction. Helmy F. Giacoman was one of the first scholars to uncover the relationship between Beethoven's Symphony no. 3 and Carpentier's *El acoso* (1956; *Manhunt*, 1959).[2] Antonio Benítez Rojo has convincingly shown the importance of classical music for understanding the same author's *Guerra del tiempo* (1958; *War of Time*, 1970). He illustrates the presence of pieces from Bach's *Musical Offering*: Bach's "Canon perpetuus super thema regium" in "Camino de Santiago" (1958; "The Highroad of St. James," 1970); the modulating themes of "Canon per tonos" and six thematic stages in "Semejante a la noche" (1958; "Like the Night," 1970); and the progressive and regressive "Canon per motom contrarium," also known as "Canon cancrizans" (crab canon), in "Viaje a la semilla"[3] (1944; Journey Back to the Source," 1970).

Other recent writers have focused on Hispanic popular music and its unique blend of Caribbean influences. The Dominican Pedro Verges published *Solo cenizas hallarás (bolero)* (1980), a novel that mixes music with political, psychological, and cultural elements and offers many perspectives of life immediately after the Trujillo years.[4] The title contains the word *bolero*, referring to the first nineteenth-century vocal synthesis of Caribbean music to come to the attention of the world. The same musical form also became the central concern of the Cuban writer Lisandro Otero in his *Bolero* (1991)[5] and Hijuelos's songs of love.

The Puerto Rican novelist Luis Rafael Sánchez writes about contemporary music. His *La guaracha del Macho Camacho* (1980; *Macho Camacho's Beat,* 1984) refers to the twentieth-century musical arrangement that brings together Spanish and African elements and combines lead and choral sections.[6] The novel reproduces the song, but its structure also reflects the same composition as it alternates between the lead singer and chorus. Both Sánchez's and Hijuelos's works conclude with a copy of the lyrics of the songs their respective narrations underscore.

Sánchez's second novel continues the theme of music and literature. *La importancia de llamarse Daniel Santos* (1988) is a novelized biography of the popular Puerto Rican singer Daniel Santos.[7] His reputation is extensive, and his work touched all those who either saw him perform or heard his music throughout Latin America and the northeastern part of the United States. Sánchez reproduces many of Santos's popular boleros, known throughout the Hispanic world and sung by almost anyone who has been in love. Moreover, he shows that Santos and his music unite Hispanics in New York with those residing in their native countries. Hijuelos's character, Néstor, also composes a bolero, "Beautiful María of My Soul," in New York, which brings fame to him and his brother César.

The tradition of writing about music in Hispanic literature is continued in the United States by Oscar Hijuelos. In *The Mambo Kings Play Songs of Love,* he discusses the popularity of the bolero, but also that of the mambo, in the decade of the fifties in New York. As a jazz musician, Hijuelos played in and patronized the same nightclubs where the Castillo brothers of the novel perform.[8]

New York played an important role in the development and promotion of the mambo in the United States. The mambo became a craze on both the east and west coasts, and each region professed to have its own Mambo King. In the early part of the 1950s, Merced Gallego, who played in San Francisco, was known as the "King of the Mambo"; in New York, Tito Puente held the honor. Puente's one-hundredth record album, entitled *The Mambo King,* released in 1991, refers not only to an earlier time but also to Hijuelos's book and to the musician's own participation in the film version of the novel, also entitled *The Mambo Kings.* Dámaso Pérez Prado became the mambo's best-known practitioner, and he played to impressive crowds in California. He was received with less enthusiasm in New York, where his technique was seen as an uncomplicated contrast between brass and reeds. The demanding New York Hispanic audience preferred musicians like Tito Puente, Arscenio Rodríguez, Miguelito Valdés, and Frank Grillo (Machito), who developed a more creative mambo style.

When the fictional Castillo brothers arrive in New York, they profit from a Latin musical environment that dates to the turn of the century, when the music industry in the United States began to record and distribute Cuban music. RCA Victor launched its record industry by featuring the music of El Septeto Habanero among its first releases; and Columbia Records did the same with the Septeto Nacional of Ignacio Piñeiro. Cuban sounds were further promoted by such well-known figures as Don Aspiazú, who made popular Moisés Simóns's "El Manicero" (The peanut vendor), and Xavier Cugat, who composed the music for and appeared in many Hollywood movies of the period. But there were other important musicians such as Rodríguez, Machito, Puente, Valdés, and Chano Pozo, the most gifted conga musician to play, who made significant contributions to Dizzy Gillespie's music and his band. The mambo spread rapidly to many nightclubs and particularly to the Palladium Dance Hall, which became the center of New York mambo as well as home to other Latin musical arrangements.

Although the mambo originated in Cuba, it was not exclusively a Latin thing. Other ethnic groups were drawn to mambo rhythms and helped to promote Caribbean music in the United States. For example, Alfred Mendelsohn (known as Alfredo Méndez) rivaled many Latino bands in popularity. Latin musicians of any stature could get jobs playing in the Catskill resort hotels in summer, entertaining a North American clientele.[9] By 1954, the mambo was popular throughout the United States and the Mambo USA band of Noro Morales, Miguelito Valdés, and Mongo Santamaría, among others, toured the country and influenced mainstream popular music. That same year, Ruth Brown's "Mambo Baby" climbed to number one on the rhythm-and-blues chart. The Latinization of rhythm and blues and of jazz continued. Cuban trumpeter Chico O'Farrill played with Benny Goodman and arranged for Dizzy Gillespie. Like other Latino musicians, the Castillo brothers played in the Catskills and toured the United States.

The mambo was invented in Cuba and was transposed to the United States, where it was played not in the manner known to islanders but with a flavor common to other musical compositions popular in the new environment. In New York, the mambo developed a unique style. John Storm Roberts explains:

As we have seen, the music was originally Cuban, but New York musicians so built on the root form as to create a New York style. The same is true of the dance. Though it has been claimed with almost certain truth that the basic steps of what became the mambo were danced in Cuba years before the dance got its name, New York Latinos, and notably the young Latino Palladium crowd, built a dance out of the beat, flowing yet bustling basic patterns and a thousand lindy-based variations. A contemporary definition in *Down Beat*, "rumba with jitterbug," put it as well as any.[10]

Like the New York adaptation of the mambo, Hijuelos's novel reflects the lives of Cubans and other Hispanics in New York and underscores the mixture of both Hispanic and U.S. cultures.

Of the Latino Caribbean narratives discussed in this study, Hijuelos's novel has the most in common with contemporary Spanish American literature written in the vernacular. He was familiar with many well-known writers and had read Jorge Luis Borges, Julio Cortázar, Gabriel García Márquez, among others, while a student of Donald Barthelme at City College.[11] Hijuelos combines literature and music, but also begins his novel in a style familiar from the works of his Spanish American counterparts. At the outset of the novel, the reader encounters Eugenio and his alcoholic uncle, César Castillo—close to the end of his life—as another rerun of the "I Love Lucy" episode featuring the Castillo brothers has just begun. In this way Hijuelos underscores the present time of the narration and the protagonist's tragic destiny. At the end, the narration returns to the present as Eugenio visits Desi Arnaz in California.

The structure I have just outlined, which begins with the end, was already evident in Mario Vargas Llosas's novel *¿Quién mató a Palomino Molero?* (1986; *Who Killed Palomino Molero?* 1987), in which the author describes Molero's death and leaves the reader to explore the motive of the crime. This structure was made popular some years before, however, by García Márquez's *Crónica de una muerte anunciada* (1981; *Chronicle of a Death Foretold*, 1982); because everyone knows about Santiago Nasar's execution, everyone is a possible accomplice. In the absence of motive, the reader is invited to continue to explore what seems a horrible and possibly an unwarranted death.

Works like *¿Quién mató a Palomino Molero?*; *Crónica de una muerte anunciada*; and *The Mambo Kings Play Songs of Love* follow a narrative structure more closely associated with Carpentier's "Viaje a la semilla" and establish an intertext between the short story and the novels. Carpentier's story line begins in the present, but he narrates it backward; that is, it starts from the most recent event, proceeds to the earliest time, and con-

cludes with the present time of the narration. "Viaje a la semilla" begins
with an Afro-Cuban figure who waves his arms and, in an act of magic, sets
time marching backward. The deceased Marqués de Capellanías returns to
life; he is an old man, then is transformed into an adult, an adolescent, an
infant; finally he reenters the womb. The regressive narration is one that
will be adhered to more closely by Julia Álvarez in *How the Garcia Girls
Lost Their Accents* (1991) as we shall see in chapter 7. Carpentier's story,
therefore, offers two beginnings and two endings, the narrative and the
chronological ones.[12]

Like Carpentier's story, *The Mambo Kings Play Songs of Love* is a recollection of the past. Just as "Viaje a la semilla" begins with the Afro-
Cuban going over the remains of a house he knew so well, Hijuelos's narration is opened and closed by Eugenio. But it is the *I Love Lucy* rerun that
causes time to be altered. The show leads Eugenio to misread his uncle's
present condition, and César to remember the past. In the end—or in the
beginning—César is alone in the Hotel Splendour, drinking and listening to
records. Memory—a synthesis of past events—is renewed by continuous
reruns of César and Néstor's appearance on the *I Love Lucy* show and the
playing of their hit single, the two representations are the high point of the
Mambo Kings' career.

Of the contemporary Spanish American authors, Guillermo Cabrera
Infante is most visible in Hijuelos's work, not only because the Cuban
American writer may have read the Cuban exile author, but because both
describe similar aspects of Cuban life and culture in two different environments. Néstor and César's background and lives and the language used to
portray their experiences appear to recall those of the characters of Cabrera
Infante's *Tres tristes tigres* (1967; *Three Trapped Tigers,* 1971). Like the
mighty duo Silvestre and Arsenio Cué, Néstor and César were born and
raised in Oriente, the easternmost province of Cuba, a region known to
Cabrera Infante, who was born in Gibara. Oriente was also the home of
other Cuban notables, like Reinaldo Arenas and Desi Arnaz. As with César
and Néstor, Silvestre and Arsenio leave the countryside during approximately the same period and travel to Havana to improve their lives.
Silvestre is a journalist, Arsenio an actor. Although they frequent many
Havana clubs, it is Eribó, a bongo player who describes his frustrated relationship with the well-to-do Vivian Smith Corona, and Estrella, a singer
who is the protagonist in the section "Ella cantaba boleros" (She sang
boleros), who represent the musical interests of the period. The bolero,
again, is the preferred composition of many writers, and it will also acquire
meaning in Hijuelos's novel. *Three Trapped Tigers* not only has many references to music, but is written in the form of an evening performance at the
famed Tropicana Club, as the master of ceremonies in the introduction
suggests, of dance, humor, and music. Metaphorically speaking, Cuba is

one big nightclub, and each of the novel's sections appears to represent one of many acts in the "club."

Hijuelos departs from Cabrera Infante's work when Néstor and César leave Havana for New York. Though staged in New York, Hijuelos's novel continues a trend that was made popular by Cabrera Infantes's story but was already evident a century earlier in Cuba's national novel, Cirilo Villaverde's *Cecilia Valdés* (1882; 1935, 1962), and continued in James Joyce's *Ulysses*. Each author provides an archaeology of the city he narrates: Villaverde and Cabrera Infante of Havana and Hijuelos of New York. Hijuelos's descriptions of New York's nightlife are reminiscent of those in Cabrera Infante's work. One work provides a guided tour of the nightclubs in Havana, the other does the same in New York, taking the reader to the different boroughs and clubs where Latin music is played. Moreover, Cabrera Infante privileges the bolero in his work; Hijuelos too finds meaning in that composition, but also in the mambo.

Translations play an important part in both works. In *The Cuban Condition: Translation and Identity in Modern Cuban Literature* (1989), Gustavo Pérez Firmat argues that Cuban culture is translational, and he explores that theme in the works of Fernando Ortiz, Nicolás Guillén, Carlos Loveira, and Luis Felipe Rodríguez. It is the same theme he discusses in *Life on the Hyphen: The Cuban American Way* (1994).[13] Cabrera Infante refers to the issue of translation by alluding to the presence of North American culture in Cuba. Hijuelos does the same by considering Hispanic culture in the United States. Cabrera Infante provides the reader with two versions of Mr. and Mrs. Campbell's visit to Havana in the section entitled "The Visitors," in which the same story is told from the point of view of each of the Campbells. Toward the end of the narration, the reader discovers that both versions are derived from a story written by one person, William Campbell, a writer from Kentucky living in New Orleans and teaching at the University of Baton Rouge. Rine Leal has done a poor translation of Campbell's story, which the editor of *Carteles*, Guillermo Cabrera Infante, deems unpublishable and assigns Silvestre to correct.[14] However, the theme of translation is made more explicit by Silvestre's phrase *tradittori* (derived from *traduttore* and *traditore*—translator and traitor—suggesting that translations betray the original whether it be from one medium or from one language to another, as we shall see later.

Cabrera Infante continues to be a model for Hijuelos, especially when he writes about the relationship between men and women in *Three Trapped Tigers*, but he is more explicit in his descriptions of the opposite sex in his *La Habana para un Infante difunto* (1979; *Infante's Inferno*, 1984), a semiautobiographical account of sexual awakening. In this novelized autobiography, Cabrera Infante describes with great detail and enjoyment the different stages of his protagonist's encounters with women, from his sexual initiation by Julieta to his passionate relationship with Margarita. The ending of *La Habana para un Infante difunto* also recalls Carpentier's "Viaje a la semilla," as the protagonist, who is in a movie house looking for romance, finds an interested partner, is transformed into Jonathan Swift's Lilliputian, or a phallus, and enters the woman's vagina, thus literally returning to the womb or the source.[15]

Like Cabrera Infante's work, Hijuelos's novel is also about sex and romance. His detailed descriptions of César Castillo's sexual encounters are spicy and at times walk a fine line between the erotic and the pornographic, into territory familiar to French critics such as Bataille and Barthes, but also to Spanish American narrators such as Manuel Puig and Reinaldo Arenas. But of course there are other interpretations of César's actions. Like the protagonists of *La Habana para un Infante difunto* and *La muerte de Artemio Cruz* (1962; *The Death of Artemio Cruz*, 1964), César is a Don Juan looking to have sex with as many women as he can. However, at the end of the novel the reader discovers that there is also a desire for a communion with his childhood and the women he knew during that stage of his life. For César, women are a barometer of his state of mind: when he is involved with many women, he feels successful; when involved with few, he feels dejected. Lydia Santos, the only woman who rejects him, is the great exception.

Hijuelos relies on Cabrera Infante's and Carpentier's stories, which end where everything begins, in the womb. César's final thoughts carry him back to his origin, to his childhood in Cuba, to his good and bad experiences with his parents, and above all, to a rediscovery of his love for his Cuban girlfriends:

> Floating on a sea of tender feelings, under a brilliant starlit night, he fell in love again: with Ana and Miriam and Veronica and Adriana and Graciela and Josefina and Virginia and Minerva and Marta and Alicia and Regina and Violeta and Pilar and Finas and Matilda and Jacinta and Irene and Yolanda and Carmencita. . . .[16]

These names may be a list of his early conquests. More important, they are associated with César's formative years and his origin, even though his thoughts return him to the present, to the dilapidated Hotel Splendour, and to the woman to whom he repeatedly made love in that room, Vanna Vane.

Although the sexual exploits of one character appear to recall that of the other, there are also important differences between the two works. Cabrera Infante uses wordplay and alliteration, a literary technique he associates with the sexual acts; Hijuelos concentrates on a language obsessed with tension, depression, and disappointment, undoubtedly reflecting his characters' lives.

Hijuelos's novel contains explicit descriptions of César's love affairs, but they are a small part of the narration. If Side A contains only one song about his sexual encounters, the entire Side B concerns his fragile state of mind; more than half the novel narrates Castillo's downfall and depression. César's numerous relationships with women can be viewed as a narrative technique that elevates the protagonist's stature, only to have him fall farther from grace, thus accentuating the idea of descent. Time is stagnant, and the instant, as a past event, is lived and relived, becoming a part of César's psyche and obsession. For both César and Néstor, depression is associated with their personal and professional failures, but also with their immigrant status.

Upon leaving the island, Néstor and César represent two types of immigrants in the United States. Néstor is the reluctant immigrant. He is tied to the past from which he cannot escape. He prefers to relive the memories left behind, those associated with his ex-girlfriend María, who abandoned him for her former lover. His mind and heart are not in the present with his wife Delorita, but back in Cuba with María, as his song "Beautiful María of My Soul" suggests. Unlike his brother, César breaks with the past and looks forward, to the challenges of the future. César detaches himself from the life he knew and embraces the North American way of living. For him, Vanna Vane, blond and blue-eyed, represents an essential aspect of the American dream he wants to attain. She is his symbolic key to opening the doors of North American society.

By following closely the lives of the Castillo brothers, Hijuelos narrates the migratory process, the contacts immigrants establish with relatives living abroad, the new friends and acquaintances, and the hard work they must endure in order to survive. The linguistic barrier is another hurdle that must be overcome, but it is ameliorated by the strength of the Hispanic community in the United States. In spite of the difficulty of being a Hispanic immigrant in the United States, the Castillo brothers become successful, mainly thanks to Néstor's pain. Unable to detach himself from the past and his love affair with María, Néstor succeeds in finding an outlet by putting his feelings to music. Néstor temporarily alleviates his suffering by composing "Beautiful María of My Soul," which he rewrites twenty-two times. With Néstor's song, the Castillo brothers achieve the notoriety they have been searching for and an invitation to appear on *I Love Lucy.*

The connection between Cuba and the United States had already been made by Desi Arnaz and Lucille Ball when they first met in May 1940, as members of the cast for the film version of *Too Many Girls,* in which Arnaz played a leading role. Desi and Lucy were immediately attracted to each other, and married in November of that same year. The public aspect of their marriage would be played out on television, before millions of

North American viewers. When Lucille Ball and Richard Denning's radio program "My Favorite Husband" was transformed into the television show *I Love Lucy*, Lucille Ball, wanting a more stable marriage with Desi, who traveled often with his band, insisted that her real husband play the same role on television. With the rapid spread of Cuban music in the United States and the popularity of Don Azpiazú and Cugat, among others, this country's public was ready to accept a certain type of Cuban image and music. Desi Arnaz represented, exploited, and promoted that image in his program: he portrayed the white, cool Latin lover and Lucy the jealous, emotional, and irrational redheaded wife.

Lucille and Desi are aptly studied by Pérez Firmat. In *Life on the Hyphen*, he dedicates two chapters to the couple and provides the reader with a close reading of the *I Love Lucy* show and of Desi's memoir, *A Book* (1976).[17] Lucy and Desi are an important part of Hijuelos's narration. Not only does the author describe a Cuban helping his compatriots, but it is probable that Hijuelos relied on some of the episodes of the *I Love Lucy* show for his own inspiration. Hijuelos was familiar with the popular television program and may even have seen "The Ricardos Visit Cuba," broadcast on December 3, 1956, or "Lucy Takes a Cruise to Havana," aired on November 6, 1957. As the titles suggest, both episodes take place in Cuba. More likely than not, he was influenced by another episode that brings Cubans and the Ricardos together, set not in Havana but in New York. The scene to which I refer in the novel takes place in 1955, but corresponds to a show that aired three years earlier, in which two of Ricky's friends visit him. "Cuban Pals" may have served as the nucleus of the story Hijuelos includes in his novel, and it is also the episode mentioned in the film version of the novel, titled *The Mambo Kings*. The program was one of the most watched episodes of *I Love Lucy*, airing on April 21, 1952. Bart Andrews summarizes "Cuban Pals" this way:

> Lucy is at a disadvantage when her husband's Cuban friends, Carlos and María Ortega, visit: Lucy's *español* is a sad sampling of pigeon [*sic*] Spanish. When she learns that "little" Renita Pérez, with whom Ricky once danced in Cuba, is arriving in town, she insists he dance again with her, claiming it will "help the good neighbor policy." What she isn't expecting is that "little" Renita has developed into a voluptuous *señorita*. Jealous, Lucy recruits Ethel, and they pose as charwomen and invade the Tropicana during rehearsals of "The Lady in Red" number, just to keep an eye on Ricky and Renita. Determined to keep the two apart, Lucy gets Fred to dress as a cabbie and take Renita on a "shortcut through Philadelphia" instead of to the club. At the Tropicana, when

Ricky introduces Renita and her usual dance partner, Ramón, who will perform the "African Wedding Dance," Lucy appears instead of the sultry Latin. It's a funny few minutes with Lucy trying to escape the clutches of the voodoo-masked Ramón.[18]

The television episode, of course, is not identical to the one in the novel, but it contains the main idea expressed in the story. Two of Ricky's Cuban friends visit him. He invites them to his house and also to sing at his club. Lucy is jealous and upset not at the men, but at Ricky who had promised her that she would sing in one of his shows. Acceding, Ricky looks over to the brothers and pronounces the most extensive Spanish monologue in the novel, which Hijuelos follows with a translation:

If you knew what I have to go through every day with this woman. These American women are enough to drive you nuts! My mother told me a million times: Ricky, never marry an American woman unless you're looking for one big headache. And she was right, I should've married that girl back in Cuba! Now there was a quiet girl who never bothered me, who knew where her bread was buttered. She wasn't crazy! She always left me alone, you know what I mean, *compañeros!* (141)

Although in the novel Ricky does not translate badly what Lucy says, his Spanish contains many grammatical errors, as Pérez Firmat has already observed in his study of this novel and other Cuban American works.[19] However, Hijuelos could have been trying to be faithful to the original show, which also contained linguistic errors. Andrews's summary of "Cuban Pals" is followed by a footnote that reads: "In the first scene, Desi Arnaz made a few mistakes while translating Lucy's English into Spanish, but he covered nicely. Watch for it."

Spanish was the original language in which Néstor composed his song and in which Hijuelos's Desi communicated with the Castillo brothers. However, it is the English language that reaches a level of fluidity and nativeness. Translation is an important issue faced by all Latinos in the United States. It is a concern that Cabrera Infante and Hijuelos address, and so does Pérez Firmat in his studies of Cuban culture *(The Cuban Condition)* and of Cuban American culture *(Life on the Hyphen)*.

Cuban culture is a translation of Spanish literature and culture, but it is also a translation of African or Afro-Cuban culture, an important component absent from Pérez Firmat's study. Cuban culture and literature can be traced to the nineteenth century, when slave masters attempted to control and subjugate their slaves, and Juan Francisco Manzano and Gabriel de la

Concepción Valdés—better known as Plácido—among other blacks and mulattos, wrote and published their works. In the contemporary period, the number of Afro-Cubans leaving the island has been small in comparison to their white counterparts, especially during the first wave of Cuban exiles. But Cuban music both on the island and on the continent contains sounds and rhythms that can be traced to Afro-Cuban culture and religion. This aspect of Cuban culture was understood by Desi Arnaz and by Hijuelos, if only in a marginal way. "Cuban Pals" mentions an "African Wedding Dance." Likewise, Hijuelos represents Afro-Cuban culture throughout the stage scenery and on the African drums: "Then the dance floor itself, and finally the stage, its apron and wings painted to resemble African drums, with birds and squiggly voodoo lines, these patterns repeated on the conga drums and on the music stands" (142). In the United States, Afro-Cuban rhythms were expressed by musicians such as Machito, Chano Pozo, and Pérez Prado and are an integral part of the mambo, rumba, son, cha-cha-chá, and salsa.

The significance of translation in *The Mambo Kings Play Songs of Love* is made clearest at the end of the novel, when the reader uncovers the Spanish and English versions of "Beautiful María of My Soul." A copy of the Spanish was found next to César's body. Eugenio recalls the translation, sung on *I Love Lucy*, as he sits in Desi Arnaz's living room. It is difficult to disagree with Cabrera Infante's understanding of the interpretative act as a betrayal, and there are significant differences and similarities between the original and the translation of Néstor's song. At first sight, one appears to be a literal translation of the other; but a close reading of both the Spanish and English songs helps to reveal how Hispanic and North American cultures intersect, a theme present throughout the novel. A study of the English and Spanish affirms the Derridian concept of displaced origin, but also questions it. As in Carpentier's story, the origin is both at the beginning and at the end. And if the past is recalled from the present, Hijuelos's novel shows that both past and present occupy the same time and space.

According to the scene on the *I Love Lucy* show, the Castillo brothers, represented by Manny and Alfonso Reyes, have just arrived from Havana, but, oddly enough, they sing in English. It is not clear whether Néstor first wrote his song in Spanish or in English, though the reader suspects the former. The song is sung in English, but it is also introduced in Spanish. If we suppose that Néstor first wrote his song in Spanish and César later translated it into English, it is the English version that is free of grammatical errors. But if we propose that the song was first composed in Spanish, then we should keep in mind that the novel was first written in English; that is, the English translation of the song came first and the Spanish is therefore a translation of the "translation." Let us study the English and Spanish versions of "Beautiful María of My Soul":

Oh, love's sadness,	¿O, tristeza de amor,
Why did you come to me?	por qué tuviste que venir a mi?
I was happy before you	Yo estaba feliz antes que
entered my heart.	entraras en mi corazón.
How can I hate you	¿Cómo puedo odiarte
if I love you so?	Si te amo como te amo?
I can't explain my torment,	No puedo explicar mi tormento
for I don't know how to live	porque no sé como
without your love . . .	vivir sin tu amor.
What delicious pain	Que dolor delicioso
love has brought to me	el amor me ha traido
in the form of a woman.	en la forma de una mujer
My torment and ecstasy,	Mi tormento y mi éxtasis.
María, my life . . .	Bella María de mi Alma,
Beautiful María of my soul,	María, mi vida . . .
Why did she finally mistreat me so?	¿Por que me maltrataste?
Tell me, why is it that way?	Dime por qué sucede de
Why is it always so?	esta manera?
María, my life,	¿Por qué es siempre así?
Beautiful María of my soul.	María, mi Vida,
	Bellísima María de mi alma.[20]

Upon comparing the two songs, we notice that the Spanish version appears to be an original. It was written by Néstor, who was tied to his Cuban past, in a language that reflects the culture he carries within, and translated by César, who understands U.S. culture. The Spanish song is handwritten and contains the appropriate musical indications on the sheet; that is, the chords in which the song should be played. The English translation was sung during the *I Love Lucy* show. However, it appears to be a translation or a transcription of the Spanish, without any musical arrangement. But if we accept the Spanish as original, written in Néstor's native language, how then do we explain the grammatical errors it contains? Does it reflect upon Néstor's level of education? For example, some of the words are missing accent marks. The *a mi?* of the second line is missing an accent over the *mí*, and *traido* on line 10 should correctly be *traído*; and *como*, line 8, is also missing an accent as in *cómo*, an error that changes the meaning of the line from the intended *how* to *as*. The same error is repeated on line 15 with *por que*, which should have been written as *por qué*. The lack of the accent changes the meaning from *why* to *because*.

Néstor's song is far from being a model composition in Spanish. Some lines appear to be forced; they do not seem to be natural Spanish expressions and may have been derived from the English. For example, line 2 reads "por qué tuviste que venir a mi?" which appears to be a translation of "Why did you come to me?" also contained in the second line. Although one may have been derived from the other, they do not say the same thing. The Spanish contains two verbs, whereas the English translates only one. The Spanish reproduces the verb *tuviste,* therefore the English line should read "Why did you have to come to me?" But if the English is the original, then the Spanish line should have been translated as "por qué viniste a mí?" In any event, the two verbs prolong the length of the song's line.

The English is also an original. As I have mentioned, the novel was written in English, and we can suspect that the song was also composed in the novel's language. The strongest argument rests on the chord indications to the Spanish song, which are written in English, suggesting that the song was composed in that language. The Spanish song contains indications such as Ami (A minor), Bmi (B minor), Dmi (D minor), and so on. In addition, the song contains the exclamation *Oh,* which is reproduced in the Spanish song as *O,* an expression more common in English than in Spanish. If this is the case, then how do we explain errors reproduced in what we now posit as the English original? The English also appears to be forced. Although the English is free of typographical or spelling mistakes, there are syntactical problems. For example, the beginning of the last stanza reads: "Why did she finally mistreat me so? / Tell me, why is it that way?" This sounds awkward to me and could be a direct translation of the Spanish. But just as the Spanish contained an extra verb in line 2, the English contains an unnecessary adverb, *finally,* absent in the Spanish.

The most compelling reason to believe that the English is an original is contained in the title, "Beautiful María of My Soul." The clue is given to us not in the novel, but in the lyrics used in the film *The Mambo Kings,* written by Arne Glimcher, with music by Robert Kraft. Before I proceed with my analysis of the title, I would like to point out a few inconsistencies between the English and the Spanish lyrics that recall those present in the novel and underscore the problems of translation. The first two stanzas of the score read as follows:

Si desco sonreir	In the sunlight of your smile,
Pienso solamente en ti	in the summer of our life.
En la magia de tu amor	In the magic of love,
En tu piel, en tu sabor	storms above scattered away.
En la isla del dolor	Lovers dreaming in the night,
Recuerdo tu calor	reaching for Paradise.
Desearia morir	But as the dark shadows fade,
	love slips away.

Cerca de ti	On an empty stretch of beach,
Un ardiente corazon	in the pattern of the waves.
Colorea mi pasion	Drawing pictures with my hand
Deseando compartir	In the sand,
El sentir de este vivir	I see your face.
En las olas de este mar	Skipping pebbles on the sea,
Sueno en la eternidad	Wishing for Paradise. Sand castles
Con cada luna vendras	Crumble below, the restless tides
Con la marea te iras	Ebb and flow. Listening to a shell,
En un caracol	Hoping for your voice.
Pienso oir tu voz	Beautiful María of my soul.[21]
La bella María de mi amor.	

Although the film lyrics are different from the ones provided by Hijuelos, the English song is original and was translated into Spanish by Antonio Banderas, Johnny Pacheco, and Gabriel Riera; however, both the English and Spanish exhibit discrepancies similar to the ones I have observed in the novel. Let us look at them more closely. The film lyrics were written first in English and read smoothly, but this is not the case with the Spanish, which we are told is a translation of the original. If we can attribute the missing accents and tilde to the nature of an English publication, marketed for an English-speaking audience—though many presses are set up for foreign characters— how do we explain other typographical or orthographic errors? First stanza, "Si desco sonreir" should read "Si deseo sonreir"; sixth stanza, "Aunque esternos separados," should be "Aunque estemos separados," and "No hay razon, porque cambiar," should be written as "por qué cambiar"; the seventh stanza, "Sin tien la eternidad," should be "Sin tener la eternidad." If the mentioned errors can be explained as typographical mistakes, common to all publications, how do we come to terms with the misuse of the subjunctive? The last stanza contains the lines "Si no te vuelva a ver / No dejaras de ser / La bella María de mi amor." In Spanish, the "If" clause should be written in the present indicative, not in the present subjunctive, followed by what appears to be the future *dejarás*. However, one can use the past subjunctive or past conditional, followed by the past subjunctive, as contained in the second line, but it is more fluid with the conditional: "Si no te volviera a ver / no dejaras (dejarías) de ser."

The best indication that the English song in the novel is the original is evident in its title, "Beautiful María of My Soul." The last portion of the title contains the word *soul*, as in "soul mates," or "to have soul," popular expressions used during the sixties. It also alludes to a particular African American music known as soul music. The title to the musical score of "Beautiful María of My Soul" is translated as "Bella María de mi Alma," which differs from Hijuelos's "Bellísima María de mi Alma." Although "Bellísima María de mi Alma" is an appropriate expression in Spanish, "[La] bella María de mi amor," as translated in the musical score, is also acceptable. Here, the translators may have chosen *amor* to continue the assonant rhyme scheme. Nevertheless, *mi amor* is a common Cuban expression. If we compare the Spanish title as it is reproduced in the novel and in the film's music, the use of "Bellísima María de mi Alma" appears to have been derived from "Beautiful María of My Soul." Moreover, Hijuelos writes the final word of the title, *Alma*, with an uppercase letter, using the format customary not in Spanish but in English.

Let us return to the novel. There are other important differences between the English and Spanish renditions of the song that should be mentioned. The third and fourth stanzas of the English version end with a refrain, which is the song's title; the Spanish stanzas do not. If we compare one with the other, in the third stanza, the Spanish refrain does not begin with the last line but with the next-to-last one, thus inverting the English, which Spanish commonly does (or vice versa). Only at the end of the fourth stanza is the title of the song replicated as it appears in the English version. But it is the third stanza that actually reproduces the English equivalent of *beautiful*; either *bella* or *hermosa* would be an acceptable translation of the word. The Spanish title of the song, which is also present at the end of the fourth stanza, contains the superlative *bellísima*, which should be translated not as *beautiful*, but as *ravishing, gorgeous*, or at least *very beautiful*. If we take into account the above information, "Beautiful María of My Soul" does not translate smoothly to "Bellísima María de mi Alma," but rather to "Bella María de mi alma," as contained in the Spanish translation of the film's score, which replaces "alma" with "amor."

This same fourth stanza contains a semantic slip. The Spanish says "Por que me maltrataste?" in which the singer speaks directly to María. The English reproduces the same line as "Why did she finally mistreat me so?" referring to María not in the first person, as the Spanish does, but in the third. An English rendition of the Spanish would be "Why did you mistreat me?" A Spanish rendition of the English would be "Por qué me maltrató?"

More likely than not, both the Spanish and the English are originals and both are translations. When composing the song, Hijuelos may have been writing in Spanish but thinking in English; or if he composed it first in English, he was also thinking in Spanish. Both languages are native and foreign to him. When he employs one language, it contains traces of the other. One signifies the other and both occupy the same space. These observations highlight the tension and mediation that take place when two cultures come together, and point toward the essence of Latino culture and literature written in the United States.

The original and the translation of "Beautiful María of My Soul" refer to the lives of the two Castillo brothers, since one can be considered a translation of the other. Néstor is tied to María and the Cuban past; César is not: he wants to immerse himself in North American culture. *The Mambo Kings Play Songs of Love* insists on recollecting the past and thereby provides the reader with possible explanations for the differences in character between the Castillo brothers. Néstor is shy and essentially a one-woman man; César is the opposite—he is aggressive and likes to be surrounded by many members of the opposite sex. As a child, Néstor suffered from asthma and was under the constant care of his mother. Unlike his brother, César was daring; he experienced sex at an early age; he had an antagonistic relationship with his father. In order to show his independence, he put at risk his relationship with his parents by learning to play the trumpet, which he accomplished by stealing rum from his father and giving it to his alcoholic teacher, Eusebio Stevenson.

Although Néstor's depression is precipitated by his loss of María, she assumes a larger significance and symbolically represents Cuba and his love for his native land. His longing for María is a desire to return to what Cuba represents: "The more he thought about her, the more mythic she became. Every ounce of love he'd received in his short life was captured and swallowed up by the image of María. (Mama, I wanted María the way I wanted you when I was a baby feeling helpless in that bed, with welts covering my chest, and lungs stuffed with thick cotton. I couldn't breathe, Mama, remember how I used to call you?)."[22]

María is the womb, the lost origin, the paradise to which Henri Baudet refers in *Paradise on Earth: Some Thoughts on European Images of Non-European Man* (1965), from which man was ejected and searches for, but to which he can never return.[23] Yet it is this sense of loss and the resulting tension between the past and the present that allows the immigrant to be creative and, in Néstor's case, to write the musical composition that brings fame to the Castillo brothers. Cuba and María can be captured and represented only metonymically, and they are transformed into a song.

In spite of Néstor's efforts to integrate himself into the new environment, total assimilation is denied to him and the other Cuban characters. Needing to come to terms with the past and become more mainstream, Néstor reads *Forward America*, by D. D. Vanderbilt; the author's name is a symbol of wealth and success. The book is about prospering in America, and Néstor has underlined the following passage:

> In today's America one must think about the future. Ally yourself with progress and tomorrow! The confident, self-assured man looks to the future and never backwards to the past. The heart of every success is a plan that takes you forward. In moments of

doubt you must remember that every obstacle is only a temporary delay. That every problem can be solved. Where there is a will there is a way. You, too, can be a man of tomorrow! (148)

The book's content, however, represents the opposite of Hijuelos's depiction of Hispanic culture and of Néstor, who looks not to the future but to the past. He did not write "Beautiful María of My Soul" as a money-making venture, but rather as an outlet for his intense emotional pain. Even when Néstor reads the book, which is a Bible of sorts, and strives to change his life, he cannot divorce himself totally from the past. The past is an obstacle he cannot overcome. Vanderbilt's book addresses only the concerns of the immigrant who is willing to divorce himself from the past— not those of one who must mediate between his native and adopted cultures. Tomorrow, for Néstor and for other Hispanic immigrants, cannot exist in isolation but only in conjunction with the past. *Forward America* has the opposite of its intended effect on Néstor. It does not point him in the "right" direction, but rather reveals him to be a failure in "today's America." Vanderbilt does not speak to Néstor's concerns, thus the book creates a deeper depression, resulting in his suicide.

In the United States, Néstor looks for a piece of the past in the present. For him, Delorita portrays a part of the Hispanic experience in a foreign environment. Néstor, Delorita, and others allow Hijuelos to describe how the Hispanic community exists and survives during the period in which the action unfolds. Even Delorita's desire to be with the Pepsodent man, whom she initially likes, arises not out of a need to assimilate into North American culture, but out of an obligation to insulate her father from the pain and frustration he encounters outside of his homeland. Considering incest, she wants to soothe her father's anguish but cannot, and is drawn to the Pepsodent man for the same masculine characteristics her father represents.

Throughout the novel Hijuelos explores the presence of Hispanic culture within a North American environment and compares the two. He measures the strengths and weaknesses of one culture against those of the other in his description of Latin versus U.S. men: César versus the Pepsodent man. I should point out that aside from the Castillo brothers, Mr. Pepsodent is the only man described engaging in any sexual activity. Although César's virility is beyond the scope of this study, his masculinity stands in contrast to that of the Pepsodent man, who wishes to seduce Delorita. Whereas César charms women into having sex with him, the conniving Pepsodent man lures Delorita into a compromising situation and forces himself on her. Faced with his aggressive urge to satisfy his manhood, Delorita resigns herself to losing her virginity. But, much to her surprise, he is unable to complete the sexual act and ejaculates prematurely.

The Pepsodent man is all teeth and smiles but has no bite. He does not compare favorably to the more sophisticated César or even to his shy brother Néstor, who know how to allure women into the bedroom and are more than capable of satisfying them. Similarly, U.S. society and culture present an attractive facade; yet beneath the surface, it is devoid of substance and meaning. In the end, not even Néstor or César is able to make the appropriate adjustments to survive in the culture of North America.

The Hispanic enclave in the United States is not strong or developed enough to save Néstor, who continues to be depressed and ultimately commits suicide. The narration is ambiguous about what has actually occurred before Néstor crashes into a tree with the car. However, I believe that the text provides enough information to suggest that Néstor is taking his own life, especially in light of the fact that he feels isolated and has contemplated suicide on more than one occasion. This is certainly what is happening when Néstor goes over the rooftop, hangs over La Salle Street, and thinks about dropping and hitting the pavement; and when he swims to a small island in the middle of the lake and begins to sink in the water (117 and 175, respectively). But in each situation Delorita's voice brings him back to his senses. Moreover, César believes that Néstor has seized the opportunity to end his life offered by the inclement road conditions. This is also the dominant interpretation of the film, as Néstor in his own way says farewell to his wife before the accident. In the novel, Néstor holds on to Eugenio for one last kiss.

Néstor's death changes César's life. César is transformed into his younger brother and acquires many of his characteristics. After Néstor's death, César is chronically depressed, takes care of Néstor's children, becomes Eugenio's surrogate father, desires Delorita, and thinks of and becomes tied to the past. He also falls in love with Lydia; unlike Vanna Vane she is not Anglo, but like Delorita and María she is Hispanic. If María represented the past for Néstor, Néstor's memory serves the same purpose for César. He is more attentive to his family in Cuba. He visits the island, sends money to his relatives, worries about them, and when the time is right, helps them to leave and to establish themselves in the United States. Even more important, César writes a version of "Beautiful María of My Soul"—not the original, but the translation as it appears at the end of the novel.

César is also drawn to Néstor's book, *Forward America*, and he too looks for solutions to his condition in Vanderbilt's understanding of the North American way. Ironically, as a recent immigrant César without knowing it had embraced Vanderbilt's prescription for success. He had put his past behind him and looked forward to the challenges of the present and future. No obstacle would stop him from achieving success. However, after Néstor's death, César is a changed man. In this part of the novel,

Forward America is associated with an industrious period in César's life, one in which he acquires some direction—paradoxically, in the form of a janitor's job. Certainly, some will argue that going from being a well-known musician with a popular song on the charts and an appearance on *I Love Lucy* to working as a custodian is not what Vanderbilt had in mind, nor can it be remotely associated with upward mobility. César has moved into the basement, a physical and spiritual downward fall. There, César feels moments of solitude and happiness, but they do not curtail his suffering. And when he finally lifts himself up and becomes the owner of Club Havana, César comes closer to achieving Vanderbilt's version of success, but it is short-lived; his personality and culture prevent him from becoming a good and rich businessman. He remembers that others need help, and instead of following a path to financial independence, César prefers to give his profits to Cuban immigrant musicians who are worse off than he. Vanderbilt would have put profits before such concerns, as César's North American business associates advise him to do. But César cannot become a Vanderbilt. His culture is distinctly different from that of North American magnates. The same sense of pride that keeps him away from organized crime and out from under the control of others also leads to his downfall. Just as Vanderbilt's book failed Néstor, it will remind César that there is a lacuna between his life and the one Vanderbilt lived and wrote about. César's drinking puts him on the road to self-destruction, which I interpret as a slow and torturous suicide. Like Néstor, who had become obsessed with María, in his old age César finally falls in love with Lydia; and like María with Néstor, she rejects him.

The emphasis on the present time of the narration as a focal point of César's life allows us to search the past in order to understand the present. But it is also important to study the present in order to come to terms with the past. César's childhood offers insights into his affairs with women. But his reclusive life in the Hotel Splendour, waiting for death to arrive, presupposes that at some point in time, his life was on a collision course.

The early migration of Hispanics to the United States, as we have seen with Bernardo Vega, provides an understanding of their continual presence in this country. And their present conditions also allow us to compare the contemporary period with the past. For Hijuelos, the decade of the mambo is meaningful as a past event, but more importantly as a reflection of the present. I would like to explore two events that unfold during the present time of the narration and that help to reveal why the mambo and the decade of the fifties were important for the writing of *The Mambo Kings Play Songs of Love.*

Let us look more closely at the novel's introduction and epilogue; that is, to the present time of the narration. The year in which Eugenio awakens César to see his father and uncle's performance on *I Love Lucy* is the same year in which Castro instigated the Mariel boatlift, opening the door for more than 125,000 Cubans to flee to the United States. Even though his life has nothing to do with politics, César is aware of the transformation of the Cuban government, which also affects the lives of all Cubans. César's interior monologue provides us with insight into his thoughts, as he names some of the musicians who escaped the island:

> Sitting in his room in the Hotel Splendour (reeling in the room), the Mambo King preferred not to think about the revolution in Cuba. What the fuck had he ever cared about Cuban politics in the old days, except for when he might play a political rally in the provinces for some local crooked politician? What the fuck had he cared when the consensus among his musician pals was that it wouldn't make any difference who came to power, until Fidel. What could he have done about it, anyway? Things must have been pretty bad. The orchestra leader Rene Touzet had fled to Miami with his sons, playing the big hotels there and concerts for the Cubans. Then came the grand master of Cuban music, Ernesto Lecuona, arriving in Miami distraught and in a state of creative torpor, unable to play a note on his piano and ending up in Puerto Rico, "bitter and disenchanted," before he died, he'd heard some people say. Bitter because his Cuba no longer existed. (259)

The distress of the musicians leaving Cuba coincides with César's own depression. Events in Cuba have indeed touched—for better or for worse—the lives of all Cubans, whether political or apathetic, living on the island or abroad, including César and including Hijuelos. According to the narration, musicians other than the ones mentioned in the above quotation were affected by events in Cuba. We are told that Celia Cruz left the island in 1967 but that musicians such as Bola de Nieve and Elena Burke remained in their native land. The revolution does affect César's life. When his mother dies in 1962, he is not able to return to Cuba and bury her. A dancer for Alicia Alonso, his daughter, Mariela, is committed to supporting the Cuban government, and that explains why she keeps her father at a distance. And although César has to raise money to get one of his brothers out of Cuba, the other decides to stay, thus continuing the fragmentation of the Cuban family.

By the time Hijuelos had published his novel and received the Pulitzer Prize, the economic situation in Cuba had worsened, mainly because of the political turmoil in Eastern Europe that toppled the communist regimes and replaced them with more representative forms of government. With the disbandment of the Soviet Union, Russia and its former allies no longer shared Castro's commitment to promoting a congress of communist deputies and became more concerned about resolving their own economic difficulties. The tense situation in Cuba, which has brought paralysis to the country, caused an increasing number of Cubans to risk their lives and travel in makeshift boats and rafts to escape to freedom.

Events during the present time of narration and of writing recall a period before Castro came to power, a time in which political corruption in the administrations of Presidents Grau San Martín and Carlos Prío Socarrás led to Batista's coup in 1953. During those events and up to 1959, Cubans migrated freely, some for political reasons, but the vast majority in search of economic opportunities in the United States. In this regard, the novel harkens back to a moment when Cubans traveled to and from the mainland with relative ease. Hijuelos's own father made frequent journeys to the United States. In an interview with Ilán Stavans, Hijuelos referred to the migratory process of his parents in a way that recalls similar movements in the narration:

> He emigrated at 15. He had a cousin in New York. As a typical youngster of the Oriente Province, he saved his money and spent six weeks with his cousin. He fell in love with the city, but had to go back to Cuba; he returned 17 years later. It was 1946, he had two sisters here (they will be the subject of a future novel): One worked as a stewardess for an airline, the other as a Macy's employee. Aside from his savings, he had received an inheritance. He had a good three or four years: he met my mother and established roots. After having children, they returned to the island, became disillusioned, and returned to New York.[24]

The present alludes to the fondly remembered past, and the characters continue a long tradition in which it was easier to travel from the Caribbean to New York than from New York to California.

Music is another ingredient for understanding the past and the present. Hijuelos's novel is about the mambo, but also about the bolero and other musical compositions played in the United States. Pérez Firmat explores the juxtaposition of the two musical compositions in the novel's title, which refers to the mambo and the bolero. "*Mambo Kings* is a literary latune—English words and Cuban music. But words and music do go together, as the mambo and bolero serve as correlates for the two dominant but discordant emotions in the book, lust and melancholy. The mambo is fast-paced, aggressive, lascivious; it is César's chant of conquest. By contrast, boleros are sad, even whining ballads whose speaker is typically passive and mournful."[25] But if the bolero points to the past of its origin and in the novel to Néstor and María, there is another musical composition that brings the reader to the present and future of Latin music in the United States. During the present time of the narration, in which Eugenio attempts to wake César up from his hangover, and in which he visits Desi Arnaz, the mambo had already been replaced by the less frantic and more subtle cha-cha-chá, and salsa had achieved its own identity. If the Latino culture in New York transformed the mambo, it made salsa into a New York phenomenon, which spread rapidly throughout the United States, to Spanish-speaking countries all over the world, and even to Japan.[26]

The Mambo Kings Play Songs of Love points to mambo and to bolero, but also to salsa. Many of the musicians and promoters of mambo in the decade of the fifties, such as Tito Puente, were also involved in creating salsa. In addition, the novel itself is made up of the same ingredients that went into making salsa a unique blend of Hispanic and North American cultures.

Like the New York mambo, salsa embodies a distinct blend of Caribbean and North American music. A review of salsa will help to explain the prominence of mambo in Hijuelos's novel. Charlie Palmieri adapted for his band the charanga sounds of Cuban bands touring in the decade of the fifties. For his band, Charanga Duboney, he found flautist Johnny Pacheco; the flute and violin, unfamiliar to other groups in the United States, became integral sounds of Palmieri's orchestra. In 1961, Pacheco formed his own group, which he called Pacheco y su Charanga. Pacheco went on to create a new rhythm known as Pachanga (combining Pacheco and charanga), a combination of charanga and jazz. Another change was introduced by Charlie's younger brother, Eddie Palmieri, and his orchestra, La Perfecta. Eddie expanded on the Cuban rhythms and added a jazz influence in the form of trumpets and saxophones. He also brought in a pair of trombones—one was that of jazz musician Barry Rogers—as the base of the melody, giving them preeminence. Palmieri had them sound hoarse and aggressive. To the trombones he added the improvisation of African drumming of the mozambique, created in Cuba by Pedro Izquierdo in the mid-sixties.[27]

Willie Colón made another contribution to salsa. Unlike the Palmieri brothers, who had studied music in a conservatory, Colón had dropped out of school and begun playing the flute, but he later gained notoriety with his trombone. In his orchestra The Company he used two trombones, but very differently from the way Palmieri employed them. His were loud and out of tune. He was accompanied by his lead singer, Hector Lavoe, who sang in a shrilling style reminiscent of the violent life in the ghetto familiar to Colón and other New York musicians. Colón preferred to be known as "El Malo," the bad one. Colón's records "El Malo" and "The Good, the Bad, the Ugly" highlight this particular stage in his salsa career.[28] Colón and other musicians later expanded their themes to include injustices in Puerto

Rico and also in the rest of Latin America. There are similarities between Colón's music and the Nuyorican style of poetry, which emerges from the ghetto, speaks to the people, and defies the dominant culture. Musicians like Colón and Eddie Palmieri, in their music and lyrics, voiced concerns similar to ones the Young Lords Party expressed.

Salsa got an important push in 1971 when Jerry Masucci, owner of the label Fania Records, approached Ralph Mercado, the new owner of the Cheetah nightclub on 52nd Street, and asked him to host the best musicians of Masucci's company—the best New York had to offer—under the heading of the Fania All-Stars. This musical extravaganza was a popular success, resulting in two albums and the film *Nuestra Cosa Latina*, directed by Leon Gast. Masucci followed the event with his 1973 Fania All Stars concert at Yankee Stadium. The event was made into a motion picture and its title, *Salsa*, was engraved forever on the music played in New York.[29] *Nuestra Cosa Latina* incorporates images already seen in the film *Right On!* depicting the urban environment in which salsa emerged and flourished. *Salsa* is more historical. It places salsa within a broader context, referring to its origins, narrating the important period from 1920 to 1950, which included important Hispanic figures such as Dolores del Río, Desi Arnaz, the Moreno sisters, Carmen Miranda, and others. During this period, rock, jazz, and soul appealed to the youth of this country, and to those musical arrangements salsa was added. In a similar manner to *Salsa*, Hijuelos's novel is a literary reconstructuon of an earlier period.

Salsa is a New York phenomenon, born of urban culture, of the marginal Hispanic and Latino community. Salsa underscores Hispanic culture in the Caribbean, but also reflects the Latino experience on the mainland: it speaks to the pains, problems, and ailments of the Latino community in New York. Different from other musical arrangements that developed in the Caribbean and enriched the lives of Hispanics living in New York, salsa was born in New York and spread throughout the Caribbean and the world. It emerges out of a unique Latino experience that combines Hispanic and North American traditions. Like salsa, Hijuelos's novel is a product of the Hispanic and Latino experience in New York. It is made up of a culture that gave rise to salsa, one that translates itself back and forth between Hispanic and U.S. cultures. The novel underscores the importance of this translation, which it represents by Desi Arnaz's translation of a scene in "Cuban Pals" and by Hijuelos's rendition of the same scene, in which Ricky speaks Spanish to the Castillo brothers and Hijuelos translates for the reader. More important, the theme of translation refers to Néstor's translation of his emotions into "Beautiful María of My Soul" and to César's translation of his brother's song; also to Glimcher's "Beautiful María of My Soul" and to Banderas, Pacheco, and Riera's translation of the same song. The New York Palladium, where the Castillo brothers played, became the privileged space in which the mambo and salsa, as music and dance, acquired their distinct characteristics. The importance of salsa during the time in which Hijuelos was writing his novel allowed him to look back to a period in which the mambo was being transformed into a New York phenomenon and consider the possible connections between it and salsa. The same musicians who contributed to mambo also led the way to the creation of salsa.

As *The Mambo Kings Play Songs of Love* explores the importance of César's rise and fall as the King of the Mambo, it also portrays what it means to be a Cuban American, as I have painstakingly shown with the study of Néstor's song. The key is presented at the beginning, when Eugenio and César view once more a rerun of *I Love Lucy*, and at the end, when Eugenio visits Desi Arnaz. Like Eugenio and César, who relive the Castillo brothers' appearance on *I Love Lucy* and their hit song "Beautiful María of My Soul," Cuban American men are nostalgic about the past. Many among the first waves of immigrants, who were forced to leave the island from 1959 to 1961, had already achieved professional success. In the United States they became obsessed with the past, and most of their conversations focused on the events of their lives in Cuba before 1959. César, but also Eugenio and Desi, continued to privilege the heydays of their professional careers.

The epilogue captures the essence of the Cuban condition in the United States. Eugenio stands to profit from the experiences of those who preceded him. As Eugenio visits Desi Arnaz's estate, he observes that Desi has recreated aspects of Cuba in his home in California. When he enters the estate, Eugenio notices

> a stone wall covered with bougainvillea, like the flower-covered walls of Cuba, and flowers everywhere. Inside the gate, a walkway to the large pink ranch-style house with a tin roof, a garden, a patio, and a swimming pool. Arched doorways and shuttered windows. Iron balconies on the second floor. And there was a front garden where hibiscus, chrysanthemums, and roses grew. (400)

Later, Desi explains his reason for living in California: "It's beautiful. I chose this climate here because it reminds me of Cuba" (402). When asking Eugenio if he has ever been to Cuba, Desi says: "Well, that's a shame. It's a little like this" (402). And as he shows Eugenio the gardens, he adds: "This garden is modeled after one of my favorite little plazas in Santiago. You came across it on your way to the harbor. I used to take my girls there. . . . Those days are long gone" (402). In addition, Arnaz's house is covered with memorabilia of Cuba and Cuban culture. But Arnaz's estate also includes elements of other cultures—North American ones—represented by his photographs of the biggest movie stars, his employment of a Mexican house servant, and the Dos Equis beer she serves.

By the time Eugenio visits Desi, Desi is a broken man. He and Lucille Ball divorced on May 4, 1960, a little over a year after Castro took power. But the marriage had begun to fall apart five years before. Lucy vividly recalled those years as unadulterated hell:

> Desi drank and I knew he went out with other women, but I didn't worry about it soon enough. The last five years were the same old booze and broads, the only change being that he was rarely at home anymore. And that was a blessing, because we didn't yell at each other when we didn't see each other.[30]

Part of Desi's divorce settlement included half of the Desilu fortune and the ranch at Riverside, where the epilogue takes place.

Toward the end of the epilogue, Eugenio has a copy of Vanderbilt's *Forward America,* the same one his father and uncle had read. The question that immediately arises is whether Eugenio will follow in his father's and uncle's footsteps, since he not only carries their blood but also identifies with them. Theirs is the same path that Desi ultimately took. Desi did look forward, found his Vanna Vane in Lucille Ball, and with her help created an empire and amassed great wealth. But, like César, he was unable to separate himself completely from his past. In fact, Desi lived the same free-spirited life known to César, one that led to isolation and downfall for both. The similarities between Desi and César are so striking that one wonders whether Hijuelos used Desi's biography as a model for constructing César's character. The similarity between the character and the real person of Arnaz seems pointed in the narrator's summary of "Beautiful María of My Soul": "A song about love so far away it hurts; a song about lost pleasures, a song about youth, a song about love so elusive a man can never know where he stands; a song about wanting a woman so much death does not frighten you, a song about wanting that woman even when she has abandoned you" (409).

Perhaps Eugenio will follow in the footsteps of Néstor, César, and Desi. Before he calls to visit Desi, he meets "one of the blondes by the pool" and they fall desperately in love. But unlike the other three, Eugenio was not born in Cuba. He was born and raised in the United States and his life represents a departure from the past, one that does not abandon it but combines it with the present. At the end of the novel, Eugenio drifts as he listens to the *I Love Lucy* episode in which his uncle and father appeared; he is transported to La Salle and Cardinal Spellman's visit to confirm sixth-graders. But the event turns into a funeral, and instead of listening to the organist playing Bach, he hears a 1952 mambo orchestra playing a bolero.

The coffin is a sign of death, the death of a culture, represented by his father and uncle. The coffin and the music recall another culture; they are reminiscent of burials attended by musicians of New Orleans, who get together and play one more time for the deceased colleague, ushering him into the next world. Relying on that cultural understanding of death, the mambo band plays a languid bolero, perhaps "Beautiful María of My Soul," providing the same departure for the Castillo brothers, represented by the coffin and satin hearts (of the *I Love Lucy* show). The novel closes with the two hearts: "Then the place is very sad, as they start carrying out the coffin, and once it's outside, another satin heart escapes, rising out of the wood, and goes higher and higher, expanding as it reaches toward the sky, floating away, behind the other" (407). For Eugenio, the culture of his father and uncle has "died," but the memory will always be with him. In the final scene, which blurs the boundaries between the real and the imaginary, between fact and fiction, he sits in Desi's living room as the *I Love Lucy* show, dreams, and images are transformed before his eyes. Also important is the mingling of different cultures, repesented by Cardinal Spellman, the funeral march with music, and the Mambo Orchestra. One heart is united with the other; one culture is blended with the other.

Eugenio's name is significant for understanding the end of the narration. He is the symbol of a beginning. His name means "well born," and *Eugenio* and *genesis* are both derived from the same Greek word *genos*, signifying beginning. Eugenio will liberate himself from the destiny of his father, his uncle, and Desi. His destiny will be different; it will successfully combine the present with the past, as Hijuelos has done with his novel. The novel starts and concludes with the present time of the narration. Eugenio represents a new start. *The Mambo Kings Play Songs of Love* is more than just a book about sex and tragedy. It embodies the Cuban experience in the United States and portrays the delicate dance and the changing rhythms, between the mambo, the bolero, the salsa—and the two cultures.

II

Both César and Néstor Castillo represent Cubans who left the homeland and migrated for economic reasons, during the decades of the forties and fifties, to the United States. Like many other immigrants before them, the Castillo brothers used the talents they had acquired on the island and became successful musicians abroad. But their inability to mediate between the Cuban past and the North American present was, to a large degree, responsible for their tragic ending. Though César and Néstor left the island twenty years before Castro's rebel army marched into Havana, they would be affected by events unfolding in present-day Cuba. Their estrangement from the island was made even more acute by the adversarial relations between the Cuban and U.S. governments, which made it difficult for them to return to the island.

Cristina García's *Dreaming in Cuban* (1992) describes the lives of more recent Cuban refugees. Castro's 1959 takeover forced an unprecedented number of Cubans to seek political asylum in the United States. García's novel follows the pattern of Cuban American works written and published in cities like New York and Miami, which have acquired a Caribbean character. Cuban exile literature is not new. Dolores, Jorge, and Pilar del Pino are part of a group of exiles who began leaving Cuba in the early to mid-nineteenth century. Intellectuals who opposed the Spanish colonial government abandoned the island and moved to safer haven in the United States, where many continued their political and literary activities.

Cuban exile writers of the nineteenth century who sought refuge in the United States, such as Cirilo Villaverde, José María Heredia, and José Martí, and others of the twentieth century such as Lino Novás Calvo, Lydia Cabrera, Reinaldo Arenas, and Antonio Benítez Rojo contribute to a tradition of Cuban literature written abroad that is as significant as the one native to the island. These and other writers were raised and educated in Cuba and had published works of fiction before fleeing their country. Cristina García represents a new wave of writers, born or raised in the United States, who write in Spanish but also in English. García was born in Havana but educated in New York during the important decades of the sixties and seventies, a time in which the youth of her adopted country were questioning the government's foreign and domestic policies. Although some of the children of Cuban exiles conformed to their parents' political ideology, others rejected it and developed their own opinions about events unfolding on the island. Some members of Areíto even opposed the U.S. blockade of Cuba and favored a dialogue with the Castro government.[31]

This portion of the chapter shows how García's novel discloses intricate layers of Cuban history, politics, literature, and culture, present on the island and in the United States. It also uncovers the works of Cuban master writers, like Cirilo Villaverde and Reinaldo Arenas, who abandoned the island and lived in exile. While abroad they presented a more objective and perhaps realistic portrayal of Cuban society than the writers who remained on the island. Villaverde was critical of the Vives government and Arenas of the Castro regime. As the author of Cuba's national novel, Villaverde identified narrative and cultural themes that other writers later developed, as Arenas's *La loma del ángel* (1987; *Graveyard of the Angels,* 1987), a rewriting of *Cecilia Valdés,* suggests. In her novel, García documents the most recent stage of the fragmentation of the Cuban family, this one created by the Cuban revolution. However, my chapter title, "Master Codes of Cuban American Culture," also refers to García's protagonist as she attempts to understand her own Cuban realities.

In writing about three generations of the Celia and Jorge del Pino family, García explores the different dimensions of the Cuban family trauma. The political events on the island forced the del Pino family to split up.

Opposition to the new government propelled Lourdes, Rufino, and Pilar to emigrate to the United States in 1961, and Pilar's grandfather, Jorge, who needed specialized medical care, to do so in 1966. Celia and the rest of the family remained in Cuba. The segmentation of the family is not unique to those opposing the Castro government; rather, given revolutionary Cuba's economic, political, and cultural relations with Soviet bloc countries, it also affected those who supported it. Celia's youngest son, Javier, volunteered to go to Czechoslovakia, where he taught biochemistry at the University of Prague and married a native of that country. In addition, Celia's grandchildren, Luz and Milagros, did not live with their mother, Felicia. Students in a revolutionary society had limited options, and many, like Luz and Milagros, were required to reside in boarding schools.

As a member of a younger generation of Cuban Americans, García struggles with her Cuban identity and presents both sides of the Cuban question without appearing to privilege one point of view over the other. In an interview with Allan Vorda, García explained her attitude toward Communism:

> I grew up in a very black-and-white situation. My parents were virulently anti-Communist, and yet my relatives in Cuba were tremendous supporters of Communism, including members of my family who belong to the Communist Party. The trip in 1984 and the book, to some extent, were an act of reconciliation for the choices everybody made. I'm very much in favor of democratic systems, but I also strongly believe a country should determine its own fate. I realize I couldn't write and be a journalist and do everything I've done in Cuba; yet, I respect the right of people to live as they choose.[32]

García's novel recognizes that the Cuban situation is complex. The author goes to great pains to distance herself from other exile writers who provide a more simplistic representation of good and evil in the lives of Cubans both in and outside the island country. She is careful to mention less typical points of view, including those of foreign supporters of Cuba's policy and dissenters on the island. García also addresses both positive and negative aspects of life in the United States.

Lourdes and Rufino are typical of the exiles who left Cuba during the first two years after Castro seized power. Their story is a common one in the exile community. The government confiscated Rufino's dairy farm, but not before a revolutionary soldier raped Lourdes on the land, a symbolic portrayal of Castro's land reform policy. Yet the rape and the wound the soldier leaves on Lourdes's stomach will mark Pilar's birth, inscribing the memory and pain of the Cuban family trauma, as we shall see.

In the United States Lourdes becomes an active anti-Communist and an astute businesswoman, determined to live the American dream. Lourdes is a loyal American. She names her second bakery Yankee Doodle Bakery, to commemorate the Bicentennial. However, Pilar, a member of Rubén Rumbaut's and Gustavo Pérez Firmat's "1.5" generation, questions her parents' values, including their opposition to the Castro government.[33] Pilar is criticized for painting a punk rendition of the Statue of Liberty to celebrate the opening of her mother's second bakery. Pilar, and by extension the author, is best understood not as a child of the anti-Communist Miami community, but as one who belongs to the anti–Vietnam War era, which was critical of U.S. imperialism. This latter point of view was prevalent among Hispanic groups living outside of Miami, in particular the Areíto group and the Puerto Rican community in New York City, where García was raised.[34] A bohemian looking to establish her own identity, Pilar wants to return to her place of birth and live with her revolutionary grandmother, Celia.

Celia is a paradigm of those who remained in Cuba and support the Castro government. Of humble origins, Celia was raised without her parents, and, like the Cuban leader, she is married to the revolution. Celia watches the northern coast for invaders and is the civilian judge of her neighborhood defense committee. But Celia's political fervor is not shared by the daughter who also stayed in Cuba. Unlike her mother, Felicia has opposed the government since 1962, the year of the Cuban missile crisis. Considered to be an unfit mother, she is sent to a work brigade, where she encounters others also punished for not supporting government policies. The novel underscores generational divisions between Celia and Felicia, but also between Felicia and her revolutionary daughters and others who do not conform to an orthodox way of life: "It was my daughter who turned me in for insisting we say grace at the dinner table," Silvia Lores complains. "That's what they teach her at school, to betray her parents. Now I'm considered an 'antisocial.'" Another member of the brigade states: "It could be worse. . . . My neighbor's son was sent off to the marble quarries on the Isle of Pines because he listened to American jazz and wore his hair too long. Now I'm not in favor of long hair, mind you, but hard labor? In that sun?"[35]

In Cuba there is pressure to embrace a Communist way of life. In the United States there is pressure to acquiesce to a conservative interpretation of U.S. politics and culture, one that Pilar rejects. This is apparent when Lourdes commissions Pilar to paint a mural of the Statue of Liberty in celebration of the opening of the second bakery, Yankee Doodle Bakery, and in commemoration of the Bicentennial. Pilar prefers to do a painting and describes her masterpiece in the following manner:

When the paint dries, I start on Liberty herself. I do a perfect replication of her a bit left of center canvas, changing only two details: first, I make Liberty's torch float slightly beyond her grasp, and second, I paint her right hand reaching over to cover her left breast, as if she's reciting the National Anthem or some other slogan.

The next day, the background still looks off to me, so I take a medium-thick brush and paint black stick figures pulsing in air around Liberty, thorny scars that look like barbed wire. I want to go all the way with this, to stop mucking around and do what I feel, so at the base of the statue I put my favorite punk rallying cry: I'M A MESS. And then carefully, very carefully, I paint a safety pin through Liberty's nose.

This, I think, sums everything up very nicely. SL-76. That'll be my title. (141)

García's rendition of Liberty is a political commentary on how immigrants are treated in the United States. The Statue of Liberty, located on Liberty Island at the entrance to New York Harbor, was a gift from the people of France to the people of the United States and celebrates their country's allegiance during the American Revolutionary War. Liberty represents freedom from oppression, and she is the first symbol immigrants see when arriving at one of the busiest ports in the United States.

Pilar's rendition sheds light on her interpretation of the North American symbol. Let us compare the two representations of the statue. Lady Liberty, designed by the Alsatian sculptor Frédéric-Auguste Bartholdi, holds an illuminated torch in her right hand; in her left, a tablet with the date of independence, July 4, 1776, written in Roman numerals. The base upon which Liberty stands contains an inscription of Emma Lazarus's sonnet entitled "The New Colossus," which includes these well-known lines: "Give me your tired, your poor, / Your huddled masses yearning to breathe free, / The wretched refuse of your teeming shore, / Send these, the homeless, tempest-tost to me: / I lift my lamp beside the golden door!"[36]

According to Pilar's painting, the statue stands left of center. The torch has been switched from the right hand to the left and is beyond Liberty's reach. The tablet with the date of independence is not important and has been suppressed. Instead, Liberty appears to be pledging allegiance to the flag while holding on to her left breast. Clearly, the painting should be read within the context of the times. There is an emphasis on leftist politics; liberty and justice are beyond the reach of immigrants; and the statue is caressing her breast, an allusion to the influence of the women's movement upon the artist. Pilar's interpretation also illustrates that freedom is still an expensive commodity in the United States. Pilar's Lady Liberty, painted with barbed wire, speaks not of freedom but of sacrifice and suffering, and even of imprisonment, concepts opposed to those she usually represents. Whereas in the past many European immigrants were welcomed to the United States, filling a rapidly developing economy's need for cheap labor, today's (Hispanic) immigrants have not been received with the same enthusiasm. Certainly Puerto Ricans, who have migrated steadily since their island was seized by the United States during the Spanish-American War of 1898 and whose numbers increased in the 1940s and 1950s with Operation Bootstrap, know all too well the isolation portrayed by Pilar's statue. Pilar's Lady Liberty is a prisoner of society and has in recent years been denied her true identity. When the painting is unveiled, visitors are offended and are critical of Pilar's artistic expression.

The novel's description of life both in Cuba and in the United States raises the question of whether liberty exists for all the people or only for some. It also suggests that both the Cuban and U.S. governments and the cultures they promote demand that everyone conform to the dominant values of their respective societies. Although there are inherent differences between the two societies, and Felicia's punishment cannot be compared to Pilar's experiences, Pilar does feel restricted in the way she can express herself, especially in a society that calls itself free. She is disillusioned by the contradiction between what the United States is and what the country is supposed to represent.

Parts of García's novel take place in Cuba, where Celia lives. Lourdes and Pilar return to the source, a theme already made popular by Alejo Carpentier's "Viaje a la semilla."[37] Their one-week visit is a result of the government's policy to promote the reunification of the Cuban community. Prior to 1978, exiled Cubans were considered "worms." But since the visit of the Antonio Maceo Brigade, a group of children of exiles, in December 1977, and the dialogue one year later, Cubans living abroad have been encouraged to travel to their country of origin. The reunification, of course, has become profitable business, because the exiled Cubans bring with them the hard currency the government desperately needs.

Other historical events in Cuba become an important subtext for the novel. For example, Pilar, the author's alter ego, is a child of the revolution; she was born January 11, 1959, ten days after the victory that forced Batista to flee the island and three days after Castro's triumphant march into Havana. More significantly, political events in Cuba frame the novel. The narration develops between 1972 and 1980 and refers to specific events in the revolution. Let us look more closely at the two dates that open and close the narration. At the outset of the novel, Celia del Pino watches the northern coast of Cuba for any sign of invaders, but the only foreign presence approaching the island is the spirit of her recently deceased husband, Jorge, who returns from New York to say good-bye. Jorge's trip prefigures the one Pilar and Lourdes will take. Celia depicts the defensive mind-set that has existed in Cuba since the Bay of Pigs invasion in 1961 and is still evident in the 1970s.

Celia is the antithesis of the Statue of Liberty, welcoming immigrants at the entrance of New York Harbor. Celia also stands by the sea, looking out, not to welcome but to fend off intruders. The events related to Celia's vigilance intensified in 1970, when Castro announced his 10-million-ton sugar harvest. In order to set a new production record, Castro mobilized the Cuban workforce, sending many inexperienced city workers to the countryside to cut sugarcane. This unprecedented effort, whose purpose was to show that the country had the political resolve to meet stated goals and display its independence of other countries, impaired the Cuban economy. Hugh Thomas states that Castro's commitment was such that it appeared that his government would stand or fall by the extent to which the projected goal was reached.[38] Although Cuba did produce a record seven-million-ton harvest, it still fell short of the government's forecast. Cuban officials found themselves on the defensive, became sensitive to criticism, and responded in a predictable manner.

The government reaction to the failed sugar harvest of 1970 helps to explain why Castro's officials chose to make an issue of the poet Heberto Padilla, whom they had detained on March 20, 1971, an event García records in her novel: "She [Mom] reads the newspapers page by page for leftist conspiracies, jams her fingers against imagined evidence and says, 'See. What did I tell you?' Last year when El Líder jailed a famous Cuban poet, she sneered at 'those leftist intellectual hypocrites' for trying to free him" (26). Padilla was accused of counterrevolutionary activities and sentenced to one month in jail. However, the Padilla affair had started three years before, when his book *Fuera del juego* (Outside of the game) (1968) won the UNEAC (National Union of Writers and Artists of Cuba) prize for poetry but was condemned by government officials for containing poems critical of the revolution.[39] The book was published along with the jury vote and a declaration by officials who attacked the book's ideological content.[40]

After the failed harvest of 1970, government officials were intolerant of dissidents both in and outside the country, and Padilla became their most visible victim. The situation escalated when intellectual supporters of the revolution living abroad published an open letter to Castro in *Le Monde*, expressing concern over Padilla's arrest.[41] Padilla was released on April 27. That evening he attended a public meeting of the UNEAC and confessed his antirevolutionary activities, accusing his wife and close friends of conspiring against the government.[42] Padilla's staged confession led to a second *Le Monde* letter in which many of the signatories of the first one denounced the Stalinist pressures placed on the poet and others to confess their revolutionary sins.[43] Castro himself went on the offensive: he accused intellectuals of collaborating with the enemy and refused entry to sympathizers now critical of government policies.[44] Cuban functionaries echoed Castro's position. As a response, the critic and poet Roberto Fernández Retamar wrote his well-known essay *Calibán* (1972), which denigrated writers now considered enemies of the revolution.[45] The Padilla affair had a profound effect on the unconditional support intellectuals living in the West had given to Castro and divided public opinion into two camps, those who defended the revolution and those who attacked it.

As *Dreaming in Cuban* opens with events that reflect the tension surrounding the failed sugar harvest and the Padilla affair, it closes with another of Castro's miscalculations—this one involving another wave of Cuban exiles. Like Oscar Hijuelos's *Mambo Kings,* García's novel refers to the events following the takeover of the Peruvian embassy in April 1980, which led to Castro's decision to open up the port of Mariel. The significance of the result was undeniable: more than 125,000 Cubans fled the island, escaping to Miami.[46] The novel's action ends with Ivanito's escape to Peru, but García is compelled to mention the Mariel boatlift, which took place after that time. Lourdes dreams about the boatlift, an event that continued the fragmentation of the Cuban family:

> That night, Lourdes dreams of thousands of defectors fleeing Cuba. Their neighbors attack them with baseball bats and machetes. Many wear signs saying, *soy un gusano,* "I am a worm." They board ferries and cabin cruisers, rafts and fishermen's boats. The homes they leave behind are scrawled with obscenities. Rogelio Ugarte, the former postmaster of Santa Teresa del Mar, is beaten to death with chains on the corner of Calle Madrid, a visa in his pocket. Ilda Limón, too, is hoarse from screaming. She found a man face down in a pool of night rain in her yard and swears it's Javier del Pino, although her eyesight is no longer so good. Her neighbors tell Ilda she's crazy, that it's not Javier but just a poor wretch who tripped on the roots of her gardenia tree and drowned. (238)

The dream uncovers Javier's death, and the ending of the novel underscores a moral and political defeat of the Cuban government. It also recalls the first Cuban exodus, in 1959-61, of which the García family was a part. Nevertheless, there is a difference between the earlier exodus and the most recent one. The first was composed mainly of middle- and upper-class adults who fled with their children; the second was made up of people of modest means and included young people who, for one reason or another, had stayed behind and had been reared under revolutionary ideology.

According to Castro, the revolution had been made for them, the future of the new Cuban society. But their efforts to leave the country represented a sound rejection of the so-called accomplishments of the revolution in favor of an uncertain future in the United States. García concludes her novel with the mass exodus of Cubans in 1980, indicating that Pilar, and for that matter the author herself, has come to terms with her position regarding the Cuban revolution. At the outset of the novel she rejects her mother's values and embraces those of her grandmother. In the end, her actions appear to say the opposite. After witnessing for herself life in Cuba, Pilar becomes independent of the influence Celia and the Cuban government had over her. She hides from her grandmother the fact that she has seen her cousin Ivanito in the Peruvian embassy, daring to leave the country.

The trip to Cuba transforms Pilar, just as the return trip to the island changed some of the members of Areíto who made up the first contingent of the Antonio Maceo Brigade. Her "journey back to the source" allows Pilar to understand her past and present and to assume an independent position, one that recognizes a delicate balance between the negative and positive attributes of the Castro government. In the end she recognizes that Ivanito must escape to freedom. Although Pilar's position ultimately coincides with that of her mother, there is no evidence to suggest that she has accepted her mother's ideological position. Just as Lourdes is unable to come to terms with her experiences in Cuba, Pilar is also marked by her life in the United States. Lourdes was raped in Cuba; Pilar was molested in New York's Central Park. The mother formulates her opinion based on what takes place in Cuba, the daughter does the same according to what happens in the United States. Unlike her mother, Pilar goes to Cuba with a positive view of the revolution, and her change is part of her own process of development. She makes her decision to help Ivanito after seeing life in Cuba more clearly and contemplating her cousin's future.

The political discourse is evident in García's novel and, as I have demonstrated, marks the beginning and ending of the narration. But we would misread *Dreaming in Cuban* if we were to focus only on the political events. Though Celia and Jorge feel differently about the policies of the Cuban government, their reactions, and those of other characters, are not exclusively political; rather, they have a psychological dimension that can be seen in the interactions of the three generations of the del Pino family. This alternate reading suggests that Cuba's problems are not simply political: there are also cultural problems, which at times are manifested in political terms. The problems are inherent in the Cuban culture and psyche, and they are manifest in the writings of both Villaverde and García.

The del Pino family and the issues they encounter recall those of the Valdés (Gamboa) family that Villaverde so eloquently described in his *Cecilia Valdés*. Although Villaverde completed his masterpiece a century before García wrote her novel, both authors observe Cuban society while living in the United States. Undoubtedly, Villaverde and García address concerns prevalent both in Cuba and in the United States. As we have seen, Villaverde wrote about slavery, an institution that was widespread in Cuba until 1886 but had been abolished in the United States in 1865. Moreover, his denunciation of a massacre of blacks, which took place during the Ladder Conspiracy of 1844, can be related to his political beliefs and activities in the United States.[47] García narrates events concerning the revolution up to the takeover of the Peruvian embassy and the Mariel boatlift, but also provides a snapshot of the obsession lived by Cuban exiles in the United States. She shows that there are distinct differences between her parents' generation and her own. Unlike her parents, who are grateful to be in the United States, Pilar is critical of mainstream U.S. politics and culture. In spite of the century that separates them, both Villaverde and García place Cuba's problems within the context of the Cuban family. Villaverde wrote about the incestuous relationship between the white Leonardo Gamboa and his mulatto half sister Cecilia Valdés; García also refers to problems that can be understood in generational and cultural terms.

The concerns expressed by García are not necessarily related to the Cuban Revolution; on the contrary, they transcend that period and existed before Lourdes and Felicia were born. They emerge from the love triangle, a theme that in Villaverde's work is represented by Cecilia, Leonardo, and Isabel Ilincheta. In García's novel the triangle is composed of Celia, Gustavo (her Spanish lover), and his absent wife, who lives in Spain; and later of Celia, Jorge, and the absent Gustavo, who has returned to his native country. Celia never stops loving Gustavo, and Jorge never forgives her for it. In an early letter to Gustavo, dated March 11, 1935, Celia makes her feelings clear:

> *Mi querido* Gustavo,
>   In two weeks I will marry Jorge del Pino. He's a good man and says he loves me. We walk along the beach and he shields me with a parasol. I've told him about you, about our meetings in the Hotel Inglaterra. He tells me to forget you.
>   I think of our afternoons in those measured shafts of light that spent light, and I wish I could live underwater. Maybe then my skin would absorb the sea's consoling silence. I'm a prisoner on this island, Gustavo, and I cannot sleep. (49)

In her August 11 letter Celia tells Gustavo that she is pregnant and adds: "If it's a boy, I'll leave him. I'll sail to Spain, to Granada, to your kiss, Gustavo." And signs it "I love you, Celia" (50). Celia does not give birth to a boy, but rather to Lourdes, whom she will resent, and stays in Cuba.

Jorge and Celia's relationship is a key to understanding the novel and is further clarified in the second of two chapters, which appears to be out of chronological order, under the heading "Daughters of Changó."[48] The previous chapter, "God's Will," narrates Herminia Delgado's point of view, and it is dated 1980. It is followed by the chapter in question, which is dated 1979 and describes a conversation between Lourdes and her husband Jorge's spirit. The next date that appears, in the same chapter, returns us to 1980, but the passage discusses events from Pilar's first-person narration. The section dated 1979 is important, not only because it underscores the magical elements in the novel but also because it is Jorge who tells Lourdes that she must return to Cuba. In addition, Jorge confesses his participation in the Cuban family drama:

> After we were married, I left her with my mother and my sister. I knew what it would do to her. A part of me wanted to punish her. For the Spaniard. I tried to kill her, Lourdes. I wanted to kill her. I left on a long trip after you were born. I wanted to break her, may God forgive me. When I returned, it was done. She held you out to me by one leg and told me she would not remember your name. (195)

In addition, Jorge tells Lourdes that her sister Felicia has died.

Even though Celia does not love Jorge, her problems were present much earlier, perhaps before she was born, and may have been inherited from her own parents. A daughter of her father's failed second marriage, Celia was separated from her parents and siblings and sent to live with her great aunt Alicia, in Havana. Celia's displacement from her own family and her need to return to the love represented by that nurturing nucleus led her to become involved in a precarious relationship with a married Spaniard, destined to fail. Her marriage to del Pino did not solve her problems but made them even worse.

The trauma that develops, perhaps of Spanish origin—represented by Gustavo and in *Cecilia Valdés* by Cándido Gamboa—takes on national characteristics. Celia does not go to Granada; rather, she stays with Jorge and his family, the Ameidas, who persecute her. The actions are expressed in racial terms, and it is here that I see another link between Villaverde's and García's novels. Celia's character is a rewriting of Cecilia Valdés. Both Celia and Cecilia are rejected by their fathers; in essence they are orphans, live with a relative, and lack guidance and economic resources. However, in García's novel, Celia is white and Jorge is dark, or so we assume because his sister and mother are.[49] Both Villaverde and García allude to the racial complexity of Cuban society. And both of their characters have tragic endings. Cecilia is committed to an insane asylum and is destined to raise her child on her own; Celia walks into the sea and commits suicide. Moreover, the names Cecilia and Celia recall each other, and Felicia's husband is named Villaverde.

In García's novel, familial and generational patterns develop to which all the characters adhere. A generational opposition exists between Celia and her two daughters, Lourdes and Felicia, and is repeated between them and their daughters, Pilar and Luz and Milagros. However, the antagonism is not clearly evident between grandchild and grandparent; on the contrary, there is an attraction that, to some degree, helps to justify the discord with the mothers: Pilar admires Celia, and although Luz and Milagros live in boarding school, Celia looks after them.

The hatred for the mother, expressed in generational terms, follows a motif already explained in Freudian terms as the Electra complex. The disdain for the mother leads to a concern for the father. Jorge and Lourdes care for each other, and Luz and Milagros look after Hugo, even though he abused Felicia and abandoned them. The interfamilial relationships also reflect the Oedipus complex. Celia has difficulty relating to her two daughters, but she is very close to her youngest son, Javier. Similarly, both Luz and Milagros think their mother is crazy, but Ivanito wants to be by her side. Meanwhile, Javier and Ivanito have difficulty interacting with their respective fathers. Although the relationships between the characters can be understood in psychoanalytic terms, they have political implications, too, suggesting the younger generation's defiance of the older, to become independent of its power and influence. This indicates that the relationship between Jorge and Lourdes and between Hugo and Luz and Milagros is based on revenge, a desire to hurt and defy the mother for the pain that they have experienced. In political terms it foreshadows a possible division among the generations of Cuba's leaders. The younger officers were not molded by the same circumstances that led members of the July 26th Movement to overthrow Batista's forces or by those that led the Partido Socialista Popular, the Cuban Communist Party, to be loyal to Soviet and Marxist ideologies. If the pattern proposed by the novel is to be continued in Cuban society, the younger political generation will inevitably turn against the older one.[50]

The generational opposition is also exemplified by the lack of communication within the Cuban family, which continues to be manifested in political and personal terms. The novel represents the lack of communication in a series of letters Celia writes to Gustavo, from November 11, 1934, until January 11, 1959, the day of Pilar's birth. The letters, meant to establish communication, are never sent: "For twenty-five years, Celia wrote her Spanish lover a letter on the eleventh day of each month, then stored it in a satin-covered chest beneath her bed. Celia has removed her drop pearl earrings only nine times, to clean them. No one ever remembers her without them" (38). The letters appear in three separate chapters, each marking a different historical period: the first dating from 1935 to 1940, the second from 1942 to 1949, the third from 1950 to 1955, and the final one, which ends the novel, dated January 11, 1959. The third group of letters, from 1950 to 1955, mixes the personal with the political as Celia becomes involved in opposition to the Batista dictatorship. The lack of communication is further accentuated by the missing letters, a majority, to which there is no reference in the novel. Only partial communication is possible. Toward the end of the narration Celia gives to Pilar the letters that García reproduces in her novel.

The letters in the novel reveal that even though Celia was married to Jorge, she maintained a continuous (emotional) relationship with Gustavo. Celia's inability to break with past memories led her to engage in a twenty-five-year double love affair with Jorge and Gustavo, which ended when her granddaughter was born and the Cuban Revolution triumphed. Celia then transferred the love she had for Gustavo to Pilar, and after the granddaughter left, from Pilar to the revolution. Jorge, jealous of Celia's relationship with Gustavo, had her committed to an asylum. In political terms, the letters portray a singular point of view, valuable regardless of the context in which they were written or whether or not they become the property of the intended receiver. Read together, the letters create their own context. Moreover, the letters indicate the lack (or partial lack) of communication and the irreconcilable differences among the members of the del Pino family—and among the members of the revolutionary government and the exile community.

In spite of the geographical distance between Cuba and the United States and the political distance between the institutions that determine the laws of each country, there are similarities between Pilar, Luz and Milagros, and Ivanito. They are Celia's grandchildren, but, just as their mothers reject Celia, Pilar, Luz, and Milagros also repudiate their own mothers and are drawn to their grandmother. Ivanito, who is close to his mother, is also under the protection of his grandmother.

More significantly, the grandchildren narrate their stories in the first person, that is, from their own point of view. All the other sections are told in the third person. It is this contrast in narration that underscores their position in society, as victims of the older generation. The younger generation is attempting to develop its own individual voice and, because of the generational differences, the younger is a symbol of the future. The children challenge the adult discourse and provide the reader with another and more personal perspective of what is described in the third person. Luz and Milagros, for example, offer the reader a view of Hugo Villaverde different from the one proposed by the omniscient narrator. Whereas Hugo is depicted as a violent and selfish individual, his daughters find him to be warm and compassionate, and they become receptive to his needs.

The use of the first-person narration also suggests an association between the grandchildren and Herminia, Felicia's childhood friend. Herminia's section, also written in the first person, describes Felicia's initiation into Santería as she completes the various stages of her preparation, which culminate in the final consecration. Herminia also narrates Felicia's death. The identity between Herminia's section and other first-person narrations is not meant to suggest that she is one of Celia's grandchildren, but to show an affinity between Pilar and Herminia, whom the protagonist visits. This section confirms that Pilar's return to Cuba was a spiritual journey; she is a daughter of Changó, the god of fire and lightning.

Santería, originally practiced by Yoruba slaves brought to Cuba, and mixed with Catholicism, represents an important part of Cuban culture on the island, but also abroad. In Cuba, Santería has been woven into the fabric of Cuban society. After the Castro takeover, it was banned as another religion opposed by scientific Marxism, but also because of the historical fear blacks represented, dating to the uprising in Santo Domingo in 1791 and reinforced in Cuba by the Aponte Conspiracy of 1812, the Ladder Conspiracy of 1844, and the Race War of 1912. In the revolution, the government forced Afro-Cuban religion underground, where, as in the nineteenth century, it continued to survive. Cuban policy changed, and in 1989 it became legal for Cubans to practice religion, including Santería. I believe that Nicaragua's unique blend of Marxism and Christianity became a more attractive model for change in Latin America than the Cuban one. Perestroika also allowed Cuban officials to recognize the need to alter their long-standing antireligion policies. The change was also a way of addressing inconsistencies within Cuban society. During the time of the narration and in the present, Cuban officials adhere to Marxist ideology. But in private many worship Afro-Cuban gods. It is widely known, as García writes, that Castro himself has been initiated into Afro-Cuban religion; he is the son of Eleggua, the god of the road.

There has been a public acceptance of Afro-Cuban religions in Cuba, but there are still color and racial divisions in the new Cuban society. Even though blacks have made economic and political gains, racial attitudes remain relatively unchanged. In Herminia's section, which reads more like an interview, the narrator speaks to this aspect of Cuban reality: "Felicia is the only person I've known who didn't see color. There are white people who know how to act politely to blacks, but deep down you know they're uncomfortable. They're worse, more dangerous than those who speak their minds, because they don't know what they're capable of" (184). Viewed in the context of the Race War of 1912, in which Herminia's grandfather and great-uncles and many other blacks were killed, life for Afro-Cubans under the revolution is much improved. However, Carlos Moore, a critic of Castro's racial policies, shows that blacks have not fared well under the revolution. They have not been given the opportunity to promote their own culture, but instead are encouraged to become culturally whiter. Afro-Cubans have been provided with the mechanisms to abandon their religious and cultural past.[51]

Herminia herself admits that her oldest son died in Angola, in the war to which many Afro-Cubans were sent to fight. Uncharacteristically, Herminia prefers to define the problem not in racial but in sexual terms, observing that men are still in charge. What Herminia fails to understand is that whites continue to be in charge; there are even more white women in high government positions than Afro-Cubans. But Herminia's words more accurately recall the situation of blacks in the United States as it is known to Pilar or to the author. They reflect the common belief that southerners usually speak their minds, whereas northerners are hypocritical and tend to mask their racial positions. In addition, García's re-creation of Herminia's narration speaks to the success with which on the surface the revolution has been able to devalue the race issue at home and abroad. It also refers to the author's greater familiarity with gender issues, promoted by the women's movement, than with those of race, advanced by civil rights organizations.

Continuing the parallel between Cuba and the United States, Santería is also present in North American culture—taken there by Cuban immigrants, most recently by the Marielitos—where it has joined Puerto Rican Espiritismo and other manifestations of Afro-Caribbean religions. In New York, Pilar is attracted to a *botánica,* where she is recognized as the daughter of Changó and, after nine days of herbal baths, understands that her destiny is to travel to Cuba. Afro-Cuban religion is not portrayed as a superstition of ignorant people, but as a vibrant element of a culture that gives meaning and a sense of purpose to society. It is perhaps her visit to the *botánica* that saves Pilar from a more serious attack by a gang of youths as she crosses Central Park.

What Alejo Carpentier defined in his introduction to *El reino de este mundo* (1949; *The Kingdom of This World,* 1957) as the magical or marvelous reality in America, a concept later associated with García Márquez and promoted in literature as magical realism, is present in Cuba and the United States and affects all of the members of the del Pino family. Afro-Cuban religions have become an integral part of Cuban culture. Lourdes is not a follower of Santería, but she is able to see her father's spirit and even talks to him. He informs Lourdes that Felicia has died and encourages her to travel to Cuba and tell Celia that in spite of his mistreatment, he loved her. This supernatural event coincides with the one Pilar experiences with

Santería. For different spiritual reasons, both Pilar and Lourdes decide to return to Cuba.

The spiritual link between Christianity and Afro-Cuban religions points directly to Felicia, whom I believe to be the most fascinating character in the novel. She is considered crazy, antirevolutionary, a fanatic of Afro-Cuban religion, a murderer, and an unfit mother. But her character offers an insight into Cuban culture and García's novel. After Felicia burns Graciela, a technique she uses to get out of an abusive marital relationship with Hugo, Celia's second daughter finds herself without memory, in Cienfuegos on July 26, 1978, married to Otto Cruz, who wants to take her to Minnesota. Felicia belongs to another world, and she attempts to reconstruct cultural codes and piece together her past and present:

> During the following week, Felicia begins to assemble bits and pieces of her past. They stack up in her mind, soggily, arbitrarily, and she sorts through them like cherished belongings after a flood. She charts sequences and events with colored pencils, shuffling her diagrams until they start to make sense, a possible narrative. But the people remain faceless, nameless. (157)

Ivanito's apparition and voice allow Felicia to bring order to her life; she kills Otto and escapes to her present. As she finds her way back to Havana, Felicia's actions recall those of Pilar, or García. In García's case, she is torn between different worlds, one of the present, the United States, and the other of the past, Cuba; one of the Cuban Revolution and the other of the exile commnunity. García left Cuba in 1961 and returned in 1984, where she claimed (in the interview with Vorda, quoted earlier) to have learned about the history of her family. The experience led her to write *Dreaming in Cuban*.[52] "Going South," a chapter title, represents for both protagonist and author a desire to go back to the roots. After his death, Rufino returns home. Lourdes does the same, against her better judgment, but recognizes that her father's encouragement expresses a spiritual connection. Pilar travels to Cuba to see the successes and failures of the revolution, not through her mother's perspective but with her own eyes, as many early refugees' children have done by joining the Antonio Maceo Brigade. The travel should be interpreted as a form of rebellion against the parents, but also as a communion with the origin of Cuban history, literature, and culture.

Like Felicia, who finds herself in a different environment, Pilar in Cuba strives to read the cultural signs, which she can make sense of only by coming to terms with the master codes of Cuban culture. Ivanito's voice is replaced by Celia's image, or, in the case of the author, by a return to the island where she was born; and only with a trip to the island can she truly understand her past—but also her present.

In her trip to Cuba, Pilar learns about her family but soon discovers that even though she was raised in the United States, she is part of a series of symmetries that bind her to her family in particular and to Cuban history and culture in general. In the United States Pilar knew that she differed from her mother and was attracted to her grandmother. But in Cuba Pilar also learns that she has much in common with Felicia, such as their shared ability to move in different environments and have contact with the spiritual world. Felicia finds the master codes in Afro-Cuban religion. Similarly, Pilar realizes that she, for better or for worse, is drawn to Cuba and Cuban culture.

The magical or spiritual elements permeate the novel and provide insight into a series of repetitions, in which Pilar herself is an important element. For example, while in the sanatorium Celia meets Felicia Gutiérrez, who killed her husband by dousing him with gasoline. Celia names her second daughter after Felicia, and the daughter repeats the crime of which her mother's friend was accused. Celia writes to Gustavo on the eleventh day of each month, the same day Pilar is born, which also happens to be Celia's birthday. Both Celia and Felicia, for separate reasons, are committed to an asylum. Celia and Felicia, in different periods, make love to their respective boyfriends, Gustavo and Hugo, in the same Hotel Inglaterra; and both relationships fail. Felicia and her second husband, Ernesto, were born on the same day and year, only minutes apart. Lourdes and Celia are on opposite sides of the political spectrum, yet each one polices the society in which she lives.

Although Pilar wants to stay away from her mother's interpretation of Cuba's internal situation, in some strange way she comes back to it. Pilar cannot avoid succumbing to Lourdes and Felicia's political and cultural perspectives. It may not be totally accidental that both Pilar and Batista are children of Changó. Pilar and Lourdes are also the daughters of Changó. And just as Lourdes and Felicia betray Celia, and Felicia betrays Hugo, Pilar will also do the same to her grandmother, leading to her grandmother's suicide.

In spite of their differences, Lourdes and Pilar return to Cuba to fulfill a mission. In the chapter "Daughters of Changó," Lourdes tells her father's spirit that she cannot return to Cuba, and he answers: "There are things you must do, things you will only know when you get there" (196). As daughters of Changó, Lourdes and Pilar's mission is to liberate Ivanito from Celia and the revolution. He is the only male child in the family and, in traditional terms, the carrier of the family name. And his departure from the island continues to underscore the fragmentation of the Cuban family: Luz and Milagros remain in Cuba, Pilar and Ivanito will live in the United States, and Javier's daughter, Irinita, resides in Czechoslovakia.

The events at the Peruvian embassy in May 1980, and their placement at the end of the novel, provide a meaningful connection between *Dreaming in Cuban* and Reinaldo Arenas's *Termina el desfile* (1981). Arenas's collection of short stories concludes with the one that gives its title to the work and is based on the takeover of the Peruvian embassy.[53] Like Pilar, Arenas experienced a change in his allegiance to the Cuban Revolution. He wrote the opening story, "Comienza el desfile" (also the original title of the collection), at the beginning of the revolution and narrates the protagonist's enthusiasm generated by the entry of rebel soldiers into his rural town. After Arenas left the island he wrote "Termina el desfile," a narrative confirming his break with the Cuban government.[54]

Of the Cuban exile writers who fled to the United States, Arenas was the most active and best known. Arenas escaped without the knowledge of Cuban authorities in the Mariel boatlift, the same event García describes at the end of her novel. In the closing moments of the novel the protagonist, referring to the takeover of the Peruvian embassy, states: "Nothing can record this, I think. Not words, not paintings, not photographs." García attempts to capture it in her narrative, but Arenas's "Termina el desfile" provides the best description of what took place during that unprecedented period. Ivanito and Pilar's presence in the Peruvian embassy recall Arenas's description of the same event, and one story serves as an intertext for the other. Let us look more closely at Arenas's story. Following the chronology of events, Arenas's protagonist runs to the embassy, a place that had been transformed into a haven, an oasis from the harsh Cuban political, economic, and social realities.

Arenas's "Termina el desfile" is a long meditation upon that tragic event and reproduces with convincing emotion what it was like to have lived inside the Peruvian embassy. Written in one continuous paragraph, in which the narration changes from first to third person, it captures the chaos experienced by the 10,000 Cubans seeking refuge. They lived in overcrowded conditions, like sardines, among the urine and feces, with pangs of hunger and thirst. Arenas states for the record that although the government did pass out eight hundred boxes of food, there was not enough to go around, and it was done in a humiliating way: soldiers stomped on the hands attempting desperately to reach whatever nourishment they could grab.

Just as Pilar is looking for Ivanito, Arenas's protagonist is also undergoing a search—first for a reptile, later for his friend, but ultimately for the elusive truth concealed within the society in which he lives. At the outset the object of the search is represented by the third-person female pronoun *she*, lost among the dirt, urine, feces, arms, and legs of the tumultuous crowd. No one has a name and each person is identified by body parts, all serving as obstacles in the protagonist's quest. *She* is a lizard, but the referent of the pronoun shifts and comes to be applied to his best male friend, who, because of the nature of the pronoun, is also his lover.

As the protagonist undergoes this multiple search, he reflects upon his life prior to entering the Peruvian embassy. The story reconstructs the past, and the reader notices that the chaos of the present is no different from that which the protagonist experiences in Cuban society. Therefore, the decision to enter the compound is not a difficult one for the many Cubans who saw their lives and standard of living deteriorate under the Castro government. The protagonist's life makes even more sense if we consider him an extension of the author and read the story alongside *Antes que anochezca* (1992; *Before Night Falls*, 1993) in which Arenas provides detailed descriptions of his imprisonment under the Castro regime. In "Termina el desfile" the reader comes to appreciate the close relationship and trust that the protagonist has with the friend for whom he is looking.

Arenas's story helps to contextualize Ivanito's life. García does not provide much information about why Ivanito left the country. Nevertheless, his actions speak louder than his words and they should be read next to those of others who were reared under the Castro government and had no other choice but to escape. The lack of freedom and the direct or indirect physical or psychological persecution are not alternatives that can be tolerated. On more than one occasion, Arenas tells us that many of those attempting to escape are young people, like Ivanito, for whom the revolution was built but whom the revolution betrays.

The theme of betrayal is present in both stories. In Arenas's story, his protagonist goes to the Peruvian embassy looking for his friend, who promised, if everything appeared to be safe, to go back to the apartment and rescue him. Believing his friend to be among the many wanting to leave the country, the protagonist transforms himself into the reptile he is also searching for and crawls and squeezes by everyone impeding his progress. Finally, he sees his friend at a distance, not inside the compound but outside, dressed in a government uniform, talking to other soldiers and laughing at what they perceive to be a comedy unfolding before their eyes. At this point in the story, the protagonist, and the reader, realize that the friend is a Castro supporter who has betrayed the protagonist. It is now clear that the government's earlier search and confiscation of the protagonist's property, including his manuscripts, were the result of information provided to the authorities by his friend, the informant. In a society like present-day Cuba, one does not know whom to trust, even when it comes to one's best friend and lover.

Arenas's story helps to uncover why Ivanito betrays his grandmother. Celia is a symbol of the revolution who has already betrayed her children. His rejection of her represents Ivanito's attempt to escape a life of contradictions with no future, his only recourse. Ivanito prefers to risk every-thing he has known and start anew, in a different society, under a different government.

Arenas's story ends with the completion of the search and the attain-ment of the truth. The protagonist finds his friend, but also the lizard. The reptile has escaped from the embassy, but, given the conditions in Cuban society, even it returns to safety and the protagonist's hand. It is no acci-dent that the protagonist finds meaning in something as common as a lizard, which has no monetary or spiritual value and is common through-out the island. The lizard symbolizes the protagonist, who has had to live and move like a reptile among the numerous obstacles, real and imaginary, placed before him. And, as he cannot with his friend, he can confide in the lizard—have it know everything yet reveal nothing. Perhaps, in the society about which Arenas writes, one can trust and befriend only the reptiles. In García's novel, Pilar enters the compound and is confronted with the same anarchy Arenas describes. Like Arenas's protagonist, Pilar finds Ivanito, but she tells her grandmother that he has already left the country.

Ivanito, the only male of his generation, is a symbol of the future of the del Pino family.[55] Let us remember that except for Ivanito, Lourdes, Felicia, and Javier have daughters. Pilar's younger brother dies in Cuba as a result of Lourdes's horseback accident, followed by the rape. Ivanito is the savior of the family, a Christlike figure who needs to be protected and rescued. In Cortázar's "Las babas del diablo" (1966; "Blow-Up" 1968) the protagonist is able to make sense of the boy's life not at the moment when he is taking the pictures, but only after he develops them. The protagonist can under-stand his participation in helping the boy escape only after the events con-clude.[56] Similarly, Ivanito's life and Pilar's presence in Cuba are meaningful in the context of the events at the Peruvian embassy, in which she under-stands a greater order and purpose and so helps him leave the island. Ivanito's escape is a rejection of what the Cuban Revolution and Celia stand for, as symbols of the present course of events. The revolution's role as a nurturing parent is called into question when the reader understands that Celia has a missing breast. Ivanito has given Celia a reason to live, and once she believes that he has fled the island, she loses her interest in life and commits suicide—perhaps as an allusion to Castro's (or the revolu-tion's) final outcome. Ivanito's escape is a way of helping Felicia and sym-bolically getting her out of Cuba; in the United States he will continue in his role and support his relatives. However, the real savior is Cristina (García) whose name is derived from Cristo (Christ), and it is her work that permanently saves Ivanito and the Cuban family tradition.

The novel ends in Cuba, and the reader is tempted to speculate as to whether Pilar has deciphered the master codes of Cuban politics and cul-ture. Has she been transformed by what she witnessed on the island and will she now be more receptive to her mother's point of view? Or will the situation in the United States force her to continue to support a critical position regarding North American culture? Although the author may not have felt the need to choose one country over the other, the novel does show that Pilar is as much a part of her Cuban past as are her relatives who live in Cuba. More important, she is not just a witness to the historical unfolding of events, but an active participant in Cuba's history. Pilar was raised and educated in the United States, but her stay in Cuba awakens a side of her that remained dormant; she comes to accept that she also carries Cuban culture within her. The last chapter, "Six Days in April," whose title refers to the time Pilar and Lourdes spent in Cuba, contains the line that gives title to the novel. Pilar narrates the section to which I refer. In it Celia gives Pilar the box of letters she wrote to Gustavo, but the section also contains a paragraph that speaks to García's experiences in Cuba:

> I've started dreaming in Spanish, which has never happened before. I wake up feeling different, like something inside me is changing, something chemical and irreversible. There's a magic here working its way through my veins. There's something about the vegetation, too, that I respond to instinctively—the stunning bougainvillea, the flamboyants and jacarandas, the orchids growing from the trunks of the mysterious ceiba trees. And I love Havana, its noise and decay and painted ladyness. I could happily sit on one of those wrought-iron balconies for days, or keep my grandmother company on her porch, with its ringside view of the sea. I'm afraid to lose all this, to lose Abuela Celia again. But sooner or later I'd have to return to New York. I know now it's where I belong—not *instead* of here, but *more* than here. How can I tell my grandmother this? (236)

Although Pilar, or García, looks at Cuba from a romantic point of view, one of a visitor not committed to staying permanently, the paragraph reveals that Cuba will always be a part of her. Pilar's Cuban experience is something she lives, feels, and dreams, but may never understand logically. It is like the letters Pilar carries back with her to New York. They are images, fragments, tropes that recall her family's past, and now of Pilar's present. And New York, which also contains bits and pieces of Cuban and Hispanic cultures, will nourish this newly found aspect of Pilar's being. Pilar will live in the United States, but she will dream of Cuba.

SIX

Dominican American Poetry
Culture in the middest

Men, like poets, rush "into the middest," in medias res, when
they are born; they also die in mediis rebus, and to make sense
of their span they need fictive concords with origins, and ends,
such as give meaning to lives and to poems. The End they imagine will reflect their irreducibly intermediary preoccupations.
They fear it, and as far as we can see have always done so; the
End is a figure for their deaths.
— Frank Kermode, *The Sense of an Ending*

OMINICANS are the most recent group of immigrants to arrive
in the United States from the Hispanic Caribbean; most reside in
New York City. Dominican migration was under way during the
Trujillo dictatorship, when those who opposed his regime sought
political asylum in the United States. Migration to the mainland increased
after the U.S. invasion of the Dominican Republic in 1965; the military
replaced the democratically elected and socialist Juan Bosch with one of
Trujillo's ministers, Joaquín Balaguer, thus reinforcing economic and political ties between the two countries. This was the same year the U.S.
Congress passed the 1965 Family Reunification Act, which allowed family
members to join their relatives living in the United States. Statistics show
that there was an increase in the number of Dominicans leaving the island
after the fall of Trujillo, and an additional rise after Bosch was elected into
office in 1963. But the numbers increased dramatically following the U.S.
invasion in 1965 and throughout the 1970s and 1980s.[1] Presently,
Dominicans are the second-largest Hispanic group in New York City, and
the fourth-largest in the United States.

A review of the decades in which Dominicans arrived in the United
States is crucial for understanding their migration to and position within
North American society. By the time Dominicans arrived in large numbers,
Puerto Ricans and Cubans had made significant political, educational, and

literary gains, mainly on the East Coast, and Chicanos had done so in the Southwest. Taking advantage of Johnson's Great Society, and in New York City of Lindsay's Mobilization for Youth, Latinos made modest gains in work-related areas and education. In the decade of the sixties, the majority of Latinos in New York were Puerto Ricans. The breakthroughs were a direct result of much confrontation between groups such as the Young Lords Party and Latino college and university students, and New York City and state officials. The creation of Latin American, Caribbean, or Puerto Rican studies programs in the Northeast responded to events in the Caribbean, but also to those taking place on U.S. campuses. When Dominicans arrived, they joined the ranks of Latino organizations and pressed for rights that also benefited them as recent immigrants. And as their numbers continued to increase, Dominicans emphasized the Dominican component of Latino culture, and they laid the groundwork for the creation of Dominican studies programs.[2]

Dominican immigrants have had to contend with the low status accorded to any newcomer, as well as that of Latinos in New York generally. Dominicans have identified with Latinos and supported them on key issues that were extant prior to their arrival in large numbers. They have joined Puerto Ricans and Cubans in championing causes such as bilingual education, multiculturalism, English as a second language instruction, and programs for students with limited English proficiency.

Dominican American literature reflects the Dominican experience both on the mainland and on the island. In some respects, Dominican literature written in the United States combines elements already seen in Cuban American and Puerto Rican American literatures. Because of their status as recent immigrants, Dominican writers tend to express themselves in Spanish and in a standard language that recalls that used by Cuban Americans who also write in Spanish. However, many Dominicans live in New York City and are dark-skinned; in this regard their experiences coincide with those of dark-skinned Puerto Rican Americans. Dominican writers have been encouraged by the successes of other minorities in documenting their experiences in the United States and have become active in publishing magazines and creating editorial houses. Whereas the means of literary production may have been off-limits to them in their country of origin, in the United States they have contributed to and profited from an upsurge of Latino literary activity.

In 1988 Daisy Cocco de Felippis and Jane Robinett published the first bilingual anthology of Dominican writings from the United States, *Poemas del exilio y de otras inquietudes/Poems of Exile and Other Concerns: A Bilingual Selection of the Poetry Written by Dominicans in the United States.* The title alludes to the recent arrival of Dominicans and proposes that they are not willing immigrants, but rather have been forced to abandon their homeland. The "exile" mentioned in the title was the result of economic changes in the Dominican Republic after the United States invaded the island. As in Puerto Rico following Operation Bootstrap, foreign investment in the industrial sector has also led to an increase in unemployment and therefore a forced migration to the United States.

The use of the word *exile* refers to the condition of Dominicans in the United States and places them culturally closer to the Dominican Republic than to their adopted country. The title suggests that if Cubans are exiles, so are Dominicans; Cubans are not the only exiles living in the United States. This explains the language used to write the poems. Except for the poems written by Julia Álvarez, they were originally composed in Spanish and translated by the editors into English. But the poems are not about exile, at least not in the way we have seen in the writings of Cuban American writers such as Ricardo Pau-Llosa and Pablo Medina. Because many of the writers have lived in the United States for some time, "exile" does not refer to their legal status, as it often does in the case of Cubans. More appropriately, it describes a political position that prevents Dominicans from assimilating into the North American environment.

The title's inclusion of the term *exile* problematizes the immigration of Hispanics to the United States. Whether Hispanic Caribbeans leave their country of origin and arrive in the United States for political reasons or economic ones is less important for understanding the impact the move has on their children. The children, who have little or no say in their parents' decision yet are profoundly affected by it, are indeed exiles. They have been taken from their country and transported to the United States, and they look to the past and desire a communion with the reality they once knew, as seen through the innocent eyes of a child. In this sense, Puerto Rican and Dominican children, like their Cuban counterparts, are also spiritual exiles.

The pressures Hispanics experience when leaving one culture and entering another, or when attempting to maintain their own identity within the context of a dominant culture, are addressed by Franklin Gutiérrez in "Helen." The poem's title alludes to William Carlos Williams's Puerto Rican mother, Elena, who lived in the United States and did not speak fluent English. More directly, the name refers to a Dominican woman who has become a symbol of an immigrant's desire to assimilate into North American society.

If the works of Puerto Rican and Cuban American poets can be divided by gender, Gutiérrez crosses this line and confronts issues that belong to women, evident in the poetic dialogue between Sandra María Esteves and Luz María Umpierre.[3] From the outset of the poem, the poetic voice notices a change in Helena, who left her homeland to reside in New York. Although the move was intended to produce a positive effect, the poetic voice sees the opposite, and expresses it with words such as *faded, buried, snow, scar,* and *collapse.* The cold weather is debilitating, and the only available heat is artificial.

> How things have changed, Helena,
> the anguished cry for a homeland
> left behind
> the first encounter with
> the tall, uniform faded towers of the empire,
> the wide avenues
> buried under immense layers of snow,
> the traffic signs,
> one way, no parking anytime, quarters only.
> The daily toils with a heater,
> with feet bumping into sleeping rugs,
> and the scar on your left knee,
> sad reminder of an escalator's collapse.[4]

Helena's willingness to put her past behind her recalls the relative ease with which Cuban American women moved into North American society. More than the men, they closed the door behind them and looked forward.

The poem's version of Dominican life in New York is distinct from the experiences of other immigrants residing in the same city. Instead of a sense of happiness and freedom, the poem conveys a lack of enthusiasm on the part of these refugees on the mainland. Gutiérrez's images are abundantly visual. Although the mainland provides a change and an opportunity to start anew, it also demands conformity. This conflict is underscored in the opposing directions present in the first stanza: up is represented by tall towers; horizontal by the wide avenues and traffic signs that instruct "one way, no parking anytime, quarters only"; and down by the collapsing escalator. The latter image is also a comment on the present society and its advanced technology. The increased weight of those wanting to move vertically has caused the escalator to collapse. The technology cannot support the weight of all the riders, so their movement is not upward but downward. In effect, not everyone can move upward.

In the second stanza, the reader is told why Helena has forgotten her past and does not have time to write home. She is enticed by the grandeur of *Intrepid Museum,* an aircraft carrier that ruled the oceans, perhaps the same one used during the U.S. invasion of the Dominican Republic in 1965, as suggested in the third stanza: "This immense ship once happened to pass by your island / just to see what was happening."[5] The first stanza ends with the scar and the collapsed escalator; the second one repeats the image with "victims of bygone years," and the third points to the land from where the victims came.

The change in Helena is most visible in her name. She is no longer Helena, but Helen, and she does not date Hispanic men, only Anglo-American ones. As in the previous stanzas, Helen's progress is offset by elements present in her adopted country. Although her Anglo-American boyfriend sleeps with Helen, he does not want to be seen in public with her, perhaps because of her dark skin or Hispanic accent. The poetic voice speaks from a Dominican perspective, but it is not free of the Anglo-American one. The concern for race that the poetic voice finds in Helen is mostly a reflection of historical events in the United States. Certainly, racial issues exist in Dominican society, even though upper-class and elite writers have omitted them from the literature. In the Dominican Republic, dark-skinned or black people are not considered Dominicans, but Haitians. Statistics show that an overwhelming majority of Dominicans are non-white. However, in the Dominican Republic Haitians are the blacks and are considered to be inferior and savage. This attitude was made brutally evident when, in 1937, Trujillo ordered the massacre of more than 15,000 Haitians who lived near the border. In Dominican society, Haitians have been transformed into Pliny the Elder's "other"—segregated physically, culturally, religiously, and economically. At the same time, the separation serves to reinforce Dominican identity.

When they travel to the United States, Dominicans are transformed into the "other," not only because they may be dark-skinned, but because they are Hispanics and do not speak standard English. In spite of the rejection by her boyfriend's mother, Helen is willing to take her chances. The risk is viewed in terms of cultural stereotypes: North American men cannot be as bad as macho Latinos. Contrary to Dominicans, Anglo-American men represent a whitening, and therefore an improvement, of the Dominican physiognomy.

By her move to the United States, Helena has been transformed and has become a monster of sorts:

> How things have changed, Helena,
> your mother misses
> the final A left out of your name
> in your last letter home.

Her boyfriend and the culture of his society have changed the Dominican Helena into the North American Helen.

The speaker is sensitive to Latina women who sleep with men from another (white) culture. His mixed feelings are evident when he refrains from calling Helena *una puta,* instead attributing the words to his friend Pedro, who is certainly the typical jealous, macho Latino. But whereas Umpierre's María Cristina is proud of sleeping around with whomever she wants, Gutiérrez's solution—like Esteves's response, "So Your Name Isn't

María Cristina"—is clouded by ethnic and cultural pride, as the speaker reproaches Helen for abandoning her roots.

Assimilation into North American culture requires the development of a selfishness not common in Caribbean society, where people tend to share what little they have. Helen learns to enjoy all the comforts of modern U.S. society. Cultural views of life are polarized. If she accepts one, she must reject the other.

> How things have changed, Helen,
> far away many are still dreaming
> and awaiting your help
> while you plan your next trip
> to Tokyo, Paris or Frankfurt.
> Letters from her beloved homeland
> tearfully left behind
> are torn
> before they are read
> because you think that they will ask you for money
> and your income for the next three years
> has already been spent.[6]

Helen thinks only of herself. She has closed the door behind her and envisions only her present and future.

The ending returns to Helena's origin and identity, which she has rejected. Her birth certificate states:

> Cabimota,
> a sector of Jimayaco
> between much hunger and little land
> province of La Vega
> half a life away from civilization
> República Dominicana.[7]

Helen has come a long way indeed, from a difficult life in the Dominican Republic to the comforts and aspirations enjoyed by Anglo-Americans. But, in the process, Helen has abandoned her identity; she has forgotten who she is and where she came from, like Pedro Pietri's Juan, Miguel, Milagros, Olga, and Manuel.[8] They did everything possible to assimilate into North American society and live the American Dream, only to find out that they were not able to overcome the obstacles society placed in their paths. In the process of change, they lost a sense of who they were, a loss that led to their physical and spiritual deaths. Helen's boyfriend cannot accept the Hispanic person that she is, and so he forces her to change. According to the poetic voice, he is interested only in her womanly attributes. As for Helen, she is willing to do whatever is necessary to belong to mainstream North American culture, even if it means forgetting about her family in the Dominican Republic.

The idea of the name change has also been treated within the Cuban American context by Gustavo Pérez Firmat in "Nobody Knows My Name." In this self-reflexive poem, the poetic voice is tired and frustrated because U.S. society demands conformity and does not respect differences. The United States is supposed to be a country that opens its doors to foreigners and treats everyone democratically, but in reality, immigrants are expected to abandon their native language and to speak English; some states have ongoing political campaigns for English only. Hispanics believe that many Anglo-Americans are not sensitive to other cultures, much less willing to learn or respect their languages. Pérez Firmat reacts in a manner typical of Nuyorican poets:

> I'm tired
> dead anonymous tired
> of getting mail addressed
> to all those people I never was:
>> Gustazo   Perez
>> Gustavio   Penley
>> Gary   Porris
>> Gus   Perry
>> Gustaf Pirey.
>
> Nobody here knows my name.
> This would never have happened in Havana.[9]

Although the personae in Pérez Firmat's and Gutiérrez's poems would undoubtedly encounter difficulties in their homelands, there at least they would not need to question their identity. In both poems, it is not being accepted for who they are that produces anger and contempt for North American culture. The poetic voices think that U.S. society demands total conformity, and that Hispanics feel the pressure to assimilate. Pérez Firmat's and Gutiérrez's poems convey an unwillingness to go from one extreme to the other and search for a hyphenated expression that modifies their identity, defined by the geographic location of Havana and the Dominican Republic. Anglo–North Americans have no tolerance for someone named Gustavo Pérez Firmat; so they transform him into Gustaf Pirey, and Helena into Helen.

The dialogue between Esteves and Umpierre on the role of Hispanic women within U.S. culture has established a benchmark from which to measure related expression by other poets, including men writing about issues that pertain to women. Gutiérrez is prominent among the latter; four of the six poems included in the anthology refer to people, and all of those have women's names in their titles.

Gutiérrez's position regarding Helena can be further understood by comparison with his "Martha at the Edge of Desire." In this poem Gutiérrez describes a well-to-do woman in the Dominican Republic: "Martha grew up watching the workers / refining petroleum at her father's plant."[10] As a woman, Martha acquires a valuable lesson that will help her later on in her interaction with men. The type of work men do significantly affects their body size and lifestyle. Therefore, if Martha wants to live well, she reasons, she needs to select the largest man, which she does at an auction. Since she assumes that large men have large sexual appetites, she makes passionate love for seven years and has seven children.

Whereas Helen seems unaware of the change she is undergoing, in the next-to-last stanza Martha experiences a conversion and realizes that bigness—defined by her husband and reinforced by the smokestacks of her father's petroleum company—is not an accurate measure of life. The implication here is that bigness is not better, but that big men also carry big problems.

Experience has changed Martha. Although she returns to the auction, the outcome is different from that in the earlier stanzas:

> That day Martha went back to the auction
> and walked among all the men
> big, small, and bigger still
> and returned to her house alone
> without anyone,
> to comfort her sons, to look them over,
> to scrub their chests, seal up their pores,
> to keep their hearts and bodies
> from beginning to grow.[11]

From a feminist viewpoint, Martha has awakened; she has become a strong and independent woman. She does not stay home and wait for a suitor, but knows what she wants and does not want. However, it can be argued that Martha is also trapped by her culture; she gives birth in seven consecutive years. But having many children is a sign of strength; she looked for a large man with whom to make love and have many children. The latter interpretation is the least plausible, because she does experience a conversion and returns home without a man to comfort her and her seven sons. Martha's liberation consists in her having a choice and deciding not to exercise it.

The end of the poem suggests an advanced state of spiritual development. For the real strength does not come in giving in to men or choosing them, as Helen and Maria Christina do, but from walking away from them as well. Martha spends the rest of her life undoing what she learned and making sure that her children do not equate the largest with the best. Although this interpretation is the dominant one, Gutiérrez is also pointing to a cycle from which there is no escape. Martha, who attempts to keep her children's bodies and hearts from growing, is only fooling herself. She may succeed for a short time; however, inevitably they will grow to the size of their father, be tall and have big hearts. Once they leave the household others will judge them by their size. Martha shows an awareness of change, but the society remains the same.

For Gutiérrez, the relationship between men and women is not autonomous, it is tied to other factors as well. The poem questions not only the values Martha learned, but also what her father represents. Martha's father epitomizes grandeur and success; he is the owner of the oil refinery, and the large smokestacks of his refinery are a metaphorical representation of his manhood. Like her husband, he is big, but not necessarily better than the others.

Gutiérrez is less complimentary to women in "María and the Others"; like "Martha at the Edge of Desire," this one takes place in the Dominican Republic. Just as Umpierre is critical of María Cristina, in "María and the Others" the poetic voice belittles María, who acts with an air of splendor unbefitting a person of her social and economic status.

The poetic voice knows María well; he follows and watches her constantly and knows what she does and thinks. He is a voyeur. In the original poem the Spanish verb *ver* is used five times, and in translation *watch* is used four times. The poetic voice is most critical of María at the end of the poem:

> Especially
> I watch her
> when she dresses up like a lady
> or better yet
> like what she believes she has always been.[12]

Although the poem may be about someone known to the poet, Gutiérrez is persistent and unyielding in his criticism of María's lifestyle and view of the world. He is not even willing to consider that her false pride may be based on her own psychological insecurities. We know that she has a vivid imagination that has allowed her to travel throughout the world. But we also know that she is poor and visits the pawnshops. It may be precisely for this reason that she needs to escape her environment and transport herself into a different world, one of make-believe and illusion. If Gutiérrez provides Martha with the power to recognize her mistakes and correct the past, he denies María any such possibility.

There is something further unsettling about this poem. The poem's title is "María and the Others." We know who María is, but who are the others? The poem refers only to María and to the poetic voice, who is fixated on María and constantly watches her. Could "the others" refer to the singular poetic voice? Or could it be María's girlfriends, who are mentioned in passing? Or is it even possible that the others include those who act like her and intimate the women in Gutiérrez's other poems? If the latter is the case, then there is a direct correlation between María and Helena, for María represents the type of person Helena was back in "Cabimota, / a sector of Jimayaco / between much hunger and little land / province of La Vega / half a life away from civilization / República Dominicana."[13]

Both Elena and María are from the same economic background; we know that María lives a lifestyle that is not sustained by her economic means. María appears to be a representation of Helena before she departed for the United States and was transformed into Helen. On the mainland, Helen turned her back on her country and culture and accepted the values of North America. If we read the two poems together, María reveals that Helen had abandoned her culture before she even left the island. The betrayal of Dominican culture and social and political identity explains the bitterness the poetic voice feels toward the two women. Although Gutiérrez can be criticized for his negative portrayal of Dominican women, his women are a representation of origin and of traditional Dominican culture and values, which are in a state of change as described in "Martha at the Edge of Desire."

The essence of migration is captured by Héctor Rivera in "The Emigrants of the Century." He starts the poem with the following lines:

> We
> the emigrants of this century
> will roam
> the earth
> with a handful of dirt
> on our chests
> without a place
> to substitute
> our homesickness
> We will gaze
> always from afar
> drawing in our eyes,
> lacerated by skyscrapers,

our last image of
a homeland[14]

The pronoun *we* refers to Dominicans, but is also applicable to Cubans and
Puerto Ricans, among other Hispanic Caribbean immigrants. Although the
emigrants are of this century, the images also allude to the previous one,
when slaves were forced to emigrate from their lands to work in the New
World. If slaves were the emigrants par excellence of the past century,
Dominicans, and other Hispanics, are the ones of this century. The handful
of dirt on the chest suggests that the emigrants carry their country close to
their hearts. But the same dirt could have been acquired by crawling or
lying on their stomachs, and thus also symbolizes their economic condition. To a large extent, the economic refugees from the Dominican
Republic and Puerto Rico are poor people from either the inner city or the
countryside, who at one time or another worked the land and have had little access to education and upward mobility. Regardless of their reasons for
abandoning the homeland, the emigrants are nostalgic and are bound to
compare their adopted country with their place of birth. The emigrants
will look for opportunities in the metropolis, represented by skyscrapers,
but they will not lose sight of their homeland.

For Rivera, the origin can be abandoned but it cannot be replaced with
another. The origin will always be present and persist. The feeling is
expressed in sexual terms from the point of view of the male, who sees it
lingering like the recently conquered woman. These lines not only reveal a
male-dominated cultural understanding of events, but also suggest that the
"We" who emigrate are mainly men who initially leave their families
behind to find a job and send money back to the motherland. Although
they become involved with other women, perhaps those from the adopted
country, the vision of their wives also lingers. The sexual conquest can be
an essential part of the emigrant's experience—one that reminds him of the
past, just as dancing the *merengue* is a way of returning to the point of
departure.

The poetic voice describes the emigration not as a conscious decision
to leave the country for another, but as a last resort, a way of surviving.
The poem raises a fundamental question. Why emigrate to a country so different from the one where you were raised, and one where you are unwel-
come, if not out of necessity?

We, the emigrants of this century,
exiled by hunger,
authenticated by loneliness,
in this land
of alien eyes,

of alien tongues,
of alienation
without a room
for our bodies
How am I to sing to you,
emigrants of this century,
inhabitants of this earth,
without tears of pain
escaping from my eyes.[15]

We should note that the speaker describes the inhabitants of the adopted country as aliens; that is, as if the emigrants were the residents and those born in the country were foreigners. This inversion reminds us that Hispanic people were present on the North American continent before the British arrived in large numbers, and implies that the emigrants of the century are now in the majority. Here "the emigrant" can be interpreted broadly to include everyone who has been exiled by hunger. Though economic emigration is a common phenomenon throughout the twentieth century, the residents are defensive and look at the emigrants with disdain.

The latter part of the above stanza, in which the poetic voice wants to speak for the emigrants of the century, recalls Pablo Neruda's journey to Machu Picchu, a source of inspiration for some of the poets discussed in this chapter. Rivera concentrates on the speaker's communion with the physical structure of the pre-Inca civilization and with the common man. The poem also suggests his need to feel their pain, hunger, and sorrow and to give them a voice. Neruda writes:

I come to speak for your dead mouths.

Throughout the earth
let dead lips congregate,
out of the depths spin this long night to me
as if I rode at anchor here with you.

And tell me everything, tell chain by chain,
and link by link, and step by step;
sharpen the knives you kept hidden away,
thrust them into my breast, into my hands,
like a torrent of sunbursts,
an Amazon of buried jaguars,
and leave me cry: hours, days and years,
blind ages, stellar centuries.

And give me silence, give me water, hope.
Give me the struggle, the iron, the volcanoes.
Let bodies cling like magnets to my body.
Come quickly to my veins and to my mouth.
Speak through my speech, and through my blood.[16]

From Rivera's perspective, the contemporary emigrants of this century are like the pre-Incas, still destined to suffer. The analogy between Rivera's and Neruda's poems, between the emigrants and the pre-Incas, can be supported; the arrival of the emigrants to the adopted country resembles the Inca experience with the Spaniards during the conquest of the New World. The Spaniards viewed the Incas as having strange eyes and speaking a strange language. The emigrants of that period displaced the native inhabitants and became the new residents. Modern history has displaced Hispanics, but the reference to aliens (or strangers) within the context of this century indicates that all the inhabitants of United States are aliens, or descendants of aliens, themselves.

The poetic voice speaks of the emigrant's experience in the United States, as in the line "the suitcase of the first traveller / to arrive at the gate." The suitcase refers to the few possessions the immigrant has, and the gate to New York Harbor, the Statue of Liberty, and Ellis Island, where so many of the early emigrants of this century landed. But within a contemporary context, the gate is also the gate of an airline terminal, permitting immigration to increase dramatically. This was the case with the Puerto Rican migration of the fifties and sixties, the Cuban in the sixties, and the Dominican in the seventies and eighties. Even though the poetic voice alludes to a specific location, Machu Picchu, the Hispanic and Amerindian experiences are in the background. Rivera's depiction of the emigrant's life and his physical description of New York City are variations of the ones Neruda employs. Rivera writes:

Emigrants of this century,
given the opportunity
to die off the tenth floor
fleeing from exile
city of the world
city of ice
city of rocks
city of opportunities
city of similes
naked city[17]

Death is ever present, in the homeland and in the adopted country. For the sake of comparison, I will cite a few lines from *The Heights of Macchu Picchu*. Rivera refers to the vertical dimension of the city in "the tenth floor" and repeats the word *city*; Neruda does the same with the appropriate images of height and grandeur and the word *stone*, a representation of the city of Macchu Picchu:

> Interstellar Eagle, vine-in-a-mist.
> Forsaken bastion, blind scimitar.
> Orion belt, ceremonial bread.
> Torrential stairway, immeasurable eyelid.
> Triangular tunic, pollen of stone.
> Granite lamp, bread of stone.
> Mineral snake, rose of stone.
> Ship-burial, source of stone.
> Horse in the moon, stone light.
> Equinoctial quadrant, vapor of stone.[18]

After Neruda celebrates the wonders of Machu Picchu, he is curious about what happened to the common man and concentrates on his existence: "Macchu Picchu, did you lift / stone above stone on a groundwork of rags?"[19] Similarly, Rivera is concerned for the downtrodden, whom he describes in terms of "drunkards who sate / their hunger on refuse . . . arrived out of hunger / at this corner of the world / where hope has died."[20]

If Neruda's concern for man, as seen in both the first and second halves of the poem, is a projection of his political beliefs, Rivera's is as well. This is particularly evident in his reference to "the new man," who will turn the previous structures upside down and set in motion a return to the origin. The concept of the "New Man" refers to the Cuban Revolution and particularly to Che Guevara's essay "El hombre y el socialismo en Cuba" (1965; "Man and Socialism in Cuba" 1968), in which he outlines the moral responsibilities of this individual who will benefit from and lead the revolution.[21] But what is troubling about Rivera's New Man is that he "will reverse our steps / on old paths,"[22] and will not go forward, as "new" or "modern" would indicate. Ultimately, he prefers to return to the point of departure.

For Julia Álvarez, as we shall see in a later section, the past is no longer what it used to be, or what it means to Dominicans on the island; she looks at it from a different perspective, conditioned by the adopted country. For others, the past is undergoing its own development and change; the society left behind has also become modern. The immigrant returns to a time and place he or she cannot recognize. Rivera's poetic voice has undergone significant changes:

> chasing the dollar
> forgetting their origin
> forgotten are the huts
> exchanged for luxury condos[23]

One hopes that Rivera's New Man will be more successful than the one the Castro government has tried to shape. Of importance is the New Man's attempt to reverse the steps of previous generations, and depending on how long he remains in the adopted country, he will again become an immigrant. Like "the first traveler / to arrive at the gate," he will pack his suitcase once more, this time to travel from the adopted country to the one he believes he left behind, which has inevitably changed. The movement to and from the mainland recalls Elías Miguel Muñoz's "Returning," which expresses the uneasiness the immigrant feels when he stays in one place for any length of time, regardless of where that place may be.[24] But in Muñoz's poem, the return is to the past of the lost childhood. If the migrant remains long enough, in Rivera's poem, he will be "authenticated by loneliness," even though he can still "seize this song." Memory always preserves the emigrant's past. Paradoxically, he will dream of a New Man who will undo the course of the history of this century's migrants. The poetic voice ends the poem by hoping that "there will be time later / to speak of other matters." He recognizes that he needs to recover the past to think of other matters, and this is the essence of the migrant's dilemma.

The need to return to a moment before the time of the emigrant's departure is expressed in Tomás Rivera Martínez's "From Here," which describes the emigrant, before leaving the house, experiencing feelings brought about by the new day. One of them is the communion with the other; another is

> Wanting to retrace time
> back to the childhood
> of the boy with a wheel and a stick
> running swiftly downhill
> Of the boy throwing a ball
> Of the boy pondering the heart
> to strike with a bouquet
> of roses in his hand.[25]

This and other desires are juxtaposed with what actually takes place in the outside world, subject to chronological time: elevators moving, machines operating, workers entering and leaving the factories, subversive activities—all these continue. The communion with their past, as we have seen in the poems of Cuban American and Dominican male writers, is not with the present time of the countries they left behind, but with the time of their childhood.

The estrangement of which Rivera Martínez speaks is also contained in "I Ask Myself," a poem about communicating with the self because there is no one else to talk to. In fact, the speaker finds himself in a society in which no one cares, a concern he repeats in the first line of each of the five stanzas. The first one sets the tone for the rest:

> Does anyone care
> it is 7 in the morning
> in this Babel of nothingness
> or if I ooze like gelatin
> on the streets
> retracing a homeland in my heart.[26]

The isolation addressed in "I Ask Myself" is experienced in the metropolis of the adopted country, but is also a result of the rupture from the homeland:

> And your letters filled with the breath of the earth
> no longer arrive
> because you have forgotten my child-like frailty
> stubbornly attached to a land where I no longer live.[27]

The feeling of total dejection, which replaces the sense of origin and innocence represented by the motherland, is what makes all emigrants in Rivera's "Emigrants of the Century" permanent travelers in constant search of a home. The only person mentioned in the poem, a significant other referred to only as *you*, has cut the umbilical cord with the owner of the poetic voice and will develop according to his own personal, cultural, and historic circumstances. Meanwhile, the destiny the poetic voice has chosen or been forced to choose, is one of continuous suffering and death, what Neruda called in *The Heights of Macchu Picchu* the "daily death." Tomás Rivera Martínez relies on the same images when he writes in "I Ask Myself":

> Does anyone care if I remain
> in bed,
> in agony's strike for a death
> afraid to arrive,
> in agony's strike
> for a death we dare not embrace,
> for fear of dying of death,

because there is no way to die of death
especially when one knows
that the other side of pain
continues to be tomorrow.[28]

Neruda writes:

It was not you, grave death, raptor of iron plumage,
that the drab tenant of such lodgings carried
mixed with his gobbled rations under hollow skin—
rather: a trodden tendril of old rope,
the atom of a courage that gave way
or some harsh dew never distilled to sweat.
This could not be reborn, a particle
of death without a requiem,
bare bone or fading church bell dying from within.[29]

There is a difference between Neruda's poem and the one written by Rivera Martínez. The "little death" seen in the first part of *The Heights of Macchu Picchu* and repeated in the second, serves to focus man's plight. At the end of the poem, the speaker will unite with the pre-Incas, as they live and speak through him. In Rivera Martínez's poem, death is continuous and it will also be present tomorrow.

The chaos of modern civilization to which Neruda refers in the first half of *The Heights of Macchu Picchu* is also captured by Guillermo Francisco Gutiérrez in his "Unlicensed Doctor in New York." The persona of the poem sells his mode of transportation, his bicycle, in an unnamed geographic location that might be identified as the Dominican Republic, packs his suitcase, and migrates to New York City. For this migrant, New York is not the city others have envisioned, whose streets are paved with gold, but rather the one described by other Latino writers, in a constant state of decomposition:

he arrived at the warehouse of drugs
and everyday crime
he walked through the complex
of sky-scrapers
and penetrated the rotten
                    apple[30]

The skyscrapers were already mentioned in Gutiérrez's poem, and drugs and crime are familiar images in the works of Nuyorican poets who also share life in the same "rotten apple."

Guillermo Gutiérrez's persona walks "In a coming / and going of streets / he arrived in Manhattan / like a robot." The immigrant's presence in and interaction with the city are described in sexual terms, as a physical penetration:

> to have sex with the city
> or with a cosmopolitan woman
> or maybe with Walt Whitman's
> mother[31]

Although the poetic voice may be alluding to the loneliness of the immigrant and his desire to find a companion, the images more appropriately refer to an interaction with North American culture; culture in Spanish is a feminine noun and can be represented by a woman. Neruda begins his poem with the poetic persona wandering aimlessly throughout the city in search of meaning, the other, and the self. He uses similar images to portray his communion with contemporary society, such as the buried tower, the hand penetrating the earth, the release of the sperm, and the rebirth of the poet. In Neruda's case, the poet is reborn blind, an allusion to Homer and his writing of the *Odyssey*. Most important, the poet's blindness produces his vision of the world in general and of Machu Picchu in particular. The pre-Inca civilization that the poet sees is not the historical Machu Picchu but the one he re-creates in his own imagination, the poetic Macchu Picchu.

But if Neruda's persona finds the meaning and purpose of life in Machu Picchu, Guillermo Gutiérrez's recognizes that his mission is in this city:

> to preach to an old woman
> racist and prejudiced.
> He arrived in the city
> loving it with its defects
> tirelessly
>   walking
> through its body[32]

By following the subject, the poetic voice takes the reader on a ride through certain parts of New York City and provides an archaeology of those areas, from Broadway to the Grand Concourse, from the Avenue of the Americas to Wall Street. The latter two locations symbolize the violence in Latin America, represented by Caupolicán's spilled blood and the corruption of Wall Street.

The poetic voice identifies the persona as *you*, and associates it with the downtrodden, like the bums mentioned in the poem or migrants traveling from "Manhattan to San Juan," "from Washington to your history / you come out of a fierce hunt." The hunt can be interpreted in political terms, as a reference to U.S. involvement in Dominican and Puerto Rican history. But the hunt is also a reference to Rubén Darío's poem "A Roosevelt" and Martí's essay "Nuestra America," in which North America is described as a hunter and Spanish America as the prey. Nevertheless, the old man in the poem is not rabid, like the other stray dogs.

About halfway through the poem the poetic voice identifies itself as being of a culture in which sick people are not abandoned, one whose traditions and customs allow others to keep them company. In Gutiérrez's poem, the poetic voice is dedicated to a profession through which he lends his voice to the sick and they speak with it, recalling the end of Neruda's poem. He arrives in search of a man:

> He has 40 buttonholes in the satellite
> of the earth
> his head is of the moon
> with virtues that channel the
>   firmament.[33]

Certainly the person he is looking for transcends any particular race or color, and is a universal man who has been oppressed. Guillermo Gutiérrez continues to express themes present in Neruda's master poem.

> I arrived at this labyrinth
>   of ghosts
> where the living were mistaken for
> the dead
> seeking a man
> of generous laughter
> of broad limbs.[34]

New York, as a representation of a postmodern society, values death above life. When money is an issue, life is more expensive than death, and it is easier to let someone die. Life and death are no longer moral or religious issues; instead they have become economic ones:

> In New York when a patient
> has no money to pay
>   they bleed him dry
> Caramba Dr. how much does it cost
> a drop in his veins
> it's a coal mine
>   it's a bauxite mine[35]

The poetic voice, who comes from a caring tradition, is a doctor without formal recognition or training, as the poem's title suggests. He does not allow the postmodern society with all its wealth to destroy his values. Perhaps the lack of formal training saves him from the destiny that has befallen other doctors who take the Hippocratic oath yet are interested only in money. The poetic persona is connected to his culture and also to nature:

> It happens that . . .
> I don't grow weary of going in and out
> your door
> Dressed in green
> with skin of ground flame-trees
> with a light not of neon
>   but of summer[36]

In this poem, the persona is always in the state of arriving; Guillermo Gutiérrez uses the verb *arrive* eight times, three of them in the first person, "I arrive." In the last stanza, the poetic voice arrives, but also enters and allows his presence to be noted:

> I enter
> maybe I'm not much
>   but here I am
> and I feel like saying
> that it's a long way
> from tropic to tropic
> this feeling
> this speaking for you
> with my throat full of stones
> and that's all.[37]

As in the ending of Neruda's poem, here the poetic voice has found his purpose; that is, to speak for those who live in isolation and do not have a voice. But unlike Neruda's, Gutiérrez's poetic voice does not have to travel or return to a time before time, before the presence of Europeans in the New World. He finds the suffering among the chaos of the modern city. The key word in the last stanza is *feel*. The poetic voice is still capable of experiencing emotion in a city that dehumanizes everyone. The feeling allows him to care, to be a doctor, and, most important, to be a poet. Yet the mention of feeling suggests that the poetic voice is not able to express the depth and complexity of the emotions that move him to bring the poem to a rapid conclusion.

II

There does not appear to be a great thematic difference between the poetry of Dominican women and that of their male counterparts. In the sections on Puerto Rican and Cuban American poets, I have observed some of the differences and showed that women poets write about their own sexuality and sexual needs. Dominican men and women poets appear to develop similar themes, which pertain to their presence in the North American society. The crossover is represented by Franklin Gutiérrez, who writes about themes that, under different circumstances, would be of interest to women too.

In Chiqui Vicioso's "Perspectives," the poetic voice is an observer of a series of events, as indicated by "one looks" and "one watches" (The Spanish repeats the verb *se mira*). The first stanza conveys a sense of fatalism; Eudocia is described as always having been a worker, convinced that the present is more important than the past. She and others have left the past behind: "For them there is no way back." Their displacement from the origin and the impossibility of returning to it are associated with Eudocia's work ethic and her need to better their future. The economic conditions of those being observed is further underscored by Rosa and her faith in the lottery. Rosa's faith reinforces the sense of permanence seen in the first stanza; furthermore, she is content to live in a dream world. If Manuel Puig was mesmerized by Hollywood movies, which he later incorporated into some of his novels,[38] so is Rosa, who like Pietri's Juan, Miguel, Milagros, Olga, and Manuel, has found a more permanent and less expensive escape in the lottery.[39] Rosa paraphrases the commercial advertising for the New York Lottery: "these dreams are better than the movies, / they cost one dollar and last a whole week."[40] The lottery is meant to transform your life overnight, to transport you from dream to reality.

The sense of loneliness and tragedy that Eudocia and Rosa experience is embodied in the third stanza by María Luisa, whose opium is the television soap operas. All the women follow a similar pattern: Eudocia escapes into her work, Rosa does the same with dreams provoked by the lottery, and María Luisa justifies her soap operas by stating, "in this loneliness they are my happiness."

In the fourth stanza, the hard-working Eudocia is multiplied in the working women; and whereas in the first stanza the geographic location is not specified and could even be the Dominican Republic, though this is the place to which the women cannot return, we now know that the setting is New York City; the working women are traveling on the subway. They are "hiding their mistreated hands, / untended nails, hiding behind glasses," perhaps because they are not used to working and now they must make ends meet in the present environment, perhaps because the work they do is labor-intensive and more demanding of them. The sense of permanence seen in the other stanza is conveyed here in the dark circles under their eyes.

Halfway through, in the fifth stanza, the poem changes. In the previous four stanzas the personae were women; in the fifth they are men. The blue-collar workers have jobs that may put their lives at risk, but they are also physically assaulted by the high-decibel sound produced by the subway. The noise recalls "the sound made by a jet's landing," as reported by the *Daily News*, which became the topic of discussion when the British-French Concorde was seeking permission to land its supersonic airplane at Kennedy airport.

Physical and moral destruction has become the resounding theme of the poem, and is most evident in the description of the street life of Latinos:

> One watches the young latinos
> "loose joints," "acid" and "loose cigarettes"
> boys of few years who lost
> their original humanity on these streets[41]

If the young Latinos have succumbed to the evils of their street environment, the Latinas too have been robbed of their childhood and have to concern themselves with the children they are bringing into the world at such a tender age. The description of New York street life is reminiscent of the works of Guillermo Gutiérrez and of Nuyorican poets such as Pedro Pietri and Tato Laviera.

Just as the poetic voice observes Eudocia, Rosa, María Luisa, the working women, the blue-collar workers, the young Latinos, and the girls, "One looks at the garbage, the trash / on 103rd Street, at the drunks; / at the people hunting for 'specials' / in the second-hand clothing stores." The perspectives offered by the poem have been gradually descending, signaled by the descriptions of the subway, which represents a physical descent, and those of the youngsters, suggesting a moral one. But the ultimate descent is described in the stanza that mentions the garbage: 103rd Street, an area known to the Young Lords in the heart of East Harlem, is a symbolic hell. Whereas all of the previous stanzas refer to one subject, the penultimate one incorporates many: the garbage, trash, drunks, and people hunting for specials. And the descent, like Dante's journey in the *Divine Comedy*, leads to a realization:

> And one begins to feel differently
> this bad air; to walk over the dead
> fighting against death itself
> to try to make a new life.[42]

In the last stanza the poetic voice recognizes the difficulty of making a new life in New York City. Although affected by the conditions, the poetic voice will not allow herself to be controlled by them. She has been transformed by the course of events. Whereas she had distanced herself from the actual problems, she is now an active participant in her environment. The poetic voice is a fighter and walks over those who have not been able to overcome their circumstances; she faces and fights death to survive, and refuses to be defeated or to become another statistic. Here we should point out the strength of the poetic voice, armed with the knowledge of how Latinos have been trapped by the environment and determined to carve a new path of life with success. The poetic voice will overcome the same fatalistic or deterministic structure that led the other Latinos to indulge in the pitfalls of North American society. Unlike the Puerto Rican Miguel Piñero, who accepted his environment with all the good and bad it entailed, Vicioso sees it as oppressive, as something she must fight to change.

The determination the speaker shows at the end of "Perspectives" is also present in "Reports," where she exerts her independence and dares to be different. The poem is composed as a dialogue between two individuals, the poetic voice and her boss. They have different positions, voices, and cultural and personal concerns. It is five o'clock, the workday is almost over, and the poetic voice has not finished the report she has promised her boss. Instead of thinking of work, the poetic voice is preoccupied with something more meaningful to her, the passage of time and the arrival of a loved one. The contrast is also between the authoritative voice of the one demanding the report and a third-person interior monologue of the one asked to provide it. The first voice demands: "It's five o'clock and you still haven't given me the report," "You promised to get me the reports today," Did you hear me?" "I'm leaving at 5:30. You have half an hour," "The half hour is almost up," "The report?"[43]

The second voice contemplates the changing colors, the sunset, a vase of flowers, preparing the house and dinner for the arrival of someone who has been absent for a significant period of time. The poem ends with two commands, which, following the structure of the poem, are also in quotation marks and should correspond to the boss's authoritative voice. But their content represents the position of the poetic voice, who says: "I didn't do it." / "Good night." If my assumption is correct and the speaker is the poetic voice, then the last two lines represent an inversion of the power structure. That is, if at the outset of the poem, one voice is powerful and the other subservient, the end of the poem makes clear that the latter voice, whose values and concerns are clearly different from those of the first voice, is also powerful. Her innermost thoughts, as expressed by the interior monologue, are more important than what her boss requests of her. Although one can propose that the poetic voice has an obligation to fulfill her responsibilities, she rebels against the legal structures that have relegated her to an inferior position. Instead of the supervisor's leaving, it is she who leaves; she usurps his power and in fact has become the boss. The poetic voice challenges the power structure and, like Umpierre, is defiant. Whereas the Puerto Rican Umpierre is motivated by her own personal needs, Vicioso's Dominican persona is thinking of herself and her sweetheart.

Unlike Umpierre, Vicioso does not see the need to reject Dominican or Hispanic culture to liberate herself. In "Wo/men" Vicioso has the opportunity to transfer her defiance of society and her boss to her relationship with men, but she does not seize it. The opposition *Wo/men*, which separates the sexes but also brings them together (for one is contained in the other), is meant to describe women with manly attributes. These are women who drape themselves in black, perhaps because they are mourning, perhaps because it is the only color available to them. It is also possible that these women, who are like men, do not know how to dress. They wear multicolored socks. Most important, the women have manly features: They are very hairy; the word is repeated three times and the idea is suggested by others. They have strong arms, hair, mustaches, and hairy legs.

At the end of the first stanza and at the beginning of the second, the poetic voice tells the reader that these women suffer and are "Sad women, who never smile / lacking teeth, lacking dreams." These women are not your typical beauty queens—they are described as monsters, neither women nor men but something in between. They have been affected by their condition and consequently lack aspirations and dreams: "Sad women, who never smile / lacking teeth, lacking dreams." The women are juxtaposed with the elements associated with earth, for they are close to nature and the farms they work; to the cabbage and other vegetables they eat and to the wool that clothes and keeps them warm; and to men, children, and tenderness. The Spanish original equates men with husbands, as in the line "woman / men, child, and tenderness." Only in the woman's relationship with her family do we notice a feeling of tenderness. The line suggests that the family is what brings out an inner and intimate emotion. The tenderness is counterposed with the strength conveyed in the last line: "iron women, rock women."

The closing of the poem returns us to the image offered at its outset. The poetic voice relies on stereotypical representations of women and men; that is, one is feminine and the other masculine. In so doing, she underpins an external vision of these women, someone everyone knows and sees, but no one really understands or bothers to appreciate. On the contrary, the poetic voice judges them as if they were members of the Plinean people. But the poetic voice also underscores an emotion associated with tenderness and the family—perhaps observed by her or projected from her own experience as a woman onto the women she is observing—which humanizes them. In this respect, Vicioso proposes that regardless of the appearance of women, they all share a common element, based on the family and the feeling of tenderness. If Maya Islas found universal meaning in her virginity, Vicioso finds it in women as the nucleus of the family, regardless of who they are or what they look like.[44]

The race issue so conspicuously absent from Dominican literature is confronted by Vicioso. She situates it in "Haiti," as she presents a different perspective of the neighboring country than the one promoted by government officials. In this prosopopoeia, Haiti is viewed with warmth and compassion. The poetic voice envisions Haiti as a virgin prior to being molested or ransacked by pirates, "to leave you thus / with your bare, round breasts / and your torn grass-skirt."[45]

In the second stanza, Haiti is envisioned prior to the disastrous consequences of the slave traffic, which turned the island, then called Santo Domingo, into a sea of human carnage. Slavers turned Haiti into the world's slave auction. Alejo Carpentier was the first Caribbean writer to provide a literary interpretation of historical events from the Haitian viewpoint, from the mid-eighteenth century until the time of the Boyer government.[46] But it was not until 1844 that Haiti lost the eastern part of the island and the Dominican Republic was created as an independent country.

Whereas in the first two stanzas the poetic voice tells the reader what she imagines Haiti to be, in the last one she sees Haiti and is able to confirm her thoughts. Haiti smiles at the poetic voice, and as Haiti is personified, the poetic voice represents the Dominican Republic; one smiles at the other, showing no animosity, but friendship. Haiti is described as a constant traveler "with your sweaty, bare feet," a natural condition that is also manifested in her artistic talents:

> Haiti who can give art a thousand shapes
> and who paints the stars with your hands
> I found out that love and hate
> share your name.[47]

Haiti's capability to paint stars with her hands suggests earthly intervention in the realm of the divine, but also points to her adeptness in bringing the two together, a quality that also speaks to her divine blessing. Just as Haiti is able to embrace the extremes that heaven and earth represent, she also unites those of love and hate. Though these extreme and powerful emotions may also refer to the country's historical cycles of oppression and liberation, the love and hate that Haiti symbolizes is made up of the country's love and the hate brought from the outside, by pirates and slave traffickers.

As we have mentioned, Vicioso's other perspective of the race issue in the Dominican Republic and Haiti is probably related to her experiences in the United States, where that issue is a feature of everyday life. Race is also evident in the two island societies, but there it is treated differently. Dominicans do not consider themselves black; for them Haitians are black. Haiti is the poorest country in the Western Hemisphere. There is poverty in the Dominican Republic, but Haitians often cross the border looking for work, and they occupy the lowest level of Dominican society. In addition, Haitians speak a different language, have a different culture, and practice a different religion, and these factors prevent them from assimilating into Dominican society. Vicioso lived in the United States, not as a member of the dominant society, but as part of a marginal one, so her situation was comparable to that of Haitians in the Dominican Republic. Her experiences on the mainland allowed her to reevaluate her country's cultural, political, and racial discrimination against Haitians. Her poem is not a condemnation, but a conciliation between two extremes, just as "love and hate / share your name."

Haiti is both love and hate. If love is associated with Haiti's natural beauty, the hate was brought first by the pirates of the first stanza and the slave traders of the second. The hate may also represent the feeling that Dominicans have for Haitians. This idea is alluded to in the poem's outlined sequence and includes the third stanza. It is Haiti who smiles at the poetic voice, which in this stanza can also represent the Dominican Republic. Each country is affected by the other. Because they share the same island, their destinies are intricately connected. From the poetic point of view, the romantic description of Haiti brings the two countries and cultures together.

III

Dominicans are indeed the most recent group of immigrants from the Caribbean, and, like recent Cuban exile writers, they write in Spanish. They recognize that although they are Dominicans and have close ties with the homeland, they share a common destiny with other Latinos in the United States. Chiqui Vicioso was raised in New York but lives in the Dominican Republic and has chosen to express herself in Spanish. Julia Álvarez was born in the United States, but returned to her parents' homeland at a young age. As her first novel, *How the Garcia Girls Lost Their Accents* (1991), indicates, she remained in the Dominican Republic until the age of ten, when she returned to her country of birth. Álvarez is the only Dominican American writer who writes in English. She has published two other novels: *In the Time of the Butterflies* (1994), about the Mirabal sisters' fight against Trujillo, and *Yo* (1997), which continues to develop the character Yolanda of her first novel.

The blending of U.S. and Latino Caribbean culture occurs in the United States, but also in the Caribbean. In Julia Álvarez's "Homecoming," the poetic voice describes her return to the Dominican Republic to attend her cousin's wedding. The poetic voice is conscious of differences; she returns not as a Dominican, but as a North American observing a mildly familiar culture.

At the outset of the poem, the poetic voice describes an unfamiliar ritual; the guards of the bride of a well-to-do family gather the jewelry of the guests so that it can be "bathed in a river whose bottom had been cleaned / for the occasion. She was Uncle's only daughter." The family's wealth is signified by their ability to change or alter nature: they clean the bottom of the river as one would scour the bottom of a swimming pool or bathtub. The obsession with bathing and cleanliness suggests a move away from the soiled river, which also characterizes poor people. Money points to a difference between those who have it and those who do not, represented in the poem by the workmen and maids. The wealthy must have guards in order to protect themselves from their workers. The wealth with which the poem begins appears to be the essence of life.

The distinction is expressed in terms of wealth but also of race. The wealthy people are "dark-skinned men" who use their money to marry "white women" and have "spoiled children." However, money is also used to narrow the gap between North America and the Dominican Republic; the Dominican daughter is marrying a "sunburnt Minnesotan." Race is an issue between the rich dark-skinned men and the white women they marry, but also between the poetic voice's biracial cousin and the "sunburnt Minnesotans." There is an attempt to associate the dark-skinned men and the "sunburnt Minnesotans," but the geographic difference between the Dominican men, who live close to the Equator, and the Minnesotans, who live in one of the northernmost and coldest states, keeps them apart. Nevertheless, if wealth is used to acquire white women, the same means is also used to acquire white Minnesotans. Wealth is the equalizer.

The poetic voice has been estranged from what was once a familiar environment. She speaks English, a skill the uncle wants her to show off to the guests, but he also finds her skinny, reflecting a cultural difference between the United States and the Dominican Republic and other Caribbean countries, where diets are different and a rounded figure is considered more attractive. The cultural difference is felt by the poetic voice, who is uncomfortable with her uncle "fondling my shoulder blades beneath my bridesmaid's gown / as if they were breasts." And the uncle who encourages his niece to return to the Dominican Republic: "*Come back from that cold place, Vermont, he said, / all this is yours!*" The "blocks of ice / to keep the champagne lukewarm," and the reference to the state of Vermont remind me of the previously mentioned state of Minnesota, and call attention to the physical and cultural differences between the inhabitants of that state and Dominicans in their homeland.

The distinction here is also climatic. The cold of the northern states is counterposed with the heat of the Dominican Republic. One tends to preserve and the other to destroy: ice is brought in to safeguard the champagne, which the heat decomposes. The wedding cake is a miniature replica of the family *rancho*, and it too is being destroyed by the heat.

> A maiden aunt housekept,
> touching up whipped cream roses with a syringe
> of eggwhites, rescuing the groom when the heat
> melted his chocolate shoes into the frosting.[48]

The maiden aunt's effort to save the cake is symbolic of the wedding between two countries, two races, and two cultures. Just as the ice preserves the champagne, the maiden aunt does the same for the cake, salvaging the groom figure from the heat. The Minnesotan will also save cousin Carmen from the heat, as well as from her culture and her country. The word *rescuing* is used to describe the maid as she touches up the groom figure. Just as the ice is rescuing the champagne and the aunt is rescuing the melting groom, so will the Minnesotan groom rescue cousin Carmen. The poetic voice's uncle wants her to return to the Dominican Republic, but she has already been rescued by the state of Vermont.

The difference drawn between the Minnesotans, Vermonters, and Dominicans is also illustrated in their dancing. The poetic voice's uncle teases her that her "merengue had lost its Caribbean." *Merengue* is the national dance of the Dominican Republic and its principal contribution to world music. Her immersion in North American culture has distanced the poetic voice from the rhythms known to her uncle's country. But the *merengue* is compared to the Charleston: "The Minnesotans finally broke loose and danced a Charleston / and were pronounced good gringos with latino hearts." From the poetic voice's point of view, there are similarities between *Caribbean* and *Charleston*, the latter of which denotes the dance but also a geographic location. Though both are geographic locations with their own cultures, both start with the letter *C*. This comparison is supported by privileging the signifiers. If the letters are counted using the Spanish alphabet, both locations contain the same number. (In Spanish, the *Ch* is considered to be one letter; both words contain nine letters.) This similarity allows the two cultures to come together, for the Minnesotans to dance the Charleston to the beat of Caribbean music, and for the Dominicans to claim that Minnesotans are "good gringos."

The above lines refers to "good gringos," suggesting that not all grin-gos are good. Certainly, some Dominicans would make a case against the gringos who invaded the Dominican Republic in 1965 and supported Joaquín Balaguer for the presidency against the popular, but leftist, Juan Bosch. But the structure of the poem, in which Minnesotans go to the Dominican Republic to marry their son to a Dominican, implies that the invasion also has a positive interpretation. This idea is furthered by the uncle's affirmation: *"Come back from that cold place, Vermont,* he said, / *all this is yours!"* Here the uncle is offering his ranch—and perhaps all of the Dominican Republic and its culture—to his North American niece upon her return, but later he decouples the proposition of giving what his country has to offer from a return to the mother country. His reversal is evident in the altered syntax of his words, when he states unequivocally, *"This is all yours."*

Just as the North is attracted to the Caribbean, the opposite is also true:

> The little sister, freckled with a week of beach,
> her hair as blonde as movie stars, was asked
> by maids if they could touch her hair or skin,
> and she backed off, until it was explained to her,
> they meant no harm.[49]

These lines are important because they confirm that the "sunburnt Minnesotan" is fair-skinned and that there are class and cultural distinc-tions, not only between the little sister and the maids but also between owners and workers. The maids want to touch the little sister's hair because it is soft and blond, but also because it resembles that of movie stars; in essence, the maids are approaching the little sister from their own cultural interpretation of the North. The little sister does the same. Although she feels comfortable on the beaches of the Dominican Republic, she is less relaxed around the maids and other common people. She, too, may be responding to her own cultural biases. More likely than not, the maids are dark-skinned and, unlike the groom's father, they have no money. Be that as it may, someone explains to the little sister that the maids mean no harm. This someone, certainly a member of cousin Carmen's family, understands both cultures and is able to translate between the cultural codes of the Dominican and North American soci-eties. But, according to the poem, the translation is only one-way; that is, there is interest only in explaining to the little sister that the maids mean no harm. There is no interest in interpreting for the maids the little sister's rejection of them.

The poetic voice describes events from a North American perspective, in terms of the cultural values that it represents. As a Dominican, she would not have noticed or been concerned for the maids. The maids are invisible to Dominicans on the island. As a North American, she is aware of their plight:

> The maids went by with trays
> of wedding bells and matchbooks monogrammed
> with Dick's and Carmen's names. It would be years
> before I took the courses that would change my mind
> in schools paid for by sugar from the fields around us,
> years before I could begin to comprehend
> how one does not see the maids when they pass by. . . .[50]

Although the poetic voice returns to the Dominican Republic, she wants to distance herself from that nation's culture. Just as the heat melts the groom and the cake, and the sun comes up, the poetic voice recognizes that she has had too much to drink, and has a vision that "the fields around us were burning." The vision of intense heat could be a reference to the slave uprising of 1791 that led to the creation of Republic of Haiti in 1804. The slaves killed the white masters and forced others to flee the island to Santiago de Cuba and New Orleans. The burning fields also refer to the climate and how it destroys or decomposes everything. The poetic voice's North American cultural upbringing allows her to see beyond the wedding and the abundant food to the space occupied by the workmen and maids. They were responsible for the success of the wedding and the happiness of the guests. The poem ends with another contrast, as the members of the wedding party eat and enjoy themselves, while the workers have nothing:

> Except the maids and workmen,
> sitting on stoops behind the sugar house,
> ate with their fingers from their open palms
> windows, shutters, walls, pillars, doors,
> made from the cane they had cut in the fields.[51]

Just as the guests are eating the cake in the shape of a ranch, the workers will digest the real ranch, the one they constructed and work to maintain.

The poet has developed a keen sense of race/class distinction by living in the United States and now observing life in the Dominican Republic. In fact, her observations about Dominican society suggest a Marxist critique of events. The workers are the ones who support the wealthy class with their labor, yet they end up with nothing. It is here that the burning fields acquire another significance: these workers might destroy all that they have built. The poetic voice's uncle makes money from the sugar his workers harvest, and they are left with the remnants of the sugar cane, that which is discarded, for their dwelling.

The poetic voice understands the conditions of the workers, from an Anglo-American rather than a Dominican perspective. This observation takes us back to the earlier line alluding to the meeting of the two cultures. That line describes the Minnesotans dancing—not the *merengue*, but the Charleston—and being "pronounced good gringos with latino hearts." Because the poetic voice is also from the North and has forgotten to swing her hips when dancing the *merengue*, her point of view allows us to consider her as a gringo with a Latino heart or, given the dialectics developed in the poem, a Latina with a gringo heart. Nevertheless, the metaphorical dance of the North American and Dominican cultures allows the reader to interpret them from two distinct points of view. The ideas expressed in "Homecoming" are also contained in Álvarez's *How the Garcia Girls Lost Their Accents*, as we shall see in chapter 7.

SEVEN

A Search for Identity
in Julia Álvarez's
How the Garcia Girls Lost Their Accents

T HE displacement of Caribbean people from their islands to the
United States, for political or economic reasons, has produced a tension between the culture of the country of origin and that of the
adopted homeland, one representing the past and the other the future of the immigrant. As time passes, the rupture with the past, strongest
in political exiles, is transformed for the immigrant into a desire to recover
a lost moment in time. But the past ceases to exist as an island reality;
rather it is interpreted from the perspective of the mainland culture.

The political migration of Dominicans from their island of origin to
the United States is contemporaneous with the fall of Rafael Leónidas
Trujillo as well as the arrival of the first wave of Cuban exiles at the beginning of the 1960s. During the dictatorship, Trujillo had absolute control
over the military, the economy, and the people, and, except for a select
group, he prevented anyone from leaving the island. During this stage of
Dominican history, those who did abandon the island, with or without the
dictator's consent, sought political exile.

The situation changed radically after the dictator's death and the U.S.
invasion of the island in 1965, which foiled any efforts to restore Juan
Bosch to the presidency or to convert the Dominican Republic into another
Communist Cuba. With the direct involvement of the United States in the
internal affairs of the Dominican Republic and its support of Joaquín
Balaguer's presidency, the number of Dominican exiles increased and the
character of their exile changed from political to economic. The
Dominican migration to the United States has steadily risen so that
Dominicans are now rapidly becoming the largest Hispanic group in New
York.[1] However, as with other immigrant groups, Dominicans have found
themselves looking back in order to understand their present and future. If
writers on the island were trying to come to terms with the Trujillo dictatorship and the U.S. invasion of their country, those who traveled to the
mainland wanted to recover a lost origin.

The Puerto Rican economic migration, associated with Operation Bootstrap after World War II, and the Cuban political exodus, related to the Castro takeover, produced a generation of Latino writers born or raised in the United States. The Dominican migration, which was first political and later economic, would also count among its participants a significant number of writers. And just as the other immigrants or sons of immigrants have documented their experiences mainly in the cities in which they live, Dominican American authors would also do the same, some of them writing in Spanish and a few in English.² In her novel *How the Garcia Girls Lost Their Accents* (1991), the Dominican American writer Julia Álvarez depicts a search for identity motivated by a tense struggle between Hispanic and North American cultures.

The political exile of the fictional García family takes place during General Trujillo's dictatorship. In re-creating the past, the narrator tells us that Carlos García, with the assistance of Mr. Victor, an American diplomat and member of the Central Intelligence Agency, planned to assassinate the ruthless Trujillo. But the plot failed when the State Department did not support the plan Mr. García had been asked to organize. Accosted by Trujillo's henchmen, Mr. García received a fellowship from the United States, allowing him to leave the Dominican Republic and work as an intern in a hospital in New York City, where he moved with his wife and four daughters.

Even though *How the Garcia Girls Lost Their Accents* is written in English and appears to have more in common with North American than Hispanic literature, the novel's structure recalls that used by Borges's Herbert Quain, who writes *April March*, invoking the inverse world of Bradley. The narrator explains:

> The worlds proposed by *April March* are not regressive; only the manner of writing their history is so: regressive and ramified, as I have already said. The work is made up of thirteen chapters. The first reports the ambiguous dialogue of certain strangers on a railway platform. The second narrates the events on the eve of the first act. The third, also retrograde, describes the events of another possible eve to the first day; the fourth, still another. Each one of these three eves (each of which rigorously excludes the other) is divided into three other eves, each of a very different kind.³

Though Quain writes nine novels, each containing three chapters, and affirms Schopenhauer's observations of the twelve Kantian categories, Álvarez also appears to sacrifice everything for the sake of symmetry. Her novel is divided into three parts, each containing five chapters.

Álvarez's structure follows more closely Carpentier's "Viaje a la semilla" (1944; "Journey Back to the Source," 1970).[4] As I have demonstrated elsewhere, Carpentier's story is narrated backward; that is, it begins toward the chronological ending of the narration and ends at the beginning, at the chronological origin of the events narrated. Similar to Carpentier's story, *How the Garcia Girls Lost Their Accents* describes the most recent events and ends with the earliest ones; that is, it begins during the 1989–1972 period, when the four sisters are adults and reside in the United States, and concludes during the 1960–1959 period, when they were young girls living in the Dominican Republic. The beginning of the narration is the end and the end is the beginning, and the novel has two beginnings and two endings, the physical and chronological ones.[5]

In Carpentier's work, the black character, a practitioner of an African religion, perhaps Melchor, with extraordinary gestures sets into a regressive motion events associated with the life and death of the Marqués de Capellanías. Like Carpentier's story, Álvarez's novel refers to the magic of African religion, expressed mainly by Chucha and Pilar, the two old Haitian women who practice voodoo. Pilar, who is present at the end of the narration, which is the chronological beginning of the story, causes Yolanda, in particular, to experience the terror of the coal shed. Yolanda is the author's alter ego, and the coal shed occupies a central space in the narration and is the source of Yolanda's nightmares. The coal shed is the space of terror, represented by Pilar's stories and the mother of the kitten Yolanda wants to raise; of pleasure, when Mundín asks her to show him her private parts; and of fiction, when she has to lie to avoid *tía* Carmen's punishment. The coal shed is the origin of memory, and the origin of the story that motivates Yolanda to return to the island, possibly to stay forever, and Álvarez to write her story, as we shall see. The novel is an attempt to understand memory, the past, and a time before the sisters lost their innocence and their accents.

How the Garcia Girls Lost Their Accents describes the exile of the García family from the Dominican Republic to the United States and the reasons why the family had to leave the motherland and travel to the mainland, where their lives continue to unfold in the present. Carlos García's action, the planning of an attack against a high dignitary, Trujillo, was a theme developed in Marcio Veloz Maggiolo's *El prófugo* (1962) but already present in Carpentier's *El acoso* (1956; *Man Hunt,* 1959). In this aspect, García's life resembles that of many nineteenth century political exiles who conspired against Spain and sought refuge in the United States, where many of them continued their struggle against the colonial government. Like the first wave of anti-Castro exiles, the Garcías are privileged and professionals. The grandfather studied in the United States, held a diplomatic appointment, and owned land where the members of the family built their homes and had servants and private guards. In the Dominican Republic, the García daughters attend a school for American children and live a North American existence. When Mr. García wins a fellowship that allows him to abandon the island, the grandfather does not consent that his son and family are to live like commoners. And on more than one occasion, the reader is told that the parents shopped only at FAO Schwarz, one of the most complete and expensive toy stores in New York City.

In the United States, the García sisters continue to receive the best education money can buy. But the situation has changed; they now experience life in the United States from a different vantage point, not as members of a privileged class associated with the Dominican Republic but as common Hispanic immigrants. The García girls are the object of discrimination both in and outside of school. Carla, the oldest, experiences rejection when a gang of boys follow her, throwing rocks and yelling "Go back to where you came from, you dirty spic!" These are the same words La Bruja uses in a section narrated by Sandi.[6] This subtext in Álvarez's novel recalls the Puerto Rican literature of the Generación del Cuarenta, which documents the life of Puerto Ricans who left the island after Operation Bootstrap was initiated, but has more in common with the works of the sons and daughters of Puerto Rican immigrants that make up Nuyorican and Puerto Rican American literature, written primarily in English. The works of poets such as Pedro Pietri and Tato Laviera and narrators such as Nicholasa Mohr and Piri Thomas and also narrator and poet Judith Ortiz Cofer document not the migratory process generated by Operation Bootstrap, but primarily the lives of Puerto Ricans once they have arrived on the mainland.[7] Álvarez's contribution to this literature reveals that North Americans do not differentiate between economic and political exiles. Nor do they distinguish between different Hispanic Caribbean groups, that is, between Cubans, Puerto Ricans, and Dominicans; the García girls are reduced to common people and are treated with disdain.

In Álvarez's work, discrimination on the part of North Americans toward Hispanics is not presented as unique but as an aspect of any migratory process, including that inside the Dominican Republic. The reaction North Americans have upon seeing Carla García is similar to the one she and other members of her family exhibit toward servants in general, and Haitians in particular, while living in the Dominican Republic. In fact, their characterizations contain racial overtones. For example, Chucha is not a "café-con-leche" Dominican, but a "blue-black" Haitian; that is, she is very black and has problems pronouncing some words in Spanish, particularly those having a "j" sound. This situation parallels that of the García girls; in the United States, the girls speak with the accent their father still has. From the point of view of a regressive narration, racial prejudice existed in the Dominican Republic well before the García family left the island to live in the United States. But the prejudice that the girls experience in the United States toward the beginning of the narration allows them to uncover an earlier one, in the Dominican Republic, toward the end of the novel.

How the Garcia Girls Lost Their Accents follows with more precision a tradition established by novels such as Pedro Juan Labarthe's *The Son of Two Nations: The Private Life of a Columbia Student* (1931), Humberto Cintrón's *Frankie Cristo* (1972), and Richard Ruiz's *The Hungry American* (1978), three works written by Puerto Ricans who were born on the island and lived in the United States and wrote their autobiographical narratives in English. Even though Álvarez's characters are Dominicans, professionals, and well-to-do, like those in the works of the mentioned Puerto Rican writers, they live with the hope of improving their lives in the United States. Álvarez's, Labarthe's, Cintrón's, and Ruiz's characters live the American dream. By contrast, works such as Piri Thomas's *Down These Mean Streets* (1967) and Jamie Buchingham and Nicky Cruz's *Run, Baby Run* (1968) portray a life of despair; their protagonists are victims of U.S. society and culture.

With the passage of time, the status of the García family becomes more permanent and their lives resemble not so much those of other Hispanics living in the United States as those of their Anglo-American counterparts. Because the family is descended from Spanish conquerors and a great-grandfather married a Swedish woman, we suppose that they had very little African blood. Indeed, Carlos García was a doctor with a generous source of income, and his daughters were able to assimilate into North American culture with little difficulty. Certainly, this was the father's plan. The children enroll in the best and most expensive schools for the purpose of losing their Spanish accent when speaking English—the answer to the novel's title, how the García girls lost their accents.

As the sisters incorporate themselves into North American culture, they suffer the same problems associated with mainstream middle- and upper-middle-class citizens. Carla is divorced and marries her psychiatrist; Sandra starves herself in order to remain slim; Yolanda does not get along with her husband, is under the care of a psychiatrist with whom she falls in love, and ends up becoming the lover of the chair of the Department of Comparative Literature where she teaches; and Sofía is pregnant from an affair with a German she met in Colombia and whom she marries. In addition, they have forgotten aspects of their Hispanic culture, and during the father's birthday party the band plays North American music.

Although they are Hispanic, the García girls have neglected their Dominican traditions and accepted U.S. culture. They are caught in the middest, as indicated in my epigraph to chapter 6, that is, between the *tick* and the *tock*, something and nothing, Genesis and Apocalypse, past and future, or between North American and Hispanic cultures.[8] The unstable lives of the sisters are related in part to the control the mother and father exert over their children. The parents do not adapt to the changing culture of the sixties and treat their daughters as if they were still living in the Dominican Republic. But the daughters are also responding to the North American environment in which they live, more liberal and permissive than the traditional one known to their parents. Certainly, Anglo-American culture plays an important role in the rebellion of the García girls. Therefore, the control the parents want to maintain over the daughters, a hallmark of Dominican culture, and the girls' need to rebel, an effect of North American society, result in cultural and personal conflicts. Like that of Cristina García's protagonist in *Dreaming in Cuban* (1992), Yolanda's search for her Dominican identity must be understood within the context of the 1960s in the United States.

The novel is narrated backward and reveals the sisters' original language and accent, the one associated not with their adopted culture but with their country of origin. The novel starts or ends with Yolanda, the North American. That is how she is perceived when she returns to the island at the outset of the novel. Similar to the way in which Nuyoricans are perceived when returning to Puerto Rico, described by writers like Miguel Algarín and Nicholasa Mohr but also Pedro Juan Soto, Yolanda is not totally accepted in the Dominican Republic. Her cousin Lucinda describes her clothes and characteristics as those of a hippie; that is, a member of the youth of the decade of the sixties who were nonconformist and experimented with drugs. She is no Dominican; she is "like a missionary, her cousins will say, like one of those Peace Corps girls who have let themselves go so as to do dubious good in the world" (3–4). Lucinda also calls her "Miss America."

Yolanda has forgotten her language; she does not speak fluent Spanish and relies on English to express herself. Yolanda and her sisters' retrospective voyage is an expression of their desire to find the original language and accent, one that has been lost in the present. Yolanda does not remember what an *antojito* is. In Dominican lexicon, *antojito* has two meanings: It refers to something you crave to eat, but also to the spiritual possession of someone's body. Yolanda embodies both referents, the Dominican and the North American ones. Her return to the island after a twenty-nine-year absence shows that she is as much North American as Dominican, if not more so. Nevertheless, Yolanda finds herself between two worlds; she belongs to both and to neither one. Her return to the island in 1989, the most recent time of the novel, symbolizes a spiritual journey in search of communion not with Dominican culture as it exists during the present time of the novel, but with a mythical past associated with her childhood. Yolanda's past compares favorably with the present of her *tía* Carmen and her cousin Lucinda. For Yolanda, her cousin is a typical Dominican model; that is, a woman of the night. She does not recognize or understand her family's culture: the chauffeur drives aunt Flor to church, and the women await their husbands' return, knowing that they will stop to see their lovers before coming home.

Yolanda is not Dominican but North American. In an essay entitled "An American Childhood in the Dominican Republic" (1987) Álvarez reveals some information about her own life. The essay could have served as the original idea for the novel or for a chapter the author excluded. In the essay, Álvarez reproduces information found in the novel. For example, she mentions that it was Mr. Victor, of the U.S. Embassy and the CIA, who persuaded Carlos García, the protagonist's father, to join the resistance against Trujillo and who later assisted him in leaving the country and obtaining a job with an international cardiovascular team.

However, the essay also provides the reader with explanations that the novel does not offer. For example, it explains Carlos's past. As a young man, Carlos participated in the resistance movement against Trujillo and sought refuge in Canada, where he lived for nine years, studied medicine, and met his wife. More important, it reveals that Álvarez is the second daughter, and that she and her older sister were born in the United States and the younger two in the Dominican Republic. Her mother said that the first two were "Americanitas" and the last two "criollas." This information would suggest that the author corresponds to Sandi, the second daughter in the novel, and not Yolanda, the third one. We should note that Sandi is the least visible character in the novel, while Yolanda plays a central role. But in order to undergo a search for her origins, in the novel Álvarez had to change her place of birth, from the United States to the Dominican Republic; therefore, she trades places with her sister and assumes the identity of the third child, who was born on the island.

A close reading of the essay and the novel shows that Álvarez altered the events of her life to create fiction. She mentions in the essay that it was her grandmother and not her father, as in the novel, who brought from the United States the mechanical savings boxes that were in style in the New York toy store FAO Schwarz. According to the essay, Mamita brought the grandchildren one with a Jonah, a boat, and a whale; another with a girl jumping rope; and for her, a man with a dog that jumped for a bone. In the novel, the savings box with the girl is for Sandi; the one with Jonah and the boat is for Yolanda; and the other, with a girl and a cloud, not mentioned in the essay, is for Carla. Álvarez does not mention the savings bank with the man and his dog in the novel, and saves it for herself; or perhaps we could attribute the bank to Sofía, who in the novel does not have one. This last idea intimates that Álvarez is also Sofía. But I propose that she is also Yolanda. In the essay, Álvarez tells us that her grandmother brought her a drum with two sticks inside, the same one mentioned at the end of the novel as belonging to Yolanda. Moreover, it was Yolanda who liked to eat guavas, and these appear in both the essay and novel.

If the novel is a search for the past of the Dominican Republic, the tone of the essay is different. The essay represents Álvarez's reunion with her place of origin, the United States; it expresses a desire to distance herself from her parents' culture in order to affirm and accept her own. Álvarez mentions that in the Dominican Republic she attended a North American school, which she preferred to the Dominican one, swore allegiance to the flag of the United States, and sang the Marine hymn. The essay concludes with the family's departure from the Dominican Republic to the United States:

"We're here!" my father said a little sadly. Despite my dark hair and coloring, despite the fact that I came from generations of Dominicans, I joined the Americans in clapping. All my childhood I had dressed like an American, eaten American foods, and befriended American children. I had gone to an American school and spent most of the day speaking and reading English. At night, my prayers were full of blond hair and blue eyes and snow and just such a plane ride as this one. All my childhood I had longed for this moment of arrival. And here I was, an American girl, coming home at last.[9]

In the essay, Álvarez finds her identity in her return home to the United States. In contrast, the novel begins (or ends) with Yolanda's return to the Dominican Republic.

The change in perspective from the essay to the novel is elucidated by their chronological relationship. The essay was published in 1987, the novel in 1991. A second autobiographical essay, which Álvarez published in 1992, is also instructive in this regard. In "Hold the Mayonnaise," Álvarez offers the reader information about her life, this time about her husband and his "two tall, strapping, blond, mayonnaise-eating daughters" and her estrangement from the younger members of her new family—this essay is a way of bridging the distance between her and "her husband's daughters." Unlike in the earlier essay, in "Hold the Mayonnaise" Álvarez identifies herself not as a North American but as a Dominican; that is, she refers to herself as if she had been born in the Dominican Republic. The desire she has as a young girl to assimilate into North American culture and society, expressed in the first essay, is not developed into a theme as an adult in the second essay. The five years that transpired between the publication of one essay and the other allowed Álvarez to recognize that her experiences and, most important, her interpretation of those experiences, have changed. In the present, she feels proud to be Hispanic. Álvarez writes in the second paragraph:

> We were also Dominicans, recently arrived in Jamaica, Queens, in the early 60's, before waves of other Latin Americans began arriving. So, when we imagined who exactly my father might possibly ever think of remarrying, only American women came to mind. It would be bad enough having a *madrastra*, but a "stepmother." . . .
> All I could think of was that she would make me eat mayonnaise, a food I identified with the United States and which I detested.[10]

Álvarez, who now dissociates herself from North American culture and identifies with Dominican culture, has become the stepmother she once feared she would have. Her stepdaughters are truly American and, in comparison, she appears more Hispanic. Álvarez, it appears, is also struggling with her Hispanic identity. Her shift in identification, from North American to Hispanic, is associated with her family situation but also with that imposed by her students and the times. In the second essay she questions her father's advice that one had to work hard to be accepted in this country: "In this age of remaining true to your roots, of keeping your Spanish, of fighting from inside your culture, that assimilationist approach is highly suspect. My Latino students—who don't want to be called Hispanics anymore—would ditch me as faculty adviser if I came up with that play-nice message" (24). Álvarez is trying to come to terms with being Hispanic or Latina; the novel speaks of a strong Hispanic tradition, and the essay of another one closely tied to a Hispanic presence in the United States. The word *Latino*, which she attributes to her family, herself, and her students, refers more appropriately to Hispanics born or raised in the United States. If we consider the information provided in the first essay, Latino is an identity Álvarez can also claim. Taking into account the changing discourses, Álvarez is North American, Hispanic, and Latina, shifts that can be explained by the time elapsed between her writings: the novel was published four years after the first essay and one year before the second one; even though the novel contains information from the first autobiographical piece, it is closer to the narrative tone of the second one.

In the novel, Yolanda returns to the Dominican Republic in search of her own Dominican identity. But North American culture has changed her forever. She arrives not as a Hispanic but as a North American. Yolanda's search is part of a process of discovering identity and pride that evolved in the decades of the sixties and seventies in the United States and brought back racial and ethnic pride to African Americans and Puerto Rican Americans, among other groups. Yolanda's search must be understood within the context of that North American cultural experience; she is an independent person but is tied to the cultural experiences of her adopted country.

As a "typical American," Yolanda imposes U.S. customs on Dominican traditions. When she arrives on the island, her first desire is to eat the wild guavas. She looks for them in the countryside, against the better judgment of her aunt, who warns her of the danger of getting lost or being kidnapped or raped. The protagonist does not return to Dominican reality, but to the past of her childhood, by means of her memory, writings, and the text.

Yolanda's return is counterposed to that of her sister Sofía; their experiences are distinct from one another. Sofía was sent to the island at seventeen, against her own free will, for admitting that the bag of marijuana the maid had found was hers. During that "punishment," Sofía suppresses the feeling of independence she has developed in the United States and accepts the ways of a Dominican woman; that is, she becomes traditional, passive, and obedient to the demands of her boyfriend, Manuel Gustavo, who is proud to assert that in the Dominican Republic, "the men wear the pants."

Unlike Sofía, Yolanda travels to the Dominican Republic of her own free will, but she cannot accept the life her cousin and aunt represent. She is attracted to and repelled by Dominican culture, and, in the present, she lives the tension that exists between North American and Dominican ways of life. Nevertheless, the text suggests that she will never abandon her independent habits, exemplified by her venture into the countryside to find guavas. When she gets a flat tire and two men approach her, Yolanda identifies herself as an American, which saves her from the danger her aunt Carmen foresaw. Let us remember that in the novel the Miranda guard does not want to help José, whom Yolanda has sent for aid, because he does not believe that at that hour of the evening a Dominican woman is out looking for guavas. Even though on her birthday Yolanda desires that her country of origin become her home, North American culture is an inherent part of her personality. Just as Eve can never return to paradise but only to a time after her downfall and ejection from Eden, Yolanda cannot go back to the past of her innocence. Yolanda's guavas are the symbolic equivalent of Eve's apple; and if the apple forced Eve from paradise, the guavas will reenforce Yolanda's desire to return to her childhood past. Although she is seeking a moment of innocence, her arrival is already contaminated by the world of adults, by the present, and by North American culture that she cherishes and that determines how she interprets the past.

Yolanda is caught between two worlds, the Hispanic and the North American. She is a multiple being. She is both North American and Dominican; she is Carla, Sandi, Sofía, and Yolanda, and she embodies the different narrative perspectives their voices represent. She is also Yolanda and not Yolanda. This idea is manifested in the novel by the multiple names used. She is Yolanda, Yoyo, Yosita, Yo, and, last but not least, the English Joe. And above all, she is *Yo*, the Spanish first-person pronoun, the *I* of the narrator. Yolanda's return to the island represents her desire to transform herself from the North American Joe to the Yolanda of her family and youth. One of her nicknames is Yoyo, which recalls the toy constantly going up and down, moving from one extreme to the other, from one culture to the other, touching upon both but not remaining a part of either one of them. The protagonist's onomastic displacement will be continuous. It characterizes a search for identity, for a voice that will offer a coherent understanding of her circumstances, but also the impossibility that any one perspective exists that can explain the complexity of her reality. She will always be Yolanda, and someone else.

Yolanda's struggle is embedded in another scene near the end of the novel, which is the chronological beginning of the narration. Yet this incident is perhaps the narrative center of the novel, because after its resolution the temporal dimension changes and the narration follows a traditional course. I am referring to the scene in which the young Yolanda enters the coal shed with her drum and contemplates taking a kitten from the mother's litter, the one with the white boots, which is distinctly different from the rest. Yolanda is not certain that if she plays with the kitten the mother will abandon it, and she consults a hunter who happens to cross their property. He states: "Well, just as your drumsticks belong inside your drum, and dowels will not do, so a kitten belongs with its mother, and no one else will do." He continues: "While a kitten is still a suckling, it cannot, now can it, be taken from its mother to be a pet? . . . To take it away would be a violation of its natural right to live" (284–85). The man convinces Yolanda to wait seven days, until the kitten is older, but she soon recognizes the hypocrisy of the hunter, who shoots at birds that have babies.

In the story, the hunter appears and disappears at the appropriate moments and may even represent the author coming to terms with her conscience. Nevertheless, Yolanda takes the cat, whom she has named Schwarz, a symbol of the items brought to her from that store, from the litter, hides it in her drum, and returns to the house pursued by the mother cat. Although there is a parallel between Yolanda and the hunter, each of whom disrupt a natural order, she is more like the kitten inside the drum. Like the kitten, Yolanda was also uprooted from her nest, her childhood (perhaps seven years too early), in the Dominican Republic. The kitten's meows and the drumbeats meant to disguise them represent a natural language and the imposed one that in the years to come will cover Yolanda's accent. Although we can assume that once Yolanda puts the kitten out the window it returns to its mother, Yolanda will spend the rest of her life searching for the origin of her past. From that moment on, Yolanda is haunted by the mother cat, a continual reminder of the incident with the kitten. The nightmares recall that past, but most important, they recall

Yolanda's own trauma, that of being taken from her natural environment, from her own litter; it is after this incident that her family moves to the United States.

By revisiting the past, Álvarez comes to terms with her trauma. After the description of Yolanda's encounter with the cats, the novel pivots; the events stop unfolding regressively and are narrated in chronological order; time is accelerated, and life appears to make sense. The novel ends this way:

> Then we moved to the United States. The cat disappeared altogether. I saw snow. I solved the riddle of an outdoors made mostly of concrete in New York. My grandmother grew so old she could not remember who she was. I went away to school. I read books. You understand I am collapsing all time now so that it fits in what's left in the hollow of my story? I began to write, the story of Pila, the story of my grandmother. I never saw Schwarz again. The man with the goatee and Kashtanka vanished from the face of creation. I grew up, a curious woman, a woman of story ghosts and story devils, a woman prone to bad dreams and bad insomnia. There are still times I wake up at three o'clock in the morning and peer into the darkness. At that hour and in that loneliness, I hear her, a black furred thing lurking in the corners of my life, her magenta mouth opening, wailing over some violation that lies at the center of my art. (290)

The mother cat is a reminder of what Yolanda did, but it is also a symbol of the psychological impact of being taken away from her surroundings at an impressionable age. It is for this reason that Yolanda, the adult, must return to the Dominican Republic, not to understand the present status of a privileged family or of a culture struggling for democracy but to confront her childhood and the past.

If the Caribbean was the first space of the encounter between Europe and the New World, where the different cultures clashed but also mixed, these same encounters were later repeated in other parts of the American continent. In the Caribbean, the coming together of the cultures has produced a conflict of identity, in which Spanish, African, Amerindian, and national components must be sorted out. When Caribbean people travel to the United States, the question of identity becomes even more complex, taking on a North American component as well. The movement back and forth between North American and Hispanic cultures has propelled Cubans, Puerto Ricans, and Dominicans into an eternal quest for identity and a perpetual dance between two cultures.

EIGHT

Postmeditation
on *Latino*, Race, and Identity

THE issue of Spanish American postmodernity and postcoloniality pertains to the Spanish-speaking countries of the Americas, but the United States has one of the largest Hispanic populations in the world and its traditions also include the migratory histories of Hispanics. In this respect, the United States is also a part of Spanish America. As we have seen throughout this study, since the nineteenth century Cubans, Dominicans, and Puerto Ricans have been seeking refuge in the United States, where Hispanic culture continues to develop and thrive.

While I am aware that postcolonial theory is based on British colonialism and that there are historical differences between it and the Spanish model in Spanish America, it gains further meaning when applied to Latinos living in the United States. Many Latinos in the United States continue to live, as Puerto Ricans do, a colonial existence within the colonizing country. Whereas Anglo-Americans profit from the American dream, Latinos and African Americans, as a group, have been kept at a distance. Yet this rejection has forced Latinos to search for an identity that reflects their condition in the dominant country. In the words of Homi Bahbha:

> The postcolonial perspective forces us to rethink the profound limitations of a consensual and collusive "liberal" sense of cultural community. It insists that cultural and political identity are constructed through a process of alterity. Questions of race and cultural difference overlay issues of sexuality and gender and overdetermine the social alliances of class and democratic socialism. The time for "assimilating" minorities to holistic and organic notions of cultural value has dramatically passed.[1]

Latino refers to a specific yet changing reality. It has a specific origin but is often used and misused, sometimes to an extreme degree, to accommodate the interests of a particular speaker. To clarify some misconceptions, I find it necessary to explore the term's historical context. *Latino* can be traced to the late sixties and early seventies, when it first appeared in the Young Lords Party 13-Point Program and Platform. Their positions attempted to decenter the center from within. The second of the thirteen points contains the word *Latino* and reads as follows:

> 2. We Want Self-Determination For All Latinos.
>
> Our Latin Brothers and Sisters, inside and outside the united states, are oppressed by amerikkkan business. The Chicano people built the Southwest, and we support their right to control their lives and their land. The people of Santo Domingo continue to fight against gringo domination and its puppet generals. The armed liberation struggles in Latin America are part of the war of Latinos against imperialism. Que viva La Raza![2]

Latino refers to political, social, historical, and racial realities that define the lives of many Puerto Ricans and other Hispanics, born or raised and educated in the United States, demanding the same rights enjoyed by Anglo-Americans. In the Young Lords Party Program and Platform, *Latino* is used synonymously with "Our Latin Brothers and Sisters"; the latter was the more commonly used expression when the platform was drafted. As I have mentioned at the outset of this study, the word *Latino* may have been derived from the Spanish language, since it has a Spanish equivalent in *Latinoamérica*—a Spanish translation of *Latin America*. But *Latino* is also a Hispanicism, a deformation and a reappropriation of the English word *Latin*. More precisely, the term is Spanglish, an English word with a Spanish pronunciation, and its signifier connotes and unites two linguistic and cultural referents.

If we look closely at the Young Lords platform, we can find other clues that help us understand the usage of the term *Latino*. The paragraph points to a common bond between "Latin Brothers and Sisters" in and outside of the United States, one that is based on oppression by U.S. imperialism and business interests. This idea recalls the internationalist position of the Young Lords Party, acquired from proponents of revolution like Fidel Castro and Che Guevara, and represented in the United States by Rap Brown and other members of the Black Panther Party. In this sense, there is a connection between oppressed Chicanos in the Southwest and Dominicans, who in 1965 witnessed a U.S. Marine invasion of their country.

There are similarities between oppressed people living in and outside the United States; however, their circumstances are also distinct. For example, Dominicans in the Dominican Republic are subjected to U.S. interest in the region, but at least they can express themselves in their own language and culture. Unlike their compatriots, Dominicans living in New

York and Chicanos in the Southwest must contend with linguistic and cultural discrimination and are reminded on a daily basis of their minority status. Newly arrived immigrants speak their native language and express their cultural values within the context of another language and culture. They attempt to preserve their identity, but within a short time, and especially in their children's generation, they lose some of their distinctive characteristics, blending with the dominant society to produce a multiplication of identities and linguistic terms.

The term *Latino* refers to oppressed people in the United States. It is derived by those who are colonized or oppressed within the colonial power looking out toward the neocolonial countries or, in the language of Homi Bhabha and others, the postcolonial world.[3] *Latino* refers to an identity postcolonial people have developed within the colonizing country—an identity that does not extend outside its geographic borders. This is especially the case with Puerto Ricans, who are a colonized people in Puerto Rico and whose experiences as such are continued and exacerbated in the United States. However, Puerto Ricans on the island are not Latinos in the same sense of the word as those living on the mainland. Latin Americans do not consider themselves to be Latinos or Hispanics; the terms do not mean the same thing within Spanish social, linguistic, and cultural contexts. They prefer to embrace a national or even regional identity. The presence of large numbers of these national groups in the United States allows Latinos to establish a bond with their counterparts in the countries of origin. In other words, Dominicans who live mainly in New York have been responsible to some extent for bringing to the attention of Latinos and Hispanics the plight of Dominicans in the Dominican Republic. Most recently, Julia Álvarez's *In the time of the Butterflies* (1994) has brought the struggle of the Mirabal sisters against the dictator Trujillo to the attention of an English-speaking audience as she translates the history of one culture into the other.

Oppression, as it is used in the platform, also has a racial connotation. The slogan "Que Viva la Raza" refers to a Chicano call for unity and identity, one that other Latinos embraced as their own, most evidently during César Chávez's grape boycott against Gallo wineries. The idea of race alludes to Vasconcelos's *La raza cósmica/The Cosmic Race* (1979) and more recently to Chicanos as descendants of Aztlán.[4] Likewise, in his "Puerto Rican Obituary," Pedro Pietri writes that "Puerto Rico is a beautiful place / Puertorriqueños are a beautiful race." *Race* is reappropriated and recontextualized beyond its biological referent. It can imply an ethnic group or national minority wanting to establish and promote its own identity within the space dominated by Anglo-American culture. The concept of race as a U.S. construct, nevertheless, is important not only to Chicanos or Puerto Ricans, but also to African Americans, and also refers to them.

Many Chicanos, Puerto Ricans, and other Latinos who live in the same conditions as inner-city African Americans are fighting the same battles against oppression and for civil rights. The relationship between blacks and Latinos is evident in Roberto Rodríguez's *X in La Raza* (1996), in which he analyzes the *X* in Malcolm X's name:

> When Malcolm X became a Muslim, he said the letter "X" represented the unknown—that it signified the African last names—prior to the European names that were imposed upon them by the slave owners. For those reasons, all Raza would also be justified in placing an "X" for their last names—to signify the indigenous names taken from us. . . . "X" could have the same value to Raza as it does to African Americans—representing the indigenous names, the language and our history that was taken from us.[5]

The word *Raza* underscores the common bond with the black race, with which the Young Lords and other oppressed minorities identified. The expression "Brothers and Sisters" is also derived from the African American linguistic referent; it speaks to the brotherhood and sisterhood among African Americans, but also between them and Latinos.

The term *Latino* is often used without the type of historical, political, and racial context I have provided. On the contrary, it has been defined loosely and often as part of rhetorical strategies by U.S. and Hispanic writers and critics who have defused its political and racial intents. Recent works of Latino Caribbean criticism have focused on one particular group or another and have referred to them not as Latinos, but by their national origin. As we have seen, Pérez Firmat's *Life on the Hyphen* (1994) researches Cuban Americans living in Miami; Juan Flores's *Divided Borders: Essays on Puerto Rican Identity* (1993) and Julio Marzán's *The Spanish Roots of William Carlos Williams* (1994) deal with Puerto Ricans on the island and the continent; and Eugene Mohr's *The Nuyorican Experience: Literature of the Puerto Rican Minority* (1982) focuses on Puerto Ricans from New York. Among such works, Ilán Stavans's *The Hispanic Condition: Reflections on Culture and Identity in America* (1995) studies the largest Hispanic minorities living in the United States: Cubans, Puerto Ricans, and Chicanos, and attempts to clarify their Latino history, culture, and identity. The title of his book alludes to Pérez Firmat's *The Cuban Condition: Translation and Identity in Modern Cuban Literature* (1989) more directly than to Jean-François Lyotard's *The Postmodern Condition: A Report on Knowledge* (1984), even though Latin America in general and Latinos in the United States provide another and more meaningful understanding of postmodernity and, as I have suggested above, postcoloniality. Stavans's first chapter, "Life in the Hyphen" confirms Pérez Firmat's influence by referring to his *Life on the Hyphen: The Cuban American Way.*

Stavans's reflections allow him to bring all Hispanics together, minimizing differences such as migratory periods and patterns, and issues pertaining to race, class, and gender. Some of his classifications are all-encompassing. He considers Mexican-born painter Martín Ramírez a symbol of all Hispanics, but more correctly Ramírez should serve as an example for those who shared his particular migratory history. The model becomes less precise once we uncover that Mexicans consider Ramírez not Hispanic or Latino, but Mexican, as indicated by the subtitle of his biography, *Martín Ramírez: pintor mexicano (1885–1960) (1989).*[6]

In his desire to cast a wide net for understanding Latinos, he asks a series of questions that include: "What distinguishes us from Anglo-Saxons and other European immigrants as well as from other minorities (such as blacks and Asians) in the United States?"[7] Stavans identifies himself as a Latino, but differentiates himself from other minorities such as blacks and Asians, omitting mention of the significant numbers of Africans and Asians who reside in the Caribbean and South America. Africans were slaves; Chinese became indentured servants; and Europeans transported both groups to Latin America and the Caribbean. Asians have lived in Cuba and Peru since the middle of the nineteenth century. Mexico also contains significant African and Asian populations.

There are marked differences between slavery and servitude in Latin America and the Caribbean and the United States, but there is also a common bond that cannot be ignored. The questions should be these: Are Afro-Hispanics and Asians of Latin American origin Latinos in the United States? Can they claim that identity while also identifying with their particular race and culture? Hispanics and Latinos are of European ancestry, but also African, Asian, Amerindian, and any possible combination. They are truly a postmodern people. While the question of power, language, and culture distinguishes Latinos from Anglo-Saxons and other European immigrants, very little should separate this group from blacks and Asians. According to the Young Lord's Party Program and Platform, there is a common struggle based on oppression, mainly that of Latinos and African Americans, but also of Asians.

In *The Hispanic Condition,* Stavans provides his own definition of Latinos and Hispanics. He uses "*Latinos* to refer to those citizens from the Spanish-speaking world living in the United States and *Hispanics* to refer to those living elsewhere. Which means that, by any account, a Latino is also an Hispanic, but not necessarily vice versa."[8] This explication allows Stavans to dedicate one chapter to Hispanic culture, starting with colonial history up to the present. Although this history may be useful to Hispanics who are in touch with their parents' culture, it is questionable that Latinos will recognize the value, since they are more attuned to U.S. culture.

Stavans's explanation is problematic. While it is not unrealistic to conceive that Anglo-Americans classify all U.S. Hispanics or Latinos as being one and the same, it is difficult to fathom that a recent immigrant changes his identity immediately upon arrival. Stavans's definition of *Latino* implies that one is Hispanic when he leaves his country of origin. But as soon as he crosses the border, or shortly thereafter, he becomes a Latino. More likely than not, a Hispanic, for example, who leaves his country and arrives in the United States is going to feel as nationalistic as when he left, and will probably remain the same for many years. It is difficult to understand the metamorphosis this traveler must undergo before taking on an identity formed by living and working in the United States.

Many Hispanics coming to the United States do not relate to Latinos and Latino culture, feeling closer to that of their home country, especially if they maintain their linguistic skills and travel regularly back and forth. This is certainly the case for Puerto Ricans from the island and those who visit the mainland, as represented in works such as Judith Ortiz Cofer's *Silent Dancing: A Partial Remembrance of a Puerto Rican Childhood* (1990). There are also many Cubans who arrived in the United States with the first wave of refugees who still feel more in tune with their island culture, even though they have lived in the United States longer than in Cuba. I do not mean to imply that a Hispanic, for example, who arrives in the United States as a young person, is educated and reared among Latinos and witnesses their mistreatment, will not acquire a Latino identity.

If we focus briefly on the history of the largest Spanish-speaking minority groups—Mexicans, Puerto Ricans, Cubans, and Dominicans—we see that they share a common element. Conditions in the country of origin, to a large extent because of the pursuit by the United States of its national and international interests, have forced many to flee their nations and seek refuge in the United States. Cubans are exiles, but so are the others in the broadest sense of the word; they were not willing immigrants, but found no alternative but to abandon their motherland and seek an uncertain future. Certainly, if these immigrants or exiles came looking for greater opportunities, their offspring have assumed an exile status, because they had no say in the decisions made by their parents. This is the case with Dominican Americans, who, according to the title of Daissy Cocco de Felippis and Jane Robinett's bilingual *Poemas del exilio y de otras inquietudes/Poems of Exile and Other Concerns* (1988) are not economic immigrants but exiles.

Searching for a master trope of Latino culture, Stavans looks for the first Latino writer and finds him in an antihero, in Felipe Alfau, who was born in Barcelona and lived also in Madrid and Guernica before moving to the United States. Stavans justifies his selection:

> Never a champion of assimilation and democracy, Felipe Alfau ought to be considered the first Latino writer who *consciously*

switched to English and did so for commercial and avant-garde artistic reasons. At an early age he decided to write in Shakespeare's tongue because Spanish seemed provincial, bucolic, for his innovative, experimental aspirations. Later, the Spanish Civil War gave a political undertone to his decision: He wanted to run away from ideology.[9]

Stavans gives meaning to Alfau's obscurity and his links to Iberian culture. The Iberian connection leads him to find further examples of Spanish writers who have written in the United States, suggesting that George Santayana, Juan Ramón Jiménez, Eduardo Mendoza, and Federico García Lorca should also be considered Latinos. In spite of Stavans's assertions, I find it difficult to believe that these writers identified with any country other than their own. Even though García Lorca wrote *Poeta en Nueva York* (1940; *Poet in New York*, 1940), he did not write about Latinos but about blacks and jews and understood them from the perspective of the marginal and often discriminated-against Gypsies of his native Andalucia.

Within the context of the Young Lords Party platform but also departing from it, Latinos living in the United States, along with their African and Native American counterparts, fought in the decade of the sixties to gain access to North American society. For example, the experience of a Puerto Rican from East Harlem, living in a broken-down tenement and attending an inferior school, has very little in common with a well-to-do Hispanic traveling to the United States to learn English and to maintain or improve his economic future. And even if we were to construct a comparable situation in which one leaves his poverty-stricken environment and finds his way to the United States, he would find the culture of his North American counterpart only vaguely familiar. In fact, he may view his travel to the United States as more of an opportunity than a continuation of his oppression.

For a Latin American, in contrast to a Latino, the immediate oppressor is likely to be not an Anglo-American but another person of the same nationality. This is evident in *Me llamo Rigoberta Menchú y así me nació la conciencia* (1983; *I, Rigoberta Menchú: An Indian Woman in Guatemala*, 1984).[10] The Amerindian protagonist reveals that her immediate exploiter is another Guatemalan. As I have mentioned, the text also shows Elizabeth Burgos's control over Menchú's interview and, consequently, over her. The question Spivak asks in her essay "Can the Subaltern Speak?" (1988) is appropriate in the context of the Latin American testimonial literature rescued but also mediated by the white writer.[11] *Me llamo Rigoberta Menchú* is as much about Burgos as it is about Menchú. With her questions Burgos guides Menchú's thinking and responses, and she later edits the text to coincide with her version of

Western culture, which may be antithetical to Menchú's language and culture. (I do not mean to imply that Menchú does not attempt to exert her own individuality; she does so by not revealing all of her family secrets.) The Spanish subtitle, "así me nació la conciencia" (so my consciousness was born), is a statement that applies more to Burgos, who was not aware of the Amerindian struggle, than it does to Menchú.[12] However, if we identify the Latino as a subaltern, how do we come to terms with her discourse? Should we also be concerned, as Fernando de Toro is, with the question "From Where to Speak?"[13] Certainly, the writer speaks in a language mediated by a dominant culture that she finds oppressive—but as a woman writer about an original culture to which she cannot return.

I am not aware of any antagonism that existed between Spain and the United States that would have forced writers like García Lorca and Jiménez to experience the less pleasant side of the American dream about which many Latinos write. On the contrary, historically speaking, Spain has assumed a privileged position, first as a colonial power in Spanish America, and later, in the 1960s, with the novels of the Boom period, as a cultural and publishing center for writers of the same region. Spain has always been central to the more marginal countries in Spanish America; however, its colonizing status brings it closer not to Spanish America but to other European powers and the United States.

If we accept the historical context of the term *Latino* as proposed in the Young Lords Party Program and Platform, in its broadest sense it refers to Latin America, not to Europe or to Spain. Though Spanish is a Latin-based language, Spain does not occupy an implicit or explicit space in the term "Latin Brothers and Sisters." The platform also refers to oppression, and it is not clear to me how this condition relates to Alfau. It becomes even more problematic if we consider race; not only is Alfau a white European, but he discriminated against blacks, as Stavans informs his reader: Alfau's "racist, antiblack, and undemocratic" attitude was a result of his "childhood education. He was taught that Africans were dirty and unhealthy and that whites were superior because Western civilization was built upon the wisdom of the Greek and Roman empires."[14] Alfau experienced life not as an oppressed, marginal member of society but as part of the privileged ruling class. This should have prevented Stavans from proposing Alfau as the first Latino author. If we did consider him a Latino, then what would we say about those Alfau felt were his inferiors? Latinos, who are marginal to mainstream society, identify with those who occupy the same space they do. If we must search for an origin, why not consider more appropriate writers, Puerto Ricans such as William Carlos Williams or Arturo Schomburg?

Latinos, as I see us, articulate a differentiated discourse; that is, an antidiscourse to the discourse of power, similar to that of blacks and slaves, as I have proposed in *Literary Bondage: Slavery in Cuban Narrative* (1990).[15] Within the context of U.S. postcolonial studies, the Latino and his oppressor occupy the same time and space. However, it is the position of the oppressed in the dominant society and the recontextualization of their parents' culture that gives meaning to their metanarrative. Postmodernity and postcoloniality gain greater relevance when we are studying Latinos.

When offering a discourse of difference within Anglo-American society, Stavans undermines Hispanics and Latinos when he states, "We suffer from a frightening absence of critical thinking."[16] This remark reveals more about the oppressors' position than about that of the oppressed. Did he mean to say "thinkers" or "thinking?" And, who are "we"? Is he referring to Latin Americans or to Latinos in the United States? Is he alluding to the lack of protein consumption, irregular diet, and poor education that inevitably affect the thinking patterns of poor Third World people? Or is he referring to thinkers like Borges, Cortázar, Cabrera Infante, or Piri Thomas, Cristina García, and other U.S. writers?

Are all Hispanics Latinos? Are South Americans or Spaniards, for that matter, who come to the United States to complete their bachelor's or doctoral degrees Latinos? Are Latinos those, born or raised and educated in the United States, who have been subjected to discrimination and prejudice and denied upward mobility? Are the conditions of Latinos closer to those of African Americans and Native Americans than to those of well-to-do Hispanics in their parents' country of origin? The questions I have raised are related to those proposed by Arif Dirlik in "The Postcolonial Aura: Third World Criticism in the Age of Global Capitalism" (1994). Though I am aware that that there are historical differences between British colonialism and the Spanish model in Spanish America, nevertheless I find his ideas appropriate to our discussion. Dirlik highlights the problem in a variety of ways.

In response to Ella Shohat's question "When exactly . . . does the 'postcolonial' begin?" Dirlik purposefully misreads it and answers: "When Third World intellectuals have arrived in First World academe."[17] This is a pertinent answer to a complex question, allowing Dirlik to provide an overview of postcoloniality, including its weaknesses. He shows that Eurocentrism is still alive but in a different form. With the decentering of Europe, Western values have been displaced to other areas, including postcolonial countries. Relying on David Harvey and Frederic Jameson's development of capitalism, Dirlik applies the same concept to capitalism, which does not reside in a particular space but is present throughout the world.

Dirlik sees no significant separation between Europe and the colonial world; what he does see is a movement of people with a more fluid notion of borders and boundaries. In addition, Third World countries are not always marginal, and those who are do not want to remain at the margin. For example, Indian intellectuals complain about living in a Third World country and aspire to be at the center of the nonaligned nations (a position Cuba has coveted since 1959). Furthermore, Iraq is an aggressive country and a threat to its neighbors, and the poor country of Somalia has successfully challenged the United States.

Shohat's question and Dirlik's answer forced me to consider other questions that are implicit in Stavans's book. If Dirlik addresses the issue of Third World critics who write from First World institutions, how shall we interpret the works of First World intellectuals in First World institutions who write about issues such as Latino identity, race, hybridity, postcoloniality, and Xicanismo?

There is an even more significant question that we should not overlook, perhaps more difficult to discern than the one I have just mentioned. In conceptualizing difference implicit in Stavans's work and in postmodern discourse, I ask: Can white Latin or Anglo-American scholars write from a perspective that reflects accurately the history of race and difference? Similarly, can white Hispanics who live in the United States articulate the interests of Latinos, Chicanos, and other minorities they claim to represent? Do their objects of study need mediation? Do we (all of us) speak from different centers of discursivity? Referring to his own question, Dirlik states: "Third World intellectuals who have arrived in First World academe, postcolonial discourse is an expression not so much of agony over identity, as it often appears, but of a newfound power." I believe that the answer is not one or the other but both. Dirlik's insight leads me to raise three other questions: Does Dirlik actually think that power is finally shifting? Is it a real power shift or only the appearance of a shift, as is so often the case? If some power is shifting, what kinds of responsibilities must the critic assume, regardless of race or color, when confronted with such powers? The latter is an important question Dirlik and other critics have not considered.

The questions I have posed should lead us to rethink the evolution and meaning of terms like *Latino, race, difference,* and *hybridity.* Postmodern criticism allows us to judge old metanarratives and construct new ones.[18] However, a study of metanarratives should not negate a recontextualization of the past. We should consider history and its discourses from the perspective of those instrumental in creating it, but also from the perspective of those who were its victims. *Race, hybridity, Latino, Xicanismo,* and other terms that will enter the discourse many not always be used with the same intent, and we must problematize them and assume the responsibility of uncovering the strategies employed by authors and critics alike. (Here I include myself.) In Latin America and in the U.S. inner cities where many Latinos live, premodernism, modernism, and postmodernism do not unfold chronologically but occupy the same time and space. I propose a recontextualization of the past and present, that is, a reappropriation of the two, in which they are read separately and simultaneously as one, allowing the critic to understand more closely how one period (and its narrative) works in terms of the other.

I would like to make one final observation about *The Hispanic Condition.* According to Stavans's definition, Hispanics live in their country of origin, and Latinos are Hispanics in the United States. If we give credence to the title, then the book is about those who live in Latin America and not about Latinos who reside in the United States. This interpretation is evident in the chapters "Ghosts" and "Toward a Self-Definition," where Stavans provides history narrated by Álvar Núñez Cabeza de Vaca and Hernando de Soto, but also by the Brazilian Jorge Amado, Argentinian Domingo Faustino Sarmiento, Mexican Octavio Paz, and others. But the book is also about Latinos: in the same chapters that deal with Hispanic writers he includes Oscar "Zeta" Acosta, Richard Rodríguez, Cherrie Moraga, Ernesto Galarza, Luis J. Rodríguez, and Piri Thomas. Is the title selected so that Stavans can provide the reader with a history of Latin America, starting with the Spanish conquest and discovery? More likely than not, the title and the content speak to Stavans's Hispanic and Latino identities.

I wonder if Stavans's search for Latino identity is autobiographical, allowing him to read literary history from his own perspective so that he can insert himself into the process he is describing. The autobiographical referent is present in Pérez Firmat's books, upon which Stavans relies for his titles and inspiration. This aspect of Stavans's reflections is more clearly stated in his conclusion, "Letter to My Child."

Stavans's double or multiple identity is evident in the displacement of his narrative *I,* which refers to his voice but also to his other lived and acquired identities. Stavans identifies with the center and the margin, with oppressor and the oppressed, with the Mexican, the Cuban, the Puerto Rican, the Chicano, the European, and the North American. He also takes on the role of a white, as he explicitly tells us in his description of an encounter with a black teenager in New York:

> Some time ago, while walking through downtown New York City, a black teenager approached me. "Hello, Mr. White Man!" he said. "You're the Devil, you know." Trying to remain calm, I decided the best thing to do was to continue walking. Although my aggressor kept shouting at me, the incident didn't turn violent. It was, nonetheless, deeply troubling to me. What incited this young man to verbally attack me, obviously, had more to do with the country's past, with slavery, racism, intolerance, and oppression, than with our mutual present. After all, it was the first time we accidentally saw each other. (But perhaps he would disagree: The present, he would claim, his and mine, is as oppressive as anything in the past.) In any case, we alone in the darkness of the

night had automatically become enemies: My whiteness was his problem; his explosive attitude was mine. In a matter of seconds we saw hatred in each other's face. Hatred, maliciousness, and hostility. I was his Other and he was mine—and to be the Other, everybody knows, is to offend, to transgress. "Hello, Mr. White Man!" To hell with *e pluribus unum*, I thought afterward. Latino, Jewish, who cares: I was simply the Other. Curiously, together my aggressor and I, a black and a Latino, represent a threat for mainstream America.[19]

Although it is not clear from the passage how Stavans, a white, represents a threat for "America," the presence of blacks is a constant reminder of the failure of the U.S. political, social, and judicial system. Neither is it clear to a New Yorker like me why an African American in the same city would consider a Latino to be white, since African Americans and Latinos interact on a regular basis and are aware of each other's plight. If Stavans is a Latino, why did he not explain to the teenager that even though he is white, his culture, the Latino one, is closer to that of blacks? Latinos and blacks are not each other's "other." On the contrary, they share many common traits that both the teenager and Stavans should have recognized. Their "other" is Anglo-America.

Stavans is also marginal and a minority, not only because he is Latino but because he is Jewish, as he notes in the quoted paragraph. The persecution of Jews throughout world history is well known. In Spanish America it became the topic of Isaac Goldemberg's captivating *La vida a plazos de don Jacobo Lerner* (1978; *The Fragmented Life of Don Jacobo Lerner*, 1976).[20] It is Stavans's Jewishness, I believe, that allows him to identify with the oppressed Latino communities. The discrimination, pain, and suffering of one group can be transposed to the other. But within a New York context, the Jewish identity becomes more complex. Although Jews have participated in and supported the civil rights movement, some African Americans and Latinos see Jews as oppressors; that is, as antagonistic to their struggle. This is particularly the case with those who stereotype Jews as owners of high-rent but run-down tenement buildings and expensive neighborhood stores. The black teenager was looking at Stavans, seeing perhaps not his Latino identity but someone from the Jewish heritage.

We can derive a lesson from Stavans's encounter with the black teenager. Identity is composed not only of how we perceive ourselves, but, equally important, of how others perceive us. For example, Piri Thomas's family saw him as another Puerto Rican member of the family, a perception he did not accept; he saw his own black identity. The same is true of Julia Álvarez's Yolanda, who returned to the Dominican Republic in search of her Dominican identity, only to find that those around her, including the members of her own family, saw her as a North American. Unfortunately, the impression we have of ourselves is not always the one others see, which is often informed by preconceived notions. In my study of Borges's "Dr. Brodies Report" and "The Other," I show that it is not so much who the other is, but the inward vision one has of the other, that prevails.[21] This may have been the case with Stavans's experience in New York. For the teenager, the other was defined by his own experience and imagination.

But there is more at stake here other than a claim to identity. It also speaks to the issue of the power Dirlik suggested. An acquired Latino identity helps provide a type of mobility and access to some levels of U.S. culture and society. Stavans's *The Hispanic Condition* describes and embodies a paradox that is currently developing in U.S. society and that will alter in some ways the interpretation I have provided of Latinos in the United States; nevertheless, it will also be consistent with the Young Lords Party Program and Platform. First, Stavans's book refers to the increased numbers of Hispanics from Spain and Spanish America who travel to the United States, often unaware of the political struggles Latinos have waged, but who nonetheless profit by inserting themselves into the same Latino discourse. Government officials and the society at large cannot, and may not want to, differentiate between those Latinos who have been deprived of social and educational services in the inner cities and privileged Hispanics who have the resources to send their children to the best schools. Second, the book refers to the contributions newly arrived immigrants are making to U.S. culture and society. Many of these newly arrived Hispanics feel an admirable gratitude and responsibility to Latinos and want to repay their debt by working to ameliorate the plight of the disadvantaged. Hispanics like Stavans are contributing to and expanding the ever-changing definition of *Latino*; they also identify with *Latino* as a concept. Such a perspective allows us to give new meaning to the internationalist position upheld by the Young Lords Party's use of the term *Latino*.

Bolívar's discourse of the Gran Colombia, a unified Spanish American continent forged by his liberation movement against Spanish colonialism, has become a reality. It was kept alive by José Martí, and in the twentieth century by Che Guevara and, in a different way, by the Organization of American States and the Pan-American Union. Above all, Bolívar's discourse has been recontextualized not in Latin America, where national boundaries continue to exist, but in the United States, where Puerto Ricans, Cubans, Dominicans, Mexicans, and Chicanos, but also Venezuelans, Peruvians, Chileans, and many other Hispanics live, study, and work, keeping their traditions alive. At the same time they also combine their cultures with those of African Americans, Native Americans, and, most important, Anglo-Americans to produce a new concept of *Latino*, race, and identity. In this regard, the United States is truly a postcolonial and postmodern nation.

Notes

Bibliography

Index

NOTES

Preface

1. I have chosen to use the terms *Cuban American, Puerto Rican American,* and *Dominican American* for the sake of consistency and to differentiate between those born or educated in the United States and those born or educated in their country of origin. I am aware that whereas Cuban Americans are relatively willing to accept their "hyphenated" experience in the United States, Puerto Ricans are less so. Like other ethnic minorities, Puerto Ricans are proud of their culture and nationality and do not consider themselves part of the mainstream North American experience. But the experience of Latinos in the United States has changed them in a profound manner so that they are indeed different from their counterparts living on the islands. In many respects, looking at their heritage involves examining not only the present conditions in the homeland but also the past and their childhood in the United States. For instance, in his *AmeRícan* (1985), Tato Laviera focuses specifically on the Puerto Rican experience in the United States, as one interpretation of the title suggests. In addition, the usage of the dual terms allows me to present those groups alongside other ethnic minorities in the United States. Classifications such as African American and Native American are widely accepted. Although I use the terms *Nuyorican* and *Dominicanyork,* they are limited to the New York experience.

I would also like to clarify that I use the term *Latino* to refer to Hispanics born or raised in the United States and *Spanish American* or *Hispanic* to refer to those born or educated in their country of origin. For a full discussion of these terms, see chapter 8.

2. Although I recognize the important role Chicano writers play in the development of Latino literature and that as a people they are treated in a manner similar to that experienced by Latino Caribbeans, their history and literature are beyond the scope of this book. Instead, I have decided to focus on writers from Cuba, Puerto Rico, and the Dominican Republic, countries that share a common location, history, and culture and whose people have also contributed to Latino literature in the United States. For an understanding of Chicanos see, for example, David T. Abalos, *Latinos in the United States* (Notre Dame: University of Notre Dame Press, 1986).

3. See, for example, Emir Rodríguez Monegal's *El boom de la novela latinoamericana* (Caracas: Editorial Tiempo Nuevo, 1972) and my two volumes of *Modern Latin American Fiction Writers, First Series* (Detroit: Gale Research, 1992) and with Ann González *Modern Latin American Fiction Writers, Second Series* (Detroit: Gale Research, 1994).

4. Even the informed critic Juan Flores does not distinguish between Hispanics and Latinos, instead grouping them all together. When referring to Hispanics or

Latinos, his studies do not differentiate among the more specific groups of Latinos and exclude Cuban Americans by omission. They are mentioned only once in passing. See *Divided Borders: Essays on Puerto Rican Identity* (Houston: Arte Público, 1993). In contrast, others such as Denis Lynn Heyck, whose anthology focuses on Mexican Americans, Puerto Ricans, and Cuban Americans, go as far as including in the definition Amerindians as well as the Spanish discoverers and conquerors of the New World. This is the case in her "Chronology of Latino Events," which starts at 10,500 B.C., with "Humans inhabit Americas from Alaska to the tip of South America." See *Barrios and Borderlands: Cultures of Latinos and Latinas in the United States* (London: Routledge, 1994), xiii–xviii. For a detailed discussion of this term, see my chapter 8.

5. *Hunger of Memory: The Education of Richard Rodríguez: An Autobiography* (Boston: David R. Godine, 1982), 151. Also cited by Flores, *Divided Borders,* 211. Although it is not my intention to criticize affirmative action, a program with many positive qualities, I do want to show how U.S. government agencies and culture fail to distinguish between Hispanics and Latinos.

6. Holly Ackerman defines *balseros* as "persons who have escaped from Cuba in small boats, on homemade rafts (balsas), or on inner tubes, in an effort to reach the United States." She adds: "They have left in sizable numbers since 1959 and form two distinct cycles: 1959–1974 and 1989–1994." "The *Balsero* Phenomenon, 1991–1994," in *Cuban Studies 26,* ed. Jorge Domínguez (Pittsburgh: University of Pittsburgh Press, 1996), 170. During the period from 1991 to 1994, 45,575 rafters were saved by the Coast Guard. Though not all rafters were allowed to enter the United States, a sizable number have. There are some writers among them, and soon there will be a corpus of works that will merit serious study.

7. See Antonio Benítez Rojo's *The Repeating Island: The Caribbean and the Postmodern Perspective,* trans. James Marannis (Durham, N.C.: Duke University Press, 1992).

8. See John Block Friedman, *The Monstrous Races in Medieval Art and Thought* (Cambridge: Harvard University Press, 1981).

9. See *The Postmodern Condition: A Report on Knowledge,* trans. Geoff Bennington and Brian Massumi (Minneapolis: University of Minnesota Press, 1984).

10. See Bill Aschroft, Gareth Griffiths, and Helin Tiffin, *The Empire Writes Back: Theory and Practice in Post-Colonial Literatures* (London: Routledge, 1989).

11. *Cambridge History of Latin American Literature,* ed. Roberto González Echevarría and Enrique Pupo-Walker, 3 vols. (Cambridge: Cambridge University Press, 1996).

12. *The Nuyorican Experience: Literature of the Puerto Rican Minority* (Westport, Conn.: Greenwood Press,1982).

13. See Flores, *Divided Borders.*

14. *Life on the Hyphen: The Cuban-American Way* (Austin: University of Texas Press, 1994).

15. *The Cuban Condition: Translation and Identity in Modern Cuban Literature* (Cambridge: Cambridge University Press, 1989).

16. *The Hispanic Condition: Reflections on Culture and Identity in America* (New York: HarperCollins, 1995).

Chapter 1

1. Álvarez Estévez, *La emigración cubana en Estados Unidos 1868–1878* (Havana: Editorial de Ciencias Sociales, 1986), 36. My translation.

2. *La Verdad,* June 15, 1878. Also cited by Álvarez Estévez, *La emigración cubana,* 160–61.

3. Ibid., 120. For a historical overview of Cubans in Florida, see Jorge Cantera and Carolina Hospital's "Florida and Cuba: Ties That Bind," in *A Century of Cuban Writers in Florida,* ed. Hospital and Cantera (Sarasota, Fla.: Pineapple Press, 1996), 1–26.

4. Álvarez Estévez states that in Key West, up to October 1878, the numbers were as high as 400 emigrants per month. Ibid., 136.

5. For a detailed discussion of Varela as author of Jicoténcal, see Luis Leal and Rodolfo J. Corttina's "Introducción," in *Jicoténcal* ((Houston: Arte Público, 1995), xv–xxxv. Also see *A Century of Cuban Writers in Florida,* ed. Carolina Hospital and Jorge Cantera (Sarasota: Pineapple, 1996), 31–32. These two works have placed Varela's contribution within the context of Cuban writing in the United States.

6. See my *Literary Bondage: Slavery in Cuban Narrative* (Austin: University of Texas Press, 1990), chap. 2.

7. See Roberto González Echevarría, *Alejo Carpentier: The Pilgrim at Home* (Ithaca, N.Y.: Cornell University Press, 1977).

8. "De Nueva York a Moscú pasando por París," *Bohemia* 41, no. 51 (1949): 80–86, 161–62.

9. For information on Novás Calvo, see, for example, Lorraine Roses, *Voices of the Storyteller: Cuba's Lino Novás Calvo* (Westport, Conn.: Greenwood Press, 1986) and Raymond Souza's *Lino Novás Calvo* (Boston: Twayne, 1981).

10. For documents on the Padilla affair, see *El caso Padilla: Literatura y revolución en Cuba,* ed. Lourdes Casal (Miami: Ediciones Universal, 1971).

11. *The Doorman,* trans. Dolores Koch (New York: Grove Press, 1991), 47.

12. For a discussion of this term, see my chapter 8.

13. "Noción de José Kozer," *Revista Iberoamericana* 56, nos. 152–53 (1990): 1247–56. Also see his *Life on the Hyphen: The Cuban-American Way* (Austin: University of Texas Press, 1994).

14. " Dancing into the Dream," *New York Times Book Review* 95, Aug. 27, 1989, p. 31.

Chapter 2

1. "'Qué assimilated, brother, yo soy asimilao': The Structuring of Puerto Rican Identity in the U.S.," in *Divided Borders: Essays on Puerto Rican Identity* 182–95 (Houston: Arte Público, 1993); also in *Journal of Ethnic Studies* 13, no. 3 (1985): 1–16, and *Casa de las Américas* 26, no. 152 (1985): 54-63.

2. "Assimilation vs. Ghettoization," *Antipode* 15, no. 1 (1983): 1–11. Cited in Flores, *Divided Borders,* 192.

3. Miguel Algarín and Bob Holman, eds., *Aloud: Voices from the Nuyorican Poets Cafe* (New York: Holt, 1994).

4. *The Spanish American Roots of William Carlos Williams* (Austin: University of Texas Press, 1994), 6.

5. Ibid., 260.

6. Ibid., 111.

7. See Francisco Cabanillas, "Lo que la música le hace al cuerpo: Entrevista con Víctor Hernández Cruz," in "Antología: Poesía hispano-caribeña escrita en los Estados Unidos," ed. William Luis, *Boletín de la Fundación Federico García Lorca* 9, no. 18 (1995): 77–93.

8. Algarín and Holman, *Aloud,* 313–14.

9. Many Nuyorican writers recognize the importance of Julia de Burgos in their works. For example, Sandra María Esteves writes a poem "A Julia y a mí," in *Herejes y mitificadores: Muestra de la poesía puertorriqueña en los Estados Unidos,* ed. Efraín Barradas and Rafael Rodríguez (Río Piedras, P.R.: Ediciones Huracán, 1980), 14–16, and Tato Laviera dedicates "Penetration" to "Sandra Esteves/Julia de Burgos" in *Enclave* (Houston: Arte Público, 1981), 51.

10. Gerald Meyer, *Vito Marcantonio: Radical Politician, 1902–1954* (Albany: State University of New York Press, 1989), 151.

11. For the political beliefs of the Young Lords Party, see their thirteen-point platform and essays contained in their *Palante: Young Lords Party* (New York: McGraw-Hill, 1971), 150.

12. For a history of the Young Lords Party, see the introduction in ibid., 8–13.

13. Ibid., 14.

14. See: "*La Carreta Made a U-Turn:* Puerto Rican Language and Culture in the United States" (with John Attinasi and Pedro Pedraza), in *Divided Borders,* 157–81. Also published in *Daedalus* 110 (1981): 193–217.

15. *Palante,* 16–22.

16. I have chosen to cite Pietri's poem as it originally appeared in *Palante.* Subsequently Pietri published the same poem but divided it into different stanzas in his *Puerto Rican Obituary* (New York: Monthly Review Press, 1973), 1–11. See *Palante,* 16. The variations in Spanish punctuation in this and other poems cited in this chapter are due to the reproduction in the texts themselves.

17. Ibid., 16.

18. Ibid., 17.

19. Ibid., 19.

20. Ibid., 20.

21. Ibid.

22. Ibid., 21.

23. Ibid.

24. Ibid., 22.

25. See "felipe luciano i miss you in africa," *La Carreta Made a U-Turn* (1979; rpt. Houston: Arte Público, 1992), 55–56.

26. See the videorecording *Right On! Poetry on Film. The Original Last Poets,* Ho-Ho-Kus, N.J.: Essenay Entertainment, 1993; and the recording *Right On! The Original Last Poets,* New York: Juggernaut, 1969.

27. See Flores, "Qué assimilated, brother, yo soy asimilao," 182–84; and Roberto Márquez, "One Boricua's Baldwin: A Personal Remembrance," *American Quarterly* 42, no. 3 (1990): 456–76.

28. César Miguel Rondón, "La salsa mensaje; o cómo fue inventado Pedro Navaja," *El Nacional* (Caracas), May 13, 1979, E-4. Also cited in Rondón's *El víncu-lo es la Salsa* (Caracas: Editorial Arte, 1980), 66. My translation.

29. "Eddie Palmieri Recorded Live at Sing Sing with Harlem River Drive," 1972, Tico, CLP 1317, side B.

30. *Memoirs of Bernardo Vega: A Contribution to the History of the Puerto Rican Community in New York*, ed. César Andreu Iglesias, trans. Juan Flores (New York: Monthly Review Press, 1984), 226–27.

31. "A Lower East Side Poem," in *Puerto Rican Writers at Home in the USA*, ed. Faythe Turner (Seattle: Open Hand Publishing, 1991), 131–32.

32. See "The Scattering of the Ashes: The Burial of a Poet," in Algarín and Holman, *Aloud*, 3–8.

33. "This Is Not the Place Where I Was Born," in Turner, *Puerto Rican Writers*, 20.

34. Ibid.

35. Ibid., 21.

36. Ibid.

37. Ibid.

38. Ibid., 21–22.

39. "A Lower East Side Poem," in Turner, *Puerto Rican Writers*, 131.

40. "The Book of Genesis According to Saint Miguelito," in *Nuyorican Poetry: An Anthology of Puerto Rican Words and Feelings*, ed. Miguel Algarín and Miguel Piñero (New York: Morrow, 1975), 62.

41. Ibid., 62.

42. Ibid.

43. Ibid.

44. Ibid., 63.

45. Flores, "*La Carreta Made a U-Turn:* Puerto Rican Language and Culture in the United States," 171.

46. See William Luis, "From New York to the World: An Interview with Tato Laviera," *Callaloo* 15, no. 4 (1992): 1022–33.

47. "Even Then He Knew," *La Carreta Made a U-Turn*, 14.

48. "Jesús Papote," in *Enclave*, 13

49. Ibid., 14.

50. Ibid., 17.

51. Ibid., 19.

52. Luis, "From New York to the World," 1026.

53. "Jesús Papote," 20.

54. "A Mongo Affair," in Algarín and Piñero, *Nuyorican Poetry*, 52.

55. Ibid., 52–53.

56. Ibid., 53.

57. Ibid.

58. Ibid., 55.

59. See *El país de cuatro pisos y otros ensayos* (Río Piedras, P.R.: Huracán,

1980). For an analysis of this essay, see Flores, "The Puerto Rico José Luis González Built," in *Divided Borders*, 61–70.

60. "A Mongo Affair," 56.

61. *Palante*, 47.

62. Ibid., 48.

63. Ibid., 50.

64. "Welcome to San Juan, Oldest City in the U.S.," in Algarín and Piñero, *Nuyorican Poetry*, 109–10.

65. These poems are present in *Yerba Buena*, and are reproduced in Turner, *Puerto Rican Writers*, 181–84.

66. "Trampling," in Turner, *Puerto Rican Writers*, 203.

67. "For Tito," in Algarín and Piñero, *Nuyorican Poetry*, 133.

68. "Trampling," in Turner, *Puerto Rican Writers*, 203.

69. "For Tito," in Algarín and Piñero, *Nuyorican Poetry*, 133.

70. Ibid.

71. "Spring Fever," in Turner, *Puerto Rican Writers*, 292.

72. "My Name is Maria Christina," in Barradas and Rodríguez, *Herejes y mitificadores*, 112.

73. Ibid.

74. Ibid..

75. Ibid., 112, 114.

76. Ibid., 114.

77. Ibid.

78. "Jesús Papote," *Enclave*, 14.

79. "My Name Is Maria Christina," in Barradas and Rodríguez, *Herejes y mitificadores*, 114.

80. "La ansiedad de la influencia en Sandra María Esteves y Marjorie Agosín," in *Woman of Her Word: Hispanic Women Write*, ed. Evangelina Vigil (1983; repr. Houston: Arte Público, 1987), 139–47.

81. "In Response," in *Y otras desgracias/And Other Misfortunes* (Bloomington, Ind.: Third Woman Press, 1985), 1.

82. Ibid.

83. Ibid..

84. See *The Locaton of Culture* (London: Routledge, 1994).

85. "So Your Name Isn't María Cristina," *Bluestown Mockingbird Mambo* (Houston: Arte Público, 1990), 32.

86. Ibid.

87. Ibid.

88. "Black Notes and 'You Do Something to Me,'" *Bluestown Mockingbird Mambo*, 75–76.

89. Ibid., 75.

90. "Mambo Love Poem," *Bluestown Mockingbird Mambo*, 24.

91. "The Feminist Viewpoint in the Poetry of Puerto Rican Women in the United States," in *Images and Identity: The Puerto Rican in Two World Contexts*, ed. Asela Rodríguez de Laguna (New Brunswick, N.J.: Transaction, 1987), 175.

92. Luz María Umpierre, "Rubbish," in *En el país de las maravillas* (Bloomington, Ind.: Third Woman, 1982), 16. Also in Barradas and Rodríguez, *Herejes y mitificadores*, 108.

93. "My Revolution," in Turner, *Puerto Rican Writers*, 293.

94. Ibid.

95. "Ending Poem," in Turner, *Puerto Rican Writers*, 9.

96. Ibid.

97. Ibid., 9–10.

98. "Sunday Morning in Old San Juan," in Turner, *Puerto Rican Writers*, 315.

99. Cabanillas, "Lo que la música le hace al cuerpo," 82–83. My translation.

100. "Going Uptown to See Miriam," in Turner, *Puerto Rican Writers*, 86.

101. Ibid., 85.

102. Ibid., 86.

103. Ibid.

104. Cabanillas, "Lo que la música le hace al cuerpo," 88–89. Cabanillas's translation.

105. "Three Days/out of Franklin," in Turner, *Puerto Rican Writers*, 89.

106. Ibid., 91.

107. "The Physics of Ochun," in Turner, *Puerto Rican Writers*, 116.

108. Ibid., 118.

109. Ibid., 116.

110. Ibid., 118.

111. See, for example, my "Caribbean Cycles: Displacement and Change," *New England Review and Bread Loaf Quarterly* 7, no. 4 (1985): 412–13.

112. "The Idea of Islands," in Turner, *Puerto Rican Writers*, 22–23.

113. Ibid., 23.

114. See *Paradise on Earth: Some Thoughts on European Images of Non-European Man*, trans. Elizabeth Wentholt (New Haven: Yale University Press, 1965).

115. "They Never Grew Old," in Turner, *Puerto Rican Writers*, 276.

116. Ibid., 227.

117. Ibid.

Chapter 3

1. For statistics on the pulmonary tuberculosis mortality among Puerto Ricans in New York City and their comparison with other countries, see: Lawrence R. Chenault, *The Puerto Rican Migrant in New York City* (New York: Columbia University Press, 1938), 114–18.

2. Ibid., 120.

3. See *Cuban Counterpoint: Tobacco and Sugar*, trans. Harriet de Onís (New York: Knopf, 1947).

4. *Recuerdos de provincia*, 1850; reprinted in *Obras* XLIX (Buenos Aires: Imprenta y Litografía Mariano Moreno, 1896).

5. For a study of Sarmiento's work as autobiography, see Sylvia Molloy, *At Face Value: Autobiographical Writing in Spanish America* (Cambridge: Cambridge University Press, 1991), 32–35.

6. Paul de Man, "Literary History and Literary Modernity," in *Blindness and Insight: Essays in the Rhetoric of Contemporary Criticism* (New York: Oxford University Press, 1971).

7. *Beginnings: Intention and Method* (New York: Basic Books, 1975), 3–6.

8. Eugene Vance, "Roland and the Poetics of Memory," in *Textual Strategies: Perspectives in Post-Structuralist Criticism*, ed. Josué Harari (Ithaca, N.Y.: Cornell University Press, 1979).

9. Vega reveals that he is conscious of comparing two historical periods: "In those days our newspapers were not as big as they are today—none were over twelve pages" (4). "They reflected the life of the whole society—or rather, of its ruling class—with uneven success, but in any case they were more truthful than they are today, for sure" (4–5). *Memoirs of Bernardo Vega: A Contribution to the History of the Puerto Rican Community in New York*, ed. César Andreu Iglesias, trans. Juan Flores (New York: Monthly Review Press, 1984). Unless otherwise indicated, all quotations are from this edition and the page numbers will appear parenthetically in the text.

10. *Advantages of Plant Location in Puerto Rico* (1967), cited in Manuel Maldonado-Denis, *Puerto Rico: A Socio-Historic Interpretation*, trans. ElenaVialo (New York: Vintage, 1972), 163.

11. See *The Oxcart* (New York: Scribners, 1969).

12. The Planning Board referred to the Puerto Rican agricultural problem in the following manner: "The goal of obtaining a source of jobs and income in the agricultural sector through the replacement of imports becomes rather difficult due to the fact that the free market [*sic*] between the United States and Puerto Rico provides that agricultural goods produced by a high technology in the United States compete with local products. And due, furthermore, to that fact that in Puerto Rico the limitation of lands available and adequate for the mechanization of production makes impossible—even with public economic assistance—the adoption of an agricultural technology similar to that of the United States." Junta de Planificación, *Informe económico al Gobernador, 1967* (San Juan: Junta de Planificación, 1968), 111, cited in Maldonado-Denis, *Puerto Rico: A Socio-Historic Interpretation,*, 159.

13. The Law of 1919 allowed the Commissioner of Agriculture to regulate emigration, giving him the following powers: "inquirir, inspeccionar, intervenir y regular las proposiciones, promesas, condiciones u ofertas hechas a los trabajadores nativos en casos de emigración; y gestionar, suscribir y hacer cumplir los contratos que se formalicen, ya sea por personas naturales o jurídicas residentes en o fuera de Puerto Rico, ya en cualquier estado de la Unión Americana o estados extrajeros, velando porque la estabilidad o repatriación de los trabajadores que se hallen fuera de la isla quede garantizada." Cited in Maldonado-Denis, *Puerto Rico y Estados Unidos: Emigración y colonialismo* (Mexico City: Siglo Veintiuno, 1976), 76. Maldonado-Denis adds: "El gobierno de Puerto Rico explícitamente declara que la protección de dicha ley no se extenderá a quienes emigren sin contrato, y dispone penalidades por el delito menos grave de violar dicha ley" (76).

14. Ibid., 52.

15. Ibid.

16. For a discussion of Sarmiento's concept of "civilization and barbarism," see his *Life in the Argentine Republic in the Days of the Tyrants*, trans. Horace Mann (New York, 1868).

17. Maldonado-Denis, *Puerto Rico y Estados Unidos*, 72.

18. Vega, *Memoirs*, 101.

19. *La Voz de Puerto Rico* lasted only one month. The first issue was published June 20, 1874.

20. Under Ramón La Villa, the first issue of *Gráfico* was subtitled S*emanario Defensor de La Raza Hispana*. However, the others were subtitled *Semanario Defensor de La Raza* on the front page, but they retained *Hispano* on the inside subtitle.

21. Salvatore John LaGumina, *Vito Marcantonio: The People's Politician* (Dubuque, Iowa: Kendall/Hunt, 1969), iv.

22. See Gerald Meyer, *Vito Marcantonio: Radical Politician, 1902–1954* (Albany, N.Y.: State University of New York Press, 1989), 144–172.

23. Charles Woodbury, "Our Worst Slum: Can We Save It from Going Red?" *American Magazine*, September 1949, 30, 32; "Marc Meets a Fighter," *Daily Mirror*, September 16, 1948, 27; "Congress Probes Marc's Vote List," *New York Daily Mirror*, November 1, 1948, 1; quoted in Meyer, *Vito Marcantonio*, 164–65.

24. LaGumina, *Vito Marcantonio*, 47–48.

25. Ibid., 137–138.

26. For an informative discussion of the kind of help Marcantonio gave Campos, see Meyer, *Vito Marcantonio*, 151 and 162.

27. Federico Ribes Tovar, *Albizu Campos: El revolucionario* (New York: Plus Ultra Educational, 1971), 93–95.

28. LaGumina, *Vito Marcantonio*, 137.

29. The socialist discourse takes precedence over the one associated with tobacco workers. When Vega arrived in New York, it was the members of the Socialist Club and not the members of the Tobacco Workers Union, Local 90, who helped him and provided assistance in obtaining employment. This was so even though Vega was a tobacco worker and carried a letter of introduction from his local in Cayey, Puerto Rico.

30. For information on Manzano's autobiography, see my *Literary Bondage: Slavery in Cuban Narrative* (Austin: University of Texas Press, 1990), 82–100.

31. See, for example, my study of Barnet in *Literary Bondage*, 199–218.

32. Juan Flores translates the same chapter as "From my hometown Cayey to San Juan, and how I arrived in New York without a watch" and in so doing eliminates the presence of the editor and underscores the testimonial character of the work. *Memoirs of Bernardo Vega*, 3.

33. Maldonado-Denis, *Puerto Rico y Estados Unidos*. See statistics on 177–78.

34. Ibid., 185.

35. Ibid., 190.

36. Ibid., 181.

37. For a study of reverse migration, see "Los que retornan," in ibid., 155–73, and José Hernández Álvarez, *Return Migration to Puerto Rico* (Berkeley: University of California, Institue of International Studies, 1967).

38. Juan Flores addresses the issue of the coming together of the Puerto Rican and African American communities. See his "'Qué assimilated, brother, yo soy asimilao': The Structuring of Puerto Rican Identity in the U.S.," *in Divided Borders: Essays on Puerto Rican Identity* (Houston: Arte Público, 1993), 182–95.

39. Ibid., 124.

40. See, for example, Houston Baker, *Blues, Ideology, and Afro-American Literature* (Chicago: University of Chicago Press, 1984), and Henry Louis Gates,

ed., *Black Literature and Literary Theory* (New York: Methuen, 1984). Also see Richard Jackson, *The Black Image in Latin American Literature* (Albuquerque: University of New Mexico Press, 1976), and *Black Writers in Latin America* (Albuquerque: University of New Mexico Press, 1979), as well as my *Literary Bondage* and *Voices from Under: Black Narrative in Latin America and the Caribbean* (Westport, Conn.: Greenwood Press, 1984).

41. See Arturo Alfonso Schomburg, *The Legacy of Arthur Alfonso Schomburg: A Celebration of the Past, A Vision for the Future* (New York: Schomburg Center for Research on Black Culture, 1986), and Flor Pineiro de Rivera, *Arturo Schomburg: un puertorriqueño descubre el legado histórico del negro* (San Juan: Centro de Estudios Avanzados de Puerto Rico y el Caribe, 1989). Because English versions of names sometimes differ markedly from the Spanish, I have chosen to retain the Spanish for Schomburg's name and for other writers included in this study.

42. "Jesús Colón" is normally written in Spanish with accents, and I have decided to preserve this spelling, which is different from the way it appears in *A Puerto Rican in New York and Other Sketches* (1961; reprint, New York: International Publishers, 1982).

43. The chronology in the book must be questioned. The essays previously published appear to be out of any chronological ordering. The sketch on "Maceo," *Daily Worker*, May 1, 1956, begins on 60; "Pisagua," *Daily Worker*, March 26, 1956, on 66; "Rivera Back In Mexico," *Daily Worker*, May 8, 1956, on 69; and "Trujillo's Fair Fear of Blood," *Daily Worker*, February 6, 1956, on 73.

44. Colón, *A Puerto Rican in New York*, 105.

45. Ibid., x–xi.

46. Ibid., 183.

47. In his "Puerto Rican Literature in the United States: Stages and Perspectives," Juan Flores offers a periodization of this literature. He places Jesús Colón's work in the second stage, from 1945–1965, and Piri Thomas's novel in the third one. See his essay in Ramón Gutiérrez and Genaro Padilla, eds., *Recovering the U.S. Hispanic Literary Heritage* (Houston: Arte Público, 1993), 53–68.

48. Census, *State of Birth of the Native Population*, 1930, table 23, 37. Cited by Chenault in *The Puerto Rican Migrant*, 60.

49. Chenault, *The Puerto Rican Migrant*, 79.

50. Meyer, *Vito Marcantonio*, 146.

51. Chenault, *The Puerto Rican Migrant*, 62–63, 89–97.

52. Ibid., 107–8.

53. For an account of Plinian races, see John Block Friedman, *The Monstrous Races in Medieval Art and Thought* (Cambridge: Harvard University Press, 1981).

54. In his "Qué assimilated, brother, yo soy asimilao," Juan Flores divides the question of identity into four parts. While some of his ideas coincide with mine, our essays clearly move in two separate directions.

55. The statistics for Puerto Rican migration show that there is a negative net migration back to the island in 1961 (-230), 1968 (-14,249), but in particular in 1972 (-34,015) and 1973 (-20,948). See Maldonado-Denis, *Puerto Rico y Estados Unidos*, 181.

56. In his works, Thomas provides a glossary that explains the Spanish and slang terms used in the books. The idea of the glossary to explain terms of a cul-

ture to a reader of a different one was also employed by authors writing about the experiences of Afro-Caribbean people. See, for example, Alejo Carpentier's *¡Écue Yamba-Ó!* (Madrid: Editorial España, 1933) and Lydia Cabrera's *El monte* (Havana: Ediciones CR, 1954).

57. *Down These Mean Streets* (1967; reprint, New York: Vintage Books, 1991), 162. Unless otherwise indicated, all quotations are from this edition and page numbers will appear parenthetically in the text.

58. Colón, "Greetings from Washington," 119–25.

59. In *Slums and Crime* (New York: Polygraphic Company of America, 1934), Halpern et al. use court statistics of arrests and convictions to show the high crime and delinquency rates among Puerto Ricans. However, in his study, Chenault points to the limitations of that type of research. See Chenault, *The Puerto Rican Migrant*, 131–41.

60. *Seven Long Times* (New York: Praeger, 1994), 220.

61. *New York Journal-American*, February 28, 1950, 3.

62. *New York Journal-American*, February 25, 1950, 1, 2. Also cited in Thomas, *Seven Long Times*, insert.

63. Wall Street special edition, *New York Journal-American*, 2.

64. Night Edition, *New York Journal-American*, 2.

65. *New York Journal-American*, February 26, 1950, L13, and February 27, 1950, 3.

66. *The New York Times*, February 26, 1950, L1.

67. Ibid., 55.

68. "A Neorican in Puerto Rico: Or Coming Home," in *Images and Identity: The Puerto Rican in Two World Contexts*, ed. Asela Rodríguez de Laguna (New Brunswick, N.J.: Transaction, 1987), 153.

69. *Seven Long Times*, 174–82.

70. The certificates are mentioned in *Seven Long Times*.

71. Thomas describes the prison scene in the following manner: "The sound of the west wall cons got more angry as they tore down the hacks' wooden stands and splintered them into clubs. It hit me inside. *Never punk out* was the code I had lived by; fear came second, rep came first. Hell, when something went down, I had been there; and if I had to hurt, I had hurt, too. So what was keeping me back? Was I afraid? Hell, no. Did I want to see the board and go home? Hell, yes! but was I a punk to want this? I didn't know" (282).

72. *Down These Mean Streets*, 321.

73. See Appendix 2, *Seven Long Times*.

Chapter 4

1. For a history of these early Cuban American groups, see the Areíto group's *Contra viento y marea* (Havana: Casa de las Américas, 1978), 10–14.

2. See, for example, *Areíto* 7, no. 26 (1981), an issue dedicated to Lourdes Casal.

3. At the end of its first year the editors of *Areíto* published a summary of their purpose, which included excerpts of their first editorials, and I reproduce it in its entirety:

A propósito de ese número con el cual Areíto cumple su primer año, nosotros, el Consejo de Dirección y los Equipos de Trabajo de la revista, quisiéramos detenernos brevemente sobre lo que hemos logrado y los obstáculos con que nos hemos tropezado en este último año, así como la razón de ser el futuro de Areíto.

La coordinación y planificación del trabajo, tanto intelectual como manual y técnico, envuelto en la publicación de una revista son, ciertamente, tareas de marca mayor. El que en torno a Areíto se haya reunido un grupo de cubanos, mayormente jóvenes, cuyo compromiso y disciplina hayan garantizado el trabajo que requiere la empresa constituye, sin lugar a duda, nuestro mayor logro.

Las condiciones en que este trabajo se ha llevado a cabo, sin embargo, no han sido siempre favorables. Primeramente, Areíto ha sido una carga económica para nosotros y nuestros colaboradores. La revista, no obstante, comienza a levantar cabeza, ya que las suscripciones y la venta van aumentando. Nuestra dispersión geográfica nos ha impedido establecer el proceso técnico de la composición, el emplanaje y la impresión en una misma ciudad y así todo, cada número que sale refleja una mejoría marcada.

Pero aún cuando todos los primeros pasos son igualmente dificultosos en cualquier circunstancia, éstos son los definitivos que ayudan a estabilizar y son ese despegue inicial necesario para desarrollar una base más firme y estable. Cabe, entonces, abordar una vez más la pregunta: por qué Areíto?

Areíto nace de un grupo de cubanos jóvenes cuyo proceso de maduración en los Estados Unidos los lleva a una revaluación de la sociedad norteamericana, de la Revolución Cubana y de aquello que conocían como 'lo cubano' en materia de valores, tradiciones e historia. Areíto fue concebida como medio de sondear su posible arraigo en algunos sectores de nuestra comunidad.

El entusiasmo y hasta la alegría con que nos escriben nuestros lectores, el aumento en la venta de la revista y la dedicación del grupo creciente que la publica prueban que las inquietudes y las ideas expresadas en Areíto no representan un fenómeno individual y aislado, sino que por lo contrario, constituyen un hecho sociológico y un proceso psicológico por el cual muchos cubanos jóvenes en este país han atravesado y por el cual otros tantos han de pasar.

Planteamos la necesidad de alcanzar una comprensión más profunda y un conocimiento más extenso de Cuba y el proceso revolucionario como un primer paso en considerar la problemática de la minoría cubana en los Estados Unidos: sus orígenes, su desarrollo y su relación con respecto a los otros grupos minoritarios y la sociedad norteamericana en general. No creemos que el asumir una posición de simpatía hacia la Revolución implique como consecuencia inevitable el traslado permanente a la isla.

Cuba es simplemente un punto de partida en el análisis que pretendemos hacer sobre nuestra situación en los Estados Unidos. La experiencia de aquellos chicanos y puertorriqueños (las otras dos grandes minorías hispano-parlantes en este país) que tienen una visión digna de su posición en esta sociedad nos enseña que, para cuadrar un análisis acertado sobre la dinámica socio-política norteamericana, es imprescindible lograr una comprensión de nuestras raíces históricas y culturales.

Como expresábamos en nuestro primer editorial (*Areíto*, año I, n. 1), nuestra cultura y nuestra historia conllevan actualmente una dimensión que está determinada por la Revolución Cubana. Por lo tanto, si no intentamos una comprensión más amplia del proceso cubano, tendríamos que renunciar a nuestra cubanidad o estancarnos en una concepción subjetiva de la misma.

Nuestra posición editorial—la de reflexionar seriamente sobre la Revolución Cubana y de así rescatar y orientar nuestra identidad nacional en su contexto actual en los Estados Unidos—no encuentra, es obvio, apoyo masivo en nuestra comunidad. En ningún momento hemos pretendido ser el vocero de la mayoría de la juventud cubana en este país ni portavoces de la máxima y única verdad.

Sin embargo, como expresábamos en nuestro segundo editorial (Coexistencialismo reprimido? *Areíto*, año I, n. 2), Areíto, por su iniciativa en comenzar a contrarrestar la visión tergiversada y distorsionada de la Revolución Cubana y de nuestra historia perpetuada por los medios masivos (del exilio), constituye la legitimación del pluralismo ideológico (en el exilio). Como tal, reiteramos que, lejos de ser "un grupito de diez o quince" representamos una corriente que se acrecienta en nuestras comunidades, particularmente en su sector más joven que, en general, no está traumatizado por el pasado.

En este próximo año, por lo tanto, nos proponemos adentrar más sobre el análisis de la minoría cubana en Estados Unidos y su futuro. El futuro de Areíto, después de todo, está estrechamente ligado a éste y en la posibilidad de comenzar a pensar en direcciones previamente veladas. ("Editorial: un recuento de nuestro primer año," *Areíto* 1, no. 4 [1975]: 52.)

4. Ibid.

5. See *Contra viento y marea,* and in particular the questionnaire that appears on 259–62.

6. *Areíto* 5, no. 17 (1978): 30. My translation. Also see Françoise Pérus, "Un testimonio excepcional," *Revista Plural,* no. 85, reprinted in *Areíto* 5, nos. 10–20 (1979): 67–68.

7. "Editorial," *Areíto* 4, nos. 3–4 (1978): 2.

8. For the brigade's itinerary, see ibid., 13–22. The issue was dedicated to the Antonio Maceo Brigade. It includes the brigade's intinerary, participants' impressions, and clippings from U.S. newspapers regarding the trip.

9. *Areíto* 5, no. 17 (1978): 30. My translation.

10. This was the case with Carlos Muñiz, a member of the Brigada Antonio Maceo and president of Viajes Varadero, who was assassinated in San Juan on April 28, 1979. See, for example, "El diálogo y la desesperación de los terroristas," *Areíto* 5, nos. 10–20 (1979): 9–11.

11. *Areíto* 5, no. 17 (1978): 5–8.

12. For details of these and other events, see Lourdes Casal, ed., *El caso Padilla: Literatura y revolución en Cuba* (Miami: Editorial Universal, 1971).

13. In 1980, Carlos Olivares Baró, author of the two reviews published in *Areíto*, joined the ranks of the Marielitos and left Cuba for Mexico, where he now resides.

14. *Handbook of Latin American Studies 44*, ed. Dolores Moyano Martin (Austin: University of Texas Press, 1982), 444.

15. Rubén G. Rumbaut, "The Agony of Exile: A Study of the Migration and Adaptation of Indochinese Refugee Adults and Children," in *Refugee Children: Theory, Research, and Services*, ed. Frederick L. Ahearn, Jr., and Jean L. Athey (Baltimore: Johns Hopkins University Press, 1991), 61. Also cited by Gustavo Pérez Firmat in *Life on the Hyphen: The Cuban-American Way* (Austin: University of Texas Press, 1994), 4.

16. See Pérez Firmat, *The Cuban Condition: Translation and Identity in Modern Cuban Literature* (Cambridge: Cambridge University Press, 1989).

17. Ibid., 153.

18. Ibid., 160.

19. *Next Year in Cuba: A Cuban Emigre's Coming of Age in America* (New York: Anchor Books, 1995).

20. Pérez Firmat, *Life on the Hyphen*, 19.

21. Carolina Hospital, ed., *Cuban American Writers: Los Atrevidos* (Princeton, N.J.: Ediciones Ella/Linden Lane Press, 1988), 16.

22. Ibid., 18.

23. See, for example, Miguel de Cervantes, *Don Quijote de La Mancha*.

24. "The Beauty of Treason," in Hospital, *Cuban American Writers*, 36. Unless otherwise indicated all the poems cited are from this edition.

25. Ibid.

26. "Terraces," 51.

27. Ibid.

28. Ibid., 51–52.

29. "Exile," 41.

30. Ibid.

31. "The Exile," 66.

32. "Returning," 140.

33. Ibid.

34. "Bilingual Blues,"   .

35. Ibid.

36. Ibid.

37. "My Graduation Speech," in *Aloud: Voices from the Nuyorican Poets Cafe*, ed. Miguel Algarín and Bob Holman (New York: Holt, 1994), 332.

38. Ibid., 333.

39. "Thanksgiving," 132.

40. "Elizabeth, New Jersey," 131.

41. Ibid.

42. "Dear Tía," 169.

43. "Arrival," 56.

44. See Roland Barthes, *The Pleasure of the Text,* trans. Richard Miller (New York: Farrar, Straus & Giroux, 1975).

45. "Arrival," 56.

46. Ibid.

47. "Your Picture, 57.

48. "Ibid.

49. "Now," 58.

50. Ibid.

51. "Elephant Ride," 93.

52. Ibid.

53. Ibid.

54. Ibid.

55. For an analysis of Kozer's work, see Pérez Firmat, *Life on the Hyphen.*

56. See Rozencvaig's introduction in *Poetas cubanas en Nueva York,* ed. Felipe Lázaro (Madrid: Editorial Betania, 1991), 13–18. Unless otherwise indicated, all the poems cited are from this edition.

57. Untitled, 27.

58. Ibid., 31.

59. Ibid., 31, 33.

60. See "Homage to the Virgins," 85.

61. "VIII," 47.

62. "XIV," 59.

63. Ibid.

64. Ibid.

65. Ibid.

66. Ibid.

Chapter 5

1. See *La música en Cuba* Mexico City: Fondo de Cultura Económico, 1946).

2. See Helmy F. Giacoman, "La relación músico-literaria entre la tercera sinfonía 'Eróica,' de Beethoven, y la novela *El acoso* de Alejo Carpentier," *Cuadernos Americanos,* no. 158 (1968): 113–29. Also see his "La estructura musical en la novelística de Alejo Carpentier," *Hispanófila* 33 (1968): 49–57.

3. See Antonio Benítez Rojo, "'El camino de Santiago' de Alejo Carpentier y el *Canon perpetuus* de Juan Sebastian Bach: Paralelismo estructural," *Revista Iberoamericana* 123–24 (1983): 293–322; "'Semejante a la noche' de Alejo Carpentier y el *Canon per tonos* de Juan Sebastian Bach: Su paralelismo estructural," *Eco* 43, no. 6 (1983): 645–62; and "'Viaje a la Semilla,' o el texto como expectáculo," *Discurso Literario* 3, no. 1 (1985): 53–74.

4. *Solo cenizas hallarás (bolero)* (Valencia, Spain: Editorial Prometeo, 1980).

5. *Bolero* (Buenos Aires: Puntosur, 1991).

6. *Macho Camacho's Beat,* trans. Gregory Rabassa (New York: Pantheon, 1980).

7. *La importancia de llamarse Daniel Santos* (Hanover, N.H.: Ediciones del Norte, 1988).

8. See Ilán Stavans, "Habla Oscar Hijuelos," *Linden Lane Magazine* (1989): 14–15. Also reprinted in *La gaceta de Cuba* (Sept.–Oct. 1993): 26.

9. *The Latin Tinge: The Impact of Latin American Music on the United States* (New York: Oxford University Press, 1979), 130.

10. Ibid., 131.

11. Stavans, "Habla Oscar Hijuelos," 14.

12. See my "Historia, naturaleza y memoria en 'Viaje a la semilla,'" *Revista Iberoamericana* 145 (1991): 151–60.

13. *The Cuban Condition: Translation and Identity in Modern Cuban Literature* (Cambridge: Cambridge University Press, 1989), and *Life on the Hyphen: The Cuban-American Way* (Austin: University of Texas Press, 1994).

14. See the ending of *Three Trapped Tigers*, trans. Donald Gardner, Suzanne Jill Levine, and Cabrera Infante (New York: Harper and Row, 1978).

15. *Infante's Inferno*, trans. Suzanne Jill Levine and Cabrera Infante (New York: Harper and Row, 1984).

16. Hijuelos, *The Mambo Kings Play Songs of Love* (New York: Farrar, Straus & Giroux, 1989), 394. Unless otherwise indicated, all quotations are from this edition and the page numbers will appear parenthetically in the text.

17. See Pérez Firmat, *Life on the Hyphen*, 23–76.

18. Bart Andrews, *The "I Love Lucy" Book* (New York: Doubleday, 1985), 248.

19. See Pérez Firmat, *Life on the Hyphen*.

20. *The Mambo Kings Play Songs of Love*. The Spanish and English versions appear on 396 and 405–6, respectively.

21. "Beautiful María of My Soul" (Secaucus, N.J.: Warner Bros., 1992).

22. Ibid., 43.

23. *Paradise on Earth: Some Thoughts on European Images of Non-European Man*, trans. Elizabeth Wentholt (New Haven: Yale University Press, 1965).

24. Stavans, "Habla Oscar Hijuelos," 14. My translation.

25. Pérez Firmat, *Life on the Hyphen*, 149.

26. Salsa has also reached Japan and is represented by the internationally famed Orquesta de la Luz, which in 1991 recorded the album *Salsa no tiene fronteras*, produced by Kiyoshi Teranishi and Sergio George.

27. See Roberts, *The Latin Tinge*, 187–91.

28. See José Arteaga, *La salsa* (Bogota: Intermedio Editores, 1990), 47–51.

29. Ibid., 31–32.

30. Andrews, *The "I Love Lucy" Book*, 217.

31. This latter position is best represented by the magazine and group Areíto, in particular during the time when Lourdes Casal was its most prominent leader. See, for example, *Areíto* 7, no. 25 (1981).

32. "A Fish Swims in My Lung: An Interview with Cristina García," in *Face to Face: Interviews with Contemporary Novelists*, ed. Allan Vorda (Houston: Rice University Press, 1993), 71.

33. See Rumbaut, "The Agony of Exile: A Study of the Migration and Adaptation of Indochinese Refugee Adults and Children," in *Refugee Children: Theory, Research, and Services*, ed. Frederick L. Ahearn, Jr., and Jean L. Athey (Baltimore: Johns Hopkins University Press, 1991); and Pérez Firmat, *Life on the Hyphen*.

34. For this point of view, see Young Lords Party and Michael Abrams, *Palante: Young Lords Party* (New York: McGraw-Hill, 1972).

35. *Dreaming in Cuban* (New York: Ballantine Books, 1992), 108. Unless otherwise indicated, all quotations are from this edition and the page numbers will appear parenthetically in the text.

36. See, for example, *Emma Lazarus: Selections from Her Poetry and Prose*, ed. Morris U. Schappes (New York: Emma Lazarus Federation of Jewish Women's Clubs, 1967).

37. *Viaje a la semilla* (Havana: Ucar, García y Cía, 1944).

38. Hugh Thomas, *The Cuban Revolution* (New York: Harper and Row, 1977), 659.

39. For a detailed account of the Padilla affair, see Lourdes Casal, ed., *El caso Padilla: Literatura y revolución en Cuba* (Miami: Ediciones Universal, 1971).

40. For the government's disclaimer, see Document no. 9, in Casal, *El caso Padilla*, 57–63.

41. See Document no. 12 in ibid., 74–75.

42. See Document no. 14 in ibid., 77–104.

43. It should be noted that Gabriel García Márquez and Julio Cortázar did not sign the second letter. For a text of this letter, see Document no. 17 in ibid., 123–24.

44. See Castro speech closing the First National Congress of Education and Culture, *Casa de las Américas* 9, nos. 65–66 (1971): 21–33. Also in Document no. 16 in Casal, *El caso Padilla*, 115–27.

45. See *Calibán* Mexico City: Editorial Diógenes, 1972).

46. For an account of the Marielitos and other Cubans in Miami see, for example, Alejandro Portes and Alex Stepick, *City on the Edge: The Transformation of Miami* (Los Angeles: University of California Press, 1993).

47. For an account of Villaverde's life and his *Cecilia Valdés*, see my *Literary Bondage: Slavery in Cuban Narrative*, (Austin: University of Texas Press, 1990).

48. The dated chapters appear in the following manner: The first appears in "The Meaning of Shells" (1974) and contains "Luz Villaverde (1976)"; it includes a description of the father. The second is entitled "Enough Attitude" (1975) and includes "Pilar (1976)." "A Matrix Light" is dated 1977. In this section Lourdes narrates life in the United States. She suspects Pilar is sleeping around and describes the mother's anti-Castro activities. The novel concludes with "Six Days in April."

49. García writes: "Celia knew that Ofelia joined her mother at her dressing table, where they sat on their bony behinds and rubbed whitening cream into their dark, freckled faces. Berta Arango del Pino left the paste on overnight to remove any evidence of her mulatto blood." *Dreaming in Cuban*, 41.

50. This idea became clear to me during a trip I took to Cuba in December 1989. At a musical event I heard a song about William Tell, sung by Carlos Valera, one of the newer members of the Nueva Trova, that referred to the generational differences. In the song, William Tell asks the son to place an apple on his head so that the father may shoot an arrow through it. The son recognizes the danger and refuses. The father, who is much stronger than the son, forces him to stand still with the apple on his head. As time passes, the son gets older and stronger and then forces the father to stand against the tree with the apple on his head.

51. See Carlos Moore, *Castro, the Blacks, and Africa* (Los Angeles: University of California, Center for Afro-American Studies, 1988).

52. Vorda, "A Fish Swims in My Lung," 65.

53. See *Termina el desfile* (Barcelona: Seix Barral, 1981), 145–74.

54. These and other aspects of Arenas's life are contained in an autobiography written after he had been diagnosed with the AIDS virus and while on his deathbed. See *Before Night Falls*, trans. Dolores M. Koch (New York: Viking, 1993).

55. This idea is valid even though Ivanito is a Villaverde, as indicated in the note Lourdes gives her nephew (p. 239). However, Lourdes writes the note in English, which Ivanito cannot read, and she changes his name to conform to U.S. tradition and culture. According to Spanish customs, Ivanito would carry his mother's and father's surnames. In the novel, Ivanito was raised not by his father but by his mother, who had assumed her maiden name, and his grandmother; and he considered himself closer to them.

56. See *Blow-Up, and Other Stories*, trans. Paul Blackburn (New York: Collier, 1968).

Chapter 6

1. See Sherrie Grasmuch and Patricia Pessar, *Between Two Islands: Dominican International Migration* (Berkeley: University of California Press, 1991), 20, table 1. Also cited by Ramona Hernández and Silvio Torres-Saillant in "Dominicans in New York: Men, Women, and Prospects" (manuscript), 45, table 1.

2. The first Dominican Studies Institute began at the City College of New York in August 1992 and was officially recognized by the CUNY Board of Trustees in February 1994. The institute's first director is Silvio Torres-Saillant.

3. See chapter 2 for a discussion of Esteves and Umpierre's discussion over the definition of a Puerto Rican woman.

4. "Helen," in *Poemas del exilio y de otras inquietudes / Poems of Exile and Other Concerns*, ed. Daisy Cocco de Felippis and Emma Jane Robinett (New York: Ediciones Alcance, 1988), 25. Unless otherwise indicated, all of the poems cited in this chapter are from this anthology.

5. Ibid.

6. Ibid., 27.

7. Ibid., 28.

8. See my study of Pietri's "The Puerto Rican Obituary" in chapter 2.

9. "Nobody Knows My Name," in *Cuban American Writers: Los Atrevidos*, ed. Carolina Hospital (Princeton, N.J.: Ediciones Ellas/Linden Lane Press, 1988), 163.

10. "Martha at the Edge of Desire," 23.

11. Ibid.

12. "María and the Others," 22.

13. "Helen," 28.

14. "Emigrants of This Century," 71.

15. Ibid., 72.

16. *The Heights of Macchu Picchu*, trans. Nathaniel Tarn (New York: Noonday Press, 1974), 69–71.

17. "Emigrants of This Century," 73.

18. Neruda, 47.

19. Ibid., 57.

20. *Emigrants of This Century,* 73.

21. "Man and Socialism in Cuba," in *Venceremos! The Speeches and Writings of Che Guevara* (New York: Simon and Schuster, 1968), 387–400.

22. I have translated the first line, since the English is different from the Spanish original. The Spanish is "que retorne nuestros pasos." The verb *retornar* has been translated as "undo" instead of as "return."

23. "Emigrants of This Century," 73.

24. For a reading of "Returning," see chapter 5.

25. "From Here," 46.

26. "I Ask Myself," 43.

27. Ibid.

28. Ibid., 44.

29. *The Heights of Macchu Picchu,* 23.

30. "Unlicensed Doctor in New York," 54.

31. Ibid.

32. Ibid.

33. Ibid., 56.

34. Ibid.

35. Ibid., 57.

36. Ibid.

37. Ibid., 58.

38. See, for example, *The Buenos Aires Affair,* trans. Suzanne Jill Levine (New York: Dutton, 1976).

39. See my study of the "Puerto Rican Obituary" in chapter 2.

40. "Perspectives," 35.

41. Ibid.

42. Ibid., 36.

43. "Reports," 37.

44. See chapter 4.

45. "Haiti," 40.

46. See *The Kingdom of This World,* trans. Harriet de Onís (New York: Knopf, 1957).

47. "Haiti," 40.

48. "Homecoming," 61.

49. Ibid., 62.

50. Ibid.

51. Ibid.

Chapter 7

1. This was made evident most recently in Enrique Fernández, Juan González and Silvana Paternostro's "Latin Rainbow: New Arrivals Create a Changing City Scene," *New York Daily News,* March 6, 1994, 36–37. I would like to thank my student, David García, for making this article available to me.

2. See Daisy Cocco de Felippis and Emma Jane Robinett, *Poemas del exilio y de otras inquietudes/Poems of Exile and Other Concerns* (New York: Ediciones Alcance, 1988).

3. Jorge Luis Borges, "An Examination of the Work of Herbert Quain," *Ficciones*, trans. Anthony Kerrigan (New York: Grove, 1962), 75.

4. See Alejo Carpentier, "Viaje a la semilla," in *Guerra del tiempo* Mexico City: Compañía General de Ediciones, 1958); "Journey Back to the Source," in *War of Time*, trans. Frances Partridge (New York: Knopf, 1970).

5. See my "Historia, naturaleza y memoria en 'Viaje a la semilla,'" *Revista Iberoamericana* no. 154 (1991): 151–60.

6. *How the Garcia Girls Lost Their Accents* (Chapel Hill, N.C.: Algonquin Books, 1991), 153, 171. Unless otherwise indicated, all quotations are from this edition and the page numbers will appear parenthetically in the text.

7. See chapters 2 and 3.

8. See Frank Kermode, *The Sense of an Ending: Studies in the Theory of Fiction* (New York: Oxford University Press, 1975), in particular chaps. 2 and 3.

9. "An American Childhood in the Dominican Republic," *The American Scholar* 56 (1987): 85.

10. "Hold the Mayonnaise," *New York Times Magazine*, January 12, 1992, 14.

Chapter 8

1. See Homi Bhabha, *The Location of Culture* (New York: Routledge, 1994), 175.

2. Young Lords Party and Michael Abramson, *Palante: Young Lords Party* (New York: McGraw-Hill, 1971), 150.

3. See, for example, Bhabha, *The Location of Culture*.

4. *La raza cósmica / The Cosmic Race* (Los Angeles: California State University, 1979).

5. *X in La Raza* (Albuquerque, N.M.: by author, 1996), 86. This idea became evident to me when discussing Juan Velasco's paper "The X-Race: Color and Identity in the Theories of Xicanismo and Me(x)icanness," in our panel on Race and the Ibero-American Cultural Self, MLA Conference, December, 1996.

6. *Martín Ramírez: Pintor mexicano (1885–1960)* Mexico City: Centro Cultural/Arte Contemporáneo, 1989).

7. *The Hispanic Condition: Reflections on Culture and Identity in America* (New York: HarperCollins, 1995), 21.

8. Ibid., 27.

9. Ibid., 175.

10. *I, Rigoberta Menchú: An Indian Woman in Guatemala*, ed. Elisabeth (sic) Burgos-Debray, trans. Ann Wright (New York: Verso, 1984).

11. "Can the Subaltern Speak?" in *Marxism and the Interpretation of Culture*, ed. Cary Nelson and Lawrence Grossberg (Urbana, Ill.: University of Illinois Press, 1988), 271–313.

12. See *Me llamo Rigoberta Menchú: Así me nació la conciencia*, ed. Elizabeth Burgos (Barcelona: Argos Vergara, 1983).

13. "From Where to Speak? Post-Modern / Post-Colonial Positionalities," in *Borders and Margins: Post-Colonialism and Post-Modernism*, ed. Fernando de Toro and Alfonso de Toro (Frankfurt: Vervuert, 1995), 131–48.

14. Stavans, *The Hispanic Condition*, 179.

15. *Literary Bondage: Slavery in Cuban Narrative* (Austin: University of Texas Press, 1990).

16. Stavans, *The Hispanic Condition*, 180.

17. "The Postcolonial Aura: Third World Criticism in the Age of Global Capitalism," *Critical Inquiry* 20 (1994): 328–29.

18. I am using the term *metanarrative* as explained by Lyotard in *The Postmodern Condition: A Report on Knowledge*, trans. Geoff Bennington and Brian Massumi (Minneapolis, University of Minnesota Press, 1984).

19. Stavans, *The Hispanic Condition*, 168.

20. *La vida a plazos de don Jacobo Lerner* (Hanover, N.H.: Ediciones del Norte, 1980). Goldemberg's novel was first published in English translation.

21. "Borges, the Encounter, and the Other: Blacks and the Monstrous Races," in *Borders and Margins*, 61–78.

BIBLIOGRAPHY

I. Primary Sources:
Latino Caribbean Literature Written in the United States

Acosta, Iván. *El super.* Miami: Ediciones Universal, 1982.

Agüeros, Jack. *Dominoes and Other Stories from the Puerto Rican.* Willimantic, Conn.: Curbstone, 1993.

———. *Sonnets from the Puerto Rican.* Brooklyn, N.Y.: Hanging Loose, 1996.

———. *Song of the Simple Truth.* Willimantic, Conn.: Curbstone, 1997.

Agüeros, Jack, et al. *The Immigrant Experience: The Anguish of Becoming American.* New York: Dial, 1971.

Algarín, Miguel. *Canción de gesta / A Song of Protest.* New York: Morrow, 1976.

———. *Mongo Affair.* New York: Nuyorican Poets Cafe, 1978.

———. *On Call.* Houston: Arte Público, 1980.

———. *Body Bee Calling from the 21st Century.* Houston: Arte Público, 1982.

Algarín, Miguel, and Bob Holman, eds. *Aloud: Voices from the Nuyorican Poets Cafe.* New York: Holt, 1994.

Algarín, Miguel, and Miguel Piñero, eds. *Nuyorican Poetry: An Anthology of Puerto Rican Words and Feelings.* New York: Morrow, 1975.

Alonso, Ricardo. *Cimarrón.* Middletown, Conn.: Wesleyan University Press, 1979.

Álvarez, Julia. *Homecoming.* New York: Grove, 1984.

———. *The Housekeeping Book.* Burlington, Vt.: Álvarez, MacDonald, Schall, 1984.

———. *How the Garcia Girls Lost Their Accents.* Chapel Hill, N.C.: Algonquin Books, 1991.

———. "Hold the Mayonnaise." *New York Times Magazine,* January 12, 1992, sec. 6, pp. 14, 24.

———. *In the Time of the Butterflies.* Chapel Hill, N.C.: Algonquin Books, 1994.

———. *Yo.* Chapel Hill, N.C.: Algonquin Books, 1997.

———. "An American Childhood in the Dominican Republic." *American Scholar* 56 (1987): 71–85.

Areíto. *Contra viento y marea.* Havana: Casa de las Américas, 1978.

Arenas, Reinaldo. *El central.* Barcelona: Editorial Seix Barral, 1981.

———. *Arturo, la estrella más brillante.* Barcelona: Montesinos Editor, 1984.

———. *Necesidad de libertad: Testimonio de un intelectual disidente.* Mexico City: Kosmos-Editorial, 1986.

———. *Persecución: Cinco piezas de teatro experimental.* Miami: Editorial Universal, 1986.

———. *La loma del ángel.* Miami: Mariel, 1987.

———. *El portero.* Málaga: Dador, 1989.

———. *Voluntad de vivir manifestándose.* Madrid: Betania, 1989.

———. *El asalto.* Miami: Ediciones Universal, 1990.

———. *Leprosorio: Trilogía poética.* Madrid: Betania, 1990.

———. *Viaje a La Habana.* Miami: Ediciones Universal, 1990.

———. *El color del verano.* Miami: Ediciones Universal, 1991.

———. *Antes que anochezca.* Barcelona: Tusquets, 1992.

———. *Adiós a Mamá.* Paris: Le Serpent a Plumes, 1993.

Armand, Octavio. *Horizonte no es siempre lejanía.* New York: Las Américas, 1970.

———. *Entre testigos.* Madrid, 1974.

———. *Cosas pasan (1975).* Caracas: Monte Ávila Editores, 1976.

———. *Piel menos mía (1973–1974).* Los Angeles: Escolios, 1976.

———. *Cómo escribir con erizo.* México: Asociación de Escritores de México, 1979.

———. *Cosas pasan.* Caracas: Monte Ávila, 1979.

———. *20 Poems.* Trans. and with introduction by Mark Stand. Caracas: Monte Ávila Editores, 1979.

———. *Biografía para feacios.* Valencia: Pre-Textos, 1980.

———. *Superficies.* Caracas: Monte Ávila Editores, 1980.

———. *With Dusk.* Trans. Carol Maier. Durango, Colo.: Logbridge-Rhodes, 1984.

———. *Origami.* Caracas: Fundarte, 1987

———. *Refractions.* New York: Sites/Lumen, 1994.

Barradas, Efraín, and Rafael Rodríguez, eds. *Herejes y mitificadores: Muestra de la poesía puertorriqueña en los Estados Unidos.* Río Piedras, P.R.: Ediciones Huracán, 1980.

Barreto, Lefty. *Nobody's Hero.* New York: New American Library, 1976.

Burgos, Julia. *El mar y tú: Otros poemas.* San Juan: Puerto Rico Printing Co., 1954.

Cachán, Manuel. *Al son del tiple y el güiro.* Miami: Ediciones Universal, 1987.

———. *Cuentos de aquí y allá.* Miami: Ediciones Universal, 1988.

Carpentier, Alejo. *¡Écue Yamba-Ó!* Madrid: Editorial España, 1933.

Carrero, Jaime. *Jet neorriqueño-Neo-Rican Jetliner.* San Germán, P.R.: Universidad Interamericana, 1964.

———. *Raquelo tiene un mensaje.* San Juan, 1970.

———. "Pipo Subway no sabe leer." In *Flag Inside.* Río Piedras, P.R.: Ediciones Puerto, 1973, 113–57.

———. "The FM Safe." *Revista Chicano-Riqueña* 7, no. 1 (1979): 110–50.

———. *El hombre que no sudaba.* Houston: Arte Público, 1982.

———. *Teatro.* San Juan, P.R.: Instituto de Cultura Puertorriqueña, 1992.

Casal, Lourdes. *Cuadernos de agosto.* New York, 1968.

———. *Los fundadores y otros cuentos.* Miami: Ediciones Universal, 1973.

———. *Palabras juntan revolución.* Havana: Casa de las Américas, 1981.

Caulfield, Carlota. *A veces me llamo infancia = Sometimes I Call Myself Childhood.* Miami: Solar, 1985.

———. *Fanaim: Poems.* San Francisco: Ediciones El y Gato Tuerto, 1985.

———. *Oscuridad divina.* San Francisco: Ediciones El Gato Tuerto, 1985.

———. *El tiempo es una mujer que espera.* Madrid: Ediciones Torremozas, 1986.

———. *34th Street and Other Poems (1982–1984).* Translated by Chris Allen and the author. San Francisco: Ediciones El Gato Tuerto, 1987.

Cintrón, Humberto. *Frankie Cristo.* New York: Taino, 1972.

Clavijo, Uva A. *Eternidad (ensayos).* New York: Plaza Mayor Ediciones, 1971.

———. *Versos del exilio.* Miami: n.p., 1975.

———. *Versos de exilio.* N.p.: n.p., 1976.

———. *Ni verdad ni mentira y otros cuentos.* Miami: Ediciones Universal, 1977.

———. *Entresemáforos.* Miami: Ediciones Universal, 1981.

———. *Secretariado bilingüe ahora.* Editorial Cernuda, 1982.

———. *Tus ojos y yo.* Miami: Ediciones Universal, 1985.

———. *No puedo más y otros cuentos.* Miami: Ediciones Universal, 1989.

Cocco de Felippis, Daisy, ed. *Sin otro profeta que su canto.* Santo Domingo: Editora Taller, 1988.

Cocco de Felippis, Daisy, and Franklin Gutiérrez, eds. *Historias de Washington Heights y otros rincones del mundo/Stories from Washington Heights and Other Corners of the World.* Bronx, N.Y.: Latino, 1994.

Cocco de Felippis, Daisy, and Emma Jane Robinett,eds. *Poemas del exilio y de otras inquietudes / Poems of Exile and Other Concerns.* New York: Ediciones Alcance, 1988.

Colón, Jesús. *A Puerto Rican in New York and Other Sketches.* 1961. Reprint, New York: Mainstream Publisher, 1982.

Comas, Ester. *Hello Stranger.* New York, 1971.

Correa, Miguel. *Peregrino sediento.* n.p., 1982.

———. *Al norte del infierno.* Miami: Editorial Sibi, 1983.

Cotto-Thorner, Guillermo. *Trópico en Manhattan.* San Juan: Editorial Cordillera, 1967.

Cruz, Nick. *Run Baby Run.* Plainfield, N.J.: Logos Books, 1968.

Díaz, Junot. *Drown.* New York: Riverhead, 1996.

———. *Negocios cuentos.* New York: Vintage Español, 1997.

Díaz Valcárcel, Emilio. *Harlem todos los días.* San Juan: Ediciones Huracán, 1978.

Espada, Martín. *The Immigrant's Iceboy's Bolero.* Madison, Wis.: Ghost Pony, 1982.

———. *Trumpets from the Islands of Their Eviction.* Tempe. Ariz.: Bilingual Press/Editorial Bilingüe, 1987.

———. *Rebellion Is the Circle of a Lover's Hands.* Willimantic, Conn.: Curbstone, 1989.

Esteves, Sandra María. *Yerba Buena.* Greenfield Center, N.Y.: Greenfield, 1980.

———. *Tropical Rains: A Bilingual Downpour.* New York: Caribbean Poetry Theatre, 1984.

———. *Bluestown Mockingbird Mambo.* Houston: Arte Público, 1990.

Fernández, Pablo Armando. *Nuevos poemas (1953–1955).* New York, Las Américas, 1956.

Fernández, Roberta, ed. *In Other Words: Literature by Latinas of the United States.* Houston: Arte Público, 1994.

Fernández, Roberto. *Cuentos sin rumbos.* Miami: Ediciones Universal, 1975.

———. *La vida es un special.* Ediciones Universal, 1981.

———. *La montaña rusa.* Houston: Arte Público, 1985.

———. *Raining Backwards.* Houston: Arte Público, 1991.

Fernández Fragoso, Víctor. *El reino de la espiga.* New York: Colección Nueva Sangre, 1973.

———. *Ser islas/Being Islands.* New York: Editorial El Libro Viaje, 1976.

Fernández-Marcané, Leonardo. *20 cuentistas cubanos.* Miami: Ediciones Universal, 1978.

Figueroa, José-Ángel. *East 110th Street.* Detroit: Broadside, 1973.

———. *Noo Jork.* New York: Plus Ultra Publications, 1978.

Florit, Eugenio. *Conversación a mi padre.* Havana: Yagruíma, 1949.

———. *Asonante final y otros poemas.* Havana: Orígenes, 1950.

———. *Antología poética (1930–1955).* Mexico City: Studium, 1955.

———. *Siete poemas.* Montevideo: Cuadernos Julio Herrera y Reissig, 1960.

———. *Hábito de esperanza: Poemas (1936–1964).* Madrid: Insula, 1965.

———. *Antología penúltima.* Madrid: Editorial Plenitud, 1970.

———. *De tiempo y agonía (versos del hombre solo).* Madrid: Revista de Occidente, 1974.

———. *Versos pequeños (1938–1975).* Miami: El Marco, 1979.

———. *Obras completas.* Lincoln: University of Nebraska, Society of Spanish and Spanish American Studies, 1982.

———. *Momentos.* Miami: Private edition, 1985.

García, Cristina. *Dreaming in Cuban.* New York: Ballantine Books, 1992.

———. *The Agüero Sisters.* New York: Knopf, 1997.

Gil, Lourdes. *Neumas.* New York: Senda Nueva de Ediciones, 1977.

———. *Vencido el fuego de la especie.* Somerville, N.J.: Slusa Editores, 1983.

———. *Blanca aldaba preludia.* Madrid: Editorial Betania, 1989.

Gómez Rosa, Alexis. *Cabeza de alquiler.* Santo Domingo: Luna Cabeza Caliente, 1990.

———. *New York City en tránsito de pie quebrado.* Santo Domingo: Editora Taller, 1993.

González, Celedonio. *El espesor del pellejo de un gato ya cadáver.* Miami: Ediciones Universal, 1970.

———. *Los primos.* Miami: Ediciones Universal, 1971.

———. *La soledad es una amiga que vendrá.* Miami: Ediciones Universal, 1971.

———. *Los cuatro embajadores.* Miami: Ediciones Universal, 1973.

———. *Que veinte años no es nada.* Miami: Ediciones Universal, 1987.

González, José Luis. *El hombre en la calle.* San Juan: Editorial Borinque, 1948.

———. *Paisa.* San Juan: Fondo de Cultura Popular, 1950.

———. *En este lado.* Mexico City: Los Presentes, 1954.

———. *Mambrú se fue a la guerra.* Mexico City: Joaquín Mortiz, 1972.

———. *En Nueva York y otras desgracias.* Mexico City: Siglo Veintiuno, 1973.

González-Cruz, Luis Francisco. *Tirando al blanco/Shooting Gallery.* Miami: Ediciones Universal, 1975.

———. *Disgregaciones.* Madrid: Catoblepas, 1986.

Gutiérrez, Franklin. *Hojas de octubre: Poemas.* New York, 1982.

———. *Inriri.* New York: Ediciones Alcance, 1984.

———. *Helen.* Santo Domingo: Editorial Santo Domingo, 1986.

———, ed. *Niveles del imán.* New York: Ediciones Alcance, 1983.

———, ed. *Espigas del siglo.* New York: Ediciones Alcance, 1984.

———, ed. *Voces del exilio.* New York: Ediciones Alcance, 1986.

Heredia, José María. *Poesías.* New York: Librería de Behr y Kahl, Imprenta de Gray y Bunce, 1825.

Hernández, Norma Iris. *Precious Moments.* New York: Parnaso, 1981.

Hernández Cruz, Víctor. *Papo Got His Gun.* New York: Calle Once Publications, 1966.

———. *Snaps.* New York: Random House, 1969.

———. *Mainland.* New York: Random House, 1973.

———. *Tropicalization.* New York: Reed, Cannon and Johnson, 1976.

———. *By Lingual Wholes.* San Francisco: Momo's Press, 1982.

———. *Rhythm, Content and Flavor.* Houston: Arte Público, 1989.

———. *Red Beans.* Minneapolis: Coffee House, 1991.

———. *Panoramas.* Minneapolis: Coffee House, 1997.

Hernández Cruz, Victor, Leroy V. Quintana, and Virgil Suárez, eds. *Paper Dance: 55 Latino Poets.* New York: Persea, 1995.

Hernández-Mijares, Julio, ed. *Narradores cubanos de hoy.* Miami: Ediciones Universal, 1975.

Heyck, Denis Lynn Daly, ed. *Barrios and Borderlands: Cultures of Latinos and Latinas in the United States.* London: Routledge, 1994.

Hijuelos, Oscar. *Our House in the Last World.* New York: Washington Square, 1984.

———. *The Mambo Kings Play Songs of Love.* New York: Farrar, Straus & Giroux, 1989.

———. *The Fourteen Sisters of Emilio Montez O'Brien.* New York: Farrar, Straus & Giroux, 1993.

———. *Mr. Ives' Christmas.* New York: HarperCollins, 1995.

Hospital, Carolina, ed. *Cuban American Writers: Los Atrevidos.* Princeton, N.J.: Ediciones Ellas/Linden Lane, 1988.

Hospital, Carolina, and Jorge Cantera, eds. *A Century of Cuban Writers in Florida.* Sarasota, Fla.: Pineapple, 1996.

Hostos, Eugenio María de. *Diario.* Havana: Cultural, 1939.

Islas, Maya. *Sombras papel: Poemas.* Barcelona: Ediciones Rondas, 1978.

———. *Altazora acompañando a Vicente.* Madrid: Editorial Betania, 1987.

Iturralde, Iraida. *Hubo la vida.* New York: Ediciones Contra Viento y Marea, 1979.

Kanellos, Nicolás, ed. *Short Fiction by Hispanic Writers of the United States.* Houston: Arte Público, 1993.

Kozer, José. *Padres y otras profesiones.* New York: Editorial Villa Miseria, 1972.

———. *Este judío de números y letras.* Tenerife, Canary Islands: Editorial Católica, Ediciones Nuestro Arte, 1975.

———. *Así tomaron posesión en las ciudades.* Barcelona: Editorial Ámbito Literario, 1978.

———. *La rueca de los semblantes.* León, Spain: Editorial Instituto Gray Bernardino de Sahagún, 1980.

———. *Antología breve.* Santo Domingo: Editorial Luna Cabeza Caliente, 1981.

———. *Bajo este cien.* Mexico City: Editorial Fondo de Cultura Económica, 1983.

———. *La garza sin sombras.* Barcelona: Ediciones Libres del Mal, 1985.

———. *El carrillón de los muertos.* Buenos Aires: Último Reino, 1987.

———. *Carece de causa.* Buenos Aires: Último Reino, 1988.

Labarthe, Pedro Juan. *The Son of Two Nations: The Private Life of a Columbia Student.* New York: Carranza, 1931.

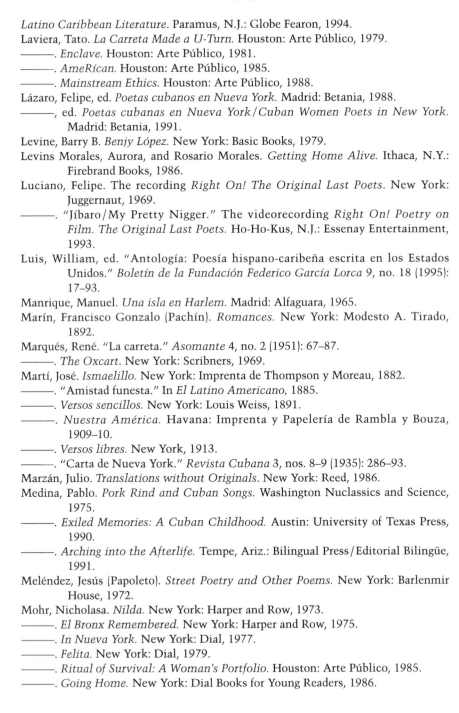

Latino Caribbean Literature. Paramus, N.J.: Globe Fearon, 1994.

Laviera, Tato. *La Carreta Made a U-Turn.* Houston: Arte Público, 1979.

———. *Enclave.* Houston: Arte Público, 1981.

———. *AmeRícan.* Houston: Arte Público, 1985.

———. *Mainstream Ethics.* Houston: Arte Público, 1988.

Lázaro, Felipe, ed. *Poetas cubanos en Nueva York.* Madrid: Betania, 1988.

———, ed. *Poetas cubanas en Nueva York/Cuban Women Poets in New York.* Madrid: Betania, 1991.

Levine, Barry B. *Benjy López.* New York: Basic Books, 1979.

Levins Morales, Aurora, and Rosario Morales. *Getting Home Alive.* Ithaca, N.Y.: Firebrand Books, 1986.

Luciano, Felipe. The recording *Right On! The Original Last Poets.* New York: Juggernaut, 1969.

———. "Jíbaro/My Pretty Nigger." The videorecording *Right On! Poetry on Film. The Original Last Poets.* Ho-Ho-Kus, N.J.: Essenay Entertainment, 1993.

Luis, William, ed. "Antología: Poesía hispano-caribeña escrita en los Estados Unidos." *Boletín de la Fundación Federico García Lorca* 9, no. 18 (1995): 17–93.

Manrique, Manuel. *Una isla en Harlem.* Madrid: Alfaguara, 1965.

Marín, Francisco Gonzalo (Pachín). *Romances.* New York: Modesto A. Tirado, 1892.

Marqués, René. "La carreta." *Asomante* 4, no. 2 (1951): 67–87.

———. *The Oxcart.* New York: Scribners, 1969.

Martí, José. *Ismaelillo.* New York: Imprenta de Thompson y Moreau, 1882.

———. "Amistad funesta." In *El Latino Americano,* 1885.

———. *Versos sencillos.* New York: Louis Weiss, 1891.

———. *Nuestra América.* Havana: Imprenta y Papelería de Rambla y Bouza, 1909–10.

———. *Versos libres.* New York, 1913.

———. "Carta de Nueva York." *Revista Cubana* 3, nos. 8–9 (1935): 286–93.

Marzán, Julio. *Translations without Originals.* New York: Reed, 1986.

Medina, Pablo. *Pork Rind and Cuban Songs.* Washington Nuclassics and Science, 1975.

———. *Exiled Memories: A Cuban Childhood.* Austin: University of Texas Press, 1990.

———. *Arching into the Afterlife.* Tempe, Ariz.: Bilingual Press/Editorial Bilingüe, 1991.

Meléndez, Jesús (Papoleto). *Street Poetry and Other Poems.* New York: Barlenmir House, 1972.

Mohr, Nicholasa. *Nilda.* New York: Harper and Row, 1973.

———. *El Bronx Remembered.* New York: Harper and Row, 1975.

———. *In Nueva York.* New York: Dial, 1977.

———. *Felita.* New York: Dial, 1979.

———. *Ritual of Survival: A Woman's Portfolio.* Houston: Arte Público, 1985.

———. *Going Home.* New York: Dial Books for Young Readers, 1986.

———. *In My Own Words: Growing Up inside the Sanctuary of My Imagination.* New York: Simon & Schuster, 1994.

———. *A Matter of Pride and Other Stories.* Houston: Arte Público, 1997.

Montes Huidobro, Matías. *Desterrados al fuego.* Mexico City: Fondo de Cultura Económica, 1975.

———. *Ojos para no ver.* Miami: Ediciones Universal, 1979.

———. *Segar a los muertos.* Miami: Ediciones Universal, 1980.

———. "Funeral en Teruel." *Verbena* 4, no. 1 (1982): 2–29.

———. "La navaja de Olofe." *Prismal Cabral* 7/8 (1982): 120–33.

Muñoz, Elías Miguel. *Los viajes de Orlando Cachumbambé.* Ediciones Universal, 1984.

———. *Crazy Love.* Houston: Arte Público, 1989.

———. *En estas tierras.* Tempe, Ariz.: Bilingual Press/Editorial Bilingüe, 1989.

———. *No fue posible el sol.* Madrid: Betania, 1989.

———. *The Greatest Performance.* Houston: Arte Público, 1991.

Novás Calvo, Lino. *Maneras de contar.* New York: Las Américas, 1970.

Núñez, Ana Rosa. *Las siete lunas de enero.* Miami: Cuadernos del Hombre Libre, 1967.

———. *Cinco poetisas cubanas, 1935–1969: Mercedes García Tuduri, Pura del Prado, Teresa María Rojas, Rita Geada, Ana Rosa Núñez.* Miami: Ediciones Universal, 1970.

———. *Viaje al Casabe.* Miami: Ediciones Universal, 1970.

———. *Los oficialeros.* Miami: Ediciones Universal, 1973.

———. *Sol de un solo día.* Miami: Editorial Márquez, 1973.

———. *Atlas poético.* Miami: Atabex, 1982.

———. *Verde sobre azul: Un Verano en Puerto Rico.* Miami: Editorial Cartel, 1987.

———. *Crisántemos, Chrysanthemums.* Translated by Jay H. Leal. Madrid: Betania, 1990.

Oliva, Jorge. *La captura y otros cuentos.* Guatemala: Unión, 1966.

———. *Donde una llama nunca se apaga.* Madrid: Editorial Playor, 1984.

Ortiz Cofer, Judith. *Latin Women Pray.* Fort Lauderdale, Fla.: Florida Arts Gazette Press, 1980.

———. *Peregrina.* New York: Riverstone, 1986.

———. *Terms of Survival: Poems.* Houston: Arte Público, 1987.

———. *The Line of the Sun: A Novel.* Athens: University of Georgia Press, 1989.

———. *Silent Dancing: A Partial Remembrance of a Puerto Rican Childhood.* Houston: Arte Público, 1990.

———. *The Latin Deli.* Athens: University of Georgia Press, 1993.

Ortiz Cofer, Judith, et al. *Triple Crown: Chicano, Puerto Rican and Cuban American Poetry.* Tempe. Ariz.: Bilingual Press/Editorial Bilingüe, 1987.

Padilla, Heberto. *La mala memoria.* Barcelona: Plaza y Janés, 1989.

Pau-Llosa, Ricardo. *Sorting Metaphors.* Tallahassee, Fla.: Anhinga, 1983.

———. *Bread of the Imagined.* Tempe, Ariz.: Bilingual Press/Editorial Bilingüe, 1992.

———. *Cuba.* Pittsburgh: Carnegie Mellon University Press, 1993.

Perera, Hilda. *El sitio de nadie.* Barcelona: Planeta, 1972.

Pérez Firmat, Gustavo. "Carolina Cuban." In *Triple Crown: Chicano, Puerto*

Rican, and Cuban American Poetry, edited by Roberto Durán, Judith Ortiz Cofer, and Gustavo Pérez Firmat. Tempe, Ariz.: Bilingual Press/Editorial Bilingüe, 1987, 121–67.

———. *Equivocaciones.* Madrid: Betania, 1989.

———. *Next Year in Cuba: A Cuban Emigre's Coming of Age in America.* New York: Anchor Books, 1995.

Pietri, Pedro. *Puerto Rican Obituary.* New York: Monthly Review Press, 1973.

———. *The Masses Are Asses.* Maplewood, N.J.: Waterfront, 1984.

Piñero, Miguel. *Short Eyes.* New York: Hill and Wang, 1974.

———. *The Sun Always Shines for the Cool.* New York: B.M.C. Productions, 1979.

———. *La Bodega Sold Dreams.* Houston: Arte Público, 1980.

———. *Plays.* Houston: Arte Público, 1984.

———. *Outrageous One-Act Plays.* Houston: Arte Público, 1986.

Poey, Delia, and Virgil Suárez, eds. *Iguana Dreams: New Latino Fiction.* New York: HarperCollins, 1992.

———. *Little Havana Blues: A Cuban-American Literature Anthology.* Houston: Arte Público, 1996.

Prida, Dolores. *Treinta y un poemas.* Brooklyn, N.Y.: Fancy Press Editors, 1967.

———. *Women of the Hour.* New York: Nuevasangre, 1971.

———. *Beautiful Señoritas and Other Plays.* Houston: Arte Público, 1991.

Reyes Rivera, Louis. *Poets in Motion.* New York: Shamal, 1977.

———. *Who Pays the Cost.* New York: Shamal, 1977.

Rivera, Héctor. *Poemas no comunes para matar la muerte.* New York: Ediciones Alcance, 1984.

———. *Biografía del silencio.* New York: Systematic Color Printing, 1985.

Rivero, Isel. *Tundra.* New York: Las Américas, 1963.

Robles, Mireya. *Hagiografía de Narcisa la Bella.* Hanover, N.H.: Ediciones del Norte, 1985.

Ruiz, Richard. *The Hungry American.* Bend, Ore.: Maverick Publications, 1978.

Sánchez-Boudy, José. *Homo sapiens.* Miami: Ediciones Universal, 1971.

———. *Lilayando.* Miami: Ediciones Universal, 1971.

———. *Los cruzados de la aurora.* Miami: Ediciones Universal, 1972.

———. *Crocante de maní.* Miami: Ediciones Universal, 1973.

———. *Orbus terrarum: La ciudad de humanitas.* Miami: Ediciones Universal, 1974.

———. *Aché Babalú Ayé.* Miami: Ediciones Universal, 1975.

———. *Pregones.* Miami: Ediciones Universal, 1975.

———. *La soledad de la playa larga, mañana mariposa.* Miami: Ediciones Universal, 1975.

———. *El corredor Kresto.* Miami: Ediciones Universal, 1976.

———. *Ekué, Abanakué, Ekué.* Miami: Ediciones Universal, 1977.

———. *Leyendas de azúcar prieta (Cabio Silo).* Miami: Ediciones Universal, 1977.

———. *El picúo, el fisto, el barrio y otras estampas cubanas.* Miami: Ediciones Universal, 1977.

———. *Los sarracenos del ocaso.* Miami: Ediciones Universal, 1977.

———. *Lilayando pal tú.* Miami: Ediciones Universal, 1978.

————. *Ninquín el cesante.* Miami: Ediciones Universal, 1978.

————. *Tiempo congelado.* Miami: Ediciones Universal, 1979.

————. *La rebelión de los negros.* Miami: Ediciones Universal, 1980.

————. *Cuentos blancos y negros.* Miami: Ediciones Universal, 1983.

————. *Cuentos de la niñez.* Miami: Ediciones Universal, 1984.

————. *Dile a Catalina que se compre un guayo.* Miami: Ediciones Universal, 1991.

————. *Partiendo el "Jon."* Miami: Ediciones Universal, 1991.

Santiago, Roberto. *Boricuas: Influential Puerto Rican Writings: An Anthology.* New York: Ballantine, 1995.

Sención, Viriato. *Los que falsificaron la firma de Dios.* Santo Domingo: Editora Taller, 1992.

————. *La enana Celania y otros cuentos.* Santo Domingo: Editora Taller, 1994.

Sierra Berdecía, Fernando. *Esta noche juega el joker.* San Juan: Biblioteca de Autores Puertorriqueños, 1939.

Silén, Iván, ed. *Los paraguas amarillos: Los poetas latinos en Nueva York.* Hanover, N.H.: Ediciones del Norte, 1983.

Soto, Pedro Juan. *Spiks.* Mexico City: Los Presentes, 1956.

————. *Ardiente suelo, fría estación.* Xalapa, Mexico City: Universidad Veracruzana, 1961.

Suárez, Virgil. *Latin Jazz.* New York: Morrow, 1989.

————. *The Cutter.* New York: Ballantine Books, 1991.

————. *Welcome to the Oasis and Other Stories.* Houston: Arte Público, 1992.

————. *Havana Thursday.* Houston: Arte Público, 1995.

————. *Going Under.* Houston: Arte Público, 1996.

————. *Spared Angola: Memories from a Cuban-American.* Houston: Arte Público, 1997.

Sutton, Lorraine. *SAYcred LAYdy.* New York: Sunbury, 1975.

Tashlik, Phyllis, ed. *Hispanic, Female, and Young: An Anthology.* Houston: Piñata Books, 1994.

Thomas, Piri. *Down These Mean Streets.* 1967. Reprint, New York: Vintage, 1991.

————. *Savior, Savior, Hold My Hand.* New York: Doubleday, 1972.

————. *Seven Long Times.* New York: Praeger, 1974.

————. *Stories from El Barrio.* New York: Knopf, 1978.

Torres, Edwin. *Carlito's Way.* New York: Saturday Review Press, 1975.

————. *After Hours.* New York: Dial, 1976.

————. *O and A.* New York: Dial, 1977.

Torres, Omar. *Conversación primera.* New York: Editorial Niurklen, 1975.

————. *Ecos de un laberinto.* New York, 1976.

————. *Tiempo robado.* Hoboken, N.J.: Ediciones Contra Viento y Marea, 1978.

————. *Apenas un bolero.* Miami: Ediciones Universal, 1981.

————. *De nunca a siempre.* Miami: Ediciones Universal, 1981.

————. *Línea en diluvio.* New York: Editorial Niurklen, 1981.

————. *Al partir.* Houston: Arte Público, 1986.

————. *Fallen Angels Sing.* Houston: Arte Público, 1991.

Turner, Faythe, ed. *Puerto Rican Writers at Home in the USA.* Seattle: Open Hand Publishing, 1991.

Umpierre, Luz María. *En el país de las maravillas*. Bloomington, Ind.: Third Woman, 1982.

———. *Una puertorriqueña en Penna*. San Juan: Masters, 1979.

———. *Y otras desgracias / And Other Misfortunes*. Bloomington, Ind.: Third Woman, 1985.

———. *The Margarita Poems*. Bloomington, Ind.: Third Woman, 1987.

Valero, Roberto. *Venías*. Madrid: Betania, 1990.

Valle, Carmen. *Un poco de lo no dicho*. New York: Editorial La Ceiba, 1979.

———. *Glenn Miller y varias vidas después*. Mexico City: Premia Editora, 1983.

Varela, Félix. *Jiconténcal*. Ed. Luis Leal and Rodolfo J. Corttina. Houston: Arte Público, 1995.

Vázquez, Miguel A. *Mejorar la raza*. Santo Domingo: Editora Taller, 1977.

Vega, Bernardo. *Memorias de Bernardo Vega*. Edited by César Andreu Iglesias. San Juan: Ediciones Huracán, 1977.

Vega, Ed. *The Comeback*. Houston: Arte Público, 1985.

———. *Mendoza's Dreams*. Houston: Arte Público, 1987.

Vicioso, Sherezada (Chiqui). *Viaje desde el agua*. Santo Domingo: Visuarte, 1981.

———. *Un extraño ulular traía el viento*. Santo Domingo, R.D.: Alfa y Omega, 1985.

———. *Bolver a vivir: Imágenes de Nicaragua*. Santo Domingo, R.D.: Editora Búho, 1986.

———. *Julia de Burgos: La nuestra*. Santo Domingo, R.D.: Editora Alfa y Omega, 1987.

———. *Algo que decir: Ensayos sobre literatura femenina, 1981-1991*. Santo Domingo, R.D.: 1991.

Vigil, Evangelina, ed. *Woman of Her Word: Hispanic Women Write*. 1983. Reprint, Houston: Arte Público, 1987.

Villaverde, Cirilo. *General López, the Cuban Patriot*. New York, 1850.

———. *El señor Saco con respecto a la revolución de Cuba*. New York: La Verdad, 1852.

———. *La revolución de Cuba vista desde New York*. New York, 1869.

———. *Cecilia Valdés*. New York: El Espejo, 1882.

———. *Cuentos de mi abuelo: El penitente*. New York: M. M. Hernández, 1889.

Vivas Maldonado, J. L. *A vellón las esperanzas o Melania*. New York: Las Américas, 1971.

Zeno, Gandía, Manuel. *El negocio: Crónica de un mundo enfermo*. New York: Powers, 1922.

II. Secondary Sources

Abalos, David T. *Latinos in the United States*. Notre Dame, Ind.: University of Notre Dame Press, 1986.

Ackerman, Holly. "The *Balsero* Phenomenon, 1991--1994." In *Cuban Studies 26*. Edited by Jorge Domínguez. Pittsburgh: Pittsburgh University Press, 1996, 169-200.

Acosta Belén, Edna. "The Literature of the Puerto Rican Minority in the United States." *Bilingual Review / Revista Bilingüe* 5, nos. 1-2 (1978): 107-16.

———. "Conversations with Nicholasa Mohr." *Revista Chicano-Riqueña* 8, no. 2 (1980): 35–41.

———. "A *MELUS* Interview: Judith Ortiz Cofer." *MELUS* 18 (1993): 83–97.

Acosta Belén, Edna, with Elsa Hidalgo Christensen, eds. "Ideology and Images of Women in Contemporary Puerto Rican Literature." In *The Puerto Rican Woman.* New York: Praeger, 1979, 85–109.

Acosta Belén, Edna, and Barbara R. Sjostrom. *The Hispanic Experience in the United States: Contemporary Issues and Perspectives.* New York: Praeger, 1988.

Algarín, Miguel. "Volume and Value of the Breath in Poetry." *Revista Chicano-Riqueña* 6, no. 3 (1978): 52–69.

———. "Nuyorican Aesthetics." In *Images and Identities: The Puerto Rican in Two World Contexts.* Edited by Asela Rodríguez de Laguna. New Brunswick, N.J.: Transaction, 1987, 161–63. Also published in *Melus* 8 (1981).

Álvarez-Borland, Isabel. "Displacements and Autobiography in Cuban-American Fiction." *World Literature Today* 68, no.1 (1994): 43–53.

Álvarez Estévez, Rolando. *La emigración cubana en Estados Unidos: 1868–1878.* Havana: Editorial de Ciencias Sociales, 1986.

Andrews, Bart. *The "I Love Lucy" Book.* New York: Doubleday, 1985.

Aparicio, Frances R. "La vida es un spanglish disparatero: Bilingualism in Nuyorican Poetry." In *European Perspectives on Hispanic Literature of the United States.* Edited by Genvieve Fabre. Houston: Arte Público, 1988, 147–60.

Aparicio Laurencio, Ángel. *Cinco poetisas cubanas.* Miami: Universal, 1970.

Ardura, Ernesto. "José Martí: Latin America's U.S. Correspondent." *Americas* 32, nos. 11–12 (1980): 38–42.

Arnaz, Desi. *A Book.* New York: Morrow, 1976.

Arteaga, José. *La salsa.* Bogota: Intermedio Editores, 1990.

Aschroft, Bill, Gareth Griffiths, and Helen Tiffin, eds. *The Empire Writes Back: Theory and Practice in Post-Colonial Literatures.* London: Routledge, 1989.

Avendaño, Fausto, ed. "Literatura hispana de los Estados Unidos." *Explicación de textos literarios* 15, no. 2 (1986–87).

Babin, María Teresa, and Stan Steiner, eds. *Borinquen: An Anthology of Puerto Rican Literature.* New York: Vintage, 1974.

Baker, Houston. *Blues, Ideology, and Afro-American Literature.* Chicago: University of Chicago Press, 1984.

———. *Black Studies: Rap and the Academy.* Chicago: University of Chicago Press, 1993.

Barradas, Efraín. "Historia y ficción: las memorias de un emigrante puertorriqueño [*Memorias (Contribución a la historia de la comunidad puertorriqueña en Nueva York)*, Bernardo Vega]." *Bilingual Review/Revista Bilingüe* 5, no. 3 (1978): 247–49.

———. "De lejos en sueños verla . . . : visión mítica de Puerto Rico en la poesía neorrican." *Revista Chicano-Riqueña* 7, no. 4 (1979): 46–56.

———. "Puerto Rico acá, Puerto Rico allá!" *Revista Chicano-Riqueña* 8, no. 2 (1980): 43–49.

———. "'Entre la esencia y la forma': el momento neoyorquino en la poesía de Julia de Burgos." *Explicación de textos literarios* 15, no. 2 (1986–87): 138–52.

———. "Martí, Emerson y Buffalo Bill: apuntes para una relectura de la obra martiana sobre los Estados Unidos. *La Torre* 3, no. 11 (1989): 459–71.

Barthes, Roland. *The Pleasure of the Text.* Translated by Richard Miller. New York: Farrar, Straus & Giroux, 1975.

Baudet, Henri. *Paradise on Earth: Some Thoughts on European Images of Non-European Man.* Translated by Elizabeth Wentholt. New Haven: Yale University Press, 1965.

Benítez Rojo, Antonio. "'El camino de Santiago' de Alejo Carpentier y el *Canon perpetuus* de Juan Sebastian Bach: paralelismo estructural." *Revista Iberoamericana* 123–24 (1983): 293–322.

———. "'Semejante a la Noche' de Alejo Carpentier y el *Canon per tonos* de Juan Sebastian Bach: su paralelismo estructural." *Eco* 43, no. 6 (1983): 645–62.

———. "'Viaje a la Semilla,' o el texto como expectáculo." *Discurso Literario* 3, no. 1 (1985): 53–74.

———. *The Repeating Island: The Caribbean and the Postmodern Perspective.* Translated by James Marannis. Durham, N.C.: Duke University Press, 1992.

Benmayor, Rina. "*Getting Home Alive:* The Politics of Multiple Idenity." *Americas Review* 17, nos. 3–4 (1989): 107–17.

Betances, Samuel. "Race and the Search for Identity." In *Borinquen: An Anthology of Puerto Rican Literature.* Edited by María Teresa Babín and Stan Steiner. New York: Vintage, 1974, 425–38.

Bhabha, Homi. *The Location of Culture.* New York: Routledge, 1994.

Binder, Wolfgang. *Puerto Ricaner in New York: Volk zwischen zwei kulturen.* Erlangen, Germany: Städtische Galerie Erlangen, 1978.

———. "An Interview with Piri Thomas." *Minority Voices* 4, no. 1 (1980): 63–78.

———. "'A Midnight Reality': Puerto Rican Poetry in New York, a Poetry of Dreams." In *European Perspectives on Hispanic Literature of the United States.* Edited by Genvieve Fabre. Houston: Arte Público, 1988, 22–32.

Blaut. J. M. "Assimilation vs. Ghettoization." *Antipode* 15, no. 1 (1983): 1–11.

Boggs, Vernon W., ed. *Salsiology: Afro-Cuban Music and the Evolution of Salsa in New York City.* New York: Excelsior Music, 1992.

Boswell, Thomas D. and James R. Curtis. *The Cuban-American Experience: Culture, Images, and Perspectives.* Totowa, N.J.: Rowman & Allanheld, 1984.

Burunat, Silvia. "Omar Torres a través de sus textos." *Explicación de textos literarios* 15, no. 2 (1986–87): 60–76.

Cabanillas, Francisco. "Lo que la música le hace al cuerpo: Entrevista con Víctor Hernández Cruz." In "Antología: Poesía hispano-caribeña escrita en los Estados Unidos." Edited by William Luis. *Boletín de la Fundación Federico García Lorca* 9, no. 18 (1995): 77–93.

Campa, Román de la. "En Torno a la crítica de la literatura cubana en Estados Unidos." *Ideologies and Literature* 4, no. 16 (1983): 276–89.

———. "En la utopía redentora del lenguaje: Pedro Pietri y Miguel Algarín." *Explicación de textos literarios* 15, no. 2 (1986–87): 32–49.

Carpentier, Alejo. *La música en Cuba.* Mexico City: Fondo de Cultura Económica, 1946.

Casal, Lourdes, ed. *El caso Padilla: Literatura y revolución en Cuba.* Miami: Ediciones Universal, 1971.

Casal, Lourdes, and Andrés R. Hernández. "Cubans in the U.S.: A Survey of the Literature." *Cuban Studies* 5, no. 2 (1975): 25–52.

Caulfield, Carlota. "Exilio, subversión e identidad en la poesía de Magali Alabau." *Latinos in the U.S. Review* 1994, 40–44.

Chenault, Lawrence R. *The Puerto Rican Migrant in New York City.* New York: Columbia University Press, 1938.

Colón, Ramón. *Carlos Tapia: A Puerto Rican Hero in New York.* New York: Vantage, 1976.

Dauster, Frank. "Image of the City: Three Puerto Rican Generations in New York." In *Images and Identities: The Puerto Rican in Two World Contexts.* Edited by Asela Rodríguez de Laguna. New Brunswick, N.J.: Transaction, 1987, 60–64.

De Man, Paul. *Blindness and Insight: Essays in the Rhetoric of Contemporary Criticism.* New York: Oxford University Press, 1971.

De Toro, Fernando, and Alfonso de Toro, eds. *Borders and Margins: Post-Colonialism and Post-Modernism.* Frankfurt: Vervuert, 1995.

Díaz Ayala, Cristóbal. *The Roots of Salsa: The History of Cuban Music.* Westport, Conn.: Greenwood, 1995.

Dirlik, Arif. "The Postcolonial Aura: Third World Criticism in the Age of Global Capitalism." *Critical Inquiry* 20 (1994): 328–29.

Esteves, Sandra María. "Ambivalence or Activism from the Nuyorican Perspective in Poetry. In *Images and Identities: The Puerto Rican in Two World Contexts.* Edited by Asela Rodríguez de Laguna. New Brunswick, N.J.: Transaction, 1987, 165–70.

———. "The Feminist Viewpoint in the Poetry of Puerto Rican Women in the United States." In *Images and Identities: The Puerto Rican in Two World Contexts.* Edited by Asela Rodríguez de Laguna. New Brunswick, N.J.: Transaction, 1987, 171–77.

——— "Open Letter to Eliana (testimonio)." In *Breaking Boundaries: Latina Writings and Critical Readings.* Edited by Asunción Horno-Delgado et al. Amherst: University of Massachusetts Press, 1989, 117–21.

Fabre, Genvieve, ed. *European Perspectives on Hispanic Literature of the United States.* Houston: Arte Público, 1988.

Falquez-Certain, Miguel, ed. *New Voices in Latin American Literature/Nuevas voces en la literatura latinoamericana.* New York: Ollantay Center for the Arts, 1993.

Fernández, Enrique, Juan González, and Silvana Paternostro. "Latin Rainbow: New Arrivals Create a Changing City Scene." *New York Daily News,* March 6, 1994, 36–37.

Fernández, José. B., and Roberto G. Fernández. *Índice bibliográfico de autores cubanos: Diáspora, 1959–1979/Bibliographical Index of Cuban Authors: Diaspora, 1959–1979.* Miami: Ediciones Universal, 1983.

Fernández Olmos, Margarite. *Sobre la literatura puertorriqueña de aquí y de allá: Aproximaciones feministas.* Santo Domingo: Editora Alfa y Omega, 1989.

Flores, Juan. "Back Down These Mean Streets: Introducing Nicholasa Mohr and Louis Reyes Rivera." *Revista Chicano-Riqueña* 8, no. 2 (1980): 51–56.

———. "'Qué assimilated, brother, yo soy asimilao': The Structuring of Puerto Rican Identity in the U.S." *Journal of Ethnic Studies* 13, no. 3 (1985): 1–16. Also published in *Casa de las Américas,* 26, no. 152 (1985): 54-63.

———. *Divided Borders: Essays on Puerto Rican Identity.* Houston: Arte Público, 1993.

Flores, Juan, John Attenasi, and Pedro Pedraza. "*La Carreta Made a U-Turn:* Puerto Rican Language and Culture in the United States." *Daedalus* 110 (1981): 193–217.

Friedman, John Block. *The Monstrous Races in Medieval Art and Thought.* Cambridge: Harvard University Press, 1981.

Gann, L. H., and Peter J. Duignan. *The Hispanics in the United States.* Boulder, Colo.: Westview, 1986.

García Lorca, Federico. *Poet in New York.* Ed. Christopher Maurer. Trans. Greg Simon and Steven F. White. Harmondsworth: Penguin, 1990.

Garrett, Charles. *The La Guardia Years: Machine and Reform Politics in New York.* New Brunswick, N.J.: Rutgers University Press, 1961.

Gates, Henry Louis, ed. *Black Literature and Literary Theory.* New York: Methuen, 1984.

———, ed. *Race, Writing, and Difference.* Chicago: University of Chicago Press, 1986.

Giacoman, Helmy F. "La estructura musical en la novelística de Alejo Carpentier." *Hispanófila* 33 (1968): 49–57.

———. "La relación músico-literaria entre la tercera sinfonía 'Eróica,' de Beethoven, y la novela *El acoso* de Alejo Carpentier." *Cuadernos Americanos,* no. 158 (1968): 113-29.

González, Flora. "The Writer as Mediator in Esmeralda Santiago's *When I Was Puerto Rican.*" *Latinos in the U.S. Review 1994,* 45–48.

González Echevarría, Roberto. *Alejo Carpentier: The Pilgrim at Home.* Ithaca, N.Y.: Cornell University Press, 1977.

———. *Myth and Archive: A Theory of Latin American Narrative.* Cambridge: Cambridge University Press, 1990.

———. *Celestina's Brood: Continuities of the Baroque in Spanish and Latin American Literature.* Durham, N.C.: Duke University Press, 1993.

González Echevarría, Roberto, and Enrique Pupo-Walker, eds. *Cambridge History of Latin American Literature.* 3 vols. Cambridge: Cambridge University Press, 1996.

González Montes, Yara, and Matías Montes Huidobro. "La novela cubana: el sitio de la palabra." *Caribe* 1, no. 1 (1976): 129–46.

Grasmuch, Sherrie, and Patricia Pessar, *Between Two Islands: Dominican International Migration.* Berkeley: University of California Press, 1991.

Gutiérrez, Ramón, and Genaro Padilla. *Recovering the U.S. Hispanic Literary Heritage.* Houston: Arte Público, 1993.

Gutiérrez de la Solana, Alberto. *Maneras de contar: Contraste de Lino Novás Calvo y Alfonso Hernández Cata.* New York: Eliseo Torres, 1972.

——. "La novela cubana escrita fuera de Cuba." *Anales de Literatura Hispanoamericana* 2–3 (1973–74): 767–89.

Halpern, Seymour, et al. *Slums and Crime.* New York: Polygraphic Company of America, 1934.

Harari, Josué, ed. *Textual Strategies: Perspectives in Post-Structuralist Criticism.* Ithaca, N.Y.: Cornell University Press, 1979.

Hernández Álvarez, José. *Return Migration to Puerto Rico.* Berkeley: University of California, Institute of International Studies, 1987.

Herms, Dieter. "Chicano and Nuyorican Literature: Elements of a Democratic and Socialist Culture in the U.S. of A.?" In *European Perspectives on Hispanic Literature of the United States.* Edited by Genvieve Fabre. Houston: Arte Público, 1988, 118–29.

Hernández Cruz, Víctor. "Mountains in the North: Hispanic Writing in the U.S.A." *Americas Review* 14, nos. 3–4 (1986): 110–14.

Hernández-Mijares, Julio. "La poesía cubana del exterior: Testimonio y recuento." *Norte* 7, nos. 3–4 (1971): 58–68.

Herrera-Sobek, María. "Identidad cultural e interacción dinámica entre texto y lector destinatario en *Mi mamá me ama.*" *Explicación de textos literarios* 15, no. 2 (1986–87): 123–37.

Horno-Delgado, Asunción. "Señores, don't leibol mi, please!!: ya soy Luz María Umpierre." In *Breaking Boundaries: Latina Writings and Critical Readings.* Edited by Asunción Horno-Delgado et al. Amherst: University of Massachusetts Press, 1989, 136–45.

Horno-Delgado, Asunción, Eliana Ortega, Nina M. Scott, and Nancy Sapporta Sternbach. *Breaking Boundaries: Latina Writings and Critical Readings.* Amherst: University of Massachusetts Press, 1989.

Hospital, Carolina. "Los hijos del exilio cubano y su literatura." *Explicacion de textos literarios* 15, no. 2 (1986–87): 103–14.

——. "Los atrevidos." *Linden Lane Magazine* 6, no. 4 (1987): 22–23.

Jackson, Richard. *The Black Image in Latin American Literature.* Albuquerque: University of New Mexico Press, 1976.

——. *Black Writers in Latin America.* Albuquerque: University of New Mexico Press, 1979.

Jefferson, Margo. "Dancing into the Dream." *New York Times Book Review* 95, Aug. 27, 1989, pp. 1, 31.

Jiménez, Alfredo. *Handbook of Hispanic Cultures in the United States: History.* Houston: Arte Público, 1994.

Kanellos, Nicolás. "U.S. Hispanic Literature in the Anglo-American Empire." *Americas Review* 14, nos. 3–4 (1986): 103–5.

——. "Toward a History of Hispanic Literature in the United Staten." In *Images and Identities: The Puerto Rican in Two World Contexts.* Edited by Asela Rodríguez de Laguna. New Brunswick, N.J.: Transaction, 1987, 236–45.

——. *A History of Hispanic Theatre in the United States: Origins to 1940.* Austin: University of Texas Press, 1990.

Kermode, Frank. *The Sense of an Ending: Studies in the Theory of Fiction.* New York: Oxford University Press, 1975.

LaGumina, Salvatore John. *Vito Marcantonio: The People's Politician.* Dubuque, Iowa: Kendall/Hunt, 1969.

Le Riverend, Pablo. *Diccionario biográfico de poetas cubanos en el exilio (contemporáneos).* Newark, N.J.: Ediciones Q-21, 1988.

Lewis, Gordon K. *Puerto Rico: Freedom and Power in the Caribbean.* New York: Harper and Row, 1963.

Lewis, Marvin. "The Puerto Rican in Popular U.S. Literature: A Culturalist Perspective." In *Images and Identities: The Puerto Rican in Two World Contexts.* Edited by Asela Rodríguez de Laguna. New Brunswick, N.J.: Transaction, 1987, 65–75.

Lindstrom, Naomi E. "Cuban American and Continental Puerto Rican Literature." *Sourcebook of Hispanic Culture in the United States.* Edited by David William Foster. Chicago: American Library Association, 1982, 221–45.

Lipp, Solomon. "The Anti-Castro Novel." *Hispania* 58 (1975): 284–96.

Loemi, Francisco, ed. *Handbook of Hispanic Cultures in the United States: Literature and Art.* Houston: Arte Público, 1993.

López, Adalberto. "Literature for the Puerto Rican Diaspora: Part II." *Caribbean Review* 6, no. 4 (1974): 41–46.

Luis, William. "Caribbean Cycles: Displacement and Change." *New England Review and Bread Loaf Quarterly* 7, no. 4 (1985): 412–30.

———. *Literary Bondage: Slavery in Cuban Narrative.* Austin: University of Texas Press, 1990.

———. "Historia, naturaleza y memoria en 'Viaje a la semilla,'" *Revista Iberoamericana* 145 (1991): 151–60.

———. "From New York to the World: An Interview with Tato Laviera." *Callaloo* 15, no. 4 (1992): 1022–33.

———. "A Search for Identity in Julia Álvarez's *How the Garcia Girls Lost Their Accents.*" In *Latinos in the U.S. Review 1994,* 52–57.

———. "Borges, the Encounter, and the Other: Blacks and the Monstrous Races." In *Borders and Margins: Post-Colonialism and Post-Modernism.* Edited by Fernando de Toro and Alfonso de Toro. Frankfurt: Vervuert, 1995, 61–78.

———. "Latin American Literature (Hispanic Caribbean) Literature Written in the United States." In *The Cambridge History of Latin American Literature,* vol. 2. Edited by Roberto González Echevarría and Enrique Pupo-Walker. Cambridge: Cambridge University Press, 1996, 526–56.

———. *Modern Latin American Fiction Writers, First Series.* Detroit: Gale Research, 1992.

———. "Reading the Master Codes of Cuban Culture in Cristina Garcías's *Dreaming in Cuban.*" *Cuban Studies 26.* Edited by Jorge Domínguez. Pittsburgh: University of Pittsburgh Press, 1996, 201–23.

Luis, William, with Ann González. *Modern Latin American Fiction Writers, Second Series.* Detroit: Gale Research, 1994.

Lyotard, François. *The Postmodern Condition: A Report on Knowledge* Translated by Geoff Bennington and Brian Massumi. Minneapolis: University of Minnesota Press, 1984.

Maffi, Mario. "The Nuyorican Experience in the Plays of Pedro Pietri and Miguel Piñero." In *Cross-Cultural Studies: American, Canadian and European Literatures, 1945–1985*. Edited by Mirko Juark. Slovenia, Yugoslavia: Ljublajaria: English Department, Filozofska Fakulteta, 1988, 483–89.

Maldonado-Denis, Manuel. *Puerto Rico: A Socio-Historic Interpretation*. Trans. Elena Vialo. New York: Vintage, 1972.

———. *Puerto Rico y Estados Unidos: Emigración y colonialismo*. Mexico City: Siglo Veintiuno, 1976.

Mantilla. Alfredo. "The Broken English Dream: Puerto Rican Poetry in New York." In *The Intellectual Roots of Independence: An Anthology of Puerto Rican Political Essays*. Edited by Iris M. Zavala and Rafael Rodríquez. New York: Monthly Review Press, 1980.

———. "Breve panorámica de las letras puertorriqueñas en los Estados Unidos." *Explicacion de textos literarios* 15, no. 2 (1986–87): 19–31.

Mantilla, Alfredo, and Iván Silén, eds. *The Puerto Rican Poets / Los poetas puertorriqueños*. New York: Bantam, 1972.

Martínez, Julio A, ed. *Dictionary of Twentieth-Century Cuban Literature*. Westport, Conn.: Greenwood, 1990.

Marzán, Julio. *The Spanish American Roots of William Carlos Williams*. Austin: University of Texas Press, 1994.

Menton, Seymour. *Prose Fiction of the Cuban Revolution*. Austin: University of Texas Press, 1975.

Meyer, Gerald. *Vito Marcantonio: Radical Politician, 1902–1954*. Albany: State University of New York Press, 1989.

Miller, John C. "Hispanic Theater in New York, 1965–1977." *Revista Chicano-Riqueña* 6, no. 1 (1978): 40–59.

———. "Cross-Currents in Hispanic Literature in the United States." In *Images and Identities: The Puerto Rican in Two World Contexts*. Edited by Asela Rodríguez de Laguna. New Brunswick, N.J.: Transaction, 1987, 246–53.

———. "Nicholasa Mohr." In *Modern Latin-American Fiction Writers, Second Series*. Edited by William Luis and Ann González. Detroit: Gale Research, 1994.

Mohr, Eugene. "Lives from El Barrio." *Revista Chicano-Riqueña* 3, no. 4 (1980): 60–68.

———. *The Nuyorican Experience: Literature of the Puerto Rican Minority*. Westport, Conn.: Greenwood, 1982.

Mohr, Nicholasa. "On Being Authentic." *Americas Review* 14, nos. 3–4 (1986): 106-9.

———. "Puerto Ricans in New York: Cultural Evolution and Identity." In *Images and Identities: The Puerto Rican in Two World Contexts*. Edited by Asela Rodríguez de Laguna. New Brunswick, N.J.: Transaction, 1987, 157–60.

———. "Puerto Rican Writers in the United States, Puerto Rican Writers in Puerto Rico: A Separation Beyond Languages." *Americas Review* 15, no. 2 (1987): 87–92. Reprinted in *Breaking Boundaries: Latina Writings and Critical Readings*. Edited by Asunción Horno-Delgado et al. Amherst: University of Massachusetts Press, 1989, 111–16.

———. "Latina Writer: A Brief Perspective." *Latinos in the U.S. Review 1994*: 23.

Molloy, Sylvia. *At Face Value: Autobiographical Writing in Spanish America.* Cambridge: Cambridge University Press, 1991.

Montes Huidobro, Matías, and Yara González Montes. *Bibliografía crítica de la poesía cubana (exilio: 1959–1971).* Madrid: Playor, 1973.

Moore, Carlos. *Castro, the Blacks, and Africa.* Los Angeles: University of California, Center for Afro-American Studies, 1988.

Moore, Joan, and Harry Pachon. *Hispanics in the United States.* Englewood Cliffs, N.J.: Prentice-Hall, 1985.

Muñoz, Elías Miguel. *Desde esta orilla.* Madrid: Betania, 1988.

Núñez, Ana Rosa. *Poesía en éxodo.* Miami: Universal, 1970.

Ocasio, Rafael. "The Infinite Variety of Puerto Rican Reality: An Interview with Judith Ortiz Cofer." *Callaloo* 17, no. 3 (1994): 730–42.

Ortega, Eliana. "Poetic Discourse of the Puerto Rican Woman in the U.S.: New Voices of Anacaonian Liberation." In *Breaking Boundaries: Latina Writings and Critical Readings.* Edited by Asunción Horno-Delgado et al. Amherst: University of Massachusetts Press, 1989, 122–35.

Ortiz, Fernando. *Cuban Counterpoint: Tobacco and Sugar.* Translated by Harriet de Onís. New York: Knopf, 1947.

Peguero, Valentina. "Japanese Settlement in the Dominican Republic: An Intercultural Exchange." In *Caribbean Asians: Chinese, Indian, and Japanese Experience in Trinidad and the Dominican Republic.* Edited by Roger Sanjek. New York: City University of New York, Asian/American Center at Queens College, 1990.

Pérez Firmat, Gustavo. "Spic Chic: Spanglish as Equipment for Living." *Caribbean Review* 15 (1987): 20–21, 36–37.

———. "Transcending Exile: Cuban-American Literature Today." *Occasional Papers Series: Dialogues.* Miami: Florida International University, Latin American and Caribbean Center, 1987, 1–13.

———. *The Cuban Condition: Translation and Identity in Modern Cuban Literature.* Cambridge: Cambridge University Press, 1989.

———. "Noción de José Kozer." *Revista Iberoamericana* 152-153 (1990): 1247–56.

———. *Life on the Hyphen: The Cuban-American Way.* Austin: University of Texas Press, 1994.

———. "Oscar Hijuelos." In *Modern Latin-American Fiction Writers, Second Series.* Edited by William Luis. Detroit: Gale Research, 1994, 148–54.

———, ed. *Do the Americas Have a Common Literature?* Durham, N.C.: Duke University Press, 1990.

Pineiro de Rivera, Flor. *Arturo Schomburg: Un puertorriqueño descubre el legado histórico del negro.* San Juan: Centro de Estudios Avanzados de Puerto Rico y el Caribe, 1989.

Portes, Alejandro, and Alex Stepick, *City on the Edge: The Transformation of Miami.* Los Angeles: University of California Press, 1993.

Prida, Dolores. "The Show Does Go On (testimonio)." *Breaking Boundaries: Latina Writings and Critical Readings.* Edited by Asunción Horno-Delgado et al. Amherst: University of Massachusetts Press, 1989, 181–88.

Ribers Tovar, Federico. *Albizu Compos: El revolucionario.* New York: Plus Ultra Educational, 1971.

Rivero, Eliana S. "Hispanic Literature in the United States: Self-Image and Conflict." *International Studies in Honor of Tomás Rivero.* Edited by Julián Olivares. *Revista Chicano-Riqueña* 13, nos. 3–4 (1986): 173–92.

———. "From Immigrants to Ethnics: Cuban Women Writers in the U.S." *Breaking Boundaries: Latina Writings and Critical Readings.* Edited by Asunción Horno-Delgado et al. Amherst: University of Massachusetts Press, 1989, 189–200.

Roberts, John Storm. *The Latin Tinge: The Impact of Latin American Music on the United States.* New York: Oxford University Press, 1979.

Rodríguez, Richard. Hunger of Memory: *The Education of Richard Rodríguez: An Autobiography.* Boston: David R. Godine, 1982.

Rodríguez, Roberto. *X in La Raza.* Albuquerque, N.M.; by author, 1996.

Rodríguez de Laguna, Asela, ed. *Images and Identities: The Puerto Rican in Two World Contexts.* New Brunswick, N.J.: Transaction, 1987.

Rodríguez-Luis, Julio. "De Puerto Rico a Nueva York: Protagonistas femeninas en busca de un espacio propio." La Torre 7, nos. 27–28 (1993): 577–594.

———. "Sobre la literatura hispánica en los Estados Unidos." *Casa de las Américas* 34, no. 193 (1993): 37–48.

Rodríguez Monegal, Emir. *El boom de la novela latinoamericana.* Caracas: Editorial Tiempo Nuevo, 1972.

Rodríguez Sardino, Orlando, ed. *La última poesía cubana (1960–1973).* New York: Hispanova de Ediciones, 1973.

———. "Cuba: Poesía entre revolución y exilio." *Revista/Review Interamericana* 4, no. 3 (1974): 359–69.

Rojas, Lourdes. "Latinas at the Crossroads: An Affirmation of Life in Rosario Morales and Aurora Levins Morales's *Getting Home Alive.*" *Breaking Boundaries: Latina Writings and Critical Readings.* Edited by Asunción Horno-Delgado et al. Amherst: University of Massachusetts Press, 1989, 166–77.

Rondón, César Miguel. *El vínculo es la Salsa.* Caracas: Editorial Arte, 1980.

Ronzencvaig, Perla. "Prólogo." In *Poetas cubanas en Nueva York: Antología breve.* Edited by Felipe Lázaro. Madrid: Betania, 1991, 7–12.

Roses, Lorraine. *Voices of the Storyteller: Cuba's Lino Novás Calvo.* Westport, Conn.: Greenwood, 1986.

Ruiz, Ariel. "Raza, sexo y política en *Short Eyes* de Miguel Piñero." *Americas Review* 15, no. 2 (1987): 93–102.

Ruiz Cumba, Israel. "Hacia una nueva lectura de *Las Memorias de Bernardo Vega.* Inti: *Revista de Literatura Hispánica,* no. 31 (1990): 50–66.

Rumbaut, Rubén G. "The Agony of Exile: A Study of the Migration and Adaptation of Indochinese Refugee Adults and Children." In *Refugee Children: Theory, Research, and Services.* Edited by Frederick L. Ahearn, Jr., and Jean L. Athey. Baltimore: Johns Hopkins University Press, 1991.

Saldívar, José David. "The Dialectics of Our America." In *Do the Americas Have a Common Literature?* Edited by Gustavo Pérez Firmat. Durham, N.C.: Duke University Press, 1990.

Sánchez-Boudy, José. *Historia de la literatura cubana (en el exilio).* Miami: Ediciones Universal, 1975.

Sandoval, Alberto. "Dolores Prida's *Coser y cantar:* Mapping the Dialectics of Ethnic Identity and Assimilation." In *Breaking Boundaries: Latina Writings and Critical Readings.* Edited by Asunción Horno-Delgado et al. Amherst: University of Massachusetts Press, 1989, 201–20.

Schomburg, Arthur Alfonso. *The Legacy of Arthur Alfonso Schomburg: A Celebration of the Past, A Vision for the Future.* New York: Schomburg Center for Research on Black Culture, 1986.

Soto, Francisco. "*El portero:* Una alucinante fábula moderna." *Inti: Revista de Literatura Hispánica,* nos. 32–33 (1990–91): 106–17.

Soto, Pedro Juan. *A solas con Pedro Juan Soto.* Río Piedras, P.R.: Ediciones Puerta.

Souza, Raymond. *Lino Novás Calvo.* Boston: Twayne, 1981.

Spivak, Gayatri Chakravorty. "Can the Subaltern Speak?" In *Marxism and the Interpretation of Culture.* Edited by Cary Nelson and Lawrence Grossberg. Urbana, Ill.: University of Illinois Press, 1988., 271–313.

Springfield, Consuelo López. "*Mestizaje* in the Mother-Daughter Autobiography of Rosario Morales and Aurora Levins Morales." *Auto/biography Studies* 8, no. 2 (1993): 303–15.

Stavans, Ilán. "Habla Oscar Hijuelos." *Linden Lane Magazine* (1989): 14–15.

———. *The Hispanic Condition: Reflections on Culture and Identity in America.* New York: HarperCollins, 1995.

Tatum, Charles A. "Geographic Displacement as Spiritual Desolation in Puertorican and Chicano Prose Fiction." In *Images and Identities: The Puerto Rican in Two World Contexts.* Edited by Asela Rodríguez de Laguna. New Brunswick, N.J.: Transaction, 1987, 254–64.

Thomas, Hugh. *Cuba: The Pursuit of Freedom.* New York: Harper & Row, 1971.

Thomas, Piri. "A Neorican in Puerto Rico or Coming Home." In *Images and Identities: The Puerto Rican in Two World Contexts.* Edited by Asela Rodríguez de Laguna. New Brunswick, N.J.: Transaction, 1987, 153–56.

Torres-Saillant, Silvio. "Western Discourse and the Curriculum." *Punto 7 Review: A Journal of Marginal Discourse* 2, no. 2 (1992): 107–67.

Umpierre, Luz María. "La ansiedad de la influencia en Sandra María Esteves y Marjorie Agosín." In *Woman of Her Word: Hispanic Women Write.* Edited by Evangelina Vigil. 1983. Reprint, Houston: Arte Público, 1987), 139–47.

Uriarte-Gastón, Miren, and Jorge Cañas Martínez, eds. *Cubans in the United States.* Boston: Center for the Study of the Cuban Community, 1984.

Vargas, Yamila Azize. "A Commentary on the Works of Three Puerto Rican Women Poets in New York." In *Breaking Boundaries: Latina Writings and Critical Readings.* Edited by Asunción Horno-Delgado et al. Amherst: University of Massachusetts Press, 1989, 146–65.

Vélez, Diana L. "'Pollito Chicken': Split Subjectivity, National Identity and the Articulation of Female Sexuality in a Narrative by Ana Lydia Vega." *Americas Review* 14, no. 2 (1986): 68–76.

Vicioso, Sherezada (Chiqui). "An Oral History (testimonio)." In *Breaking Boundaries: Latina Writings and Critical Readings.* Edited by Asunción Horno-Delgado et al. Amherst: University of Massachusetts Press, 1989, 229–34.

Vigil, Evangelina, ed. *Woman of Her Word: Hispanic Women Write.* 1983. Reprint. Houston: Arte Público, 1987.

Vorda, Allan. "A Fish Swims in My Lung: An Interview with Cristina García." In *Face to Face: Interviews with Contemporary Novelists.* Edited by Allan Vorda. Houston: Rice University Press, 1993.

Waldinger, Roger, D. *Through the Eye of the Needle: Immigrant and Enterprise in New York's Garment Trades.* New York: New York University Press, 1986.

Watson-Espener, Maida Isabel. "Observaciones sobre el teatro chicano, nuyorriqueño y cubano en los Estados Unidos." *Bilingual Review/Revista Bilingüe* 5, nos. 1–2 (1978): 117–25.

Young Lords Party and Michael Abramson. *Palante: Young Lords Party.* New York: McGraw-Hill, 1971.

Zapata, Miguel Ángel. "Breve lectura de la poesía de Carlota Caulfield." *Latinos in the U.S. Review 1994,* 62–64.

INDEX

William Luis, professor of Spanish at Vanderbilt University, is the author of several works, including *Literary Bondage: Slavery in Cuban Narrative* (1990). Born and raised in New York City, he is widely regarded as a leading authority on Latin American, Caribbean, Afro-Hispanic, and Latino U.S. literatures.

DANCE BETWEEN TWO CULTURES

was composed electronically using
Trump Mediaeval types, with displays
in Carlton and Type Embellishments Two.
The book was printed on 50# Natural Antique acid-free,
recycled paper and was Smyth sewn and cased in Pyroxilyn Linen
Grade B cloth over 88-point binder's boards, with head bands and
80-pound Multi Color endleaves, by Rose Printing Company.
The dust jacket was printed in four colors by
Vanderbilt University Printing Services.
Book and dust jacket designs are the work of Gary Gore.
Published by Vanderbilt University Press
Nashville, Tennessee 37235